Social History of Africa

PEOPLE ARE NOT
THE SAME

Social History of Africa Series
Series Editors: Allen Isaacman and Jean Allman

PEOPLE ARE NOT THE SAME

Leprosy and Identity in Twentieth-Century Mali

Eric Silla

HEINEMANN
Portsmouth, NH

JAMES CURREY
Oxford

Heinemann
A division of Reed Elsevier Inc.
361 Hanover Street
Portsmouth, NH 03801–3912

James Currey Ltd.
73 Botley Road
Oxford OX2 0BS
United Kingdom

Offices and agents throughout the world

ISBN 0-325-00005-0 (Heinemann cloth)
ISBN 0-325-00004-2 (Heinemann paper)
ISBN 0-85255-680-2 (James Currey cloth)
ISBN 0-85255-630-6 (James Currey paper)

British Library Cataloguing in Publication Data
Silla, Eric
    People are not the same : leprosy and identity in twentieth-century Mali.
    (Social history of Africa).
    1. Lepers — Mali — Social conditions 2. Leprosy — Mali — History — 20th century
    3. Mali — Social conditions
    I. Title
    362.1'96998'0096623
    ISBN   0-85255-630-6   (James Currey paper)
                  0-85255-680-2   (James Currey cloth)

Library of Congress Cataloging-in-Publication Data
Silla, Eric.
    People are not the same : leprosy and identity in twentieth-century Mali / Eric Silla.
    p.   cm. — (Social history of Africa)
    Includes bibliographical references and index.
    ISBN 0-325-00005-0 (cloth). — ISBN 0-325-00004-2 (pbk)
    1. Leprosy—Mali—History. I. Title. II. Series.
RC154.8. M42S56 1988
362.1'96998'0096623—dc21

97–39954
CIP

Cover design by Jenny Jensen Greenleaf
Cover photo: "Saran Keita," 1996, by Eric Silla.
Docutech OPI 2004

CONTENTS

LIST OF PHOTOGRAPHS
AND MAPS

ACKNOWLEDGMENTS

Research for this book was funded with a Fulbright-Hays Award for Doctoral Research Abroad (1992-93) and a Social Science Research Council Pre-Dissertation Research Fellowship (Summer 1991). A U.S. Department of Education Jacob Javits Fellowship provided important support during the writing stage.

I would like to thank all the individuals mentioned in the List of Informants who made this project possible in Mali. The former leprosy patients were especially generous with their time and insight. Fousseyni Sow, secretary of the Association Malienne des Handicapés de la Lèpre, deserves particular recognition for voluntarily arranging interviews and integrating me into Djikoroni's community of former patients. The following individuals also introduced me to former patients in their respective communities: Demba Bane in Ouéléssébougou, Ahmed Dédaou (Cledi) in Timbuktu, Bill Mosely and Julia Earl in Falan, Father Bernard de Rasilly in San, Farko Sango in Macina, and Fousseyni Sow in Kita. I would also like to thank Drissa Diallo and the Institut de Médecine Traditionnelle, as well as Klena Sanogo, the Institut des Sciences Humaines, and the Centre National de Recherche Scientifique et Technologique for formally authorizing my research.

At the Institut Marchoux, Dr. Pierre Bobin, Dr. Leopold Blanc, and Famory Keita provided instrumental assistance at different stages. Dr. Tiendrebeogo and Mamadou Hamed Cissé enthusiastically made the historical photographs available. The staff at CEDRAB in Timbuktu generously assisted me with archival research; Mahmoud Zouber was especially helpful and hospitable. Without Hamou (Mahmoud Mahamane Dédéou), I would never have been able to locate the few but illuminating Arabic manuscripts which discuss leprosy. The staff at the following archives and libraries also greatly facilitated my research: Centre Djoliba (Bamako), ENSUP (Bamako), Archives Nationales du Mali (Bamako), Archives Nationales de Sénégal (Dakar), Centre des Archives d'Outre-Mer (Aix-en-Provençe), and the Bibliothèque Nationale (Paris). Sister Louise Fricoteaux's efficiency and dedication made work at the White Sisters' Archives in Rome an absolute joy and yielded me some of the most fascinating and informative documentation used in this study. Father François Renault similarly assisted me at the White Fathers' Archives. Kevin Sturr deserves thanks for his help in producing the map.

For very warm hospitality, I thank Doral, Judy, Megan, and Amanda Watts; David and Eleanor Huggins; Dr. Famory Fofana and his family; and Jennifer Siemon. William Crowell, Gaoussou Mariko, and the rest of the U.S.I.S. staff at the United States Embassy provided critical administrative and logistical support. I am also grateful to Victoria Rovine and Assita Sissoko.

Informal conversations with family, friends, and colleagues in Mali, Europe, and the United States helped me to refine my thinking continuously. For constructive criticism on different drafts, I thank Mary Jo Arnoldi, Tim Cleaveland, Jacalyn Harden, Anwei Law, Michele Mitchell, Rebecca Shereikis, Ricki Shine, Benjamin Soares, Stuart Strickland, Michael Tetelman, and especially Diana Wylie. Paul Converse at the Johns Hopkins School of Public Health and Dr. Wayne Myers at the Armed Forces Institute of Pathology provided well-needed perspective from their respective fields. Jean-Loup Amselle at the Ecole des Hautes Etudes in Paris also contributed useful suggestions for my discussion of identity.

Stacey Suyat deserves special thanks for periodic assistance in the field, discussing ideas, and proofreading. My dissertation committee members Jonathon Glassman and Ivor Wilks offered valuable commentary on the thesis from which this book derives. Most importantly, my advisor John Hunwick read over earlier drafts and pushed me at every step towards the highest standards of scholarship.

Heinemann editors Jean Hay, Allen Isaacman, and their two anonymous readers deserve much praise for their invaluable comments.

I owe special thanks to my parents who have consistently provided the moral support necessary for independent and inspired intellectual development.

ABBREVIATIONS

Admin.	Administrateur
AEF	Afrique Equatoriale Française
AIM	Archives de l'Institut Marchoux
AMI	Assistance Médicale Indigène
AMA	Assistance Médicale Africaine
AMLM	Association des Malades Lépreux du Mali
ANM	Archives Nationales du Mali
ANS	Archives Nationales du Sénégal
AOF	Afrique Occidentale Française
ARFF	Association Raoul Follerau Française
CAOM	Centre des Archives d'Outre-Mer
CEDRAB	Centre de Documentation et de Recherches Ahmad Baba
Comm.	Commandant
DDS	Diaminodiphenyl sulfone
ENSUP	Ecole Normale Supérieure (Bamako)
FOM	France d'Outre-Mer
Gouv.	Gouverneur
H-S-N	Haute-Sénégal-Niger
ICL	Institut Central de la Lèpre
IM	Institut Marchoux
OCCGE	Organisation de Coordination et de Coopération Contre les Grandes Endémies
PB	Archives des Pères Blancs
RAMD	Rapport Annuel de la Mission à Djikoroni
RMA	Rapport Médical Annuel
RMM	Rapport Médical Mensuel
RS	Rapport Semestriel
SB	Archives des Souers Blanches
SGAMS	Service Général Autonome de la Maladie du Sommeil
SGHMP	Service Général d'Hygiène Mobile de Prophylaxie
SPL	Service de la Prophylaxie de la Lèpre
USRDA	Union Soudanaise–Rassemblement Démocratique Africain

GLOSSARY

Note on Spelling and Pronunciation: In the colonial period, French officials imposed an often misleading orthography to spell local names of both people and places. For example, *Faladyé* is actually pronounced *Falajé*. The letter *é* has also been used to represent two fairly distinct vowel sounds. The resulting spellings remain in use today, although Mali's Direction Nationale de l'Alphabetisation Functionnelle et la Linguistique Appliquée (DNAFALA) has since developed an official phonetic orthography. As also noted in the List of Informants, I preferred to use spellings which are familiar to most people or which facilitate easy pronunciation for the reader. Bambara terms are therefore spelled according to their appearance in Bailleul's dictionary, while place names are spelled according to their appearance in the *Official Standard Names* approved by the U.S. Board on Geographic Names (1965 edition) or on the Michelin map for West Africa. In a few instances, it seemed more appropriate to use the conventional English spelling for places such as Timbuktu (in French, Tombouctou) and Guinea (Guinée). Bear in mind that many of these spellings do not always correspond to actual pronunciation and that, in any case, the same words and names are often pronounced differently by Malians themselves.

bagi	Bambara term for one form of leprosy.
banaba	Most common Bambara term for leprosy.
banabato	Bambara term for leper.
al-baras	Arabic term for one form of leprosy.
bilen	Bambara term for a reddish patch or lesion appearing on the skin. Also the word for red.
CFA	Common currency used in most former French colonies.
dalilu	Bambara term referring to specialized knowledge or power.
farafin	Bambara term for African. Literally, "black skin."
farajè	Bambara term meaning "white skin." Rarely used. See *toubab*.
furakèla	Generic Bambara term for healer.
al-judham	Arabic term for one form of leprosy.
kaba	Bambara term for tinea, a skin condition which, in Mali, is often confused with leprosy in its early stages.
kòmò	Male initiation society.
kuna	Bambara term for one form of leprosy.
kunato	Derogatory Bambara term for leper.
toubab	A colloquial term used in most local languages when referring to a European. (Pronounced "too-bob.")

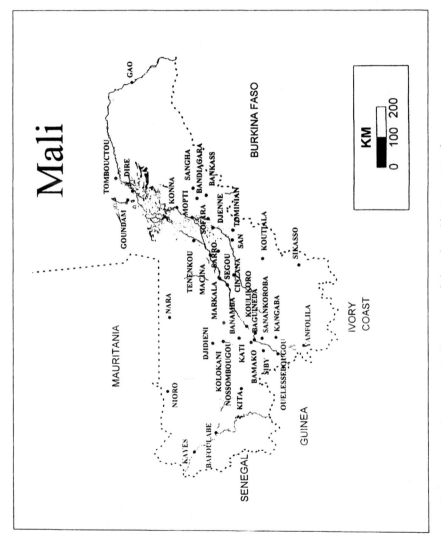

MAP 1: Principal towns and villages in Mali [produced by Kevin Sturr]

INTRODUCTION

The example of leprosy patients in twentieth-century Mali helps clarify two universal human experiences: the physical transformation of one's body and the related transformation of one's identity. Few of us imagine such experiences as historical events. Their deeply personal nature seem better suited for the fields of medicine, psychology, sociology, or philosophy. This book challenges such an assumption by relating transformations of body and identity to broader historical change in its more conventional sense—that is, change marked by "big" events such as migrations, technological innovations, colonialism, and coups. The book begins with an account of one woman's life and then gradually elaborates the larger context in which she and others acquired identities rooted in leprosy.

For most people in the United States and Europe today, leprosy (Hansen's Disease) is little more than a metaphor for deformity and stigma or a curiosity from the biblical/medieval past.[1] The disease plays virtually no role in day-to-day life, and some individuals are even surprised that it still exists in our time. Nonetheless, the people described in these pages underwent changes which, as humans, we all undergo to one degree or another, either through age, injury, or disease. In that one sense, we share a common history even though we may not share a common language or culture. The reader need not identify with the place or people in order to identify with their experiences.

Though often different in form and meaning, the experience of illness is no more or less a part of life in Africa than it is anywhere else. It is central to the human condition and therefore an ideal subject for making African history accessible to a wider audience. This book presents a glimpse of the African past which is multidimensional and human, a glimpse rarely offered in newspapers and on television. Here we find no valorous empire-builders like Sundiata, no daring resistors to colonial conquest like Samory, and no heroic nationalists like Nkrumah. There are, instead, only men and women, imperfect and nearly invisible in history, much like ourselves. We find, for example, Africans who were just as capable of prejudice, fear, and indifference as were Europeans. We also find Africans who continued to enjoy moments of happiness in spite of staggering hardship. Through their example we can move beyond the popular media image of Africa as a disease-ridden continent of misfortune and

---

1 In contemporary Europe and the United States, many patients and health care professionals consider the term "Hansen's Disease" less stigmatizing than "leprosy." They also consider "leper" derogatory and prefer "Hansen's Disease patient." Patients in Mali, however, continue to use the Bambara terms *banaba* and *banabato* which translate best into "leprosy" and "leper." For this reason, the more acceptable Western terms seemed inappropriate for the Malian context.

understand its people, regardless of their social rank, as significant and complex historical actors.

In researching this book between 1992 and 1993, I conducted nearly two hundred interviews with former leprosy patients and health care workers in Mali. My archival sources included French colonial documents in Bamako, Dakar, and Aix-en-Provence as well as mission records in Rome. In Timbuktu I studied Arabic manuscripts which yielded insights into conceptions of leprosy dating to as early as the sixteenth century. To synthesize such disparate sources into a single coherent analysis, I consulted a body of theoretical, historical, and medical literature not normally applied in the same context. As explained in the following introduction, this literature helped me to situate the lives of a small and hidden minority within the larger patterns of human experience.

Illness in Africa

Contemporary perceptions of illness in Africa partly derive from a body of literature whose origins extend back several centuries. These perceptions are often limited by a scarcity of local perspectives, especially those of patients. One underlying purpose of this book, therefore, has been to expand the range of perspectives. This section briefly explains how the literature at our disposal developed over time, while the next section describes how I endeavored to redress some of its limitations.

For the precolonial period, sources on African health and medicine are scarce and unreliable. Written almost entirely by outsiders, most early accounts associated the geographical and cultural remoteness of sub-Saharan Africa with illness and other forms of abnormality. The eleventh-century Arab geographer al-Bakri, for example, described the present-day region of southern Mauritania and northwestern Mali as follows: "The countryside of Ghana is unhealthy and not populous, and it is almost impossible to avoid falling ill there during the time their crops are ripening. There is mortality among strangers at the time of harvest."[2] Al-Bakri, however, spent most of his life in Cordoba, never once laying eyes on the African lands he vividly described.

In al-Bakri's day, virtually all of sub-Saharan Africa consisted of non-literate societies which preserved and transmitted knowledge of themselves orally. Ancient Egyptian, Hellenic, and Ethiopian societies left behind relatively rich documentation of their cultures and customs. This documentation enabled later generations in even the most distant lands to learn about these societies through their inhabitants' own words. Only with the gradual spread of Arabic literacy beginning in the twelfth and thirteenth centuries did sub-Saharan African peoples begin creating their own texts. Even then, literacy was limited to populations bordering the Sahara and to small groups of traders who circulated in the interior.

---

2 Nehemia Levtzion and J. F. P. Hopkins, eds., *Corpus of Early Arabic Sources for West African History* (Cambridge: Cambridge University Press, 1981), 81.

From the few surviving Arabic texts, it would be possible to learn more about how medical culture in the Sahel developed in the centuries preceding colonial conquest. Historian Ismail Abdalla, for example, writes on the mixing of Islamic and indigenous medicine in northern Nigeria.[3] Beyond his and a handful of other studies, however, this subject has received little attention. While researching in Timbuktu, I came across several large medical texts composed by local scholars between the seventeenth and nineteenth centuries. Many of them are little more than manuals of remedies, but some could nonetheless provide deep insights into local conceptions of health and disease. As a later chapter will reveal, attitudes towards health and disease also appear in seemingly non-medical texts such as legal treatises. Even local histories such as the well-known *Tarikh el-Fettach* occasionally offer glimpses of medical culture in passing. This seventeenth-century account mentions, for example, a saint's tomb frequently visited by "lepers" and other diseased individuals searching for cures.[4] All of these sources await careful examination by researchers with medical interests.

In West Africa, at least, Africans did produce written knowledge about themselves, some of which was medical in nature. Did this knowledge then circulate outside the region? Again, without sufficient studies, we cannot adequately answer this question. The work of several contemporary scholars reveals that learned persons across North Africa read works by West African writers, most notably Ahmad Baba.[5] These works primarily addressed legal and religious issues, although one can imagine that medical texts found their way across the desert as well. In the end, however, most people in the Arab world learned about Africa from Arab authors, traders, and travelers, or from their African slaves. John Hunwick and Bernard Lewis, both contemporary historians, explain how this outsider's perspective gave rise to prejudices and fears similar to those later harbored by Europeans.[6]

Until Portuguese ships first sailed along the West African coast in the mid-fourteenth century, Christian Europeans had virtually no firsthand knowledge of West Africa. Their perspective derived from Arab and Hellenic writings and often focused on more sensational details such as cannibalism.[7] Many Europeans were therefore predisposed to recognize and record the strangest aspects of Africa's physical and cultural environment when they finally made contact. Unaccustomed to the climate

---

3 Ismail Hussein Abdalla, "Islamic Medicine and its Influence on Traditional Hausa Practitioners in Northern Nigeria" (Ph.D. dissertation, University of Wisconsin, Madison, 1981); see also his article, "Diffusion of Islamic Medicine into Hausaland," in Steven Feierman and John Janzen, eds., *The Social Basis of Health and Healing in Africa* (Berkeley: University of California Press, 1992).

4 Mahmoud ibn al-Mukhtar Kati, *Tarikh el-Fettach*, translated by O. Houdas and M. Delafosse (Paris: Ernest Leroux, 1913), 170–72.

5 Mahmoud Zouber, *Ahmad Baba de Tombouctou (1556–1627), sa vie et son oeuvre* (Paris: G.-P. Maisonneuve et Larose, 1977).

6 John Hunwick, "A Region of the Mind: The Arab Invention of Africa," unpublished paper (17 February 1993); Bernard Lewis, *Race and Slavery in the Middle East, An Historical Enquiry* (New York: Oxford University Press, 1990).

7 Eldred D. Jones, *The Elizabethan Image of Africa* (Washington: Folger Books, 1971); Peter Mark, *Africans in European Eyes: The Portrayal of Black Africans in Fourteenth and Fifteenth Century Europe* (Syracuse: Syracuse University, Foreign and Comparative Studies Program, 1975).

and as yet unexposed to new diseases, they were understandably preoccupied with health conditions, which they usually described as dangerous.

In the fifteenth and sixteenth centuries, European doctors were still learning "their" medicine from Arabic and Greek texts. Perhaps they would have been open to acquiring African texts if such works had been available. Literacy, however, was confined to the West African interior. Virtually no African society on the coast could present Europeans with written texts documenting their medical knowledge. From the very beginning, then, this knowledge was filtered and recorded by Europeans who often misunderstood what they observed. By the time they finally reached West Africa's more literate regions in the nineteenth century, most Europeans had lost the curiosity of earlier generations and took little interest in local medical texts written in Arabic. Notions of racial and cultural superiority had even blinded them to the non-European origins of their own intellectual traditions.

Most of what we now know of early African medicine and health conditions derives from the scattered and slipshod observations contained in European travel accounts.[8] Several historians have mined these accounts very effectively, reconstructing what they can.[9] In the end, though, old descriptions of African diseases and practices tell us more about the European observers than their African subjects. As convincingly argued by scholars such as Philip Curtin and Jean and John Comaroff, most Europeans formulated their medical knowledge of Africa as part of their broader racial theories and imperial ideologies.[10] Images of a continent overrun by disease nurtured the perception of African medicine as ineffective and primitive. The notion that Europeans, armed with a superior science, must venture into the Dark Continent to rescue its population from disease crystallized in the 1800s. During that century many Europeans read popular travel accounts which often depicted scenes of "natives" beseeching the European adventurer for medical assistance.[11]

In the latter half of the nineteenth century, Europeans went to Africa more often as colonizers than simply as traders and explorers. Professional doctors then assumed primary responsibility for monitoring the disease environment both as observers and practitioners. Though accorded a separate status, these "men of science" were as much agents of imperial enterprise as were foot soldiers

---

8 See, for example, the classic accounts: William Bosman, *A New and Accurate Description of the Coast of Guinea* (1705, reprint New York: Barnes and Noble, 1967); and Thomas Winterbottom, *An Account of the Native Africans in the Neighborhood of Sierra Leone, To Which is Added an Account of the Present State of Medicine among Them* (1803; reprint, London: Frank Cass and Co., 1969).

9 See, for example, Donna Maier-Weaver, "Nineteenth Century Asante Medical Practices," *Comparative Studies in Society and History* 21, 1 (1979): 63–81; Raymond Mauny, "The Antiquity of Vaccination in Africa," *Présence Africaine* 36, 8 (1961); and Frederick Quinn, "How Traditional Dahomian Society Interpreted Smallpox," *Abbia* XX (1968): 151–66.

10 Jean and John Comaroff, *Of Revelation and Revolution: Christianity, Colonialism, and Consciousness in South Africa*, Vol. 1 (Chicago: University of Chicago Press, 1991); Philip D. Curtin, *The Image of Africa: British Ideas and Action, 1780–1850* (Madison: University of Wisconsin Press, 1964).

11 For more general accounts of Africa's popular image, see William Schneider, *An Empire for the Masses: The French Popular Image of Africa, 1870–1900* (Westport: Greenwood Press, 1982), and Annie Coombes, *Reinventing Africa: Museums, Material Culture, and Popular Imagination in Late Victorian and Edwardian England* (New Haven: Yale University Press, 1994).

and missionaries.[12] Indeed, in French West Africa, virtually all doctors belonged to the military.

Colonial medicine from conquest until independence in the 1960s is poignantly documented in contemporary historical literature.[13] Collectively, this literature illuminates two general points which are worth bearing in mind as one reads this book. The first point relates to the European impact on Africa's disease environment. The second centers on the role of medicine as a form of social control.

For "strangers"—to use al-Bakri's word—new lands do pose tangible health risks. As the survivors of "traveler's diarrhea" know all too well, the human body can suffer in some way when exposed to new viruses and bacteria for the first time. However, in the often panicked preoccupation with their own health, strangers tend to project the image of their sickliness onto the society or environment which surrounds them. They forget that strangers in their own land may fall prey to new illnesses in a similar fashion. They also tend to overlook the ailments which they themselves may be spreading to their hosts. For example, Europeans first arriving in the Americas endured "fevers" of every sort while at the same time introducing smallpox to a tragically vulnerable population which would perish by the millions within a matter of decades.[14] Europeans also carried diseases between two otherwise distant locations, such as the transmission of cholera from India to the Americas and Africa in the nineteenth century. In a similar fashion, non-European Muslim pilgrims to Mecca have also been known to spread disease.

Human activity, even at its most basic level, partly determines how microorganisms live and circulate. As demonstrated by countless cholera epidemics throughout history, the disposal of bodily waste can dramatically affect overall health conditions. Europeans in Africa were therefore more than just passive vectors and receptors of pathogens. As soon as they stepped onto the continent and began constructing homes, clearing forests, or even simply trading, they directly influenced the transmission of local illnesses. Any activity which provoked large-scale migration or war—the slave trade, for example—contributed in some way to the circulation of disease. Physical and social disruptions of communities most likely disrupted pre-existing indigenous methods of disease control as well.

The history of sleeping sickness provides us with one of the clearest examples of how European activity reshaped the disease environment. Also known as trypanosomiasis, this disease is provoked by a parasite which resides in human hosts and is transmitted by a small fly requiring very specific types of vegetation. The movement

---

12 European men carried out virtually all the early imperial tasks, with the exception of missionary work which also involved women.

13 For detailed histories of colonial medical administrations, see Rita Headrick, *Colonialism, Health, and Illness in French Equatorial Africa 1885–1935* (Atlanta: African Studies Association Press, 1994); Ann Beck, *A History of British Medical Administration of East Africa, 1900–1950* (Cambridge: Harvard University Press, 1970); Jean-Paul Bado, *Médecine coloniale et grandes endémies en Afrique 1900–1960: lèpre, trypanosomiase humaine et onchocercose* (Paris: Editions Karthala, 1996); Danielle Domergue-Cloarec, *Politique coloniale française et réalités coloniales: la santé en Côte d'Ivoire, 1905–1958* (Toulouse: Association des Publications de l'Université de Toulouse-Le Mirail, 1986); and, for Portuguese Africa, M. Shapiro, "Medicine in the Service of Colonialism" (Ph.D. dissertation, University of California, Los Angeles, 1983).

14 William McNeill, *Plagues and Peoples* (New York: Doubleday, 1976).

of human hosts can spread the disease to any location in which the fly is present. Studies of French, Belgian, and British colonies all present convincing evidence that, in provoking migration and disrupting vegetation, Europeans facilitated the outbreak of sleeping sickness epidemics.[15] Malaria and yellow fever are similarly spread between human hosts via an insect, the mosquito, which breeds and feeds under very particular conditions. However, historians have not yet assessed to the same depth the impact of colonial activity on these two diseases.[16]

As already suggested, humans tend to view the Other—someone who is different in some way—as being less healthy or hygienic. Religious, racial, and class ideologies exemplify this tendency by linking physical and moral impurity together. One becomes "dirty" by eating forbidden foods or associating with forbidden people. Medical historian Sander Gilman has written extensively and eloquently on this subject, revealing, for example, how illustrators and sculptors rendered the physical appearances of the insane differently from those of "normal" individuals.[17] Gilman and countless other scholars have also elucidated the manner in which male observers viewed females as more frail and prone to illness. Megan Vaughan describes a similar Western medical view of colonial African subjects.[18] As revealed in later chapters, people in Mali likewise explained physical "abnormality" in terms of social behavior and vice versa.[19]

These perceptions of the Other usually involve a blindness to the pathologies connected with one's own social practices. As many cancer patients know, the risk of contracting diseases, albeit different ones, can be as great in Western industrial cities as it is in seemingly squalid African villages. In colonizing Africa, Europeans not only transformed the pre-existing disease environment, they introduced new forms of social organization and all their associated pathologies. The historian Randall Packard provides some insight into this phenomenon in his study of tuberculosis and industrialization in South Africa.[20] More such studies are needed, however, before we can adequately assess this particular aspect of Europe's impact on African health.

15 John Ford, *The Role of the Trypanosomiases in African Ecology: A Study of the Tsetse Fly Problem* (Oxford: Clarendon Press, 1971); Helge Kjekshus, *Ecology Control and Economic Development in East African History: The Case of Tanganyika, 1850–1950* (London: Heinemann, 1977); Maryinez Lyons, *The Colonial Disease: A Social History of Sleeping Sickness in Northern Zaire, 1900–1940* (Cambridge: Cambridge University Press, 1992); and Meredith Turshen, *The Political Ecology of Disease in Tanzania* (New Brunswick: Rutgers University Press, 1984). See also Chapter 2 in Megan Vaughan, *Curing Their Ills: Colonial Power and African Illness* (Stanford: Stanford University Press, 1991), and scattered sections in Bado, *Médecine coloniale*.

16 Some articles on this subject are: William Cohen, "Malaria and French Imperialism," *Journal of African History* 24 (1983): 23–36; Claude Pulvenis, "Une Epidémie de fièvre jaune à Saint-Louis du Sénégal (1881)," *Bulletin de l'IFAN XXX*, Ser. B, 4 (1968): 1353–73; and Christophe Wondji, "La Fièvre jaune à Grand Bassam (1899–1903)," *Revue française d'histoire d'outre-mer* 59 (1972): 205–239.

17 Sander Gilman, *Picturing Health and Illness: Images of Identity and Difference* (Baltimore: Johns Hopkins University Press, 1995); *Disease and Representation: Images of Illness from Madness to AIDS* (Ithaca: Cornell University Press, 1988); and *Difference and Pathology: Stereotypes of Sexuality, Race, and Madness* (Ithaca: Cornell University Press, 1985).

18 Vaughan, *Curing Their Ills*.

19 In nineteenth-century America, many people associated cholera with immorality. See Charles Rosenberg, *The Cholera Years in 1832, 1849, and 1866* (Chicago: University of Chicago Press, 1962).

20 Randall Packard, *White Plague, Black Labor: Tuberculosis and the Political Economy of Health and Disease in South Africa* (Berkeley: University of California Press, 1989). See also Mark DeLancey, "Health and Disease on Plantations of Cameroon, 1884–1939," in. Gerald Hartwig and K. David Patterson, eds., *Disease in African History: An Introductory Survey and Case Studies* (Durham: Duke University Press, 1978).

In short, the "African" diseases which Europeans monitored as colonial powers were, to a large degree, a consequence of their own presence, either as vectors of new diseases, disrupters of African societies and ecologies, or creators of industrial enterprises. This point does not mean, as advocates of "noble savage" theories often believed, that Europeans infected a once healthy African population living in harmony with nature. Like all humans, Africans fought wars, cleared forests, migrated, and suffered diseases long before Europeans ever knew the continent existed.[21] When they arrived, Europeans merely introduced a dramatically new component to that process.

Since human activity and disease are intertwined, any attempt to control individual or public health inevitably involves some type of social intervention or regulation. For example, in the United States doctors often prescribe changes in diet or lifestyle as frequently as they do medicines or surgeries. In Mali healers advise their patients in a similar fashion. Such social responses to disease open the door for all sorts of interventions conducted in the name of better health. Very often the professed medical rationale becomes lost in the confluence of other political or economic factors. In 1996 the United States Armed Forces proposed the expulsion of personnel carrying HIV regardless of whether they manifested any signs of AIDS. This proposal, however, did not threaten individuals carrying all sorts of other viruses or bacteria. Clearly, the perception of AIDS as a costly, debilitating, and gruesome sexually transmitted disease common among homosexuals and drug users played a large role in shaping the military leadership's thinking.

Social interventions based on medical pretexts were as common in colonial Africa as they were (and still are) anywhere else. Several historians have written illuminating accounts of this phenomenon as it occurred throughout the continent. In nineteenth- and early twentieth-century South Africa, for example, the justification for racial segregation rested in part on professed concerns for public health.[22] In the Belgian Congo at the beginning of the century, government agents rounded up and isolated thousands of individuals in an attempt to control sleeping sickness.[23] In French West Africa, the colonial government attempted to restrict the movement and employment of Africans diagnosed with "contagious" diseases.[24] Asylums in British Nigeria likewise incarcerated Africans identified as "mentally ill."[25] Overall, the extraordinary power wielded by colonial governments allowed medical professionals to intervene socially to a greater degree than in their countries of origin.[26]

In elucidating these two major points—the European impact on the disease environment and medicine as social control—much of the historical literature

---

21 On the subject of precolonial environmental practices in Africa, see Robert Harms, *Games Against Nature: An Eco-Cultural History of the Nunu of Equatorial Africa* (Cambridge: Cambridge University Press, 1987).

22 Maynard Swanson, "The Sanitation Syndrome: Bubonic Plague and Urban Native Policy in the Cape Colony," *Journal of African History* 18, 3 (1977): 387–410; and "'The Asiatic Menace': Creating Segregation in Durban, 1870–1900," *International Journal of African Historical Studies* 16, 3 (1983): 401–421. See also Chapter 7 in Packard, *White Plague*.

23 Lyons, *The Colonial Disease*, 38–39.

24 Bado, *Médecine coloniale*, 120.

25 Jonathan Sadowsky, "Imperial Bedlam: Institutions of Madness and Colonialism in Southwest Nigeria" (Ph.D. dissertation, Johns Hopkins University, 1993).

26 Shapiro argues this point vehemently for the Portuguese colonial context. Shapiro, "Medicine...".

cited above challenges the lingering perception of colonialism as a blessing for Africa in matters of health.[27] The millions of injections and quarantines perhaps spared much of the continent's population from certain diseases, but all the other consequences of colonial rule, such as industrialization and migration, created other health risks for the same populations. As the literature also demonstrates, colonial medicine was inseparable from the larger colonial enterprise and its other less charitable endeavors such as racial segregation and forced labor.

We know a great deal about colonial medicine largely because of the extensive documentation left behind. That same documentation, however, provides little reliable insight into how Africans understood and cared for their own health during this same period. Much like earlier travel narratives, colonial records create an impression of a people devoid of their own medicine and in desperate need of European assistance. The records also focus on health issues which concerned colonial governments but not necessarily their subjects. Occasionally a doctor or administrator did acknowledge the existence of African healers and medicines. He might have even noted some medicinal plants or provided a glimpse at African beliefs and attitudes.[28] These scattered and often superficial observations hardly suffice for reconstructing African experiences to the same depth as European ones.

In general, the only Europeans who demonstrated a substantive interest in this subject were anthropologists and ethnographers. Their original mission largely aimed at documenting the ways of "primitive" colonial subjects whose cultures were expected to disappear as Europe's "civilizing mission" advanced. Several classics of anthropology such as Evans-Pritchard's *Witchcraft, Oracles, and Magic among the Azande* (1937) provided the richest and most reliable written accounts of African healing the world had ever seen up until that point.[29] Many contemporary scholars continue to rely on these works when piecing together the "African side" of medical history. Maryinez Lyons, for example, incorporates observations from Evans-Pritchard's study into her account of sleeping sickness in the Belgian Congo.[30]

By the 1960s, when colonialism in most places officially ended, medical anthropology had emerged as a distinct sub-field. Many studies of African healing have since become more nuanced and self-critical. John Janzen's *Quest for Therapy* (1978) advances the notion of plurality for understanding how communities cope collectively with an individual's illness. Within this framework, we observe healing as a process involving

---

27 For example, Lyons writes in her Introduction, "colonization was accompanied by undeniable benefits for many Africans. Western biomedicine must be considered an outstanding example of such benefits." (*The Colonial Disease*, 5.) For a more critical view on the mystique of "jungle doctors," see Vaughan, *Curing Their Ills*, Chapter 7.

28 For example, a number of colonial doctors published catalogues of medicinal plants, such as Louis le Clech and Jean Vuillet, "Plantes médicinales et toxiques du Soudan Français," *Annales d'Hygiène et de Médecine Coloniales* (1902): 223–57.

29 Edward Evan Evans–Pritchard, *Witchcraft, Oracles, and Magic Among the Azande* (Oxford: Clarendon Press, 1937). Others include Margaret Field, *Religion and Medicine of the Ga People* (New York: Oxford University Press, 1937) and G. W. Harley, *Native African Medicine* (Cambridge: Harvard University Press, 1941).

30 Lyons, *The Colonial Disease*, 162–98. Bado's account of indigenous medical beliefs and practices also derives entirely from archival sources and ethnographies. (Bado, *Médecine coloniale*)

many people, not simply the medical practitioner and patient.[31] Such scholarship has also facilitated more critical examinations of European medicine. In *Curing Their Ills* (1991), Megan Vaughan analyzes colonial medical discourse and practice in a manner "normally reserved for 'indigenous' [African] healing systems."[32] European medicine thereby appears less as the paradigm of objective rationality and more like any other human endeavor riddled with imperfections, inner contradictions, and strongly subjective assumptions.

Throughout the postcolonial period, the study of "traditional" medicine has also received active encouragement from many African governments. Mali, for example, established in 1968 an official agency for researching and producing indigenous pharmaceuticals. In an attempt to standardize and professionalize this medicine, it has even opened special clinics for healers. Hundreds of reports, articles, books, and theses now document African healing methods and conceptions of disease to an extent never imaginable even thirty years ago.[33] They are produced by both Africans and Europeans working either independently, for governments, or for non-governmental organizations. Though not widely circulated, this literature can also provide the outside world with some important insights into how people in Africa understand and experience disease.

The numerous studies at our disposal are informative, yet frequently lack historical perspectives derived from patient experiences. Anthropological literature in particular tends to dwell on the healing process in its most narrow sense rather than on the far-ranging social implications of illness. As a result, illness often appears as an experience with little connection to political change. This literature also centers on the present or recent past without adequately situating the subject within the context of long-term historical developments. One can only probe in so many directions at a time, so these limitations should be construed as openings to new research rather than as faults.

A Patient-Centered Approach

Like much of the existing literature, my research project also began as an historical study of healers rather than patients. My interest partly originated from my experiences in Mali as a Peace Corps volunteer. Wherever I went, there always seemed to be a neighbor or relative with therapeutic skills of one sort or another. A member of my host family, for example, once treated my hand which I had scraped and bruised playing soccer on a rocky field devoid of grass. I was also intrigued by the extensive medicinal herbs and animal parts found in virtually every market in Mali. Returning

---

31 John Janzen, *The Quest for Therapy: Medical Pluralism in Lower Zaire* (Berkeley: University of California Press, 1978). See also Harriet Ngubane, *Body and Mind in Zulu Medicine* (London: Academic Press, 1977) and, more recently, Didier Fassin, *Pouvoir et maladie en Afrique: anthroplogie sociale dans la banlieue de Dakar* (Paris: Presses Universitaires de France, 1992).

32 Vaughan, *Curing Their Ills*, x.

33 Some examples for Mali: E. J. Adjanohoun et al., *Contribution aux études ethnobotaniques et floristiques au Mali* (Paris: Agence de Coopération Culturelle et Technique, 1985); Piero Coppo and Arouna Keita, *Médecine traditionnelle: acteurs, itinéraires thérapeutiques* (Trieste: Arti Grafiche Noghere, 1990); and Dominique Traoré, *Médecine et magie africaine* (Paris: Présence Africaine, 1983).

as a researcher a few years later, I wanted to learn more about what I had, until that point, only superficially observed. A few works such as Pascal Imperato's *African Folk Medicine* already provided an overview of "Bambara" medical practices and beliefs but, like many studies of its kind, lacked historical perspective. I originally planned to uncover that perspective by interviewing "traditional healers."

A preliminary two-month inquiry quickly demonstrated substantial shortcomings to that approach. Then, as now, I envisioned "social history" as an endeavor which uncovers the transformation of individuals and their relations with each other. The healers I met, however, were more comfortable and enthusiastic discussing their science rather than their social relations. Well aware of the growing interest in traditional medicine, they also seemed to perceive me as just another researcher wanting to learn the techniques of their craft. Overall, these trial interviews yielded few insights into illness as a broader social experience.

Another problem stemmed from my initial limited understanding of healing in Mali. Unlike doctors or nurses, "healers" do not constitute a recognizable social group or professional class. As Chapter 3 reveals, medical knowledge and skills have always been diffused widely across society. Individuals who do possess these abilities tend to be specialists rather than generalists. One woman, for example, may be adept at treating stomach ailments but unable to deal with respiratory conditions. Certain identifiable social groups such as blacksmiths and hunters have historically maintained reputations as custodians of medical knowledge and skills, but they have never monopolized healing to the same degree as doctors in Western societies today. In short, "healer" as I originally conceived the term did not match local realities in Mali.

The final significant shortcoming resulted from a narrowness in my understanding of an "African" perspective. At the time I feared that any study involving European institutions and activities would detract from my goal of explaining how Africans understood and experienced disease. Although potentially illuminating for the continent's broader history, a study of European practices represented to me an admission of defeat. We already knew so much about the European side of African history thanks to an abundance of European sources. It seemed almost a call-of-duty to collect other forms of data and redress this imbalance as much as possible. In the course of my preliminary research, however, it became increasingly evident that nearly a century of active contact with Europeans had already transformed indigenous medical culture. In one town, San, one of my "traditional" healers turned out to be a retired government nurse. Practically everybody in the town also told me to visit an old European missionary widely regarded as an expert on African medicine. I eventually found him at the Catholic mission dispensing both African and European medicines to a line of impoverished patients. Another healer in that town boasted about his European clients and about his jaunts to Paris and Kinshasa. Though initially confusing and frustrating, my encounters with these individuals made it clear that any investigation of African perspectives would require thorough assessment of European influences.

Such realizations gradually helped me to develop a different approach. While perusing old documents from the French colonial health administration, I came across several reports describing a 1945 patient "revolt" at Bamako's leprosarium. This institution, the Institut Marchoux, still exists today, though it no longer isolates patients as it once did. It also now researches and treats other dermatological conditions in addition to leprosy. Still skeptical of a study centered around a European institution, I visited the old leprosarium and arranged to interview an elderly former patient, Makan Traoré, who lived in the neighborhood. The interview lasted only an hour, but it yielded far more insight into the experiences of illness and healing than any of my previous conversations with traditional practitioners. It also yielded a perspective not contained in the documents that I had gleaned at Mali's national archives.

Through this interview I arrived at three crucial realizations which served as the basis of my new approach. First, a study centered on patients would reveal a wider spectrum of medical beliefs and practices, not just those associated with healers. Second, focusing on only one disease would free me to look beyond the narrow sphere of healing and consider the broader social implications of illness. Third, patient interviews complemented by archival sources would enable me to assess more precisely the influence of specific European institutions on Malian society. They would likewise enable me to assess the often overlooked Malian influences on European practices. Overall, this approach satisfied most of my self-imposed criteria for a historical study of illness in Mali.

Like any method, however, my patient-centered approach had its own shortcomings. In total, I conducted about 190 interviews, most in the lingua franca Bambara with former patients now listed in the back of this book. These interviews took place in different locations throughout Mali in the course of a year. They included both men and women from virtually every ethnic/linguistic group. In the first month, Fousseyni Sow, the young secretary of a patient's association (which a later chapter will describe in detail), helped arrange most of my meetings in Bamako. He sat in on the initial interviews, occasionally interrupting to articulate my questions in clearer Bambara or to clarify answers. After that first month, however, I conducted virtually all interviews without the presence of an interpreter or assistant of any kind.[34] This approach usually facilitated a more relaxed and open dialogue.

After a few attempts, I found that reliance on a standard list of questions as well as the presence of an audio recorder stifled conversation. Instead, I took notes on paper and posed impromptu and informal questions which accommodated the specific details of each informant's life history. For example, interviews with individuals who begged tended to dwell on mendicancy, whereas interviews with former patients in rural areas often focused on their experiences with mobile nurses. In nearly all cases, informants were eager to share their life histories with me. Whenever someone exhibited discomfort with a particular question or the interview in general, I immediately changed course to maintain an air of friendly conversation and mutual respect. In Djikoroni, I also spent considerable time visiting past and future informants socially. In this way, I developed a rapport with many, some of whom became friends.

With the exception of one woman who needed money for food, I never paid cash to informants as some researchers do. Instead, I presented them with individual color portraits which I took with a Polaroid or thirty-five millimeter camera. (In rural areas cameras were usually unavailable, while in urban areas

---

34 In the Timbuktu area, however, I relied on a translator to communicate with Songhay (the lingua franca) speakers.

photographs were prohibitively expensive for most people.) As some individuals stated themselves, the photographs demonstrated respect and friendship in addition to my appreciation for their assistance. In Djikoroni, where I saw many informants regularly, I often presented people with fruit, kola nuts, peanuts, tea, and other simple items as is the custom among friends. As a sign of friendship, they too often gave me such items. Before leaving Mali, I organized a small farewell banquet to honor several informants who had also become good friends.

Interviews with "non-lepers" were also conducted on my own either in French or Bambara. A few actually began as informal conversations. In most cases, I wanted to learn more about a specific program or event rather than document life histories. For example, retired nurses and doctors informed me about their experiences with a mobile treatment campaign, other government officials helped explain police roundups of beggars, and indigenous healers offered insight into local medical practices. I recorded only two interviews on audiotape while all others were documented with handwritten notes typed up later in the day.

In the course of my conversations with former leprosy patients, I sought, as a listener, to balance their particular manner of expression with my own need for coherent meaning. Rather than simply pose questions and record answers, I pushed people to explain their inconsistencies or omissions. Sometimes individuals would revise or deepen stories related earlier in the interview. In this way, it became apparent that, like all of us, these individuals viewed their pasts unclearly and in many different ways. If a man said that he had felt shame with the onset of his disease, then I noted down the specific word, *maloya*, and sought to elucidate what it meant. Often, the word changed meaning as the discussion progressed. We worked together to interpret the past, and the resulting notes represented a synthesis of his recollections and my provocations rather than a word-for-word transcript of his testimony. Notes from each interview constituted the first of many stages of translation and distillation from which this book is the final product.

Without transcriptions of recorded texts, this book lacks "direct quotes" which would have colored the analysis with my informants' own words. This feature does not mean, however, that their perspectives are under-represented. When any of us relates stories from the past, we often contradict ourselves or forget critical details. Our listeners meanwhile demand more coherence and ask questions to clarify such ambiguities. Stories transmitted conversationally, therefore, are negotiated. Our "voices" are at once reflections of our own thoughts and responses to our listeners.

My primary goal centered on communicating patient perspectives to a general audience far removed from the small world of leprosy patients in Mali. Translations of fragmentary sentences lifted from very complex dialogues did not strike me as the most coherent or accurate way to achieve this goal. Grappling with similar methodological challenges, historian/anthropologists Moore and Vaughan write, "local people's representations of and interventions in a particular situation are not necessarily evident simply in speech or linguistic form." Local perspectives, in their view, are often more effectively reflected as "practices rather than as discourse."[35] For similar reasons, this book focuses on life events rather than the language used to described them.

---

35 Henrietta Moore and Megan Vaughan, *Cutting Down Trees: Gender, Nutrition, and Agricultural Change in the Northern Province of Zambia, 1890–1990* (Portsmouth, N.H.: Heinemann, 1994), xxii–xxiii.

Most of the direct quotes appearing in this book were recorded in the more distant past. Since they too resulted from some type of negotiation with the reader or listener, these words are no more "authentic" or "truthful" than what I would have recorded in interviews. Nonetheless, they reflect very specific attitudes at a given place and moment and serve as useful artifacts for reconstructing past perspectives in all their complexity. Most quotes from the colonial period originate from reports and publications written by European doctors, administrators, and missionaries. In a few rare cases, African patients left behind their own words which do appear in this book, along with passages from postcolonial documents written by African officials. However exciting to read, quotes out of context rarely communicate their full meaning. A scholar's task therefore lies in the translation and interpretation of that meaning rather than the mere transmission of words.

The actual individuals selected for interviews also imposed certain limits on this book. Aside from a handful of health-care workers and healers, virtually all my informants were leprosy patients, many of whom eventually became my friends. While I attempted to present as many perspectives as possible, a patient bias runs throughout the book. For example, most of what we learn about indigenous beliefs and practices comes from the patients themselves, not from "healthy" members of Malian society. In other words, I did not interview other family members or villagers to understand better their perceptions of leprosy and its sufferers. I also did not extensively research other diseases whose example might have rounded out our understanding of leprosy. However, by devoting most of my attention to patients, I achieved a level of trust and intimacy which might not have been possible otherwise. My bias is therefore quite deliberate and justified, given the general absence of patient perspectives.

Though extremely diverse in terms of ethnicity, religion, gender, and geographical origin, the individuals interviewed represent only a fraction of the thousands who lived with leprosy in Mali during this century. My informants tended to be recognized socially in some way as "lepers." Most had also left their homes and resettled close to treatment centers in towns. What the label of "leper" means exactly will become more apparent in the course of this book. For the moment, I need only acknowledge that many people carrying the leprosy bacillus avoided the label altogether or remained in their often isolated villages. Only a handful of such individuals appear in these pages.

Furthermore, the book focuses primarily on the largest and most visible patient community located in the Djikoroni quarter of Bamako. For logistical reasons, I was unable to familiarize myself as deeply with the many other smaller communities scattered around Mali. Most of Djikoroni's population is either Malinké or Bambara, the two dominant ethnicities in the region. Virtually everyone in the community, regardless of ethnicity, speaks either Malinké or Bambara. For this reason, a Malinké/Bambara perspective dominates the overall history. A more substantive discussion of ethnicity and identity follows in the next section.

Finally, my reliance on interviews resulted in some problems with this book's chronology. Few informants narrated the stages of their lives giving precise numerical dates. The historical events with which they marked those stages also tended to be very localized: for example, the year of a sister's marriage or a local famine. This manner of marking time made it extremely difficult for me to impose my own chronology on their stories. Most often, I could situate their lives only in terms of a few momentous events such as independence or a military coup. As I became more familiar with Djikoroni's local history, events such as the arrival of a new director also became convenient markers of time. For those accustomed to understanding historical change in terms of precise dates, certain parts of this book which rely primarily on the interviews may appear as timeless descriptions. One must bear in mind, then, that this impression results largely from the particular way my informants viewed the past.

Identity and Stigma

The stories related by former leprosy patients opened my eyes to the broader historical significance of their illness. What began as an investigation of health and medicine gradually evolved into a more complex study of social identity, a concept which seemed most appropriate for interpreting their experiences. My research thereby corroborated a notion well-articulated by anthropologist/historian Jean Comaroff: "The context of healing affords privileged insight into the relationship between individual experience and the sociocultural order, a relationship which lies at the heart of social transformation."[36] Patient histories revealed that leprosy-related experiences in twentieth-century Mali involved more than just visits to healers and doctors. Those experiences were bound up with larger developments affecting the whole of Malian society and Francophone West Africa. They were also connected with global changes involving other people far removed from the continent. Though limited to a small minority of sufferers, leprosy was an historical phenomenon in the broadest sense and had far-ranging implications.

Today, the concept of identity appears in many contexts ranging from theoretical mathematics to ethnic politics.[37] In this book, I understand identity as a definition or conception of self based on a particular set of attributes—such as physical appearance, gender, occupation, or religion—shared by others. Identities, of course, are as infinite as the attributes themselves and depend entirely on context. In the course of a single day, one's identity shifts repeatedly. For example, the same man can be a waiter, father, brother, uncle, actor, Frenchman, Catholic, and Parisian—each identity is as replete with complex social meaning as the other. We face the challenge of sorting through this endless chaos of identities in search of those which merit analysis. We are ultimately interested, not in the identities in and of themselves, but in the circumstances which engendered them. In other words, we seek an understanding of how certain attributes dominate social organization more than others, and how some

---

36 Jean Comaroff, "Healing and Cultural Transformation: The Tswana of Southern Africa,"*Social Science and Medicine* 15B, 3 (1981): 367–78.

37 My own thinking on identity was partly influenced by the following works: Philip Gleason, "Identifying Identity: A Semantic History," *Journal of American History* 69, 4 (March 1983): 910–31; Jean-Loup Amselle, *Logiques métisses, anthropologie de l'identité en Afrique et ailleurs* (Paris: Editions Payot, 1990); Benedict Anderson, *Imagined Communities, Reflections on the Origin and Spread of Nationalism* (New York: Verso, 1991); Jonathan Rutherford, ed., *Identity: Community, Culture, and Difference* (London: Lawrence and Wishart, 1990); Jacques Derrida, *Writing and Difference*, translated by Alan Bass (Chicago: University of Chicago Press, 1978); Stuart Hall, "Ethnicity: Identity and Difference," *Radical America* 23, 4 (1989): 9–20; and Martin Heidegger, *Identity and Difference*, translated by Joan Stambaugh (New York: Harper and Row, Publishers, 1969).

identities empower individuals socially while others weaken them. To achieve this end, we must study the specific historical conditions in which they develop.

For most of this century, ethnolinguistic identities have appeared as the driving force behind social organization in Mali and elsewhere in Africa. Journalists world-wide still reinforce this notion daily in their reporting of African events. Such identities no doubt existed in Mali long before colonization, but in documenting them, Europeans projected a social order which did not always correspond with reality.[38] This projection has persisted in one form or another to this day.

Many scholars regard Mali as the heart of the "Mande world." In the same manner that "Judeo-Christian" or "Greco-Roman" loosely describe European cultures, Mande serves as a broadly inclusive term for labeling peoples, languages, and cultures with common origins located in the Mali Empire of the thirteenth and fourteenth centuries. Today, notable examples of Mande culture can be found in Gambia, Senegal, Guinea, Côte d'Ivoire, Burkina Faso, Mauritania, and Mali. Several historians speculate that Old Mali's capital lay in the vicinity of the Niger River about ninety kilometers south of the present-day capital Bamako.[39] People who live in this area refer to their ethnicity (*siya*) as Malinké (Maninka) and trace their ancestry to the Empire or its descendants. The area also enjoys a reputation for its griots or bards who perform historical epics about Old Mali's founder, Sundiata, or other figures of the past. Malinké peoples live primarily in southern and western Mali, northeastern Guinea, and southeastern Senegal. In most cases they speak mutually intelligible dialects of a language also called Malinké.

In central-southern Mali, especially around the Niger River and its tributaries, live another Mande people who generally identify their ethnicity as Bambara (Bamana). This identity derives in part from the Bambara states of Ségou and Kaarta which covered the area in the eighteenth and nineteenth centuries. Ethnologists also consider Bambara peoples as Mande, because their language and Malinké are closely related and mutually intelligible, much like Italian and Spanish. In the colonial and postcolonial periods, Bambara served as the dominant lingua franca and "Bamana" culture became very influential.

Like many all-inclusive labels, Bambara and Malinké hardly describe the tremendous variations in ethnic identity. Soninké peoples (Maraka) often claim origin in the Ghana Empire which once occupied the regions of southern Mauritania, northern Senegal, and northwestern Mali roughly between the eighth and twelfth centuries. Technically, their language belongs to the Mande family, but it is no more mutually intelligible with Malinké than English is with Italian. Though still living in greatest concentration in this region, many have dispersed throughout West Africa primarily as traders and migrant workers. Some "Maraka" peoples, for example, claim Soninké origins, but have been living for centuries among Bambara peoples around the Niger River near Ségou. They speak Bambara as a first language and farm as their primary occupation.

---

38 Terence Ranger, "The Invention of Tradition in Colonial Africa," in Eric Hobsbawn and Terence Ranger, eds., *The Invention of Tradition* (Cambridge: Cambridge University Press, 1983), 211–62. See also Amselle, *Logiques métisses*.

39 David Conrad, "A Town Called Dakalajan: The Sunjata Tradition and the Question of Ancient Mali's Capital," *Journal of African History* 35, 2 (1994): 355–77.

"Fulani" (Fula, Peul, or Fulfulde) speaking peoples exemplify this complexity to an even greater degree.[40] Many historians believe that they originated in the far western regions of West Africa—perhaps in northwest Guinea—and gradually migrated eastward over the centuries. Today they live scattered across the Sahel and savannah from Senegal to Sudan. Their languages belong to a separate family and, much like Mande dialects, are mutually intelligible in some but not all cases. As a result of much nomadism and migration, multiple Fulani identities exist in Mali. For example, Fulani peoples living in Bandiagara may descend from those who once made up the Macina State of the early nineteenth century or those who came with Umar Tall's invasion from Fouta Djalon (in present-day northern Guinea) a few decades later. Some are pastoralists while others are sedentary farmers. In southern Mali many people are Fulani in name only—they do not even speak the language—much like fourth-generation Germans in the United States. Like the Maraka among the Bambara, they have lived among Malinké peoples for centuries and, to a large degree, share a common culture. In short, these same types of complex variations exist for all Malian "ethnicities," whether Dafing, Dogon, Bobo, Bozo, Minianka, Moor, Senufo, Songhay, or Tuareg.[41]

In recent decades, many researchers have questioned the importance and definition of ethnolinguistic identities in Africa. There now exists an extensive literature documenting a wide variety of past and present identities from different perspectives. With locally written Arabic manuscripts, for example, historians have analyzed transformations in West African Muslim communities during the nineteenth century.[42] Such studies help us to infer the meaning of precolonial religious identities. Many other historical works offer insights into the changing meaning of slave status throughout the continent.[43] Studies of migrant laborers in South Africa at the turn of the century reveal the effects of industrialization. Women have also received more attention from scholars interested in gender-based attributes.

In Mali, both local and foreign researchers have expanded their focus in similar ways. Social identities associated with inherited professional status—bards, blacksmiths, hunters, "noble" farmers, and "slaves"—demonstrate the same kinds of complex variations manifested in ethnic labels.[44] For example, recent scholarship questions the assumption that all bards (griots or jeliw) occupied an "inferior" rank in village society.[45] Other research explores the nature of identities rooted in gender,

---

40 For a fuller discussion of Fulani identity in Mali, see Amselle, *Logiques métisses*. Amadou Hampaté Ba and J. Daget, *L'Empire Peul du Macina* (Paris: Mouton and Co., 1962); John Grayzel, "The Ecology of Ethnic-Class Identity among African Pastoral People: The Doukoloma Fulbe" (Ph.D. dissertation, University of Oregon, 1977); and David Robinson, *The Holy War of Umar Tall: The Western Sudan in the Mid-Nineteenth Century* (Oxford: Clarendon Press, 1985).

41 See Amselle, *Logiques métisses* for a further discussion of Mali's ethnic complexity.

42 Robinson, *The Holy War*.

43 For Mali, see Richard Roberts, *Warriors, Merchants, and Slaves: The State and Economy in the Middle Niger Valley, 1700–1914* (Stanford: Stanford University Press, 1987).

44 David Conrad and Barbara Frank, eds. *Status and Identity in West Africa: Nyamakalaw of Mande* (Bloomington: Indiana University Press, 1995). Gerald Cashion, "Hunters of the Mande: A Behavioral Code and Worldview Derived from a Study of Their Folklore" (Ph.D. dissertation, Indiana University, 1984); and Patrick McNaughton, *The Mande Blacksmiths: Knowledge, Power, and Art in West Africa* (Bloomington: Indiana, University Press, 1988).

45 Conrad and Frank, *Status and Identity*.

[handwritten: complex - many identity factor options]

religion, and newer forms of occupational status such as government employment.[46] All of these studies enable us to appreciate better the multiple and changing meanings of identity in Mali.

When I first contemplated a study of medicine and disease in Mali, I knew nothing about the extent of Djikoroni's community of former and current leprosy patients. One saw "lepers" frequently on Bamako's streets, but they usually blended into the crowded urban landscape. In the market center or near the Friday mosque, such individuals gathered to solicit alms along with other handicapped or indigent individuals. Few, if any, of my Malian friends and acquaintances knew much about these people either. It appeared that lepers stood outside Malian society—a status which I the foreigner experienced myself, though in a considerably different manner. While listening to their stories, I realized that, like all people, individuals who lived with this disease had a specific past which could be studied, and that understanding this past might help us to recognize these seemingly anonymous urban faces as real human beings with a deep sense of self and community. Like people who shared a common language or religion, they too had an identity rooted in a common attribute.

The degree to which leprosy defined one's overall identity changed over time and varied from individual to individual, community to community. Often in conversation former patients themselves explained these variations with the simple Bambara expression, "People are not the same" (*Mògòw tè kelen*). If a woman remained married to her healthy husband while all other leprosy patients in her village lost their spouses, she would invoke the expression to explain the exception. Leprosy never fully displaced all one's other identities, whether rooted in language, religion, gender, or inherited professional status. Nonetheless, it often affected other critical attributes to the point of changing those seemingly fixed identities. For example, leprosy often impeded marriage and work, two fundamental components of personhood (*mògòya*) for both men and women.

Overall, while leprosy affected each individual differently, it almost always reduced one's social power in some way. Identities which diminish social power (most commonly, access to resources or institutions) are often understood under the rubric "stigma."[47] Stigma derives from the ancient Greek word describing the bodily signs once used to mark individuals of particular moral status such as

---

46 François Constantin, "Constructing Muslim Identities in Mali," in Louis Brenner, ed., *Muslim Identity and Social Change in Sub-Saharan Africa* (Bloomington: Indiana University Press, 1993); Maria Grosz-Ngate, "Bambara Men and Women and the Reproduction of Social Life in Sana Province, Mali" (Ph.D. dissertation, Michigan State University, 1986), and "Hidden Meanings: Explorations into a Bamana Construction of Gender," *Ethnology* 28, 2 (1989): 167–83; and Lansine Kaba, *The Wahhabiyya: Islamic Reform and Politics in French West Africa* (Evanston: Northwestern University Press, 1974).

47 My thinking on stigma was partly influenced by the following works: Erving Goffman, *Stigma: Notes on the Management of Spoiled Identity* (New York: Simon and Schuster, 1963); Stephen C. Ainlay, Gaylene Becker, and Lerita M. Coleman, eds., *The Dilemma of Difference: A Multidisciplinary View of Stigma* (New York: Plenum Press, 1986); Z. Gussow and G. S. Tracy, "The Phenomenon of Leprosy Stigma in the Continental United States," *Leprosy Review* 43, 1 (1972): 85–93; Ann Jacoby, "Felt Versus Enacted Stigma: A Concept Revisited, Evidence from a Study of People with Epilepsy in Remission," *Social Science and Medicine* 38, 2 (1994): 269–74; and Nancy Waxler, "Learning to be a Leper: A Case Study in the Social Construction of Illness," in G. Mishler, ed., *Social Contexts of Health, Illness, and Patient Care* (Cambridge: Cambridge University Press, 1981).

slaves or criminals. In his often-cited book on the subject, Erving Goffman defines stigma as a discrediting attribute which "constitutes a special discrepancy between virtual and actual social identity." Virtual identity comprises everything expected of individuals to qualify them as "normal," and actual identity is what people are in real life.[48]"Normals" then regard people with a stigma as "not quite human."

> On this assumption we [normals] exercise varieties of discrimination. . . . We construct a stigma-theory, an ideology to explain his inferiority and account for the danger he represents, sometimes rationalizing an animosity based on other differences, such as those of social class. We use specific stigma terms such as cripple, bastard, moron in our daily discourse as a source of metaphor and imagery, typically without giving thought to the original meaning. We tend to impute a wide range of imperfections on the basis of the original one . . .[49]

Sociologists Ainlay and Crosby similarly interpret stigma as a "process by which people catalog difference." Encounters between stigmatizers and stigmatized "trigger ordering activities." Like the making of laws, the creation of stigma is a "facet of the human need for order."[50] To understand a particular stigma, therefore, we must study the different forms of discourse and social practice in which it is embodied.

The role of difference in shaping identity is well documented for many other attributes, both physical and social. Sander Gilman elucidates this phenomenon vividly, revealing deep links between, for example, racial stereotyping and medical definitions of illness and madness. In his view, "The resulting basic categories of difference reflect our preoccupation with the self and the control that the self must have over the world."[51] Fears of "disease, pollution, corruption, and alteration" thereby underlie the proclivity to identify ourselves and each other. As this book reveals, this proclivity manifests itself as much in Africa as it does in Europe or anywhere else.

Leprosy has served as the basis of social identity in seemingly unconnected places and times ranging from medieval Europe to contemporary Mali. This widespread pattern stems from the disease's tendency to impose distinct physical attributes when left untreated. Much like skin color, these attributes often become markers of difference which facilitate the patient's separation from others. This phenomenon fits into a larger pattern of exclusion well described by sociologist Lerita Coleman: "Certain physical characteristics or illnesses elicit fear because the etiology of the attribute or disease is unknown, unpredictable, and unexpected." People want to separate themselves from the stigmatized in order to "reduce their own risk of

---

48 Goffman, *Stigma*, 1–3.

49 Ibid., 5.

50 Stephen C. Ainlay and Faye Crosby, "Stigma, Justice and the Dilemma of Difference," in Ainlay, Becker, and Coleman, eds., *The Dilemma of Difference*, 19–20. For an interesting study of difference as a component of ethnic identity in an African society, see Alma Gottlieb, *Under the Kapok Tree: Identity and Difference in Beng Thought* (Bloomington: Indiana University Press, 1992).

51 Gilman, *Difference and Pathology*, 23. For a similar analysis of the treatment of African-Americans, Jews, and homosexuals, see Barry Adam, *The Survival of Domination, Inferiorization and Everyday Life* (New York: Elsevier North-Holland, 1978).

acquiring the stigma. By isolating individuals, people feel they can also isolate the problem."[52] Writer Susan Sontag similarly observed, "Any disease that is treated as a mystery and acutely enough feared will be felt to be morally if not literally contagious."[53] The following chapters will examine this phenomenon as it occurred in twentieth-century Mali.

The Biology of Leprosy

Leprosy's sensational and confused history partly arises from its biological attributes and the complexity of its treatment. Before examining the disease's specific social consequences in Mali, we should briefly consider its physical effects.[54] As subsequent chapters reveal, the two dimensions of the disease are directly interrelated. This discussion provides a general sense of what happens to one's body with the onset of the disease. The rest of the study explores what happens to one's self.

Contemporary Western medical literature associates leprosy's attributes with *Mycobacterium leprae* (commonly referred to as *M. leprae* or Hansen's bacillus), an organism belonging to the same family of mycobacteria responsible for tuberculosis. Unlike most other bacteria, *M. leprae* resides within its host cell and can take as many as twelve to thirteen days to replicate. Researchers once believed that only humans carried the bacillus but have since found it in nine-banded armadillos, Mangabey monkeys, and chimpanzees. The bacillus also cannot be cultivated artificially in a laboratory, thereby hindering its study and the development of antibiotics.

Contrary to popular belief, *M. leprae* is not easily transmitted. Medical specialists, in fact, still do not agree on how individuals actually acquire the disease. Some speculate that the bacillus can enter the body through the respiratory tract, the skin, and possibly even the gastrointestinal system. While the bacillus can survive for some time in soil and is carried by the animals mentioned above, it most likely passes from one human host to another. How this occurs exactly remains uncertain. A medical handbook published by the Hawaii Department of Health states, "Most people infected with *M. leprae* never develop any illness. Of the four or five percent of exposed individuals who do develop the disease, the majority will have spontaneous resolution of their infection."[55]

Risks of infection are thought to increase only by living in close contact with an untreated person for a prolonged period of time. While the disease is not hereditary, a patient's family members are at greatest risk because they share living

52 Lerita Coleman, "Stigma: An Enigma Demystified," in Ainlay, Becker, and Coleman, eds., *The Dilemma of Difference*, 225–28.

53 Susan Sontag, *Illness as Metaphor* (New York: Farrar, Straus, Giroux, 1977), 6.

54 This brief medical discussion of leprosy derives in part from readings of recent issues of the *International Journal of Leprosy* and *Leprosy Review*, as well as from the following medical texts: Richard Frankel, "Hansen's Disease, A Synopsis for Health Care Professionals" (Honolulu: Hawaii Department of Health, 1991); Robert Hastings, *Leprosy* (Edinburgh: Churchill Livingstone, 1994); and E. H. O. Parry, *Principles of Medicine in Africa*, 2d ed. (Oxford: Oxford University Press, 1984).

55 Frankel, "*Hansen's Disease*," 6.

quarters.[56] Nobody can yet explain why the illness develops in some people and not others, although some researchers speculate it may depend on the "functional capacity" of the immune system or on genetic factors. Most specialists agree that the risks of contracting leprosy from another person are extremely small, especially when compared with other diseases such as smallpox, measles, and meningitis.

If one does not fight off the infection, then it may take anywhere from two to four years to develop visible symptoms of the illness. (In some cases, incubation periods can last as long as forty years.) *M. leprae* usually infects skin and nerve cells first, so initial symptoms appear as discolored cutaneous lesions (sometimes called patches) with decreased sensitivity. The lesions are not uniform and often vary in color, texture, elevation, sensitivity, symmetry, and size. All of these depend on the type and duration of illness. Clinical diagnosis can be effected through detection of thickened nerves, loss of sensitivity in the lesion or centers of nerve distribution, and the presence of discolored lesions. Laboratory diagnosis can be achieved by examining slit-skin smears for the bacilli, although, in the tuberculoid form, lesions tend not to harbor enough of these organisms for easy identification.

Today, medical specialists recognize different forms of leprosy which they describe in terms of a spectrum bounded at one end by the tuberculoid form and by the lepromatous form at the other. Tuberculoid leprosy usually results in people with well-developed immunity; bacilli infect only one or a few sites in the skin and peripheral nerves. While few in number, these bacilli do cause swelling and early damage to these sites.

In the lepromatous form, weaker immunity allows bacilli to multiply and spread through the blood to all parts of the body. The widespread nerve and tissue damage, however, occurs much later and more gradually. Bones and organs such as the eyes, nose, testes, and larynx may also suffer. Given the higher concentration of bacilli, the lepromatous form is more contagious and considered the more common source of transmission. Most types of leprosy fall in between the two ends and are usually identified as borderline tuberculoid, mid-borderline, and borderline lepromatous; they display mixed characteristics depending on their position on the spectrum. In its earliest stage, before one can determine its specific form, the disease is called "indeterminate."

Leprosy's peculiarities stem partly from its tendency to change over time. With sufficiently strong immunity, tuberculoid forms can heal spontaneously without treatment. The familiar term "burnt-out"—as in Graham Greene's *A Burnt-Out Case*—refers to this process. If immunity weakens, however, bacilli multiply and tuberculoid forms become more lepromatous. Untreated lepromatous leprosy usually worsens steadily, while borderline cases can move in either direction.

Beyond the exaggeration of its contagiousness, the greatest confusion over leprosy surrounds its physical effects on the body. Popular images of lepers disseminated in literature, visual arts, and film portray individuals with severe disfigurement,

---

56 K. George, K. R. John, J. P. Mulingil, and A. Joseph, "The Role of Intrahousehold Contact in the Transmission of Leprosy," *Leprosy Review* 61, 1 (1990): 60–63. See also Elizabeth Duncan, "Leprosy and Procreation—A Historical Review of Social and Clinical Aspects," *Leprosy Review* 56, 2 (1985): 153–62.

shriveled and leathery skin, collapsed noses, and stumps for hands. Jokes usually play on the assumption that lepers inevitably lose body parts. In reality, the bacillus does not mysteriously eat away one's flesh as these images suggest. Rather, the classic effects of leprosy result as indirect consequences of permanent damage in infected nerves or skin cells.

Since infection is limited to only a few sites, skin damage is not always evident in tuberculoid cases. At first, lesions may be discolored, dry, scaly, and hairless, but, over time, they can disappear on their own. Though tuberculoid leprosy can heal spontaneously, it nonetheless causes permanent nerve damage if untreated. Sensory and motor "deficits" in the fingers, toes, elbows, and soles make those atrophied parts less sensitive to pain, pressure, and temperature and, as a result, they become more easily wounded and damaged. Wounds give way to other infections and sores which can destroy appendages like fingers and toes. Nerve damage can also cause fingers to claw.

In the long term, lepromatous leprosy is far more devastating and causes the more classic symptoms. Bacilli multiply in the numerous lesions, thereby making the skin waxy and producing nodules. Eventually the face becomes pendulous, and if the infection spreads to the nasal cartilage, the bridge of the nose can collapse. A raspy voice results from bacilli in the larynx, while infected cells in the marrow weaken the bones and facilitate distorting fractures as well as absorption of the phalanges (another cause for seemingly amputated fingers). Bacilli can also enter the cornea and iris, setting off a variety of potentially blinding disorders. Infected testes atrophy and become sterile. In addition to all these complications, patients also suffer from the sensory and motor deficits and their devastating consequences as described above.

Each person mentioned in this book physically suffered leprosy in a different way. One of the most severely disfigured men had no lips, nose, toes, or hands, yet he could still amble about with partial sight. In contrast, another man missing both legs showed hardly any disfigurement at all; from the waist up he looked relatively healthy. The borderline tuberculoid form is most common in Mali and West Africa, so there are actually very few "classic" lepromatous patients to be seen. Of those interviewed, only a handful had collapsed noses or were severely disfigured. Most people did exhibit one sign or another: missing or clawed fingers or toes, a limp, blindness, an artificial leg, or perhaps a slight deformity of the face. However, outsiders unfamiliar with the disease would not immediately identify many of them as lepers since these signs are not always obvious. In fact, a number of people actually displayed no outward signs at all, and I would never have known that they had leprosy if they had not been identified for me.

Since all forms of leprosy can cause permanent nerve and tissue damage, physical disfigurement often continues even without the actual presence of the bacillus. After spontaneous healing or a cure from treatment, a person with sensory loss in the feet, for example, must always be on guard for injury and infection. In an environment such as Mali's where people do not have easy access to protective shoes or antibiotics, that person stands a great chance of losing toes or the whole foot at some later point in life. He no longer has leprosy in a biological sense, but he will always suffer its physical effects.

Leprosy in a Global Context

In many Western societies today, the word "leprosy" conjures an assortment of images centered on the disease's physical and social effects.[57] It often serves as a metaphor for defilement, stigma, and social ostracism.[58] While this study focuses on the changing meaning of leprosy in Mali, it seemed appropriate to inform Western readers about the historical origins of their own understanding of the disease. The following discussion also situates this study in the larger context of leprosy's global history while providing some background to the perspective of European officials when they first encountered the disease in Africa.

As the world's most widely circulated and read texts, the Old and New Testaments constitute the single greatest influence on past and present conceptions of leprosy. Ironically, the words translated as "leprosy" in those texts did not exclusively mean the disease we know today. The Hebrew word *Zaraat* in the Old Testament referred to ritual as well as physical impurity. Inanimate objects like houses and utensils could also have *Zaraat*. In Ancient Greek *lépra* derived from the adjective *lépros* (rough, scabrous) and, in Hippocratic writings, designated a variety of skin ailments including vitiligo and eczema; its meaning varied from author to author. Mirko Grmek, a French medical historian, argues that Greek physicians were not familiar with true leprosy at the time and that no single Greek word designated that specific disease. *Lépra* did not mean leprosy and, in the first Greek translations of the Old Testament, this term was used to translate *Zaraat*.[59]

Most scholars do agree that leprosy as a biological phenomenon existed as early as the ancient period. Sanskrit texts dating from around 1500 B.C. and Egyptian papyri dating from 1300 to 1000 B.C. mention diseases whose descriptions are thought to match our own of leprosy.[60] Grmek argues that leprosy first arrived in Greece and the Roman Empire only in the first century A.D. when it became known as *elephantiasis*, which did not denote what we call elephantiasis today. From that point onwards leprosy gradually spread throughout Europe. By the fourth century, *elephantiasis* and *lépra* had become synonymous. Church officials attending the Second Synod of Orleans (549 A.D.) then designated the second term for leprosy, while physicians began using elephantiasis for the completely unrelated disease caused by filarial worms.

---

57 This brief historical discussion of leprosy outside Africa derives from relevant works listed in the bibliography, but primarily from material collected from Mirko Grmek, *Disease in the Ancient Greek World*, translated by Mireille and Leonard Muellner (Baltimore: Johns Hopkins University Press, 1989); Philip Kalisch, "An Overview of the History of Leprosy," *International Journal of Leprosy* 43, 2 (1975): 129–44; and Olaf Skinsnes, "Notes from the History of Leprosy," *International Journal of Leprosy* 41, 2 (1973): 220–33

58 For an interesting discussion of disease metaphors, see Sontag, *Illness as Metaphor* and, by the same author, "AIDS and Its Metaphors," *New York Review of Books* (27 October 1988): 89–100.

59 See also J. L. Verbov, "Biblical Leprosy—A Comedy of Errors," *Journal of the Royal Society of Medicine* 83 (1990): 127–28.

60 Grmek, *Disease*, 159. Given leprosy's highly diverse and mutable symptoms, however, it is easy to construe any number of afflictions, especially tertiary syphilis, as leprosy. Most scholars agree that the Sanskrit texts clearly identify leprosy, but some now doubt a similar interpretation of the Papyrus Ebers from Egypt.

The social reactions towards people believed to carry leprosy epitomized a tendency in Europe to persecute threatening social groups usually considered "different" by some arbitrarily identified characteristic.[61] Unlike any other disease, this one thoroughly transformed one's social identity to the point of being named by it. While a man with gout remained a man, a man with leprosy became a leper. As early as the sixth century, lepers found themselves placed in special "houses" or hospices. Sundry state and papal edicts subsequently imposed "social death," prohibited marriage or authorized divorce, and mandated the isolation of lepers outside their communities. Many churches forced them to wear distinctive clothing or carry wooden clappers with which they could warn others of their approach. Lepers were also buried in separate cemeteries. (As we shall see, some of these responses resemble those in Mali.)

One incident occurring in Toulouse in 1321 demonstrated the severity of this persecution and its effects in forming a recognizable social class of lepers. In that year a French inquisitor exposed a plot to "overthrow Christendom" perpetrated by lepers, instigated by Jews, and encouraged by none other than the Muslim "King of Granada and Sultan of Babylon." The lepers were reported to have renounced Christianity and poisoned wells so that all Christians would become lepers. In response, angry mobs had rounded up and executed a number of lepers and Jews. Philip V ordered the arrest of Guillaume Agasse, the head of a local leper colony, who then confessed to the plot and implicated several others. By the time Agasse received a life sentence, many of those others had been burned at the stake.[62]

It remains uncertain as to whether everyone called a "leper" in medieval Europe actually suffered from the precise disease we know today. Some historians argue that descriptions from that time correspond sufficiently to our own, while others believe that medieval lepers included people with other skin diseases and tertiary syphilis (characterized by the collapsed nose). Studies of skeletons exhumed from leper cemeteries indicate that those individuals most likely had the disease, but such limited evidence can not possibly verify the conditions of the thousands of others who suffered the same fate. Registries from leprosariums indicate that lepers became most numerous in Europe between the eleventh and fourteenth centuries. From the fifteenth century onwards, their numbers steadily decreased and, in the eighteenth century, vacant leprosariums were transformed into asylums for a new breed of persecuted outcast, the insane.[63]

Like so many other aspects of this disease, the epidemiological history of leprosy is confused and controversial. Of those who take medieval diagnosis seriously, some believe that its spread resulted from overcrowding, poverty, or the Crusades. More skeptical historians attribute the numerous well-populated leprosariums to the particular hysteria of those times. The gradual near-disappearance of leprosy between

---

61 For further exposition of this subject, see R. I. Moore, *The Formation of a Persecuting Society: Power and Deviance in Western Europe, 950–1250* (New York: B. Blackwell, 1987).

62 Malcolm Barber, "Lepers, Jews, and Moslems: The Plot to Overthrow Christendom in 1321," *History* 66, 216 (February 1981): 1–17. For fuller accounts of leprosy in medieval Europe, see Saul Brody, *Disease of the Soul: Leprosy in Medieval Literature* (Ithaca: Cornell University Press, 1974); and P. Richards, *The Medieval Leper and His Northern Heirs* (Totowa, New Jersey: Rowan and Littlefield, 1977).

63 Michel Foucault, *Madness and Civilization: A History of Insanity in the Age of Reason*, translated by Richard Howard (New York: Vintage Books, 1988), 3–7.

[handwritten in margin: many "leper" accounts leprosy-like]

the fifteenth and nineteenth centuries only adds to the confusion, especially when we consider that no cure existed until 1948.

Nearly all scholars agree that, even if the reported number of leprosy cases in the Middle Ages was inflated by misdiagnosis, the disease's incidence clearly declined. Notions of improved living conditions and nutrition, often used as an explanation, hardly correspond to reality for most people. The quality of life for a nineteenth-century London laborer seemed no better than that for a thirteenth-century Toulouse peasant. Some scholars suggest that the Black Plague of the fourteenth century either killed off most human hosts (those most vulnerable to leprosy) or provided plague survivors with immunity.[64] Such explanations are highly speculative, and, to this day, doctors and historians cannot explain why leprosy waned as a major public health problem in Europe while it remained a scourge in other places such as Africa and Asia.

Since, by the eighteenth and nineteenth centuries, leprosy had become quite rare in Europe except for a few scattered places such as Norway and Portugal, interest in the disease derived more from historical and literary curiosity than from direct observation or medical apprehensions.[65] Encounters with leprosy patients were generally limited to those few people who lived abroad. For example, Dutch colonists opened a leprosy hospital in Sri Lanka in 1708 to control what was perceived as a growing problem.[66] In 1776 the Spanish governor of Louisiana similarly authorized the removal of leprous children from New Orleans, and twenty-three years later, a leprosy hospital opened in the rear of the town.[67] With the exception of these localized cases, the disease was of relatively little concern to European governments.

Several developments in the nineteenth century, however, renewed their preoccupation. First, Norway began implementing aggressive measures to assess and then eradicate leprosy from its population. In 1832 a government commission conducted the first survey of lepers, and a decade later the doctors Danielssen and Boeck formulated new and more precise clinical descriptions of the disease. Second, an "outbreak" of leprosy in Hawaii in the early 1860s dramatically revived fears of its contagiousness and spurred the British government to study the disease's prevalence in its colonies, especially India.[68] In 1873, just when European governments began intensifying their colonization efforts in Africa and Asia, the Norwegian doctor Armauer Hansen identified the leprosy bacillus.

Hansen's discovery intensified fears of contagion and inspired a revival of leprosariums which would last for at least the next eighty years. In 1897 the first International Leprosy Congress in Berlin, the same city where European powers had carved out their respective African colonies thirteen years earlier, endorsed policies

64 Stephen Ell, "Plague and Leprosy in the Middle Ages: A Paradoxical Cross-Immunity?" *International Journal of Leprosy* 55, 2 (1987): 345–50.

65 Brody, *Disease of the Soul*, 190.

66 Nimal Kasturiaratchi, "Interaction of Medical Systems and the Cultural Construction of Leprosy in Sri Lanka" (Ph.D. dissertation, Princeton University, 1989), 352–3.

67 Zachary Gussow, *Leprosy, Racism, and Public Health: Social Policy in Chronic Disease Control* (Boulder: Westview Press, 1989), 44.

68 Ibid., 69–72 and 82.

already or about to be implemented in scattered places around the globe. In 1865 the Hawaiian government passed an act mandating the forced isolation of lepers. Between 1866 and 1905, 5,800 people (mostly Hawaiians) were sent to Molokai, a "leper colony" made famous by Father Damien who confirmed the public's fears of contagion by contracting the disease himself. Dr. Hansen's discovery of the bacillus prompted the Norwegian government to pass the 1877 Act for the Maintenance of Poor Lepers and the 1885 Act on the Seclusion of Lepers which respectively authorized compulsory hospitalization for "impoverished" lepers and the isolation of all others.[69] In 1894 the Louisiana Home for Lepers opened near New Orleans. Staffed by the Catholic Sisters of Charity, the Home precipitated new public concern for leprosy in the United States. This concern culminated in 1905 with the introduction of a Congressional bill (passed in 1917) mandating isolation.[70] Japan enacted similar legislation in 1907 requiring the establishment of several leper colonies in its different prefects.[71] In 1909 the Second International Leprosy Congress in Bergen reaffirmed the policy of isolation and even recommended removal of children from leprous parents.[72]

Today, the popular images of lepers and their "colonies" derives as much from the Biblical and medieval pasts as they do from these more recent segregation efforts. In novels such as Graham Greene's *A Burnt-Out Case* and Kathryn Hulme's *The Nun's Story* (also made into a film starring Audrey Hepburn), the leprosarium evokes pathogenic horror and medical heroism. In films such as *Papillon* and *City of Joy*, maimed leprosy patients assist healthy European protagonists in their physical and spiritual escapes. The well-known travel writer Paul Theroux similarly demonstrates his masculine daring in a cynical description of his sexual encounter with a female leprosy patient in a Malawian treatment center.[73] Leper jokes and even references to Molokai and Father Damien reach still larger audiences through television shows such as *The Simpsons* and *Seinfeld*. Collectively, these sensational accounts represent leprosy as an incurable disease of the imagination, the distant past, or distant lands. This effect then enables journalists to run intriguing stories about "the last leper" or old isolation centers such as Carville or Nagashima, Japan which still exist.[74]

In most Western societies, identities associated with leprosy derive primarily from these diverse sources ranging from the Bible to television shows. Most people do not have direct contact with former or current patients, since their numbers are rather small and many conceal themselves or their conditions. Most people therefore do not know that this disease has been curable with sulphone-based antibiotics since the 1950s. Occasionally leprosy survivors attempt to assert their own identities publicly, as Kalaupapa's residents do when they lead tours of their settlement on

69 Ibid., 96 and 77.
70 Ibid., 131–56.
71 Skinsnes, "Notes," 226.
72 Ibid., 226.
73 Paul Theroux, "The Lepers of Moyo," *Granta* 48 (1994): 127–91.
74 Rick Bragg, "Lives Stolen by Treatment, Not by Disease: The Last Lepers," *New York Times*, 19 June 1995, 1(A) and 6(B); Valerie Reitman, "Banishment of Lepers in Japan May End, But Not the Anguish," *Wall Street Journal*, 19 March 1996, 1(A) and 10(A).

Molokai, Hawaii.[75] Some have also published their memoirs or related their life histories to other researchers.[76] In the end, however, such scattered voices cannot possibly compete with those projected in the mass media.

Leprosy in Africa and Mali

Leprosy in Africa has been a far more visible part of day-to-day life throughout the century. For Mali's colonial period, the frequency of misdiagnosis, statistical manipulations, and patients' hiding from doctors preclude any reliable estimation of the disease's incidence.[77] Before the introduction of antibiotics in the 1950s, the colony probably had no more than forty cases per 10,000 (Mali's population had grown from roughly two million in 1900 to four million at independence in 1960).[78] However, this number most likely varied wildly from locality to locality. In 1990, there were 12,817 registered cases of the disease in Mali alone with an incidence of 13.48 cases per 10,000 people (for a population of between nine and ten million).[79] These numbers do not include the uncounted thousands who, though "cured" clinically, still suffer the handicaps and physical signs which make them "social" lepers. Often concentrated in or around treatment centers similar to Carville or Kalaupapa, many of these past and present sufferers have joined together to exert greater control over their social identities. Contact with European institutions strongly influenced those identities but, as this book reveals, only in conjunction with indigenous attitudes and practices.

Despite the disease's continued prevalence in Africa, we lack in-depth historical studies which elucidate the transformation of patient identities to the same depth as the literature for the Western context. The few existing accounts are brief and rely primarily on European or non-patient perspectives.[80] Several anthropological and public health studies do describe recent conditions adequately but offer little historical context.[81] For example, Josephe Camara, a social worker at the Institut Marchoux in

75 I met several residents during an informal visit to Kalaupapa in April 1995.

76 Olivia Breitha, *Olivia: My Life of Exile in Kalaupapa* (Arizona Memorial Museum Association, 1988); Ted Gugelyk and Milton Bloombaum, *Ma'i Ho'oka'awale: The Separating Sickness* (Honolulu: University of Hawaii Foundation and the Ma'i Ho'oka'awale Foundation, 1979).

77 Bado extensively documents the unreliability of French colonial medical reports. He similarly argues that it is virtually impossible to specify leprosy's incidence in the colonial period. Bado, *Médecine coloniale*, 132, 186, 188, 245, and 253.

78 In 1919, for example, official estimates placed the incidence at between one and three percent for Haute-Sénégal-Niger. Bado, *Médecine coloniale*, 200.

79 For more epidemiological information on Mali and other countries see World Health Organization, *Weekly Epidemiological Record* 67, 21 (1992): 153–60. See also S. K. Noordeen, "A Look at World Leprosy," *Leprosy Review* 62, 1 (1991): 72–86.

80 Richard Pankhurst, "The History of Leprosy in Ethiopia to 1935," *Medical History* 28 (1984): 57–72; John Iliffe, *The African Poor: A History* (New York: Cambridge University Press, 1987), Chapter 12; Megan Vaughan, *Curing Their Ills: Colonial Power and African Illness* (Stanford: Stanford University Press, 1991), Chapter 4; P. Glyn Griffiths, "Leprosy in the Luapula Valley, Zambia," *Leprosy Review* 36, 2 (1965): 59–67. See also scattered references in Bado, *Médecine coloniale* and Domergue-Cloarec, *Politique coloniale*.

81 Harm Schneider, *Leprosy and Other Health Problems in Hararghe* (Haarlem: n.p., 1975); Ailon Shiloh, "A Case Study of Disease and Culture in Action: Leprosy Among the Hausa," *Human Organization* 24, 2 (1965): 140–47.

Bamako, studied the social reintegration of the institute's patients, but his otherwise illuminating thesis yields few insights into the past.[82] Numerous "in-house" histories by health workers or missionaries focus more on their own contributions than on African experiences. *Can Ghosts Arise?* by A. MacDonald extols in religious language the achievements of the Itu mission colony in Nigeria.[83] Guy-Michel Nebout, son of a former French Institut Marchoux director, concentrates on the development of different European medical treatments in his account of the institute.[84] Overall, such accounts provide important information on European activities but little on the perspectives of African patients. To my knowledge, the only work which presents this perspective is a novel, *The Modern Common Wind*.[85] Though fictional and set in Kenya, the patient experiences it describes resonate closely with those documented in this book.

Like all identities, those rooted in leprosy underwent profound transformation in colonial and postcolonial Mali. This book draws on patient interviews as well as colonial and mission records to elucidate that transformation from different perspectives. It argues that the transformation occurred as a result of specific historical developments related to the disease itself as well as to broader political life. In part, it addresses Megan Vaughan's call for a study which reveals "how far biomedical practices made a difference to people's understanding of themselves."[86]

In most cases, leprosy's social and physical effects—such as limits on marriage and work—disrupted many key attributes required for more mainstream identities anchored in lineage, profession, and ethnicity. The patient communities which formed around government treatment centers became the basis of new collective identities distinct from those associated with a life of individual isolation in more rural areas. Though once deprived of social and economic power in their villages, many leprosy patients used their new communities to secure greater control over their own lives. These developments fit into a broader pattern of seemingly marginal individuals "coming to consciousness" by forming their own groups, either by choice or by force. They represent, in the words of one sociologist, "the translation of commonality into community."[87]

82 Josephe Camara, "Les problèmes psychosociologiques de la reinsertion des lépreux" (*Mémoire*, Psycho-Pédagogique, Ecole Normale Supérieure, Bamako, 1987).

83 A. MacDonald, *Can Ghosts Arise?: The Answer of Itu* (London: British Empire Leprosy Relief Association, 1952). See also Electra Dory, *Leper Country* (London: F. Muller, 1963); and Knud Balslev, *A History of Leprosy in Tanzania* (Nairobi: African Medicine and Research Foundation, 1989).

84 Guy-Michel Nebout, "L'Institut Marchoux ou 50 ans de lutte contre la lèpre en Afrique Noire" (*Thèse*, Ecole de Médecine, Université de Paris VII, 1984).

85 Don Bloch, *The Modern Common Wind* (London: Heinemann, 1985). Bocquene's "autobiography" of a Cameroonian Fulani nomad with leprosy also offers the perspective of one individual but only in the context of more general ethnographic data. Henri Bocquene, *Moi, un Mbororo, autobiographie de Oumarou Ndoudi, peul nomade du Cameroun* (Paris: Editions Karthala, 1986).

86 Vaughan, *Curing Their Ills*, 203.

87 Adam, *The Survival of Domination*, 12. Researchers have described similar phenomena occurring among disabled peoples in the United States: for example, see Renee Anspach, "From Stigma to Identity Politics: Political Activism among the Physically Disabled and Former Mental Patients," *Social Science and Medicine* 13A (1979): 765–73; and Joan Susman, "Disability, Stigma, and Deviance," *Social Science and Medicine* 38, 1 (1994): 15–22.

Photo 1:   Saran Keita with grandchildren (1993) [Photograph by Eric Silla]

One common notion of identity centers on its role as an "artifact" of interaction between the individual and society.[88] The life histories collected for this study present over 160 examples of this interaction as it related to leprosy. However, distilling those examples into a single coherent analysis without homogenizing individual experiences posed a significant methodological problem. The opening chapter partly resolves this problem by presenting the entire life of one woman, Saran Keita. Saran's biography introduces us to the "individual" side of the interaction and balances the larger social history presented in the subsequent chapters. It reveals a succession of events which eventually resulted in Saran's joining a community of lepers. In the context of her entire life, leprosy appears as a dominant but by no means sole component of her multiple and ever-changing social identities. We see Saran not simply as a leper, but as a villager, daughter, wife, farmer, mother, grandmother, and healer as well. Such was the case for everyone else mentioned in this history, but the analytical focus of the other chapters precludes an equally detailed and comprehensive elucidation of each of their lives. Saran's biography captures the actual complexity of an individual's life which is often lost in writing the collective history of a larger group.

---

88 Gleason, *"Identifying Identity."*

1

The Life of Saran Keita

Saran Keita and I first met during the early stages of my research in November 1992. At the time she set her age at eighty years old, but, as for so many people from her generation, time passed in terms of life's stages and local events, not numerical years. Certain details from her life story—the birth of her first child around the time of Mali's independence (1960), for example—suggested that she might have been younger, perhaps in her early seventies. As our conversations (all in Bambara/Malinké) deepened in the ensuing year, it became all the more apparent that precise chronology played little role in her vision of the past. Nonetheless, Saran articulated a keen sense of historical change both in herself and the world around her. Her seemingly timeless anecdotes ultimately balanced my own historical perspective, which derived from more limited interviews with other former leprosy patients and from archival sources.

Of all the individuals consulted for this study, Saran in particular attracted my attention through her warmth and expressiveness. She recognized my curiosity and indulged it. Over time we developed a spirited friendship which superseded our original researcher/informant relationship. Her stories covered a wide range of experiences revealing the changing meaning of leprosy in both her remote rural village of Gwansolo (near Siby) and the capital city of Bamako, located fifty kilometers to its northeast. As one of Djikoroni's oldest residents, she had witnessed the transformation of a small community of leprosy patients into a dense urban quarter populated by roughly 50,000 people with absolutely no connection to the disease.

In the Introduction, I partly defined identity as the ongoing transformation of self resulting from the organization of society on the basis of difference. Understanding that transformation requires an examination of its occurrence on both an individual and social level. This chapter therefore examines one woman's experiences to illustrate how individuals internalized the social changes described in subsequent chapters. On a broader level, it captures a side of history which, according to other Africanist scholars, deserves more attention. Steven Feierman and John Janzen, for example, argue that studies of health and medicine should consider the "relationship between the most intimate sphere of people's everyday lives and overarching political and economic power."[1] Frederick Cooper similarly urges that social

---

1 Feierman and Janzen, "Introduction," *The Social Basis*, 12.

historians include the "texture of people's lives" and their "complex strategies of coping."[2]

The following "biography" distills Saran's anecdotes, observations, and reflections into a seemingly coherent narrative which conceals the inevitable inconsistencies and ambiguities of orally related stories. (A word-for-word transcription, if one existed, would only confuse the general reader and obscure the larger meaning of her life.) One person's biography also exposes only a small portion of a much larger process of social change. In the end, Saran's life history raises more questions than it answers. Were Saran and her sister unique, or were all leprosy patients in the region treated this way? Was this treatment particular to their village or to all Malinké peoples? What caused families, communities, and governments to respond as they did? How did others understand and react to leprosy? Answering these and other questions requires a wider analytical scope which ensuing chapters will provide.

Saran's Story

Masama Keita arrived at Mankan's compound in Gwansolo one last time to see Mankan's daughter, Hawa. The bridewealth paid, it seemed to everyone that the two would soon be married. On that last visit, though, Masama learned of several red patches which had recently formed on Hawa's forehead. *Banaba*, people said, "caught her." *Banaba* was the "big disease," leprosy, so Masama immediately called off the marriage. A wife with leprosy could give it to him and, as everyone knew, the disease might eventually prevent her from working in his household.

This change in circumstances left the problem of the bridewealth. Though Masama was from a distant village near Kangaba, he nonetheless farmed fields very close to Gwansolo. That was, in fact, how he first came to know Hawa. With the marriage canceled, however, he still couldn't bear the awkwardness of asking for the bridewealth back. Instead, he pointed to Hawa's younger sister, Saran—who was just a child then—and requested that she be married to him when she came of age. Mankan Keita agreed.

Mankan himself was a successful farmer, one hardly familiar with misfortune. Belonging to the venerated though enigmatic hunter's society, he possessed the secret knowledge (*dalilu*) for protecting himself from gunshot. Fellow villagers often enlisted him to ward off bad spirits, and, when thieves came to the village fields to steal corn, he caught them by casting a paralyzing medicine. As a young man, Mankan had also traveled widely to other regions. Traveling was an experience highly esteemed by villagers, almost a right of passage for *kamalenw*, young men desirous of adventure and reputation. In her early years, Saran saw that such men would disappear for a few dry seasons and then return with money and new habits, like sleeping on a bed frame made from bramble.

Through the 1870s Gwansolo belonged to Samory Touré's expansive Malinké empire, responsible for enslaving its enemies and exporting them to the Bambara

---

2 Frederick Cooper, "Conflict and Connection: Rethinking Colonial African History," *American Historical Review* 99, 5 (December 1994), 1533.

state of Ségou. The *toubabs* (Europeans), however, gradually occupied the region, so that by 1887 Samory's control was limited to areas east of the Niger River. Five years later Samory moved his empire even further back to what is today southeastern Mali and northern Côte d'Ivoire and Ghana. During these turbulent times Mankan occasionally worked as a guide leading the *toubabs* around the Mandingue Hills in their campaigns against the resilient African king. One of his missions with the *toubabs* brought him to Kankan, a Malinké town about 260 kilometers south of Gwansolo (in present-day Guinea). There he met Nasira Diakité, who became his first wife. Later, in Gwansolo, he married a second woman, Sokona Kamara from Bankumuna, a nearby village. Together they had fourteen children. Hawa was Nasira's first daughter, Saran her fifth and last.

With the "big disease" now written across her forehead, Hawa could no longer enjoy the attention of young healthy men. Her family tried to marry her to an old man whom they said was her only chance at wifehood. She refused. As on other occasions when a girl rejected betrothal to a man she disliked, Hawa's family tied her up and threatened to force her upon him. She was unconcerned. They could even cut her throat, she said, but she would never accept that man. They relented, only to attempt later to pair her with a blind man. She again refused with the same steadfastness. One day a leper named Adama from a nearby village appeared in Gwansolo hoping to meet the woman with *banaba*. Hawa found him to her liking and agreed to marry. They had a son and a daughter, but shortly thereafter a hunter mistakenly shot Adama dead while he was strolling through the bush. Hawa then lost all hope of ever marrying again in Gwansolo.

During this time, the 1910s and 1920s, Gwansolo was little more than a farming village. Every rainy season the young men and women returned to the fields. The women would sit on the side, clapping and cheering the men as they hoed and seeded in unison in a straight line stretching across the field. Young children occasionally joined them. Hawa's and Saran's mother, for example, beat any of her own sons or daughters who dared not work. She said that not working would make them lazy and useless. At harvest time, everyone stored their millet, rice, and *fonio* in granaries made of mud and thatch. People consumed what they produced and rarely sold their grains (as they did many years later when money became more common for paying taxes and buying goods).

Saran and Hawa learned their female duties from their mother, who shared household responsibilities with eleven other adult women living in Mankan's compound. Each of these women prepared the family meal on a different day. During the farming season they and the young girls would carry the prepared food out to the fields and shout "Hello! Hello! Come eat!" as they set the bowls down for the men beneath a shade tree. A man would never prepare food on his own. Even on nights when the *kòmò* (male initiation society) met, and women and children had to stay inside their huts, the women would merely prepare dinner beforehand and leave it out for the men. While men provided the cereals which formed the base of their meals, women bore the responsibility of procuring condiments used in the sauce. To this end they farmed peanuts, hibiscus, and tomatoes in their own plots. They even farmed some of their own rice and *fonio* which they sold for pocket money. Women also prepared the shea butter, the only cooking oil used then, which demanded much time and strenuous effort. A man's duty to his wife stopped at supplying cereals. For other needs, she had to fend for herself.

Though the *toubab*s technically had controlled this area since the late 1880s, they hardly ever appeared in Saran's village. The very first *toubab* she saw was an official who arrived in Siby (probably in the 1920s) to unseat Jentènè, the local *farafin* (African) ruler.[3] For many years, every family in Gwansolo had to pay Jentènè the *nyo suma*, a head tax of sorts consisting of two buckets of millet for each member of the compound. In addition to the millet, they supplied him with shea butter and chickens. Jentènè also routinely forced the young unmarried women of the surrounding villages to re-plaster the walls of his adobe compound. The *nyo suma* apparently burdened Hawa's and Saran's father, Mankan, so much that he once "sold" two of his sons, Madu and Namari, to traders from near Bafoulabé in order to procure quick cash and reduce the number of dependents in his compound.[4] One day the *toubab* appeared in Siby and summoned everyone from the surrounding villages. A loud horn announced the meeting, and Saran, still just a young girl, went along with the others. The official proclaimed the abolition of the *nyo suma* and then led an expedition which chased down Jentènè, killed him, and destroyed his house. For fifteen days, villagers celebrated and rejoiced over the turn of events.

In those early days, Saran didn't know what to make of these *farajèw* (white-skinned people). On one hand, they took people like her brother Jogo by force into their army, but, on the other, they relieved her village of the *nyo suma*. On another occasion they helped exterminate the grasshoppers which, in years past, had periodically destroyed their crops, leaving people to eat the bark of the *sinjan* or *bulancè* trees or simply starve to death. Saran hardly ever saw *toubab*s, however, and they remained a mystery to her for many years.

By the time Saran turned fifteen, Masama was no longer the young and bold hunter-farmer whom everyone remembered. Having aged so, he had long since lost interest in Saran and allowed his younger brother, Janko, to take her. Janko was a strong and powerful man, head of the hunter's association. Saran's father agreed to the marriage and Saran moved to their village, Tigu. There she found people to be as friendly and welcoming as her own villagers.

At some point in the second year of her marriage, a reddish patch called a *bilen* (literally, "red") appeared on Saran's brown forehead. *Bilenw* (plural) ordinarily aroused little concern, since many villagers had them from time to time. Janko, however, summoned Tigu's most reputable healer, Bala Kamara, for a thorough diagnosis. Bala initially identified her condition as *kaba* (a fungal infection), but then applied a medicine directly on the patch to make sure. Within a few hours her skin began

---

3 Jentènè was most likely a *chef de canton* originally installed by the French. The French administration relied on such chiefs, who often came from "traditional" hierarchies, to carry out policies such as the collection of taxes, the recruitment of forced labor, and military conscription. The French did not pay them, but allowed them to collect their own taxes and extort labor from their subjects. Uncooperative chiefs or those who abused their privileges were often deposed. As a child, Saran may not have known how Jentènè had come to power in the first place. See the section on "Administrative Chiefdoms" in Jean Suret-Canale, *French Colonialism in Tropical Africa, 1900–1945*, translated by Till Gottheiner (New York: Pica Press, 1971), 79–83.

4 The colonial government had technically outlawed slavery by this point, but the practice of "pawning" off dependents during crises appears to have continued. The individuals who "bought" his sons may have had some prior relationship with Mankan. Though no "slave trade" exists today, impoverished households in Mali still send young dependents to other families to work in exchange for food and shelter.

blistering; a few days later it turned into a sore. Bala then informed Saran and her husband that it was not *kaba* after all but "the big disease," *banaba*.

Saran wept as Janko told her that she could not remain in his household. He insisted that the disease might spread to him. With no other refuge, she wandered out into the bush and constructed a small thatched shelter. Normally, only individuals with smallpox isolated themselves in this way. Most villages in this region shunned lepers but never banished them outside the village. The thought of returning to her family in Gwansolo did cross her mind, but she couldn't face the shame of divorce. Instead, she remained in Tigu, spending nights alone on a goat skin beneath the shelter. During the day, when Janko was away in the fields, she would return to the compound. She did everything possible to avoid him since, when he did see her, he often brought out his whip and beat her. In time, Janko married another woman.

When Saran first ran out into the bush, Janko's father had given her a small amount of millet. She subsisted on this supply until she was able to plant and harvest her own grain and peanuts. On a few occasions, Janko came and robbed her of even this food, claiming that he deserved it as compensation for the bridewealth. Janko's mother eventually took pity. She insisted that Saran sleep on a mat in her hut rather than alone in the bush. She also forbade her son from beating his leprous wife, instructing him to return her to Gwansolo if he really didn't want her.

Saran lived this way for two years, dividing her time between her mother-in-law's hut and her isolated shelter. Her condition progressively worsened. Janko had long since forbidden her from cooking, but now with open sores, she could no longer even work for herself. People in Tigu didn't want a leper walking about in their village. They prohibited her from eating meat or fish, claiming that those foods would aggravate her condition. Saran became increasingly withdrawn and preferred the seclusion of the bush to the community of others in which she felt so much shame (*maloya*).

One day, a madman (*fato*) appeared in front of Saran while she was sitting beneath her shelter. Having heard that he had killed and decapitated thirteen people, she tried to frighten him away by boasting that her husband was a reputable hunter. He quickly fled, only to reappear a few days later, this time while she was fetching water at a nearby creek. When he threatened to kill her if she dared cross over, Saran ran back to Tigu and told everyone about the encounter. They immediately sent out Bala Kamara, the man who first diagnosed Saran, to cut the madman's throat. Embarrassed by Saran's precarious life in semi-isolation, they also convinced Janko to divorce his wife for good and return her to Gwansolo.

Back in her mother's compound, Saran's life hardly improved. Other villagers in Gwansolo discouraged her from even trying to marry again. She and her older sister, Hawa, slept together in their mother's house apart from others. They took their meals alone and had their own utensils; it was said that leprosy spread through food and water. Ordinarily, women of her age prepared meals along with other adult women in the compound, but Saran and Hawa were excluded from this activity. They also cultivated rice alone with their mother. Visitors to their family's compound rarely greeted them, and old friends withdrew from their lives. Few people dared insult them directly, although they could scarcely sit down without driving others away. No other disease or condition provoked such treatment. Hawa eventually ran away to the "big town" (*duguba*, Bamako) where people said that lepers like herself could receive medicine and shelter from the *toubabs*. After she left, Gwansolo's gossips said that the *toubabs* in Bamako had killed her.

As a leper, Saran could not participate in women's social activities. This particular exclusion dispirited her more than any other. Every four years Siby's women held a festival during which men danced with wooden mortars gripped between their teeth and women gathered in circles for their own rhythmic performances. A *jelimuso* (griot or praise singer) sang the women's praise, calling out one *jamu* (family name) at a time. A wrinkled and gray village matron meanwhile tightly rubbed the arms of each honored woman, whispering incantations up and down their length. As the drumbeats quickened and the *jelimuso's* singing grew louder and more shrill, the honored woman would break out into exuberant dance. In the center stood a cauldron of steaming hot sauce. If the woman was deemed strong enough, she dipped her arm into the pot, grabbed a piece of meat, and ate it immediately. Only those who achieved this without burning their skin or suffering pain were allowed to participate. The villagers restrained those whose hearts "pounded too much" or whose spirits "broke" too often. Once, when Saran herself was of very strong character, she participated without anyone's objection. Now, however, the "big disease" confined her to the periphery of the women's circle.

Even though Saran, "the leper," lived a life very different and separate from others, she continued to receive the basic support and sustenance due all members of the family, whether sick, old, or invalid. Nobody actually begged in Gwansolo. At worst, destitute villagers without any family discreetly received leftover rice from other families. Overt begging was considered an embarrassment to the entire village. True, members of Saran's family feared for their own health, yet they would never cast her out and leave her to beg for food.

Periodically, Saran's parents also sent her for prolonged treatment with Kalifa Keita, a hunter-healer living near Gwansolo in the village of Konkani. For three years he treated her with medicines which caused vomiting but scarcely improved her health. Claiming to protect her from other villagers, he often locked her in a hut out in the bush when he went away. Saran couldn't tolerate such severe isolation and broke out one day, fleeing back to her village for good.

After that episode, her family sent her to Jomaga Keita, another healer who resided in Gwansolo itself. Jomaga began his remedy on one arm first. He applied a medicine which caused severe blistering. He also prepared a solution made from boiled leaves for Saran to drink. A day later, a scab formed. After two weeks, the leprosy patches disappeared with the scab. Jomaga then applied his medicines on the other arm and, in weeks following, treated each of her limbs and body parts in similar intervals. Though effective, Jomaga's medicine was very painful and tired Saran considerably.

Every dry season many villagers (including Jomaga) journeyed to the hills in Guinea where they prospected for gold. Wanting to continue treating his patient, Jomaga invited Saran to join him, his wife, brother, and sister-in-law on the journey. This was the first time she ventured to other *jamanaw* (countries). After walking for one week they reached a village just beyond Kourémalé. There they settled in a large compound with other prospectors and panned gold from streams emanating from the mouths of old mines, perhaps those which once belonged to the great Mali Empire. People said that many spirits lived at those mouths. Jomaga and his family took large rocks and pounded them into gravel from which they then washed the precious metal. Occasionally they found chunks as large as berries. Dyula traders stood ready at hand to trade grain for the gold, which they carried away to distant towns. In the evenings men drank beer but never allowed the women to touch a drop, insisting that they would quarrel and fight under its influence.

Unlike her family and the other villagers in Gwansolo, Jomaga put Saran to work both at the mines and in the compound. Her diligence so impressed him that he desired her as a second wife, making his first wife, Kaaba, bitterly jealous. One day, as Saran was pulling water from an old mine shaft, Kaaba pushed her from behind and fled. Those who had witnessed this act found Saran unconscious and bleeding at the bottom of the shaft. The chief of the mines chased down Kaaba and brought her and Jomaga to meet with Saran. Kaaba publicly chided her husband for wanting to marry a leper, claiming that the "big disease" could spread to her as well. Though Saran appeared nearly cured at the time, everyone counseled her to return to Gwansolo lest she fall victim again to Kaaba's jealousies. She accepted their advice. In subsequent years, Saran returned to mines in other places, but only with her brother Masiri. On such expeditions she found enough gold for a set of earrings which she had made by a smith in her village.

Throughout this time, Saran's life in Gwansolo remained bleak. Her family continued to forbid her from eating meat and fish, while other villagers always feared her disease. Saran never knew what caused her illness until the day an old woman named Nankan Koné fell ill and was visited by a conjurer of spirits. In the course of drumming and dancing, the conjurer informed Nankan that sickness fell upon those who did not confess to their acts of sorcery. Nankan then called in Saran's family and related her story of how, many years earlier, she had grown jealous of Hawa and Saran for being such hard workers. Nankan had waited for the hot season when the nights seemed to swelter more than the days. She knew that this was a time of year when rusty laterite rocks absorbed all the sun's ferocity only to release it at dusk. For this reason, everyone slept outside in spite of their increased vulnerability to the sorcerers who stalked them at night. Nankan had obtained the necessary ingredients from a sorcerer, and then cast the leprosy-inducing medicine upon Hawa, Saran, and their brother, Jogo who somehow eluded the fate of his sisters. Nankan's confession came too late; she died a few days later.

For Saran, however, knowing the cause of her disease hardly alleviated the daily pains which came with being a leper. It seemed that she would suffer these pains indefinitely. One day, however, Gwansolo's chief announced that the *toubabs* were coming to inspect the skin of all the villagers. Several people with skin diseases including leprosy hid in the bush, fearing that the *toubabs* would capture and kill them. Long weary of her social isolation, Saran thought it better to die at the hands of *toubabs* than continue to suffer as she did. She lined up and the *toubabs* recorded her name. Though Jomaga's medicine had originally yielded the desired result of removing the patches from her skin, Saran found that, over time, the blemishes reappeared; in her eyes, *farafin* (African) medicine could never cure the "big disease."

During their visit, the *toubabs* invited Gwansolo's lepers to a place in Bamako where they could receive medicine, food, and shelter. Skeptical villagers said that Africans would only die in such a place, but Saran had recently learned that her sister Hawa had been living there happily for several years. Her brother Jogo, who had settled in Bamako's Hamdallaye quarter after completing his forced military service, also assured Saran that this *toubab* leprosy center was safe. Unable to marry or live a normal life, Saran finally left Gwansolo for good in 1939 and walked north down the red laterite road to Bamako.[5] Maybe the skeptical villagers were correct, she thought, but anything, even death, would be better than her present situation.

After two days of travel, she came upon a cluster of small adobe huts and a few stone block *toubab* buildings situated on the north side of the road. This was the *dokotoro so*, the "doctor's house," the place where *toubab*s treated lepers, known officially as the Institut Central de la Lépre. To the south, in the kilometer-wide space between the road and the Niger River, only a handful of compounds sat scattered among a hodgepodge of bush and fields. And further down the road, as she would later see for herself, stood the growing town of Bamako.

Saran proceeded to one of the stone buildings where she met Aldiouma Kassibo, a tall young nurse from a Bozo village in the north. He recorded her name on a large ledger before leading her to a white room with tables and shiny silver instruments. There a *toubab* doctor named Beaudiment examined her, removing a small piece of her skin for analysis. Kassibo then took Saran to a small hut in one of the four little hamlets on the hospital grounds and presented her roommate, an old woman from Ségou named Musokoroba Bagayogo. Later, she also found her sister, Hawa, who was now married to a leper named Soulaymane Traoré. As instructed by Kassibo, Saran reported the next day to the stone building, where she lined up with other patients for her first painful *piquiri* (injection) of gorli, an oil made from a seed imported from Guinea and Côte d'Ivoire.[6]

Some Institute residents claimed that this harsh medicine had killed several patients as well as infants breastfeeding from their injected mothers. In those early years, each of these deaths provoked a few escapes. Although Saran similarly believed that her sister's husband Soulaymane died from his treatment, she continued to report faithfully for her injection every three days. The possibility of a cure warranted the pain and risks. As time went on, the *toubab* doctors and *farafin* nurses also appeared to improve their once injurious healing techniques. Many of Saran's patches gradually vanished while her strength returned.

The abundance of generosity and companionship which she found at the Institute contrasted noticeably with the scarcity of "good people" (*mògòw nyuma*) in her old village. On the Institute grounds Saran found herself for the first time in the company of many people—three or four hundred it seemed—all suffering from the same disease. Some endured far greater consequences such as stubbed fingers or even an amputated leg. Together they formed a community in which Saran took comfort. Every day she lined up with the others at the storehouse where the chief of the patients' village distributed abundant rations of rice, meat, and milk. For some time Saran refused to touch meat, still believing that it would aggravate her illness. In the end, though, the *toubab* doctor convinced her that eating meat would improve her health.

In 1942, Beaudiment, the *toubab* doctor who had first examined her, left the Institute to serve in the war. His replacement was known among the patients as "Laviron" or "Labiron" depending on one's linguistic inclinations. As Beaudiment's assistant, this *toubab* had already developed a reputation for severity. Without hesitation he cut

---

5 Saran could never specify the precise year, so this date is an approximation based on other details which I've been able to periodize.

6 Chapter 6 describes this medicine in more detail.

the rations of those who missed their injections. Laviron believed that hard work and a clean environment facilitated healing. He therefore ordered the able-bodied patients to weed and sweep the grounds or to cultivate millet in the adjacent fields. Refusal brought about mild beatings. Despite the abundant rations, a number of patients often escaped into town to beg for cigarettes or "kola nut" money. Laviron became furious whenever he found such patients on Bamako's streets. Those who violated the cardinal rule against leaving the Institute without permission also faced the punishment of cut rations. In the eyes of many patients, Laviron was nothing but a mean (*ka farin*) *toubab*. Saran, however, respected him for his commitment to maintaining the Institute's cleanliness and order. She felt that the *toubab*s who constructed and operated the Institute had mercy on lepers. If it weren't for them, these unfortunate victims would have just died in their villages or alone in the bush.[7]

Once she regained her strength, Saran began working along with other Institute residents. Her chore consisted of pounding gorli seed in a mortar. Other patients then cooked it into an oil which they then gave to the Institute personnel for final processing. Ultimately, this oil made its way into Saran's and other patients' skin through a sharp syringe. Saran later found work cleaning one of the *toubab* doctor's houses. There, for the first time, she observed the differences in diet between *toubab* and African children. (In her view, the *toubab* children ate very little.) Years later, when the doctor and his family moved away, Saran inherited their iron bed.

Near the end of the Second World War, Saran married Bakari Kamara, another leprosy patient from the Siby region. The *toubab*s had brought him by force to the Institute long before Saran. After treatment, he settled in the growing community of lepers rather than return to his less tolerant village. With an honorary payment of ten kola nuts, he had acquired a plot of land from Basala Koné, Djikoroni's chief, from whom the Institute had also purchased its lot. Bakari then constructed a compound and cultivated rice and millet in adjacent fields.

Bakari asked Laviron to release Saran so that they could marry. The doctor agreed, provided that she continue her treatment on a regular basis. Always convinced of the efficacy of the *toubab* medicine, Saran easily agreed to this condition. She moved out of the patients' quarters and into Bakari's compound on the other side of the road. Saran joined her husband in cultivating his fields. There was plenty of unused land then, so they were able to work in the best parcels along the river. Saran also often collected mangoes out in the groves in Wowoyanko, the place where the *toubab*s had long before defeated Samory in their conquest of the Niger basin and Bamako area.

Throughout his tenure, Laviron remained a controversial figure for many of the patients. They felt unnecessarily burdened by his obsessions with cleanliness and a strictly enforced injection schedule. Those who worked complained that their wages were only a quarter or fifth of what laborers received in Bamako. On Sundays, some patients had to haul rocks, used for new Institute buildings, from the neighboring hills. The war between the *toubab*s and Germans also caused a reduction in their rations. The frustrations of many patients culminated one day just before the end of

---

7 Out of context, this praise for *toubab*s may appear as flattery for the *toubab* interviewer. However, Saran, like many informants in Djikoroni, usually expressed these sentiments when comparing her experiences at the Institute with more severe difficulties encountered in her village and, much later, under African rule.

the war, when they organized a demonstration and marched on Laviron's office. One patient invited Saran and her husband to participate. Both refused, believing that the protesters lacked a genuine cause. Later Saran heard that Bamako's police broke up the demonstration and that Laviron expelled some patients.

Never once desiring to live again in Gwansolo, Saran nonetheless maintained close contact with her family and some villagers. A few years after she entered the Institute, a childhood friend from Siby, Saran Koulibali, suddenly appeared for treatment as well. Her husband belonged to the same family as Saran Keita's first husband, Janko, but he never wanted a divorce. They went to Djikoroni together with their children and remained for three years before returning to Siby. Saran Koulibali felt less ostracized in her home village. She settled permanently in Djikoroni only years later, when her husband died and she suffered a relapse.[8]

Over time, Saran Keita gradually befriended more and more patients from places far from the world she left behind in Gwansolo. She once joined a women's association whose members were of many different ethnicities (siyaw). This association organized social events such as dances on special occasions. From her friend, Kanko Fofana, she learned that the Malinké in the region of Bafoulabé treated their lepers more mercifully. Those people, whom Kanko referred to as the "Khassonké Malinké," didn't fear contagion the way her own people, the "Malinké of the hills," did. Kanko was able to eat with others from the same bowl and permitted to consume meat and fish. She also participated in the farming "parties" organized by the village women.

When Mali "took" its independence in 1960, Bakari and Saran were undergoing treatment with an antibiotic pill swallowed every fifteen days. This medicine proved much more effective than earlier ones such as *gorli* which had left most patients vulnerable to relapses months or years later. Around this time, Saran finally had her first child, Kadiatou, and then her second, Modibo. In spite of the improved medicines, however, leprosy had already taken its toll on Bakari who went blind one day while searching for firewood in the nearby bush. Saran believed that *jinn* (spirits) were responsible. Since he could no longer farm, he began begging in Bamako with the help of his children, who led him around the streets with a stick. On ordinary days he usually collected leftover dried rice, often enough to feed his family. On Fridays he also collected money near the mosque. Bakari tried to convince his wife to join him in begging so that they could better provide for their children. She refused, because she was unable to bear the humiliation. After about two years of begging, her husband returned one day with a can full of the leftover rice mixed in with feces. Saran broke down and cried, vowing to work their fields herself and forbidding him from ever begging again.

The scarcity of money gradually wore Saran down to the point that she had to withdraw from important activities such as the women's association. Like so many of Bamako's inhabitants, she also had to support additional dependents. After her second husband, Soulaymane, died, Saran's sister Hawa married Seri Nyambèlè and had three more children. Seri had been at the Institute since it opened, and he enjoyed a reputation as a community leader. A few years after independence, however, he tired of Hawa and expelled her from his compound. By that time she had

---

8 Saran Koulibali, 27 March 1993.

only one surviving daughter, whose husband also had leprosy. The three of them then moved in with Saran and Bakari.

In 1968, the year Moussa Traoré took power of Mali in a coup d'état, doctors at the Institute informed Saran that she was cured and no longer needed treatment. Like so many happy moments in her life, this one was short-lived. That same year her sister Hawa died from an infection after doctors amputated her leg. Saran's husband, Bakari, also expired a short while later. After the deaths, Hawa's daughter and son-in-law immediately assumed control of Saran's entire compound, claiming it for themselves. Saran lost all her possessions, including the gold earrings made by the Gwansolo smith years earlier. She tried to reclaim ownership through the Bamako tribunal, but ended up with little more than a narrow plot beside the larger compound. The daughter and her husband eventually sold their share and moved to an emerging community several kilometers down the road to Siby. Saran persevered and built new dwellings in the narrow plot.

By 1992, the year Saran and I met, Djikoroni had become merely another densely populated Bamako neighborhood. Few of the quarter's residents had any connection to the Institute. A maze of single-story adobe and cement-block compounds stretched from the road to the river, crowding Saran's compound on all sides and destroying most of the nearby farmland. A scarcity of fields and the fatigue of old age compelled Saran to abandon farming altogether. For several years she sold vegetables in the local market, an activity which provided her with some spending money as well as important social contact with the rest of the community. In the early 1980s, however, she underwent an operation on her stomach at one of Bamako's hospitals. Her two-week stay cost about two-thirds of what her son later made in a month of teaching. The first operation failed, so she had to return to the hospital for another two weeks. After the second operation the doctors warned her against eating red pepper or kola nut. They also instructed her to avoid prolonged exposure to the sun, which meant she could no longer sit in the market. From then on, her main income derived from leasing rooms in her adobe compound. Saran's son-in-law also cultivated a small garden plot which the Institute provided for needy former patients; its produce supplemented her income.

Years earlier, Saran's daughter, Kadiatou, had gotten married and moved to another section of Djikoroni to live with her husband. Like most children of leprosy patients, she remained free of the disease and eventually had two healthy children of her own. Recent chronic fatigue, however, prevented her from assisting Saran with household chores. Her husband was also partially deaf. Kadiatou never attended school, because Saran wanted her at home. Her brother, Modibo, meanwhile enjoyed extensive education. He briefly considered becoming a police officer or an agent for "santrama," the internal security service, but Saran vehemently discouraged him from such dangerous and dishonorable professions. After graduating from a Bamako teacher's college in 1988, he lived unemployed for four years and then found work at a primary school near Nioro, a Sahelian town more than four hundred kilometers northwest of Djikoroni. His young wife and child stayed behind in Saran's care.

With Modibo far away and Kadiatou busy with her own affairs, Saran spent most of her days at home watching grandchildren and receiving visitors. Most of her close friends were former Institute patients like herself, although younger women in Djikoroni occasionally visited with their infants whom she treated for different illnesses. Her reputation as a healer even attracted mothers from other Bamako neighborhoods and local marabouts (spiritual healers of sorts) wanting to learn more about medicinal plants. Saran first learned her remedies years before, during periodic visits to her second husband's mother who also treated infants in Siby. Warned that charging money jeopardized the cure, Saran never relied on healing as a source of income.

In the course of her life, Saran observed the spread of sorcery. Her father's generation once knew the secrets (*dalilu*) necessary for keeping its practitioners under control, but later generations lost interest. Of all Saran's siblings, only Jogo bothered to learn how to counteract the "animals of the night" (*subaganw*, sorcerers). Saran pointed to greater death and misfortune in Bamako as evidence of this change. One morning during one of our conversations, her friend Fatoumata arrived in a hurry to announce that she was abandoning her husband whose brutality had become unbearable. Fatoumata was taking her children to Ségou where they could all live safely in her parents' compound. Saran sobbed at the news, covering her face with her hands. She later commented that young people were no longer "serious people" (*mògòw sèbè*).

Fatoumata's husband had a drug problem which caused him to behave irrationally and violently. The drugs came from Guinea along the same road which Saran once traveled from Gwansolo and Siby. In the past, Fatoumata had simply fled to Saran's compound for protection. One time, though, her husband arrived with a knife which he wielded at Saran, who had barricaded the door behind which Fatoumata was hiding. Much like her father long before, Saran protected herself with a spell which prevented the man from entering her hut and his knife from penetrating her skin. When Fatoumata ran away for good, Saran repeatedly muttered to herself, "Drugs ruin the mind. Drugs ruin the mind." (*Droguw bè hakili tiyèn.*)

Saran first met Fatoumata during her stay in the Bamako hospital for the stomach operation. Fatoumata's husband worked at the Institute where he often pilfered leprosy medicines (DDS) to sell on the side to "cured" patients like Saran who constantly feared a relapse of their disease; too many of their friends had lost fingers, toes, and legs long after completing treatment. Saran herself suffered from periodic skin rashes which flared up most severely in the hot season. She believed that the pills, which cost fifty CFA (about fifteen U.S. cents) each, assuaged her random ailments and protected her from losing limbs. Since their effectiveness required prolonged consumption lasting several days or weeks, Saran usually purchased at least twenty at a time. Even non-lepers, especially tired farmers, found these antibiotics very effective against their periodic illnesses.

Incidents such as Fatoumata's ordeal reminded Saran of how much the world around her had changed for the worse. Her tenants frequently paid no rent until her son, Modibo, returned from his distant teaching post. One man escaped in the night, still owing for his last four months. Saran also argued frequently with her daughter-in-law who lived in the compound but refused to do chores. Mali itself appeared to have fallen apart ever since the *farafin* regained control. Once well supplied with food and medicine under the *toubabs*, lepers like herself now felt abandoned and barely able to support their families. Even Saran's relatives in Gwansolo suffered from food shortages when rains became scarce. In an ironic reversal of fate, they turned to Saran for assistance.

In spite of all the hardship caused by her disease and the difficulties of living without money in an expensive city, Saran remained cheerful and jovial. She was poor, but by no means weak or helpless. She never hesitated to engage in physically demanding work like re-plastering her mud walls or chopping wood. When an urban development project threatened her gardens and those belonging to other lepers, she actively participated in the meetings of a recently formed patients' association. Like many elder women in Bamako, she maintained a wide circle of friends who visited frequently. In short, Saran belonged to a community in which she felt accepted and valued.[9]

Conclusion

Saran's life exemplifies many of the principal historical developments studied in this book: most notably, the long process through which she and her sister became identified socially as lepers. This process began in her village and intensified through her migration to Djikoroni. Her experiences at the hands of indigenous healers and *toubab* doctors defined her as a patient, but it was through interactions with others in society that her identity as a leper assumed its wider meaning. In particular, contact with other leprosy sufferers instilled her with a new sense of community. This community in turn shaped the manner in which she experienced the momentous changes of colonialism and independence. We must now turn our attention to this larger history.

---

9 Saran never asked for gifts or money. As friendly gestures, I occasionally brought her small things like fruit or empty jars for her medicines. After deciding to use Saran's story as a chapter for this study, I felt a professional obligation to remunerate her more adequately. In our sundry discussions about money and how to make it, she often wished for a pushcart which, when leased out, would provide a modest though steady daily income of about fifty cents. Before leaving Mali, I gave her son enough cash to buy her a cart. He wrote less than a month later to inform me of the purchase and express thanks on behalf of his mother.

2

Leprosy in Precolonial Mali

A scarcity of sources for Mali's precolonial past severely limits our ability to situate Saran Keita's experiences within a deeper historical context. Most surviving documents as well as Malian oral traditions tend to focus on political developments, shedding little light on the social consequences of disease. We can only assume that as Malian societies changed, so did their health practices. The spread of Islam, for example, no doubt transformed local conceptions and responses to disease as it had in northern Nigeria. How this actually occurred, however, remains unstudied. This chapter, therefore, draws primarily on existing secondary literature to summarize the origins of Mali's complex social landscape and its dominant political, ethnic, and religious identities. Relying on only a handful of fragmentary examples from Arabic manuscripts and oral/linguistic materials, it then offers some insight into the origins of "local" attitudes towards leprosy and its sufferers.

However limited, this evidence clearly suggests that the disease transformed people's identities long before French occupation. Leprosy qualified as a stigmatizing attribute through its negative connotations and its capacity to diminish social power. The evidence also suggests that, even in early history, identities rooted in leprosy derived from knowledge and belief accumulated across great physical and temporal distances. The legacy of this murky past will emerge more clearly as the following two chapters examine the full range of patient experiences in twentieth-century rural Mali.

A Political Overview

In the fourteenth century—around the time when Europeans struggled against leper and Muslim "plots to overthrow Christendom"—the region of present-day Mali was the site of a medieval empire bearing the same name.[1] This vast empire (ca. 1200–1400) extended from the Sahara's borders to the edge of the rain forests in the south. Originating in the

---

1 The following summary of Mali's history is based broadly on the following works cited in the bibliography: Ba and Daget, L'Empire Peul; William Brown, "The Caliphate of Hamdullahi 1818–1864: A Study in African History and Tradition" (Ph.D. diss., University of Wisconsin, Madison, 1969); Nehemia Levtzion, Ancient Ghana and Mali (London: Methuen, 1973); Levtzion and Hopkins, Corpus; Pascal Imperato, Historical Dictionary of Mali (Metuchen, New Jersey: Scarecrow Press, Inc., 1986); Roberts, Warriors, Merchants, and Slaves; Richard Roberts and Martin Klein, "The Banamba Slave Exodus of 1905 and the Decline of Slavery in the Western Sudan," Journal of African History 21, 3 (1980): 375–94; Robinson, The Holy War; and J. Spencer Trimingham, A History of Islam in West Africa (London: Oxford University Press, 1962).

Guinea mountains, the Niger River flowed through the empire's center until it reached the desert, at which point it bent southward and flowed towards the Atlantic through what is today Niger and Nigeria. The western half of the river connected several highly diverse peoples speaking a number of different languages.

Aside from the Niger, its tributaries, and a few clumps of jagged and rocky hills, no major natural barriers divided the relatively flat land. Thin forests in the south quickly gave way to a sparse Sahelian landscape marked only by scattered baobab trees and termite mounds. In the rainy season between May and October, this landscape became green and lush; in the dry season it became pale, dusty, and desert-like. Such an environment, endowed with an easily navigable river, facilitated extensive trade networks and mixing of populations. For centuries, local traders transported gold and slaves from the forests to trading centers on the desert's edge. For the return trip south, these traders brought salt, horses, glass beads, and manufactured goods imported from the Arab world. The trans-Saharan trade networks connected Mali with the Muslim/Arab states of North Africa and the Middle East. Over time, port towns such as Timbuktu and Djenne became centers of Islamic learning and Arabic letters as well as trade. Several Malian kings even made the pilgrimage to Mecca, visiting other cities along the way. In 1324, for example, the now legendary Mansa Musa stopped off in Cairo, where his enormous wealth made for much gossip and supposedly depressed the local price of gold.

Like the previous Soninké Empire of Ghana (ca. 500–1200 A.D.), the Mali Empire eventually disintegrated and gave way to smaller states or other empires such as Songhay (ca. 1400–1600 A.D.) which occupied the zones between Timbuktu, Djenne, and Gao. Mali nonetheless left a lasting cultural and linguistic legacy observable even today. Its history and kings are remembered through detailed oral traditions kept and performed by griots (bards) throughout West Africa.

Much of old Mali's prosperity resulted from its control of sub-Saharan trade routes and gold reserves. After the Portuguese opened trade with the West African coast in the fifteenth century, the importance of the Niger valley and port towns like Timbuktu declined steadily. The Moroccan invasion and occupation of Timbuktu and other parts of the Songhay Empire in the late sixteenth century accelerated the region's economic and political deterioration. In the eighteenth and nineteenth centuries, coastal states and empires such as Asante (in present-day Ghana) and Dahomey (in present-day Benin) became the new political and economic powers in West Africa. The trans-Saharan trade continued into the early twentieth century but only at a trickle.

For most of the eighteenth and nineteenth centuries, the region around the Niger River remained somewhat unstable, and fragmented into relatively small states which enjoyed only brief periods of expansion before giving way to a competing state or internal disintegration. The Bambara states of Kaarta (in the region 150 kilometers north of Bamako) and Ségou endured for a little more than a century until they fell in 1857 and 1861 respectively to Al-Hajj Umar Tall, a Fulani Muslim reformer who tried to organize the region into a vast Islamic polity extending from what is today northern Guinea to Timbuktu and the Bandiagara Plateau. Umar Tall died in 1864, but his jihad continued and took over another Fulani Islamic state, Macina.[2] At its peak earlier in the century, Macina controlled the area between Djenne, Timbuktu,

---

2 This state should not be confused with the contemporary town which bears the same name but is not in the same area.

and the Bandiagara Plateau. Umar Tall's own empire eventually became fractured by rivalries among his successors.

These two centuries of regional instability and economic weakness made the region vulnerable to first manipulation and then invasion by France. Though present on the coast for four centuries, European explorers did not reach West Africa's interior until the early 1800s when they saw the Niger River for the first time. At first, the French forces based in Senegal preoccupied themselves only with opening up and controlling trade routes to the interior. Relying on local African recruits, they gradually moved towards the Niger River and reached Ségou in 1890. By 1893, the leader of Umar Tall's disintegrating state fled to what is today Northern Nigeria.

At that point, only one major independent African polity remained. In the region of present-day southern Mali and northern Côte d'Ivoire and Guinea, Almamy Samory Touré had rapidly established his own state through military conquest conducted in the last decades of the nineteenth century. He originally signed a number of agreements with French military administrators, but, after repeated abrogations, the Dyula king openly and directly challenged their presence. The end of his endeavors began with his 1883 defeat in a battle fought just outside Bamako. In 1898 French troops captured Samory Touré in northern Côte d'Ivoire and exiled him to Gabon. France thereby secured its colony, which was renamed several times over the years: most notably, Haut-Sénégal-Niger and Soudan Français.

When the French arrived, the region around the river was already undergoing dramatic social and cultural transformation. In establishing his state, Umar Tall attempted to repress both non-Muslim religious and cultural practices as well as what he considered unorthodox Islamic customs. Since the days of the Mali Empire, Islam had been confined to political and economic elites. Trade networks often overlapped with scholarly networks. Umar Tall sought to spread Islam into the historically marginal agrarian communities and to force Muslim elites to be more orthodox and join his religious "brotherhood." Drawing inspiration from the Sokoto Caliphate in what is today northern Nigeria, leaders of the Macina state attempted their own social and economic reforms. Samory Touré also sought to transform society—not simply control it—by reorganizing agricultural production.

At the turn of the century, most of the population practiced subsistence agriculture or pastoralism, although plantation-like farms in the Middle Niger Valley used slave labor provided by the recent turbulent wars. The wetter regions in the south supported cereal crops (such as corn, millet, sorghum, and rice) better than the drier areas in the north. In spite of particularly poor lateritic soils and sparse rains, northerners did manage to cultivate enough food to last through the year. Periodic disasters like droughts or grasshoppers, however, could cause food shortages in both the north and south. The dryness of the north kept out disease-carrying insects like the tsetse fly and thereby favored the breeding of cattle, sheep, and goats.

While particular ethnicities predominated in certain zones—for example, Malinké in southern Mali—no single group occupied its own distinct and contiguous territory as one often imagines. The social landscape was not unlike that of Eastern Europe before the First World War when pockets of economically and socially stratified peoples speaking different languages, following different religions, and claiming different origins lay interspersed over large regions loosely controlled by states or empires with which they did not necessarily share any overt connection. When the French arrived, this social landscape underwent still another transformation, perhaps more profound than any of the preceding ones.

Leprosy in Arabic Manuscripts

The sources used in the writing of Mali's precolonial history provide few insights on leprosy and its sufferers. For this reason, it is impossible to determine how or when the disease became endemic in the region. Through the flourishing trans-Saharan trade with North Africa (between the eleventh and fifteenth centuries), travelers from West Africa probably became familiar with the disease even if it did not exist in their own communities. For example, al-Bakri, the eleventh-century Arab geographer mentioned earlier, noted the presence of "lepers" in Sijilmasa, a North African Saharan port town with close ties to the Ghana Empire on the southern side of the desert.[3] As another example, a scholar from an unspecified location in the Sahel (perhaps Agadez in present-day Niger) expressed concern over leprosy's contagiousness in a late fifteenth-century letter to the well-known Egyptian scholar al-Suyuti.[4]

Scattered legal texts from the regions bordering the southern Sahara reveal some local familiarity with the disease from at least the sixteenth century onward. In communities following the Maliki school of Islamic law (the only school present in West Africa), leprosy, along with "madness" (al-janun) and impotence, often constituted sufficient grounds for divorce. Al-Risala, the tenth-century text from which Maliki law derives, first stipulated these conditions.[5] Leprosy, therefore, appears frequently in legal discussions concerning al-khiyar, "the right of withdrawal" from marriage.[6]

One sixteenth-century text composed in Timbuktu contains the most extensive of these discussions. It reveals a fairly complex understanding of the disease derived from both local observation and imported ideas. Its author, Ahmad Baba, was a prolific scholar who became known in North Africa and Egypt for his works on Islamic theology and jurisprudence. Drawing on classical Arabic works including those of Ibn Sina (Avicenna, whose writings served as the foundation of European medicine), Ahmad Baba employed two terms for leprosy, al-baras and al-judham. In most literature of the time, the second term specifically designated the amputating forms

---

3 Levtzion and Hopkins, *Corpus*, 65.

4 John Hunwick, "Notes on a Late Fifteenth-Century Document Concerning 'al-Takrur'," in Christopher Allen and R. W. Johnson, eds., *African Perspectives: Papers in the History, Politics, and Economics of Africa Presented to Thomas Hodgkin* (Cambridge: Cambridge University Press, 1970), 19 and 25. Citing prophetic traditions, al-Suyuti replied, "The belief that certain diseases are infectious is false."

5 Ibn Abi Zayd al-Qayrawani, *Al-risala* (Algiers: Editions populaire de l'armée, 1990), 125. Quite interestingly, some people in Buna Sawane's village believed that Islamic law did not permit divorce in cases of leprosy (Buna Sawane, 26 October 1992)

6 *Al-khiyar* is a legal term also meaning "refusal" or "right of choice."

of the disease while the first term referred to all others. Ahmad Baba further distinguished two types of *al-baras*, "black" and "white," and claimed that their symptoms were different. He associated the black type with the onset of *al-judham* and considered it "safer," while the white type resembled *bahaq* (vitiligo) in color and was more dangerous.[7]

Ahmad Baba referred to both *al-baras* and *al-judham* as "defects" (*al-ʿayub*), but regarded only the former in its "white" form as unquestionably entitling the wife or husband of the victim to divorce. By citing well-known Maliki scholars such as al-Lakhmi and Ibn al-Hajib, Ahmad Baba demonstrated the diversity of opinion surrounding *al-judham*. Some of these scholars argued that divorce was justified for a woman even if her leprous husband was not "monstrous" or experiencing the "absence of feeling" associated with later stages of the disease. The possibility of the disease spreading to the spouse or to the children and their "progeny" supported this reasoning. Ahmad Baba noted the example (which he either observed himself or pulled from a secondary source) of a leprous woman whose husband never developed the disease but most of whose children did. Others, however, argued that *al-judham* did not justify divorce if the couple had children. The curability and less damaging nature of *al-baras* also obviated the need for divorce. One scholar asserted that there was no "right of withdrawal" for even *al-baras* unless it was "hideous."[8]

Michael Dols, a historian of medieval Arabic medicine, interprets *al-baras* and *al-judham* as signifying respectively tuberculoid and lepromatous leprosy. In his view, the verb root of the latter meant "to cut" or "to mutilate" and therefore designated the more devastating lepromatous form.[9] Ahmad Baba's legal treatise, however, clearly considers *al-baras* the more threatening type and therefore a more justifiable cause of divorce. As Dols himself acknowledges, these different terms were not used consistently in Arabic literature, so their precise meanings must always be drawn from actual context.

Ahmad Baba's discussion of this subject was considerably more researched and complex than similar ones made by subsequent local Muslim scholars in the eighteenth and nineteenth centuries. One manuscript composed in 1848 addressed the question of whether or not a man had the "right of withdrawal" after discovering that his wife was sick. The author affirmed that there was no right unless she had madness, either of the two forms of leprosy, or syphilis. He added that if the husband decided to divorce her anyway, he was obligated to return her dowry.[10] In response to a similar question concerning a leprous (with

7 Ahmad Baba al-Tinbukti, "Fasl al-khiyar," *Manh al-Jalil ʿala Mukhtasar Khalil* (ca. 1600, copied 1106 A.H./1694 A.D.), No. 5661, Folios 83–85, Center de Documentation et de Recherches Ahmad Baba (CEDRAB), Timbuktu.

8 Ahmad Baba, *Manh al-Jalil*, Folios 83-87.

9 Michael Dols, "The Leper in Medieval Islamic Society," *Speculum* 58, 4 (1983): 893; for a full discussion of leprosy in Arab societies, see also Dols, "Leprosy in Medieval Arabic Medicine," *Journal of the History of Medicine* 34 (July 1979): 315–33.

10 Muhammad b. al-Mukhtari b. al-ʿAmshi, *Nawazil* (1199 A.H./1848 A.D.), No. 4064, Folio 14, CEDRAB, Timbuktu. The same question and answer appears in Anbuya ibn al-Talib ʿabd al-Rahman, *Majmuʿ li-Nawazil al-Takrur* (1236 A.H./1821 A.D.), No. 627, Folios 30–32, CEDRAB, Timbuktu.

al-judham) husband in "monstrous" condition, another nineteenth-century scholar argued that the wife was entitled to a divorce because of the "severe threat" posed by his sores.[11]

In all these manuscripts, both forms of leprosy are listed as "dreaded diseases" (*al-amrad al-mukhawfa*) along with madness and syphilis. Interestingly, some scholars either did not mention impotence, as had Ahmad Baba, or included other ailments such as "the cough" (*al-su'al*) and tuberculosis (*al-sill*).[12] One text discusses these diseases in such a way to suggest that their "prolonged" (*mutatawil*) nature is what justifies divorce.[13] Another text explains that illnesses which persist "in bed" and inhibit intercourse are considered "dreaded."[14] Even though scholars appeared to have blindly perpetuated laws created centuries before, they nonetheless infused them with their own logic. They rationalized leprosy as a cause of divorce on the basis of any number of its perceived attributes.

However limited in detail, these manuscripts reveal leprosy's stigma for at least some Muslim communities long before colonial rule. This stigma derived in part from specific legal codes which diminished the sufferer's social power. Other factors no doubt contributed to the stigma as well, but evidence of them lies buried in the manuscripts like needles in a haystack. For example, while I was conducting research in Timbuktu, one local scholar, Mahmoud Mahamane Dédéou, recalled seeing a discussion of leprosy in a seemingly unrelated chapter of another legal text. The manuscript itself was copied in 1850 from a text most likely composed much earlier, perhaps in the eighteenth century. It consisted of a series of questions posed by a Djenne scholar to a colleague in Timbuktu. The particular discussion of leprosy concerned a very common Arabic grammar example which illustrates the use of the conjunction "and" (*waw*): "Do not eat fish and drink milk."[15] This example appeared long before in the writings of Sibawayhi (d. ca. 796), the principal founder of Arabic grammar. It became a fixture in many subsequent manuals, and, to this day, students of Arabic from Cairo to Timbuktu are familiar with it.[16] Al-Burtali, an early nineteenth-century Mauritanian scholar from Oualata, employed the same example in his grammar which is still used widely in the Timbuktu region.[17]

The discussion in the legal text begins with the Djenne scholar asking if there was medical truth imbedded in the grammar example. His Timbuktu colleague replies that he found no evidence in Arabic scientific writings to support the belief that fish with milk provoked illness. However, he did hear that the inhabitants of an island (presumably on the Niger River) abhorred eating fish with milk because

11 Ibn Muhammad b. al-Mukhtar b. al-Qasri, *Nawazil* [ca. 1800s], No. 603, folios unnumbered but passage contained in chapter on *al-khiyar*, CEDRAB, Timbuktu.

12 Muhammad ibn Bakr b. al-Hashim al-ʿAlawi (d. 1098 A.H./1687 A.D.), *Nawazil* [ca. 1600s, copied 1356 A.H./ 1937 A.D.], No. 277, Folio 37, CEDRAB, Timbuktu.

13 Anbuya ibn al-Talib, *Majmuʿ li-Nawazil al-Takrur*, 32. See also Abu ʿabd Allah al-Mustafa b. Ahmad b. ʿAthman b. Mawlud al-ʿAlawi, *Nawazil* [undated], No. 277, Folios 78–82, CEDRAB, Timbuktu.

14 Al-Warzazi, *Nawazil* [undated], No. 2749, Folios 32–33, CEDRAB, Timbuktu.

15 "La' ta'kul al-samak wa tashrub al-laban."

16 The grammar written by Ibn Ajurum (d. 1323), for example, uses the same example.

17 Ahmad al-Jayyid ibn al-Talib Muhammad b. Abu Bakr al-Sadiq al-Burtali (d. 1230 a.h./1815 a.d.), *Sharh al-Ajurmiyya* (ca. 1800), No. 5629, CEDRAB, Timbuktu. This is an exposition of Ibn Ajurum's work.

they believed such a diet caused leprosy. Allowing the questioner to draw his own conclusions, the Timbuktu scholar notes that none of these inhabitants was infected with the disease.[18] In closing, he advises that, in regards to fish and milk, people not consume one before digesting the other.[19]

This text documents another aspect of leprosy's stigma. In addition to provoking divorce, leprosy represented a contemptible consequence of breaking a dietary taboo. There was nothing distinctly Malian about this belief. Much like other forms of medical knowledge, this one reflected a synthesis of local and imported ideas. A British missionary working in Hausaland (northern Nigeria) in the late nineteenth century observed that over half his leprosy patients avoided fish because they believed it would worsen their conditions.[20] From the same area, a handbook of medical advice written in Arabic verse corroborated this belief.[21]

Fish avoidance had, in fact, existed long before among ancient Egyptians and was also documented by the Greek geographer Herodotus.[22] Catfish in particular belonged to a category of bottom-dwelling fish generally classified as taboo.[23] According to Jewish Talmudic tradition, eating fish in the spring predisposed one to leprosy.[24] Drawing on Indian sources, Ibn Sina (Avicenna) warned in his eleventh-century *Canon* that eating fish with milk caused "chronic diseases like leprosy."[25] In addition to their presence in West African centers of learning such as Timbuktu, Ibn Sina's writings greatly influenced medieval European medicine. Bernhard de Gordon, a well-known fourteenth-century doctor in Montpellier (France), reiterated Ibn Sina's warning in his writings.[26]

---

18 That this scholar found the absence of leprosy on the island significant strongly suggests the disease's notable presence in Timbuktu.

19 Saᶜid al-Habib Baba b. Muhammad al-Hadi al-Wadani al-Tinbukti, *Ajwiba* (early 1800s, copied 1266 A.H./ 1850 A.D.), CEDRAB, No. 1038, 20. The poetic nature of the grammar example, which does not carry over into the literal English translation, no doubt facilitated its retention and made it something of an adage, perhaps even among those who could not read. Equivalent versions existed in other languages. In the thirteenth century Bernhard de Gordon wrote, "Comedere lac et pisces eadem mensa inducit Lepram." (Skinsnes "Notes," 224.) A sixteenth-century collection of French proverbs contained the phrase, "Aprés poisson laict est poison." (Gabr. Meurier, *Trésor des Sentences* (sixteenth century), quoted in M. Le Roux de Lincy, *Le Livre des Proverbes Français* [Paris: Adolphe Delahays, 1859].) Even the American Ben Franklin warned in his *Poor Richard's Almanac* (1742), "After Fish, Milk do not wish." (Burton Stevenson, *The Home Book of Proverbs, Maxims, and Familiar Phrases* [New York: The Macmillan Company, 1948].)

20 Charles Robinson, *Hausaland* (London: Sampson Low, Marston and Company, 1897), 150.

21 Manuscript No. 836, Falke Collection, Northwestern University, Evanston, Illinois.

22 William Darby, *Food: The Gift of Osiris* (New York: Academic Press, 1977), 394.

23 Douglas Brewer, *Fish and Fishing in Ancient Egypt* (Warminster, England: Aris and Phillips, 1989), 17.

24 Alan Unterman, *Dictionary of Jewish Lore and Legend* (London: Thames and Hudson, 1991), 78; Emil G. Hirsch, "Fish and Fishing," *The Jewish Encyclopedia*, Vol. 5 (New York: Funk and Wagnalls Co., 1903), 403.

25 O. Cameron Gruner, *A Treatise on the Canon of Medicine of Avicenna, Incorporating a Translation of the First Book* (New York: Augustus M. Kelley, 1970 [1st edition, 1930], 406; Darby, *Food*, 400. A manuscript copy of Ibn Sina's *Canon* can also be found at CEDRAB in Timbuktu.

26 Skinsnes, "Notes," 220 and 224.

Leprosy in Language

With only the most limited documentation such as these Arabic manuscripts, historians of Africa often rely on linguistic evidence and oral traditions to piece together the precolonial past. Tal Tamari, for example, meticulously studies the diffusion of particular terms to understand the precolonial significance of identities rooted in inherited professional status.[27] G. Waite similarly reconstructs a medical history of East-Central Africa.[28] The time constraints for my own research project prevented an in-depth analysis of this sort. Nonetheless, several easily retrievable examples help round out our sense of leprosy's meaning in precolonial Mali.

Like the Arabic manuscripts, the terminology for leprosy among Bambara and Malinké peoples suggests a familiarity with the disease which predates colonization. Although literacy was far less developed and widespread in southern regions, many people possessed, much like Ahmad Baba, a fairly precise understanding of the disease's different forms. Beyond the somewhat vague and all-inclusive term *banaba* ("the big disease"), they used the more descriptive words of *bagi* and *kuna*. *Bagi* referred to the condition characterized by the formation of nodules on the skin and, like Ahmad Baba's definition of *al-baras*, was often considered the more severe of the two forms. *Kuna* generally referred to the disease in its stage when body parts appeared to amputate spontaneously and therefore corresponded roughly to *al-judham*. As in the Arabic texts, the existence of these Mande terms suggests an early awareness of the disease's different forms.

Most people known to suffer from *banaba* probably did have leprosy, but, as in Europe at that time, it was possible to confuse the disease with other ailments. In its early stages, leprosy resembled a skin condition called *kaba* which translates roughly as tinea.[29] In English, tinea applies to any number of different fungal skin infections causing leprosy-like patches. More knowledgeable observers, however, could distinguish *banaba* from *kaba* by flicking the patch with one's fingers or a small instrument in order to test for decreased sensitivity which is specific only to leprosy.[30] At a glance, one could also mistake leprosy for syphilis, since both sometimes destroy nose cartilage in their advanced stages.[31] Only a passing stranger, however, would

---

27 Tal Tamari, "Linguistic Evidence for the History of West African 'Castes,'" in Conrad and Frank, eds., *Status and Identity*.

28 G. M. Waite, "The Indigenous Medical System in East-Central African History" (Ph.D. dissertation, University of California, Los Angeles, 1981).

29 Other researchers have also found *kaba* used in this loose sense. Djigui Diakité observed, as I did, that some people employed the more descriptive terms *kabafin* and *kabajè* for the "black" (hypopigmented lesions) and "white" (vitiligo) forms of the condition. Quite interestingly, this terminology resembles that used in the Arabic manuscripts. Djigui Diakité, "Essai sur les traditions sanitaires et médicinales Bambara du Bélédougou" (*Thèse*, Ecole de Médecine, Bamako, 1988), 56; Ibrahima Diarra, "Contribution à l'étude de quelques aspects des dermatoses en médecine traditionnelle au Mali" (*Thèse*, Ecole de Pharmacie, Bamako, 1991), 2.

30 Diagnosis in medieval Arabic medicine similarly involved pricking lesions with a pin. Dols, "Leprosy in Medieval Arabic Medicine," 325.

31 Tuareg peoples employed the same word, *amaxaras* (pronounced "amagaras") for certain forms of syphilis as well as vitiligo, leprosy, and other skin ailments. Mohamed Ousmane, "La médecine traditionnelle tamachèque en milieu malien" (*Thèse*, Ecole de Médecine, Bamako, 1981), 23, 40–41, and 54.

make this kind of misdiagnosis because the earlier symptoms of leprosy and syphilis are not at all similar.

The uses of these different terms, of course, varied depending on the nature of one's medical understanding. *Banaba* and its equivalent in other languages served as lay terms for leprosy. *Bagi* and *kuna* were more specialized. Kasoume Tangara (b. 1910), a Bambara healer residing in Macina, learned how to distinguish *banaba* from *bagi* from his father, who also specialized in treating leprosy. According to the father, ordinary people assumed that both terms referred to the same disease, but healers like himself understood things differently. *Banaba* and *kuna* described the same disease, whereas *bagi* caused deformations of the nose and was more contagious since it carried higher concentrations of *banakisèw* (literally meaning "illness seeds" or, figuratively, "germs"). *Bagi* could evolve into *banaba* and vice versa. *Kaba* could evolve into *banaba* as well.[32]

As another example, one Bambara proverb distinguished the two forms of leprosy as follows: "For *kuna* there are remedies, but for *bagi* there are none."[33] The collector of this proverb observes that, in Malinké, all forms of leprosy were called *bagi*. In Bambara, however, *kuna* referred to the "amputating" form and *bagi* to the "nodular" form. Though debilitating, *kuna* was considered less serious, so people were more comfortable employing the term in proverbs. Also according to the collector, *bagi* rarely appeared in proverbs because it referred to a more threatening condition and therefore was less polite.[34] As this and the preceding examples illustrate, the precise meanings of the different terms were not uniform within Malinké- and Bambara-speaking communities.

The English language generally does not allow the construction of a single identifying term for people with diseases. Leper is one exception. No equivalent term for leper exists for people with cancer, polio, Lyme Disease, or other chronic illnesses. Instead, one uses phrases like "cancer patients" or "people with cancer." Languages spoken in Mali, however, allowed the labeling of people on the basis of a disease or some other attribute. *Banabatò* referred to someone with *banaba* in the same manner that *nyonitò* indicated a person with *nyoni* (smallpox). In Bambara and Malinké, *-tò* served and still serves as a general suffix for referring to individuals by some distinguishing attribute:for example, a *kòlibatò* refers to a person who experiences *kòli* (ruin or misery). Similarly, in Songhay, individuals with *wicir ber* ("the big disease") were known as *wicir ber koy*, the last word indicating possession. In this one linguistic sense, leprosy hardly differed from other diseases as it did in English.

Other usages, however, effectively enabled people to treat the disease differently in speech. In general, one avoided the more clinical names, *kuna* and *bagi*, since both *kunatò* and *banabagitò* served as insults. *Banabatò* (literally, "the sick one") broadly indicated someone ill from any ailment, not just leprosy. Its meaning depended entirely on context and inflection, unlike *kunatò* and *banabagitò* which, even as individual words, graphically evoked the deformities caused by the disease. *Banabatò*

---

32 Kasoume Tangara, 18 February 1993.

33 Monseigneur Molin, *Recueil de proverbes, bambaras et malinkés* (Molineaux: Les Presses Missionnaires, 1960), 122.

34 This interpretation would mean that *kuna* referred to the tuberculoid and *bagi* to the lepromatous forms. This obviously contradicts the interpretation of the Arabic terms.

was accepted as a politer usage for leprosy patients. Though intended to minimize insult, the alternative term implied a condition too unpleasant for words.

The extensive use of the topic of leprosy in proverbs in Mali also suggests a substantial familiarity with the disease prior to the twentieth century. For non-literate peoples, philosophical thinking was and still is often encoded in proverbs employed in a variety of contexts ranging from casual discourse to serious dialogue to oral literature. Today, elderly villagers are notorious for filling their speech with one proverb after another, thereby rendering themselves incomprehensible to younger "uneducated" town-dwellers. As in written literature, leprosy's appearance in proverbs created a preconceived identity to be projected onto actual sufferers whether or not it matched their own circumstances. These proverbs generally emphasized the disease's disabling or disfiguring attributes and thereby contributed to its overall stigma.[35]

The most common proverbs focused specifically on a sufferer's decreased sensitivity in the hands and feet. For example, one Bobo proverb stated, "When dancing, the leper is without difficulties, but what happens when he stops?" Playing on the image of lepers unwittingly injuring their appendages, it warned that one does not recognize the consequences of his or her acts until after their completion.[36] A similar Bambara proverb cautioned one against shortsightedness: "If you see a leper who forgot his sandals, it's because the ground beneath his first steps was good."[37] In other words, the leper fails to realize that, without sandals, his last steps will be far more painful than his first. One Minianka saying likewise instructed one to know one's place: "A leper's place for walking is not on the hill." Hills in Mali are often rocky and therefore more likely locations for leprosy patients to injure themselves.[38]

The stereotype of fingerless lepers also served as a useful device for communicating lessons on human nature. In one Bambara proverb, missing fingers made a person vulnerable to false generosity: "You are not depriving a leper of food by giving him un-decorticated millet; at the same time, you are not giving him anything either." A leper has no use for millet which he is unable to thresh and prepare for eating.[39] The following proverb similarly played upon a leper's presumed inability to wear rings to describe false friendship: "One befriends a leper, because one knows that, if he finds a ring, he will give it to you. However, if the leper dares to hang the ring from the cord around his neck, one breaks with him."[40] Still another Bambara proverb denounced blatantly false accusations: "We accuse lepers of everything, but it is a patent lie to say, 'In passing, the leper took a handful of my peanuts.'" In other words, everybody knows that lepers have no hands for stealing.[41] As a final example,

---

35 I was only able to locate collections of Bobo, Minianka, Malinké, and Bambara proverbs. This does not mean that other peoples did not use lepers in their proverbs.

36 Bernard de Rasilly, private collection of Bobo proverbs, San, proverb no. 659.

37 Molin, Recueil de proverbes, 123.

38 Jean Cauvin, L'Image, la langue, et la pensée, vol. II, recueil de proverbes de Karangasso (St. Augustin, Germany: Anthropos-Institut–Haus Volker und Kulturen, 1980), 74.

39 Molin, Recueil de proverbes, 124.

40 Ibid., 125.

41 Ibid., 123.

the Minianka expression, "You are as happy as lice in the hair of a leper," plays on the assumption that, without fingers, lepers can't pick out their lice.[42]

Much like the association of leprosy with food taboos, some proverbs portrayed the disease as a person's most dreaded fate: "The leper asks you to chase away the flies; but who attracts them more than anyone else?" This Bobo proverb criticized people who complain of misfortune which is their own doing.[43] As a final example, the Minianka expression equivalent to "salt in the wound" was "You have added leprosy to all my misfortune."[44]

Conclusion

Without the evidence of actual leprosy cases, we can only speculate how these beliefs and attitudes translated into practice before colonization. We have no way of determining, for example, the frequency of divorces sanctioned by Islamic law. Nor can we know how or when the many proverbs evolved. As the following chapters reveal, the disease's stigma survived the dramatic political, social, and technological transformations of the twentieth century. The actual manner in which this stigma played out in people's lives, however, changed considerably. To understand how this happened, we must consider patients' experiences within the context of their villages as well as the government institutions which eventually drew them away.

---

42 Cauvin, *L'Image*, 52.
43 De Rasilly, proverb no. 518.
44 Cauvin, *L'Image*, 17. For similar proverbs in Senegalese society, see Fassin (1992), 130.

3

Becoming a Leper

Saran Keita became a leper the day Bala Kamara placed his leaves on her patch and pronounced his diagnosis. The meaning and implications of this identity, however, changed considerably over time. Beginning with her husband's hostile reaction, Saran underwent a series of experiences which gradually reinforced her separation from the community. These experiences culminated in her migration to the Institut Central de la Lépre in Bamako.

During the course of the twentieth century, leprosy sufferers throughout Mali endured similar transformations of their social identities. The specific events and causes behind these transformations varied, but they almost always resulted in a definition of self based on the disease. As illustrated in Saran's story, this process occurred both outside and inside the context of government institutions. This and the following chapter examine the process as it occurred in rural agrarian societies. The remaining chapters then consider the institutional contexts.

Although life in Mali changed dramatically in the course of the century, many of the primary components of rural leper identity endured. For example, the attitudes and beliefs underpinning leprosy's stigma lasted well beyond the widespread introduction of antibiotics in the 1950s. Mali today remains an agrarian society with virtually no industrialization. Changes in attitude and practice have not occurred in a linear fashion, such that many individuals with leprosy continue to experience forms of social isolation which earlier generations also encountered.

The evidence presented in this chapter derives from interviews with former and current patients whose ages ranged roughly from thirty-five to eighty-five. Every one of these individuals fell under the influence of government treatment programs at some point in their lives. This chapter considers their experiences before that moment, focusing on the principal factors behind their disease's stigma.

Recognizing the Disease

Rural Leprosy

Throughout the twentieth century, most rural leprosy patients received their first diagnosis from family or community members. This act initiated a process of identity transformation as people applied pre-existing knowledge to real and observable conditions. Such knowledge resulted from a hodgepodge of lived and communicated experiences rather than a fixed and coherent system of ideas. As suggested in the previous chapter, it had developed historically in conjunction with leprosy's long presence in the region. The actual moment of diagnosis varied according to factors specific to each individual, but, in the long-run, provoked very similar patterns of response, described later in this chapter.

In most cases, the disease began as a coin-sized patch (lesion) on the skin, usually appearing first on the forehead or arms. On dark skin the patch assumed a reddish hue which, as noted in Saran's story, engendered the Bambara name, *bilen*. Severe aches and fever, such as those experienced by Maré Sidibé in the 1950s while working in his fields, could also accompany the appearance of patches.[1] Family or community members often noticed the patch before the individual, especially if mirrors were not available. Sometime in the late 1940s, Issaka Traoré learned about two patches on his back from a woman who noticed them as they were returning from their fields.[2] A friend pointed out Chaka Théra's patches on his leg in a similar setting during the late 1960s.[3] Given the severity of the sun and heat, farming necessitated scanty dress which left large parts of skin exposed for others to view. Those few people who did not farm at all, such as traders or town dwellers in Djenne, could intentionally or unintentionally conceal patches beneath turbans and long robes. In the end, however, other activities would force them to expose their conditions to others. Demba Doumbia, for example, received diagnosis in the course of his circumcision retreat in the late 1930s.[4]

Not everybody interpreted the presence of a patch as a sign of leprosy. Some people simply ignored it until later symptoms appeared. Others considered it to be *kaba* (mentioned in the previous chapter) or some other skin irritation which occurred frequently, especially in the hot season. Indeed, distinguishing *kaba* from *banaba* required careful examination and some prior knowledge of the disease. A patch had appeared on Koko Kanta's forehead during his late adolescence in the 1950s. His maternal uncle, Moussa Nyumata, identified it as leprosy, but then called in a healer who challenged the diagnosis saying it was *kaba*. After some time, however, the patch grew and confirmed Moussa's original diagnosis.[5] In a similar case, patches appeared on Bala Samaké's back in the early 1920s, when he was ten. His father called it leprosy, but other people in the village insisted it was *kaba*. Only when his condition worsened a few years later did the actual disease become clear.[6]

The ability to diagnose leprosy did not rest with any single group of people or type of individual. In Lafiara (near Tominian), villagers usually deferred to elders when someone manifested symptoms.[7] Mamadou Koulibali's village trusted only

1 Maré Sidibé, 9 November 1992.

2 Issaka Traoré, 5 November 1992.

3 Chaka Théra, 21 March 1993.

4 Demba Doumbia, 27 November 1992.

5 Koko Kanta, 16 February 1993.

6 Bala Samaké, 2 December 1992.

7 Alu Toléma, 28 November 1992.

hunters for distinguishing leprosy from *kaba*.[8] The ability to diagnose usually developed with direct experience. Since leprosy occasionally disappeared from a village for an entire generation or two, people often lacked that experience and relied on outsiders such as itinerant traders. If nobody was capable of diagnosis, then only the development of other characteristic symptoms would signal the disease's presence to the patient and others in the community.

The secondary physical effects of advanced leprosy (described in the Introduction) facilitated recognition. The loss of fingers, the appearance of open sores, and the weakening of limbs revealed the disease to nearly everyone, even those who could not recognize it from a patch. Diseases such as malaria and dysentery had symptoms common to many others, but the signs of advanced leprosy were unique. Only rare cases which healed spontaneously without causing permanent nerve and tissue damage could go unnoticed.

In summary, recognizing leprosy often occurred in several stages beginning with the identification of an abnormal patch by the patient or others. Associating this patch with leprosy depended on the skill and knowledge of the observer. Beyond gossip, public recognition of the disease usually coincided only with the appearance of more visible signs such as damaged fingers or open sores. The ability to distinguish leprosy's different forms clearly existed but only among more observant or well-trained individuals.

A Contemptible Consequence

An identity based on leprosy resulted largely from popular beliefs about its causes and from responses to its physical effects. Often the two became confused as healthy individuals rationalized their revulsion and fears with etiological assumptions which did not necessarily follow what they actually observed. In other words, the "intellectual" responses to leprosy partly explain the "practical" responses, both of which shaped the experiences and feelings of those infected by the disease. The wide circulation of belief also illustrates the degree to which "knowledge" had diffused across great cultural and temporal distances.

The complexity of disease etiology arises in part from the disjuncture between explaining what can happen and what has already happened. For example, medical scientists point to fatty diets as a potential cause of some cancers. When cancer does develop in a specific patient, however, actual causality becomes much more uncertain. We realize that not all consumers of fatty diets develop cancer and not all cancer cases result from fatty diets. Leprosy in Mali posed a similar challenge in which "before-the-fact" explanations differed dramatically from those posited "after-the-fact." The connections between disease and behavior further complicated people's understanding.

---

8 Mamadou Koulibali, 12 March 1993. In Bambara societies, hunters were often the custodians of medical knowledge. For more details on hunters, see Cashion, "Hunters of the Mande."

In nearly all languages spoken in Mali, people referred to leprosy as the "big disease" *(banaba)*.[9] With such a name and reputation, it served as a useful device for warning people against forbidden or undesirable practices, such as eating without having washed after sexual intercourse (a particularly Islamic taboo common in the north) or sleeping beneath a full moon.[10] One of the most common before-the-fact explanations raised the specter of leprosy to bolster taboos against sexual intercourse during menstruation. It was said that a child conceived during menstruation risked developing leprosy later in life.

The long history of taboos against menstrual intercourse throughout the world prevent one from reliably identifying their origins in Mali. For example, Jewish Talmudic traditions established the same correlation between menstrual intercourse and leprosy.[11] Muslims and Arabs had similarly reinforced the prohibition with religious teachings and written texts. The belief also circulated orally among non-literate peoples in the form of prophetic traditions.[12] Being so widespread, it inevitably varied in specific meaning. Alassana Maiga, a Songhay healer from the Diré region, learned from his father in the 1960s that intercourse just after the completion of menstruation but before ritual washing also put the child at risk for leprosy.[13] In the 1990s some people in Tuareg communities still associated menstrual intercourse with vitiligo.[14] This taboo also circulated well beyond the historically Muslim communities in the north. In the Bambara village of Moromoro, an old hunter-healer named Hamisa Koulibali advised newlyweds in the 1950s and 1960s not to break it.[15] Kasoume Tangara, the Bambara healer mentioned in Chapter 2, had also learned from his father in the 1920s that leprosy resulted in the fetus when semen and menstrual blood (or simply "white" vaginal fluid) mixed.[16]

As noted in the previous chapter, one of the most common before-the-fact explanations attributed leprosy to the consumption of mudfish (catfish), either alone or with milk. This belief existed most strongly among peoples inhabiting the regions along the Niger River, especially the Bozo, who historically worked as fishermen and boatmen. As one of many examples, people in Koko Kanta's Bozo village, Tongué (near Sarro), avoided fresh mudfish with milk out of fear of

---

9 *Wicir ber* in Songhay, *marad al-kabir* in Hassaniyya (an Arabic dialect spoken in Mauritania and neighboring parts of Mali such as Timbuktu), *waté koré* in Soninké, and *nwamowdo* in Fulfulde (spoken by Fulani peoples).

10 Hamadou Sow, 19 October 1992; Mamadou Koulibali, 17 February 1993. Haidara also documented some of these beliefs as well as those concerning intercourse during menstruation and eating mudfish and goat, all of which will be discussed next. Lalla Badji Haidara, "Prevention et contrôle des endémies majeures par les practiciens traditionnels" (*Thése*, Ecole de Pharmacie, Bamako, 1986), 33. People in what is today Burkina Faso also associated the breaking of sexual taboos with disease. Bado, *Médecine coloniale*, 25.

11 Unterman, *Dictionary of Jewish Lore*, 147.

12 Hamadou Sow, 19 October 1992. Interestingly, Hamadou also heard of a prophetic tradition which warned that sleeping with a woman outside would beget a thief. Though circulated orally, prophetic traditions are assumed to be documented in texts. This assumption enhances their perceived authenticity.

13 Alassana Maiga, 25 April 1993.

14 Ousmane, *"La médecine traditionnelle tamachèque,"* 54.

15 Mamadou Koulibali, 12 March 1993

16 Kasoume Tangara, 18 February 1993

contracting the "big disease." Leprosy patients in particular avoided it because the fish was said to aggravate their condition. Koko himself ate only smoked mudfish while growing up in the 1940s and 1950s.[17] Hamadou Sow (b. 1956), a man whose family and ancestors were known for treating leprosy, explained that Fulanis in his area considered all people to be carriers of this disease, but that certain activities, including eating mudfish with fresh milk, caused its manifestation in particular individuals.[18]

In certain contexts, this belief bolstered well-established taboos which people sought to rationalize in different ways. Hamadou Sow learned of a frequently performed "experiment" in which one placed a mudfish in a calabash of milk overnight. The resulting appearance of blood and maggots closely resembled leprosy's effects on humans.[19] One community visited by a French researcher, probably in the 1920s, explained the specific avoidance of mudfish in terms of a local legend. The legend attributed the rivalry between particular clans to a dispute between two brothers. Upon returning from a long journey, they arrived at the Niger River but were unable to cross because they did not have a canoe. A mudfish appeared and offered to transport them. When the first brother reached the other side safely, he instructed the fish not to carry the other, whom he said was violent and cruel. The fish did so anyway. When the second brother arrived safely on the other side, he killed the fish with his saber and offered half to his brother. The first brother refused and proclaimed that thereafter none of his descendants would ever touch the flesh of that fish again.[20]

In addition to exemplifying the nature of before-the-fact explanations, the milk/fish taboo illustrates the seemingly immeasurable degree to which beliefs circulated or recurred in vastly different cultural and temporal contexts.[21] The previous chapter already noted the long history of this belief in Arabic and medieval European medical literature. As in Mali, certain variations survived well into the

---

17 Koko Kanta, 16 February 1993. In some places, such as Aljuma Guindo's Dogon village near Bankas and Silvestré Kamaté's Bobo village near Tominian, people believed that goat meat as well as mudfish aggravated a leper's condition even though they were not considered causes in and of themselves. Also recall that Saran Keita's village stopped serving her meat under the same pretext. Aljuma Guindo, 5 April 1993; Silvestré Kamaté, 23 March 1993.

18 Hamadou Sow, 19 October 1992. The belief circulated in many different forms. In Koko Kanta's village and many others, people smoked the fish to make it edible. Alassana Maiga, on the other hand, learned from an old Bozo man that eating mudfish without boiling it or removing its gills put one at risk for *kaba* but not necessarily leprosy. Alassana himself trusted this knowledge because "Bozo know fish well." For those in Falela Keita's village near Kita, simply eating unsmoked mudfish, even without milk, would give one leprosy. Some beliefs emphasized mudfish consumption as a direct cause while others merely identified it as a food which would aggravate a pre-existing case. In other words, healthy people could eat it. See Alassana Maiga, 25 April 1993; Falela Keita, 28 November 1992; and Kasoume Tangara, 18 February 1993.

19 Hamadou Sow, 19 October 1992. Ousmane Abocar heard of the same experiment performed in Goundam. Ousmane Abocar, 6 November 1992.

20 Dr. Cazanove, "Les Conceptions magico-religieuses des indigènes de l'AOF," *L' Hygiène sociale* [ca. 1920s or 1930s], CAOM, Agence FOM 384, 2083. One should also note that mudfish had significance in other parts of West Africa, demonstrated most notably in the art of Benin society.

21 See Eric Silla, "'After Fish, Milk Do Not Wish': Recurring Ideas in a Global Culture," *Cahier d'Études Africaines* 144 (1996). See also Bado, *Médecine coloniale*, 61.

twentieth-century, even in the Americas. For example, folklore documented in African-American communities revealed an enduring aversion to eating fish with milk. While the specific association with leprosy disappeared, this particular diet was still considered a potential source of illness or poison.[22] In a controversial book published in 1906, the British doctor John Hutchinson specifically attributed fish consumption to the spread of leprosy.[23] Some western doctors insisted on this connection as late as the 1960s.[24]

The pervasion across continents and through centuries of fish/milk avoidance and its connection to leprosy exposes the complex origins and patterns of belief shaping a leper's identity in Mali. Its specific meaning depended largely on contextual factors and its conformity to other beliefs. The explanatory legend and experiment mentioned above underscored the contemptibleness of mudfish which, in other instances, people clearly associated with the contemptible disease leprosy. Fish/milk avoidance characterized the unsystematic and syncretic nature of before-the-fact etiological beliefs. In general, these beliefs were not confined to particular ethnicities or religions and not known by all people in a given society. Though documented and propagated in written texts accessible only to elite scholars, the fish/milk taboo circulated orally as well. Both this and the menstruation taboos demonstrated the tendency of similar beliefs, regardless of their different origins, to overlap and reinforce each other.

God, Snakes, and Sorcerers

Though these beliefs described in the previous section were widespread, not one informant reported a case of a person actually contracting leprosy from any of the supposed "causes." In other words, before-the-fact etiologies influenced a leper's identity only in so far as that they reinforced the dreadfulness of the disease by linking it with forbidden behaviors. After-the-fact explanations differed considerably, because they rarely assigned responsibility to the patient.

In most cases, people attributed actual occurrences of the disease to "God's work" (*alla ka bara*). In Lassana Diakité's village in the 1930s and 1940s, for example, it was believed that everyone had leprosy but only those chosen by God developed

---

22 For some specific examples, see Wayland D. Hand, Anna Casetta, and Sondra B. Thiederman, eds, *Popular Beliefs and Superstitions, A Compendium of American Folklore* (Boston: G.K. Hall and Company, 1981), 265 and 381; Randolph Vance, *Ozark Magic and Folklore* (New York: Dover Publications, 1947), 115; and Norge Jerome Winifred, *Food Habits and Acculturation: Dietary Practices and Nutrition of Families Headed by Southern-Born Negroes Residing in a Northern Metropolis* (Ph.D. dissertation, University of Wisconsin, 1967). More recently, Jacalyn Harden, friend and colleague, heard of the taboo from her grandmother and from members of the Florida A&M University community.

23 Jonathan Hutchinson, *On Leprosy and Fish-Eating: A Statement of Facts and Explanations* (London: Archibald and Constable and Co., Ld., 1906); Robinson, *Hausaland*, 149; and Skinsnes, "Notes," 220 and 224.

24 See the following articles by Meny Bergel: "New Lights in Leprosy," *International Journal of Leprosy* 26, 1 (1958): 64–66; "Influence of Various Pro-Oxidant Nutritional Conditions on the Growth *In Vivo* of M. Leprae," *Leprosy Review* 30, 1 (1959): 153–58; "The Hutchinson Dietetic Hypothesis of Fish Eating as a Cause of Leprosy. A Reappraisal in the Light of the Influence of Pro-Oxidant Nutritional Conditions," *Leprosy Review* 31, 4 (1960): 302–304; and "Leprosy and Nutrition," *Leprosy Review* 37, 3 (1966): 163–66.

the symptoms.[25] This belief predominated in Muslim communities, especially those in the north with deep historical ties to Islamic and Arabic culture. Further to the south in Bambara, Bobo, and Malinké communities where Islam became influential only in the past one hundred years, people anchored etiologies to more tangible phenomenon. As one common example, they connected the disease to chance encounters with a particular species of snake. One day (ca. 1930s), while perching himself in a tree during a hunt, Jasig Traoré fought off a snake which had "flown" towards him from a branch. After killing it, he inadvertently stepped on the place where it had passed. Not long after, the first signs of leprosy appeared.[26] People in Duba Traoré's Bambara village near Kolokani said (in the 1960s and 1970s) that this particular species of snake gave people leprosy with its saliva.[27] In Alu Tolèma's (b. 1927) Dogon village near Tominian, cutting the snake's tail, being exposed to its saliva, or merely stepping on its path caused leprosy.[28] In general, these kinds of explanations were rare, perhaps because they depended on coincidental encounters with snakes.

More often, after-the-fact explanations focused responsibility on one's enemies. Snakes as well as salamanders served as the primary ingredients for "medicines" which sorcerers (*subaganw*), usually motivated by jealousy, applied to their victims' food or bed to give them leprosy.[29] Much like Saran Keita, Madu Sako (b. 1910s) and Jean-Baptiste Dembélé (b. 1930s) both believed that they had contracted the disease this way.[30] In many cases, other people's children were at once sources and victims of jealousy. Unable to produce children with his wife, Sanjako Nyagaté once told his brother, "I'm giving your son leprosy because I don't have children." This occurred in the 1920s in their Soninké village near Nioro.[31] The capacity to work hard and be successful also provoked similar acts of jealousy. Haraba Dembélé believed that she caught leprosy in the 1930s from those who had become envious of her ability to harvest much cotton. As the disease progressed, she could no longer work because it ruined her hands.[32] In a similar instance, Misajé Doumbia gave Jeriba Doumbia leprosy in the 1930s because the latter "worked a lot."[33] This kind of jealousy occurred frequently among co-wives. Nantènè Keita (b. 1924) became infected as a child because a co-wife resented Nanténé's mother's diligence in the household.[34]

25 Lassana Diakité, 5 April 1993.

26 Jasig Traoré, 22 April 1993.

27 Duba Traoré, 9 December 1992.

28 Alu Tolèma, 28 November 1992.

29 Sorcerer translates from *subaga* (literally "night animal"). It is the least confusing but not necessarily the best term. In English, "sorcery" suggests secretive occult practices and obscures the more complicated but overt social dimensions in the Malian context. See Robert Launay, "The Division of Witchcraft Labor among the Dyula," paper presented at the Annual Conference of the African Studies Association, Toronto, 1994.

30 Madu Sako, 11 November 1992; Jean-Baptiste Dembélé, 21 March 1992.

31 Malè Sissoko, 24 February 1993.

32 Haraba Dembélé, 15 February 1993.

33 Jeriba Doumbia, 30 November 1992.

34 Nantènè Keita, 6 February 1993.

As discussed later in this chapter, leprosy interfered with one's ability to reproduce and work hard, two of the most important sources of status in the agrarian communities throughout the region. Unable to do either, many lepers experienced intense shame. They and those around them understood the acts of sorcery committed against them as retaliation for their individual success. Some people even explained the more general prevalence of leprosy in their communities as a direct result of an increase in acts of sorcery, presumably provoked by their village's collective success.[35]

Lepers and their families did not simply attribute the disease to sorcery because they felt victimized. Many perpetrators actually confessed to their deeds. Fatoumata Sylla contracted leprosy shortly after rejecting her first fiancé, Mari Diarra, and marrying another man. Years later when her condition became very severe, Mari confessed (probably around the 1960s) to giving her the disease.[36] Sanjako Nyagaté stated his intentions of giving his brother's son leprosy at the outset, but most sorcerers did not confess until much later, often just before death as in the case of Misajé Doumbia (d. ca. 1960).[37] If the specific sorcerer was not known, then occasionally an observer would admit to having seen one stalking the victim's premises. A friend of Karounga Doumbia's father had seen a sorcerer leaving Karounga's hut just around the time his disease developed in the 1960s.[38]

God and sorcery were the two most dominant after-the-fact explanations, although, in a few cases, people believed that one could inherit leprosy. Mba Juko (b. late 1910s), for example, heard from elders in Siguiri (located in present-day Guinea) that leper parents were likely to beget leper children.[39] Quite similarly, village elders explained Fuseni Diakité's illness in the 1950s with the fact that some of his ancestors also had it.[40] This explanation worked best when a patient's parent or relative was known to have suffered the same disease. Even when people did not single out heredity as an actual cause, the presence of leprosy within a family gave some coherence to an otherwise unexplainable phenomenon. For example, when asked to explain his disease, Koko Kanta mentioned that his mother had leprosy before he was born (ca. 1940).[41] Bakari Kamara (b. 1920s) similarly noted that his mother lost her hands from leprosy and that his younger brother died from it.[42]

In most cases, however, people lacked the evidence to substantiate heredity as a cause. Elders in Mori Tangara's village, for example, observed in the 1920s and 1930s that individuals contracted leprosy usually without any parent or ancestor ever having had the disease.[43] Adama Traoré tried first to understand the cause of his illness (in the 1940s) by finding other cases within his family. None existed, so he

35 Sira Traoré, 21 April 1993; Musomari Nomogo, 21 April 1993. Charles Bird and Martha Kendall situate the resentment of individual over-achievement within the larger context of Mande culture. "The Mande Hero," ed. Ivan Karp and Charles Bird, *Explorations in African Thought* (Bloomington: Indiana University Press, 1980): 13–24.
36 Mamadou Koulibali, 12 March 1993.
37 Jeriba Doumbia, 30 November 1992.
38 Karounga Doumbia, 15 December 1992.
39 Mba Juko, 22 April 1993.
40 Fuseni Diakité, 4 November 1992.
41 Koko Kanta, 16 February 1993.
42 Bakari Kamara, 22 April 1993.
43 Mori Tangara, 20 January 1993.

concluded that sorcery was responsible.[44] Etiological beliefs based on heredity could
have easily stigmatized a leper's children and thereby prevented them from marrying "healthy" individuals. However, this occurred in only a few rare cases, primarily
in the north where genetic assumptions predominated: for example, Bouré Maiga's
(b. 1950) community in Goundam.[45] The fact that most children were not stigmatized like their leprous parents suggests that the belief in heredity was not widespread or taken seriously.

Both before-the-fact and after-the-fact etiologies shaped the multiple meanings
of leprosy in society. The disease's association with contemptible practices accentuated people's dread of the disease. When it did occur, pointing to God, snakes, or sorcerers deflected responsibility away from the patient. Sorcery enabled people to
rationalize the tragedy of being handicapped and stigmatized. It also reminded others that the "victim" was once able-bodied and hard-working. Notions of heredity
demonstrated a similar though less common tendency to make a rather confusing
and seemingly arbitrary fate more coherent. Together, the examples presented in this
section reveal how a variety of factors ranging from dietary beliefs to the ability to
work influenced conceptions of the disease and contributed to their inconsistencies
both with each other and with observable reality. More abstractly, the remarkably
wide distribution of common beliefs and the specificity of their meaning in particular
contexts illustrate the process of how people reconciled received knowledge with
their direct observations.

Seeds of Sickness

The preceding discussion of etiologies conspicuously avoids the issue of contagion, largely because people in Mali never attributed specific leprosy cases to
infection by another person. Although some individuals said that leprosy could
spread between humans, they never cited transmission as an actual cause of the
disease. As with before-the-fact explanations, people who believed in contagion
rarely if ever observed direct evidence of it. On their surface, social responses to
lepers suggest a widespread belief in contagion, but the reasoning employed to
explain them reveal the action of more complex sentiments. In other words, contagion served only as a vague and random rationalization for exclusionary practices.
This section examines the meaning of those practices as they transformed one's
social identity.

Relatively few people conceived of leprosy's contagion in any detail. Kasoume
Tangara (b. 1910), the Bambara healer mentioned earlier, learned from his grandfather that when healthy and infected persons sleep in the same room, the latter should
rise first in the morning. "Seeds of sickness" (*banakisèw*) emanate from the patient's
body during the night and float out of the hut. In the morning these seeds collect near
the door like cobwebs and wait to infect the first person to pass by. The infected individual must leave first lest the "seeds" enter the healthy person.[46] Like the etiological

44 Adama Traoré (Kita), 22 April 1993.

45 Bouré Maiga, 17 December 1992.

46 Kasoume Tangara, 18 February 1993.

beliefs, this conception existed in slightly varying forms throughout the region among people of different ethnicities. Hamadou Sow (b. 1956), Nègè Barri (b. 1920), and Malè Sissoko (b. 1918) had heard similar theories in their respective villages near Mopti, Pita (Guinea), and Nioro.[47] In Hamadou Sow's version, women risked infecting men more easily than vice versa because men always slept near the door, where the seeds gathered, and women slept near the wall.[48]

Most notions of contagion, however, were less defined and served as vague rationalizations for actions rooted more in disgust than mindful concern for public health. In nearly all communities people ate collectively from common bowls in the same manner that families in Western societies often eat at the same table. Leprosy patients with open sores, however, usually found themselves unwanted at these bowls and had to eat alone. In Asata Tangara's village (ca. 1940s and 1950s), people did not consider leprosy contagious but felt that the disgusting nature of open sores warranted isolation.[49] Dramane Dembélé ate alone when his sores appeared around 1950 but rejoined the communal bowl when they healed.[50] In general, families rarely imposed this form of isolation on individuals without open sores. As an exception, healthy people in Malè Sissoko's village stopped drinking from the same cup and eating from the same bowl upon the slightest indication of the disease (ca. 1920s and 1930s).[51] Saran Keita's story revealed similar behavior.

The example of Kasoume Tangara's village in the early part of this century poignantly illustrates the powerful effect of open sores on attitudes and actions. Believing in the importance of the community's "solidarity," villagers ordinarily did not ostracize lepers who only had patches; healthy people allowed them to eat from the same bowl in spite of the widely believed health risks. Community solidarity became less important, though, if sores appeared; in such cases the individual ate alone. According to Kasoume, the combination of perceived risk and disgust proved too strong for loftier principles.[52] Leprosy similarly interfered with a variety of other important social activities beyond sleeping and eating. In many instances, infected individuals were not allowed to sell food; some even avoided the market altogether.[53] Lepers in Bè Diarra's village used proxies to sell their goods and, when buying things, usually dropped money in a bowl rather than hand it directly to the seller (in the 1920s and 1930s).[54] Whenever Madu Sako washed in a local creek in the 1920s, others told him to go downstream.[55]

Disgust and fear of contagion also frequently affected a leper's participation in important ritual activities. In non-Muslim villages, men often belonged to initiation associations known as *kòmò* or *jo*. Such associations met in secret and, among other things, served as forums for social bonding (usually through communal beer

47 Hamadou Sow, 19 October 1992; Nègè Barri, 23 December 1992; Malè Sissoko, 24 February 1993.

48 Hamadou Sow, 19 October 1992.

49 Asata Tangara, 17 February 1993.

50 Dramane Dembélé, 9 April 1993.

51 Malè Sissoko, 24 February 1993.

52 Kasoume Tangara, 18 February 1993.

53 Karounga Doumbia, 15 December 1992; Kama Doumbia, 25 November 1992.

54 Bè Diarra, 12 November 1992.

55 Madu Sako, 11 November 1992.

drinking) and the transmission of practical and occult knowledge. A leper's involvement in such associations depended on the particular attitudes of other members. In the 1930s, Sengu Traoré and Mori Tangara continued participating in *kòmò* activities—such as drinking beer from the same calabash as others—despite their illness.[56] A leper once even served as *kòmò* chief in Jasig Traoré's village in the 1940s.[57] In contrast, leaders of the *nya* ceremonies (somewhat akin to the *kòmò*) in Dramane Dembélé's village ordered lepers with open sores to drink beer from a separate calabash (ca. 1930s and 1940s).[58] Though Brèma Koulibali (b. 1914) also participated in *kòmò* activities, he was too "shamed" (*maloya*) to participate in the beer drinking and chicken sacrifice.[59]

The exclusion of lepers from mosques in Muslim villages also depended on the prevailing attitudes of religious leaders or the community as a whole. In spite of many forms of ostracism, Malè Sissoko still prayed with others in the 1930s; his imam instructed the villagers that "God permitted it" (*alla sònna*).[60] Adama Traorè chose on his own to pray outside because he feared disgusting fellow worshippers (ca. 1940s).[61] Alassana Maiga's community sternly prohibited individuals with open sores from entering, claiming that, "if you dirty your clothes you dirty the prayer." However, if the sores disappeared, then a leper could resume praying inside.[62] Whenever Fatoma Kamaté attempted to pray in his village mosque in the late 1950s, other men became disgusted and told him to leave.[63]

While frequently ostracized in the course of daily activities, virtually no leprosy patients experienced physical isolation or banishment from their villages. Of everyone interviewed for this study, only one person, Saran Keita, suffered this fate. People rationalized their mistreatment of lepers by saying that the disease was contagious, yet they rarely went to the extreme of completely isolating patients as they sometimes did to people with smallpox, a recognizably contagious disease. At worst, lepers ended up on the periphery of a family compound, and not necessarily because everyone believed that they were a health-risk. Aminata Traoré's mother died while Aminata was still a child in the 1930s. When Aminata developed leprosy, her father's other wife insisted, in spite of his protests, that Aminata sleep alone in a hut behind the compound. Since the wife also prohibited her from eating with the family, the father delivered Aminata's meals to the hut.[64]

The disruption of daily and ritual activities greatly affected a leper's changing identity and mirrored the disruption of his or her relations with others. Overall, very few people reported cases of direct verbal abuse of lepers. Such behavior was often considered improper. As isolated examples, both Chaka Théra (1960s) and Sabari

---

56 Mori Tangara, 20 January 1993.

57 Jasig Traoré, 22 April 1993; Joseph Koulibali, 8 December 1992.

58 Dramane Dembélé, 9 April 1993.

59 Brèma Koulibali, 19 January 1993.

60 Malè Sissoko, 26 February 1993.

61 Adama Traoré, 22 April 1993. In Makan Dembélé's village, shame similarly caused lepers to pray behind the village mosque. Makan Dembélé, 22 April 1993.

62 Alassana Maiga, 25 April 1993.

63 Fatoma Kamaté, 21 March 1993.

64 Aminata Traoré, 6 April 1993.

Sokoba (1940s) received insults from children yelling *"Kunatò! Kunatò!"* ("Leper! Leper!") whenever they walked about in their respective villages.[65] Such behavior occurred primarily in Bobo communities, although in Issa Traoré's Bambara village near Bougouni (1940s and 1950s), lepers were insulted and spat upon by people in the market who also called out, *"Kunatò! Kunatò!* Children are not given to *kunatòw!"* [66] This insult played on the assumption that lepers were not deserving of spouses. Similarly, people insulted lepers in Yusufu Diarra's (b. 1933) Bambara village for not being able to work, calling them "ruined people" (*mogow tiyenna*).[67] Though rare, such insults focused on the disease's interference with one's abilities to reproduce and work which, as already noted, were the critical factors in explanations of sorcery. In a few rare cases, children of lepers received insults.[68]

Most often individuals with leprosy felt insult through behavior rather than words. Whenever Félicité Thèra (b. 1940s) seated herself near others, they abruptly stood up and walked away. Félicité believed that their fears provoked them to spit after her as well. No other condition—not even madness—incited this treatment.[69] Ousmane Traoré (b. late 1920s) observed that fearful children fled lepers in his village because they were "different."[70] Both Malè Sissoko and Soulaymane Sidibé (b. 1925) simply lost their friends.[71] Like eating collectively, handshaking reinforced community bonds between people. Since this act involved physical contact, people in many communities rarely extended their hands to lepers.[72] Michel Traoré found that elders in the 1930s never touched his hand but young people were less fearful and more friendly.[73]

Specific behavior, of course, depended on the nature of relationships between lepers and others before the disease's appearance. Friends and family often (though not always) displayed more concern than strangers. In some communities, people concealed their feelings to avoid insulting lepers and disrupting community solidarity. For example, healthy people in Farima Doumbia's (b. ca. 1917) village shook the hands of lepers with open sores by grabbing their wrists, a practice followed even in ordinary circumstances when eating or work dirtied one's hands.[74] Despite warnings from others, one of Mamadou Diallo's childhood friends remained his playmate (ca. 1930s).[75] Many other lepers also had one or two loyal companions.

Nothing emphasized the permanency of a leper's identity more than the practice among Bobo and Dogon communities of burying lepers in the bush away from "healthy" dead people. In such communities, leprous corpses often wound up inside

65   Chaka Thèra, 21 March 1993; Sabari Sokoba, 21 March 1993.

66   Issa Traoré, 7 April 1993.

67   Yusufu Diarra, 21 March 1993.

68   Moussa Diakité, 14 November 1992.

69   Félicité Thèra, 22 March 1993.

70   Ousmane Traoré, 25 November 1992.

71   Soulaymane Sidibé, 4 December 1992; Malè Sissoko, 24 February 1993.

72   Malè Sissoko, 24 February 1993.

73   Michel Traoré, 17 November 1992.

74   Farima Doumbia, 1 December 1992.

75   Mamadou Diallo, 9 April 1993.

cliffs, baobab trees, or termite mounds.[76] For Sabari Sokoba, the prospect of such a burial caused him as much anguish and shame as the practices and beliefs which affected his more immediate day-to-day life.[77] Bobo people often buried their dead inside their homes but many feared that including lepers might spread leprosy within the village or prevent the rains from coming. Sometime in the early 1950s, the body of Hamourou Tolèma, a leper in a Dogon village near Tominian, was buried between boulders and covered with mud and rock.[78] Aside for these particular communities, however, this burial practice was not very widespread in twentieth-century Mali. At most, communities would not wash the leper's body as happened in Moussa Diakité's village (ca. 1930s and 1940s). "If they didn't want to touch a leper when he was alive," he said, "then they certainly wouldn't want to touch him when he was dead."[79]

Overall, few people knew of the "seeds of sickness" as related by Kasoume's father and grandfather. Behavior and practices which, on the surface, suggested genuine fears of contagion exposed vaguer sentiments rooted in disgust. Though motivated by different factors, these responses collectively defined lepers as different from others. In this sense, the dread of leprosy derived as much from the disease's degrading social consequences as it did from the devastating physical effects.

Marriage and Divorce

Of all the social responses, the exclusion from marriage best illustrates how leprosy transformed one's social identity. The legal manuscripts mentioned in the previous chapter document this practice in Muslim communities for at least three or four centuries before the colonial era. In both Muslim and non-Muslim communities throughout the twentieth century, contagion served as an amorphous and ill-defined concept for rationalizing the draconian penalty of denying one a spouse. Disability constituted an even more convincing and tangible excuse, especially in agrarian communities highly dependent on manual labor of all kinds. Although some individuals continued working for their families in spite of amputated fingers or feet, most people considered leprosy a handicapping disease.[80] Whatever the stated cause, exclusion from marriage deepened one's social isolation.

The specific opinions on how leprosy should affect one's ability to marry varied widely between communities or individual families. In the end, however, most practices confined one to a marginal status. In Jasig Traoré's (b. 1913) and Nakan Doumbia's (b. ca. 1942) villages, lepers were encouraged to pair themselves with other lepers rather than with healthy individuals.[81] Leprous women in Dramane Dambélé's

76 Aljuma Guindo, 5 April 1993; Arabaha Thèra, 22 March 1993; Chaka Thèra, 21 March 1993; Félicité Thèra, 22 March 1993.

77 Sabari Sokoba, 21 March 1993.

78 Alu Tolèma, 28 November 1993.

79 Moussa Diakité, 14 November 1992.

80 Mori Tangara, 20 January 1993.

81 Jasig Traoré, 22 April 1993; Nakan Doumbia, 17 November 1992.

(b. 1923) village could marry "healthy" old men or those with some defect; leprous men, on the other hand, could not find wives at all.[82] Bala Doumbia (b. 1912) heard that, in Samory's time (the last thirty years of the nineteenth century), lepers often received slaves as wives. (He knew of one such case in a neighboring village.[83]) Only in rare instances did the disease not intrude on marital practices. In Gabriel Konaté's village, people considered leprosy the "work of God" and therefore not a viable justification for exclusion (ca. 1930s and 1940s).[84] Mori Tangara (b. 1919) observed that even lepers with open sores found healthy spouses. He himself received his first wife long after his leprosy developed.[85]

Although many men and women throughout Mali suffered the same fate, the articulated reasons for it also assumed many forms. As illustrated in Saran Keita's story, her sister Hawa's marital arrangement fell apart when leprosy patches appeared on her skin; her fiancé feared the disease itself as well its potential effect on her ability to work. Belief in transmission from parent to child prevented marriage in Soulaymane Fofana's village (in the 1940s).[86] In Lambido (near Nioro), Malè Sissoko could not find a wife and Kaba Nyagaté a husband, because people believed that leprosy could spread from one spouse to another.[87] In most cases, however, notions of contagion only partly affected thinking on marriage. Former spouses of lepers were not ordinarily considered infected and (like Saran Keita's husband) easily found other people to marry.[88] Lassana Diakité (b. 1933) explained that prolonged illness resulted in poverty such that, without tools and money, one could never marry.[89] The undesirability of lepers in Sita Dembélé's village as late as the 1970s derived from the widespread assumption that the disease was incurable and that, sooner or later, such persons would be unable to work.[90]

Variations in power relations between individuals within a family and community also contributed to leprosy's unsystematic effect on marriage. Saran Keita's husband shunned her immediately upon diagnosis but did not divorce her until others in the community intervened and returned her to her parents. Fellow villagers pressured Silvestré Kamaté's wife to divorce him in the early 1950s, but she refused. Since her father had given her to Silvestré, she felt obligated to remain in the marriage.[91] Tongo Bagayogo initially refused to marry Magara Sidibé around 1961 because she feared catching his disease. Her father, however, beat her until she accepted.[92] In contrast, women in Baguinéda (1930s–1940s) were allowed without question to refuse

---

82 Dramane Dembélé, 9 April 1993; see also Makan Dembélé, 22 April 1993.

83 Bala Doumbia, 22 November 1992.

84 Gabriel Konaté, 2 April 1993.

85 Mori Tangara, 20 January 1993.

86 Soulaymane Fofana, 2 February 1993.

87 Malè Sissoko, 24 February 1993.

88 As a rare example, healthy women divorced from leprous husbands in Goundam were said to have difficulty marrying. The ease of remarriage for healthy men divorced from leprous wives, however, suggests a selective application of contagion theory to social practice. Bouré Maiga, 17 December 1992.

89 Lassana Diakité, 5 April 1993.

90 Sita Dembélé, 25 March 1993. Lasine Berté's wife left him the day of diagnosis for the same reasons. Lasine Berté, 16 November 1992.

91 Silvestré Kamaté, 23 March 1993.

92 Magara Sidibé, 2 February 1993.

marriage or initiate divorce if their husbands were infected.[93] One informant observed that women often provoked divorce from their leprous husbands by refusing to work in the household. Polygamy, of course, provided men with alternatives to divorce. Bouréma Traoré, a marabout in a village near Baguinéda (ca. 1940s or 1950s), simply married another woman rather than abandon his leprous wife.[94] The presence of children could also spare one from divorce in spite of leprosy.[95]

The following example illustrates in greater detail how others in one's family or community affected leprosy's impact on marriage. When Dawda Koita first learned of his disease in the late 1950s, he told nobody except his parents who would fetch his medicines for him in the bush. For years Dawda prepared and applied these medicines in private every morning. Though still not cured, he eventually married Mayuma Dambélé without informing her of his illness. Dawda succeeded in concealing his disease from everyone until the day his cousin Musa Koita discovered him taking these medicines and asked questions. Musa was a good friend and Dawda did not want to lie to him. The strength of this friendship, however, failed to prevent Musa from immediately telling Mayuma that her husband had the form of leprosy which "cut fingers." He warned her that, if she continued to live with Dawda and have children by him, she too would be "caught" by the disease.

Mayuma did nothing initially, but Dawda found her crying every morning. After a few months, he grew tired and began hitting her, imploring that she stop. He suspected that these were "sorcerer's tears" (*subaga kasi*) and consulted his father for advice. His father in turn asked his mother to intervene. She agreed and one day approached Mayuma who then finally admitted to knowing about Dawda's leprosy. Dawda's mother tried to persuade her that she had no reason to fear his disease because it was God's work and therefore not contagious. Mayuma did not agree. At that point Dawda told his father to return Mayuma to her parents. His father refused, saying that everyone would then know about the disease. Mayuma herself offered to stay with Dawda if they could sleep on different mats. Dawda considered her proposal an indignation and refused. One day he returned to his house and she was gone.[96]

Leprosy's interference in marriage poignantly illustrates the vicious circle in which individuals found themselves. In most agrarian communities, people perceived marriage and children as the only means for maintaining economic stability and one's status as a full member of adult society. Often considered a debilitating disease, leprosy denied one access to these means. Its social and physical handicaps thereby reinforced each other, increasing the risks of long-term destitution. In other words, leprosy simultaneously rendered one physically and socially different from others. Exclusion from marriage exemplifies the self-fulfilling nature of difference in social organization.

---

93 Adama Traoré, 26 November 1992.

94 Ibid.

95 Kasoume Tangara, 18 February 1993. As an exception, people in Issa Traoré's village sanctioned divorce even if one had children. Issa Traoré, 7 April 1993.

96 Dawda Koita, 23 August 1993.

Shame

When reflecting on the past, many people who became lepers in their villages described their feelings with one word, "shame" (*maloya*).[97] More than any other word, this one revealed how people internalized and understood their experiences. The specific causes of shame varied from individual to individual, but the repeated use of the word suggested their common fate. Shame encapsulated their sense of difference and inferiority. It expressed the essence of their relationship with society, the status of their transformed identities.

Most often, shame resulted from the prolonged inability to work like normal individuals in the fields or household. Leprosy's devastating physical effects also accentuated one's differentness. Chaka Théra (b. 1950), for example, attributed his shame to the disappearance of fingers; Ferdinand Jessana (b. 1926) faulted the flies which often swarmed about his deteriorating flesh.[98] During his interview, Fatoma Kamaté (b. 1933) descended to all fours to demonstrate how the sores on his hands and feet forced him to eat alone "like a dog" and crawl about "like a child."[99] People usually articulated their feelings in terms of their suffering the disease alone. When the distinctive open sores appeared on his skin in the 1930s, Kabiné Traoré suddenly became conscious of his status as the village's only leper.[100] Mba Juko (b. 1923) likewise felt alone since nobody else in her family, ancestors included, ever had the disease.[101]

With the phrase "you yourself are shamed" (or "you alone are shamed," "*I yèrè bè maloya*"), many individuals assumed responsibility for their feelings rather than blame them on others. Fanta Koita (b. 1928) observed that leprosy ruined her youth, made her different, and interfered with work, but she insisted that a leper's shame came from within.[102] Moussa Sokoba (b. 1940) explained that when leprosy intensified "you began to smell, and you knew that this smell would bother others, since it bothered even yourself." To avoid disgusting people, one withdrew into the compound or hut for most of the day and avoided celebrations. In Moussa's view, one's "grief" (*hami*) resulted primarily from this self-imposed withdrawal.[103] Nouhoum Koulibali (b. ca. 1930s) and Bakari Kanoté (b. 1921) similarly spent entire days alone in the bush (*kungo*) to minimize contact with their fellow villagers.[104]

The nature and level of one's shame depended on circumstantial factors and personal belief. Most people recognized the diversity of feelings induced by the disease with the phrase "people are not the same" (*mògòw tè kelen*). At one extreme, lepers suffered intense humiliation, often to the point of tears as happened to Yusufu Diarra

---

97 For further discussion of *maloya*, see Grosz-Ngate, "Hidden Meanings," 170–71.

98 Chaka Thèra, 21 March 1993; Ferdinand Jessana, 21 March 1993.

99 Fatoma Kamaté, 21 March 1993.

100 Kabiné Traoré, 16 December 1992.

101 Mba Juko, 22 April 1993.

102 Fanta Koita, 14 March 1993.

103 Moussa Sokoba, 18 February 1993; see also Malè Sissoko, 24 February 1993, and Lasine Berté, 16 November 1992.

104 Nouhoum Koulibali, 5 November 1992; Bakari Kanoté, 5 November 1992.

(b. 1933) and Fatoma Kamaté, both men.[105] Madu Sako (b. 1917), the man mentioned above whom villagers ordered to bathe downstream, nearly hung himself for fear of suffering the same stigma endured by his leprous grandmother who did not receive proper burial when she died.[106] In describing their social experiences, most lepers tersely but emphatically stated, "I was tired of it!" (N'sègènna kojugu!)

At the other extreme, individuals such as Haraba Dembélé (b. 1913) believed that leprosy was not disgraceful because one could not control it.[107] Aminata Tall (b. 1923) similarly found no reason to be humiliated, because God gave her the disease.[108] In Balafonci Diarra's village (ca. 1900–1930), lepers effectively remained full members of the community. Although illness caused one to feel out of place among the healthy, elders insisted that leprosy was "God's work" and therefore not shameful. In their view, everyone carried the disease, but lepers simply possessed more of it.[109] Occasionally lepers learned to transform their marginal status for their own benefit. When Nanyuma Koulibali (b. 1920s) could not marry in her village, her father constructed a separate hut where she slept and ate alone. At night, however, men— even married ones—visited her. In return for her attentions, many of them helped cultivate her fields which she could no longer maintain alone because of her disease. One leprous man wanted to marry her, but she refused, preferring her unique independence to a more constraining life with a man.[110]

The varied expressions of feeling underscore the multiplicity of meanings of social practice and behavior even for lepers themselves. Although most people considered leprosy an unavoidably shameful experience, they nonetheless recognized the possibility of other feelings. In the end, however, all lepers acknowledged their sense of difference from the rest of society. Within that difference rested the foundation of their social identities.

Conclusion

Many of the experiences described above were not exclusive to leprosy sufferers. Sorcery and "God's work," for example, were used to explain other illnesses and conditions such as diarrhea and blindness.[111] Griots and members of other professional castes also supposedly faced separate burial in baobab trees and termite mounds.[112] In her study of contemporary Bambara societies, Maria Grosz-Ngate observed that "outside status" (with respect to one's husband's kin group) constituted an important component of women's identities.[113] In many villages, the insane (fatòw) experienced social isolation, because they ate and slept either alone or with other

---

105 Yusufu Diarra, 21 March 1993; Fatoma Kamaté, 21 March 1993.

106 Madu Sako, 11 November 1992.

107 Haraba Dembélé, 15 February 1993.

108 Aminata Tall, 5 April 1993; see also Nèkoro Traorè, 19 May 1993.

109 Balafonci Diarra, 19 November 1992.

110 Adama Traoré, 13 November 1992.

111 For a comprehensive list of the uses of sorcery, see Traoré, Médecin et magie africaine.

112 Conrad and Frank, Status and Identity.

113 Grosz-Ngate, "Hidden Meanings," 176.

stigmatized people including lepers.[114] Some communities recognized the contagiousness of smallpox and measles patients by isolating them outside the village
until they either recovered or died.[115] As noted earlier, Muslim scholars often
included madness and impotence with leprosy as grounds for divorce.

Epilepsy in particular seems to have caused as much fear and stigma as leprosy.
According to many informants, people believed that this disease was transmitted by
the sufferer's saliva and therefore highly contagious. In Arabaha Théra's Bobo village, lepers and epileptics ate alone and could not marry.[116] In another community, an
epileptic woman never found a husband because she periodically suffered sei-
zures.[117] Hawa Dambélé's husband divorced her because he believed that, as an epileptic, she would not be able to cook or bear children.[118] In some cases, lepers with
open sores were allowed to eat from the communal bowl if they used a gourd as a
spoon, but epileptics were systematically forbidden.[119]

This chapter previously explained how leprosy's reputation as a handicapping
disease greatly influenced social responses. Aside from moments of actual seizure,
epilepsy did not ordinarily prevent one from one working. Its relatively bizarre
manifestations, however, caused much fear. Much like a leper's sores and smells, an
epileptic's saliva became the cause and object of avoidance. As Brèma Touré
explained, people shunned epileptics only when they "dropped to the ground."[120]
Both leprosy and epilepsy were somewhat rare diseases with distinct and repugnant
effects which could recur throughout a patient's life. As such, they provoked greater
stigma than more common diseases of limited duration and effect: for example,
malaria or dysentery.

The role of disabilities in shaping social conceptions of and reactions to leprosy
suggests that other handicaps also carried stigma. For example, Jasig Traoré observed
that blindness often prevented one from marrying, while Abdoulaye Diarra similarly
noted that it caused divorce among recently married couples.[121] In other communities, polio and impotence also justified divorces.[122] Most people, however, found that
handicaps alone did not shame their victims as severely as leprosy. In Buna Sawane's
village, for example, blindness or physical handicaps caused by accident did not prevent marriage or stigmatize their victims like leprosy.[123] Stories of handicapped yet
noble individuals triumphing over their adversaries (often found in historical epics)
reveal that not all disabilities were discrediting. Most notably, the epic relating the
formation of the Mali Empire portrays its founder, Sundiata, as a cripple throughout

114 Mbajala Traoré, 22 April 1993; Félicité Thèra, 22 March 1993.
115 Aljuma Guindo, 5 April 1993; Malè Sissoko, 24 February 1993.
116 Arabaha Thèra, 22 March 1993.
117 Issa Traoré, 7 April 1993.
118 Chaka Thèra, 21 March 1993; see also Kasoume Tangara, 18 February 1993.
119 Bernadetti Traoré, 11 March 1993; Musomari Nomogo, 21 April 1993.
120 Brèma Touré, 2 April 1993. For a contemporary study of attitudes towards epilepsy, see Ousmane Sala-
     manta, "Étude épidémiologique de l'épilepsie dans l'arrondissement central de Bandiagara" (Thèse,
     Ecole de Médecine, Bamako, Mali, 1989).
121 Jasig Traoré, 22 April 1993; Abdoulaye Diarra, 27 November 1992.
122 Mariame Doumbia, 23 November 1992; Bakari Borè, 22 March 1993.
123 Buna Sawane, 26 October 1992.

his childhood.[124] In Mali today, some people consider it good luck to have a physically handicapped individual, usually a polio victim, in the household.[125]

Though similar to other diseases in terms of its perceived contagiousness or resulting handicaps, leprosy was unique because it involved both these elements at once. A combination of physical and social deterioration transformed lepers into the least desirable members of their agrarian communities. Unlike fatal or short-term afflictions, leprosy lasted a lifetime, steadily limiting one's ability to work and live with others. The example of rural Mali suggests that leprosy's seemingly universal stigma grew out of the disease's interruption of agrarian life rather than simply its perceived grotesqueness, as is popularly assumed. Perhaps this may partly explain why the disease provoked similar reactions in medieval Europe.

---

124 Djibril T. Niane, *Sundiata: An Epic of Old Mali*, translated by G. D. Peckett (London: Longmans, 1966).

125 Colleague Rosa De Jorio heard this while conducting research in Ségou Bambara communities (private conversation, March 1993). None of my informants ever mentioned examples of this phenomenon actually occurring in their villages. It would be hard to believe, indeed, that agrarian communities highly dependent on field labor for survival would consider paralysis an asset. At best, this might have occurred in wealthy communities or towns such as Ségou, the former capital of the nineteenth-century Bambara state.

4

Becoming a Patient

When Saran Keita's condition worsened, she consulted healers near her village. The pursuit of indigenous medical treatment partly defined her life as a leper, leading her to people and places she wouldnot have otherwise encountered. Over the years, Saran bounced between hope and despair as she repeatedly tried new cures only to suffer relapses. Beyond the possibility of physical recovery, these cures represented her only chance of returning to a "normal" social existence. Their failure threatened her long-term health as well as her identity as a full member of Gwansolo's community.

Throughout the twentieth century, the search for a cure constituted a life-long journey involving varied attempts at African medicine prior to consultation with European practitioners. The journey often began well after the first diagnosis. Saran's story vividly demonstrated how patches could appear without the company of more familiar indications of sickness such as fever or fatigue. This aspect of leprosy enabled many people to postpone medical intervention until symptoms became more severe.

Experiences with indigenous healing changed in the course of the century, but only minimally when compared with the changes affecting European practices described in later chapters. In most cases, the specific medicines remained the same. Before the widespread introduction of antibiotics in the late 1950s, the few leprosy patients who underwent European treatments temporarily avoided African ones; they believed that pursuing both at the same time would be harmful. If the European medicine proved unsuccessful or unpleasant, then they would stop it completely before resuming local remedies. From the 1950s onward, the efficacy of European antibiotics did gradually draw many patients away from African healing altogether. Such individuals, however, tended to reside near government clinics in towns and administrative centers. As a result of limited infrastructure and supplies, those in more isolated areas continued to consult their own healers first. One man interviewed for this study lived in a hamlet so remote that, as late as 1993, he still resorted to "traditional" medicines when government nurses failed to renew his supply. Only patients with easy and steady access to European antibiotics permanently abandoned African healing for their disease.[1]

---

1 We should bear in mind that this pattern for leprosy does not necessarily apply for other diseases. The role of indigenous medicine for each particular ailment differed depending on the quality, access, and expense of European alternatives.

Like the responses described in the previous chapter, clinical experiences with indigenous healing contributed to the formation of leper identities. These experiences varied considerably, even within the same village. Diverse factors such as availability, family politics, religion, and geography all influenced the selection of remedies. Searching for a cure engaged patients in multiple medical "relationships" with people ranging from one's mother to an unfamiliar healer in a distant village, each one employing different methods. While some medical practices derived from well-developed "systems," others belonged to a more amorphous body of general knowledge passed on orally in these predominantly non-literate societies. Leprosy could last a lifetime, so patients often availed themselves of several healing alternatives not necessarily related to each other or to those used for other diseases. Rather than study each alternative in isolation, this chapter identifies the broader patterns of clinical experience. It first considers the diffusion of leprosy-specific medical knowledge and the permeability of ethnic and religious boundaries for medical practice. It then briefly examines the physical effects of the most common leprosy remedies and the nature of patient-healer relationships. Later chapters will examine patients' subsequent experiences with practitioners of European medicine.

Healers and Their Remedies

More than anything else, patients' clinical experiences with indigenous "healers" reveal a wide distribution of medical knowledge in Mali. In Europe, healing had become the preserve of professional doctors by the twentieth century—after years of political maneuvering.[2] In Mali, however, medical knowledge and skills remained dispersed throughout society in such a way that no single group monopolized the field to the same degree. As a result, virtually anyone, even patients themselves or a family member, could learn and administer a remedy. As a child in the 1910s, Musa Yirango observed his grandmother treating herself with a solution of boiled bark and roots. He applied the same remedy to himself about thirty years later when his own illness developed.[3] In the 1950s, Umu Katilé similarly treated herself with medical knowledge transmitted by her grandmother.[4] Both Sabari Sokoba and Dramane Touré underwent therapy administered by their fathers before consulting other healers in the 1940s.[5] In a few rare cases, such as that of Bintou Koulibali in the 1960s, a patient's parent was already an established healer known for treating leprosy.[6]

If nobody within the immediate family could treat leprosy or home remedies proved unsuccessful, then patients looked for healers within their own villages. Malé Sissoko fell ill as a young child in the early 1920s and immediately consulted Sika

2 On the early professionalization of European medicine, see for example, Matthew Ramsey, *Professional and Popular Medicine in France, 1770–1830* (Cambridge: Cambridge University Press, 1988); Ivan Waddington, "General Practitioners and Consultants in Early Nineteenth-Century England: The Sociology of an Intra-Professional Conflict," in John Woodward and David Richards, eds., *Health Care and Popular Medicine in Nineteenth Century England* (New York: Holmes and Meier Publishers, 1977).

3 Musa Yirango, 20 December 1992.

4 Umu Katilé, 15 February 1993.

5 Sabari Sokoba, 25 March 1993; Dramane Touré, 16 November 1992.

6 Bintou Koulibali, 22 March 1993.

Tunkara, a village healer who attracted leprosy patients from the surrounding area.[7] Ousmane Traoré similarly consulted a marabout (a type of Muslim healer described below) in his village of Tun (near Bandiagara) during the late 1950s.[8] In rare cases, individuals like Mamadu Diallo and Nouhoum Koulibali underwent treatment from itinerant healers passing through their communities.[9] Most people, however, knew that leprosy required prolonged treatment and avoided such cursory encounters. Healers themselves considered traveling undignified and preferred to receive patients at their homes rather than solicit them.[10]

Since leprosy occurred far less frequently than other diseases such as malaria or dysentery, relatively few people possessed the specific skills or knowledge for treating it. Many patients were therefore encouraged to venture further away to find those who did. When Kabiné Traoré contracted leprosy in the 1930s, his mother solicited suggestions from other villagers before sending him to a healer living about a two-hour walk away.[11] Nènènkoro Balo's mother similarly escorted him regularly to a marabout on the opposite side of the Niger River in the 1950s.[12] Following his mother's recommendation, Mori Tangara traveled two days on foot to Koutiala where he spent two years in the early 1940s with a healer.[13] Namaké Keita—who developed leprosy after retiring from the French army with which he fought in the First World War—learned of a healer from travelers returning from the gold fields near Kangaba. In spite of the nearly three-hundred-kilometer trip, Namaké himself spent two months with the healer who apparently succeeded in curing him.[14]

The tendency of patients throughout Mali to cross perceived ethnic and religious boundaries revealed a willingness to make use of different alternatives. Muhammad al-Her, a Tuareg man from the Kel Horma "tribe," consulted a Fulani marabout in the late 1960s outside his home community near Timbuktu.[15] Moulaye Ahmed Baber, a Timbuktu scholar born in 1914, affirmed that Muslims could undergo treatment by non-Muslims as long as the latter's medicines derived from substances permitted in Islam. On many occasions, members of his community consulted him on the permissibility of receiving "non-Muslim" treatment.[16] Though from a solidly Muslim family and the son of a respected Djenne marabout, Dramane Touré was allowed to receive treatment (in the 1940s) from an old non-Muslim Bambara healer recommended by another leprosy patient.[17] Jakini Cissé similarly visited non-Muslim healers near Ségou during the early stages of his illness in the 1940s. He believed that "God

---

7 Malè Sissoko, 24 February 1993.

8 Ousmane Traoré, 25 November 1992.

9 Mamadu Diallo, 1 April 1993; Nouhoum Koulibali, 5 November 1992.

10 Sidiki Koulibali, 25 June 1991.

11 Kabiné Traoré, 16 December 1992

12 Nènènkoro Balo, 22 January 1993. Working in a very religious context, marabouts usually employed both Islamic charms and local medicines.

13 Mori Tangara, 20 January 1993.

14 Falela Keita, 28 November 1992.

15 Muhammad al-Her, 26 December 1992. Though a tainted and misleading term in English, "tribe" is the best translation of the Arabic word *qabiliyya* used to describe these branches of Tuareg nomads.

16 Moulaye Ahmed Baber, 28 December 1992.

17 Dramane Touré, 16 November 1992.

willed" people to heal themselves in any way possible, especially with plants.[18] In other cases, non-Muslims consulted Muslim healers. Bawa Sokoba, who was both Bobo and non-Muslim, obtained medicines from a Muslim marabout in order to treat his nephew in the early 1950s.[19]

The healers consulted by leprosy patients varied from individuals who just happened to know of a few remedies to those who regularly practiced their knowledge and were publicly recognized for their skills. Bambara and Malinké speakers commonly referred to medicines as *fura*, which literally meant "leaf," the most common pharmacopoeial ingredient. Individuals who applied medicines were called *furakélaw* (literally, "those who do the leaf") in the same manner that farmers were known as *cikélaw* ("those who do the farm work"). While many people, especially elders, knew and employed remedies and were therefore vaguely considered *furakélaw*, a few social groups possessed specific reputations for healing. Most notably, hunters and blacksmiths learned medicines as part of their ongoing training, as did members of initiation societies such as *kòmò*.[20] One of Jean-Baptiste Dambélé's healers, for example, was a blacksmith.[21]

In communities with significant Muslim populations, marabouts (*moriw*) also maintained reputations as healers. Their remedies were pharmacologically similar to those employed by non-Muslims, but their manner of application differed considerably and included Islamic practices such as the recitation of Koranic passages. Like hunters and blacksmiths, marabouts were not exclusively healers. Their activities included religious instruction, leading prayer groups, resolving legal questions, and administering blessings. Some marabouts were well-read scholars and relatively "orthodox" Muslims, but others were only perfunctorily literate and performed "occult" services such as divination and the making of magical charms. Reliance on charms, incantations, and other mystical devices, however, easily jeopardized a marabout's credibility for complicated diseases like leprosy. Makan Traoré, for example, believed that marabouts could not treat the disease as effectively as practitioners of what he called "Bambara" healing.[22]

In contrast to these occasionally negative reputations, marabouts in communities such as Timbuktu often reached high levels of erudition. Mouhamad Abdoulaye Boularaf (b. 1909) obtained his knowledge from classical Arabic medical guides including al-Suyuti's *Kitab al-Rahma*. He also consulted works on prophetic medicine as well as locally written texts such as the *Shifa' al-Asqam*. For three years Mouhamad studied with Moor scholars in Oualata (Mauritania) where, in his view, all the "great" doctors of Arabic medicine resided. As a prominent religious scholar in Timbuktu, Mouhamad never assumed a public identity as a healer. Nonetheless, he applied his extensive medical knowledge to treating family members and giving medical advice and prescriptions to others in the community.[23] Arabic medicine was also influential in western Mali. In his village near Kayes, Buna Sawane consulted

---

18 Jakini Cissé, 28 January 1993.

19 Sabari Sokoba, 21 March 1993.

20 See McNaughton, *The Mande Blacksmiths.*

21 Jean-Baptiste Dambélé, 21 March 1993.

22 Makan Traoré, 9 August 1991.

23 Mouhamad Abdoulaye Boularaf, 29–30 December 1992.

(in the late 1940s) Demba Yugo Tugura, a healer of Moorish origin who was literate in Arabic and possessed many books.[24] Arabic manuscript collections such as those taken by French invaders at the end of the nineteenth century and those now housed in Timbuktu's Centre Ahmad Baba contain many voluminous works on medicine including Ibn Sina's *Canon* and al-Suyuti's writings.[25]

Like patients, healers also crossed ethnic and religious boundaries in their searches for knowledge. A long history of such crossings contributed to the commonality of certain practices employed by people of different ethnicities. Ousmane Traoré, for example, found that Dogon and Bambara healers throughout the century employed essentially the same plants.[26] Bagna Yattara, a Timbuktu marabout born in 1918, praised non-Muslim Bambara practitioners for their expertise in medicinal plants and other remedies.[27] Extensive travel no doubt facilitated the diffusion of knowledge. A number of other Timbuktu marabouts such as Alpha Baba Cissé (b. ca. 1930) studied with Fulani marabouts in Ténenkou situated about four hundred kilometers to their south-west.[28] Nyankoro Traoré, Adama Traoré's Bambara healer in the 1930s and 1940s also traveled frequently away from the Bamako region, befriending other "animist" healers in order to learn their medicines.[29]

The following example poignantly illustrates the extent of diffusion and heterogeneity of medical culture in Mali. Ya Umaro, Ali Baba Cissé's great-grandfather, was originally from the Malinké village of Kangaba but settled in Wa (northwestern Ghana) on his way to Mecca in the mid-nineteenth century. He was learned in "Malinké medicine" and even composed his own book of healing in Arabic. Ali's father also became a healer and received leprosy patients from throughout the Wa region. Today, Ali himself (b. 1945) practices medicine in Bamako but maintains an ethnic identity rooted in Wa rather than his ancestral Malinké society.[30] This circulation of learned individuals throughout central West Africa dates to the early days of the gold trade in the thirteenth and fourteenth centuries when scholarly networks began overlapping with trade routes. Such a long history of intellectual exchange further justifies this analysis of local medical culture as a whole rather than in more discrete units like Muslim marabouts or Bambara blacksmiths.

The healers consulted by leprosy patients outside of their villages were in most cases male *furakèlaw* with widespread reputations. As a rare exception, Issa Traoré's healer in the early 1950s was an old woman.[31] While a few practitioners specialized only in leprosy, most treated a variety of illnesses. Gabriel Konaté's healer in the 1940s, for example, handled ailments of the head, lungs, and back in addition to

---

24 Buna Sawane, 26 October 1992.

25 Interestingly, this part of Malian medical culture shares common roots with European medicine which, in the medieval period, developed in part from these same classical Arabic texts.

26 Ousmane Traoré, 25 November 1992

27 Bagna Yattara, 14 July 1991.

28 Alpha Baba Cissé, 14 July 1991.

29 Adama Traoré, 26 November 1992. "Animist" is often used as a catchall term for non-Christian and non-Muslim "indigenous" religions. Like "tribe," it is stylistically convenient but not entirely appropriate.

30 Ali Baba Cissé is not related to Alpha Baba Cissé. For a fuller and fascinating history of Wa, see Ivor Wilks, *Wa and the Wala, Islam and Polity in Northwestern Ghana* (Cambridge: Cambridge University Press, 1989).

31 Issa Traoré, 7 April 1993.

leprosy.[32] Mansonyan Kunaté (d. 1972), a Malinké healer in Guinea, also treated epilepsy and madness, two other stigmatizing conditions.[33] Occasionally an entire family or village maintained a reputation for curing lepers. Many members of Hamadou Sow's Fulani family acquired the requisite knowledge from their parents and grandparents and, for at least a century, had attracted patients from throughout the Mopti region. Leprosy patients in the area also frequented the Fulani village of Denga and the Bozo village of Sawona.[34] Garbakoyra, a Songhay–Bozo village situated on a river island near Goundam, similarly attracted many leprosy patients throughout the century.[35] Between the 1940s and 1970s, several Bambara informants visited healers in Konjan, a village near Cinzana.[36]

In short, patients consulted a wide variety of individuals for their cures. The dispersion of medical knowledge ensured that no one group monopolized the treatment of leprosy as doctors gradually did in Western societies. The disease's chronic nature and the diversity of people able to treat it drew most patients into a lifetime of clinical encounters extending outside their own families, villages, religions, or ethnicities. The permeability of such boundaries in the medical context demonstrated their limited meaning as a basis for organizing social life, especially for people with leprosy. The knowledge employed by healers also permeated these boundaries.

We should bear in mind that this pattern of boundary crossing has been observed in other African societies.[37] In precolonial Tanzania, for example, patients generally pursued "multiple forms of healing." Practitioners themselves "traveled widely in the course of their training," and this pattern "led systematically to an awareness of varieties of healing as an open set of alternatives." [38] A similarly amorphous boundary between "Islamic" and "non-Islamic" medicine also existed in northern Nigeria.[39] Studies of that region reveal an absence of discrete "medical systems" to the point of seeming "anarchic." From a patient's perspective, supposed cultural differences between available systems hardly mattered to patients searching for the most effective cures.[40]

Patients and Their Bodies

From a patient's point of view, the most significant aspect of their encounters with indigenous healers involved the further transformation of their bodies. Medical treatments usually centered on the removal of patches and sores, the primary indicators

---

32 Gabriel Konaté, 2 April 1993.

33 Majan Fofana, 16 December 1992.

34 Hamadou Sow, 19 October 1993.

35 I was unable to visit this village, but most people in and around Timbuktu (both patients and non-patients) knew of it as a healing center.

36 Laye Koulibali, 5 November 1992; Adama Traoré, 13 November 1992; Seni Koulibali, 16 February 1993.

37 "Introduction," in Feierman and Janzen, *Social Basis*, 2–3.

38 Steven Feierman, *Peasant Intellectuals: Anthropology and History in Tanzania* (Madison: University of Wisconsin Press, 1990), 101 and 110.

39 Abdalla. " Islamic Medicine" and "Diffusion of Islamic Medicine" in *Social Basis*.

40 Murray Last, "The Importance of Knowing about Not Knowing: Observations from Hausaland," in Feierman and Janzen, *Social Basis*, 402–403.

of disease and difference. As already suggested, these treatments were remarkably uniform throughout the region in spite of ethnic and religious diversity among their users. The principal pharmacological ingredients also remained largely unchanged throughout the century. Whether applied externally or taken internally, these often painful medicines reinforced one's sense of physical abnormality. Patients generally experienced little more than temporary improvement such that their identities deteriorated in conjunction with their bodies.[41]

The numerous remedies applied to the skin demonstrate a widespread belief that the disease resided primarily on the body's surface. Patients often washed with solutions made from specific leaves, roots, or bark collected in the bush. In a few cases, healers used a vulture's head or added chickens, fish, or salamanders to otherwise vegetarian mixtures.[42] The rarity of some substances required that people such as Koko Kanta's healer, working in the late 1950s, travel several days to find them.[43] Preparation involved drying and pulverizing the ingredients into powders or soaking them in clay jars of water, usually for periods of fifteen days. One of the most common treatments involved the application of a plant-derived caustic substance which caused the patch to blister and fall off with the resulting scab. A slight variation of that treatment involved the use of shallow incisions, a technique also documented in an account of medieval Arab medicine.[44] In contrast to this preoccupation with healing skin, many treatments included the repeated ingestion of solutions also derived from plants. For example, Komogoba Sako (in the 1930s) frequently boiled leaves from the *néré* tree (*Parkia biglobosa, néré de Gambie*), drank part of the solution, and then washed with the rest.[45]

Marabouts often combined these "non-Muslim" remedies with religiously imbued practices. Working in the 1940s, Madu Marigo's marabout wrote talismanic phrases (*nasi*) on a wooden tablet, washed the ink into a calabash, added a leaf, and then let the solution sit for fifteen days. Madu then washed with and drank the solution in the early mornings.[46] Also working during these years, Demba Yugo Tugura, a Mauritanian marabout based in a village near Kayes, began treating his leprosy patients simply by spitting over the affected areas and muttering incantations. When patches multiplied, he searched, like most other healers, for the necessary plants in the bush (*kungo*).[47]

---

41 Discussions of medical practices in Africa often become encyclopedic when they address specific remedies and pharmacopoeias. Many researchers have already and are currently studying the technical aspects of medicines used in Mali. For the benefit of general readers, this section examines only the broader social meaning of those medicines. As a consequence, it omits the rich technical details revealed in nearly every patient interview. See relevant works in the bibliography for further discussions of medicine in Mali.

42 Mamadou Dama, 27 October 1992; Silvestré Kamaté, 23 March 1993; Fatoma Kamaté, 21 March 1993.

43 Koko Kanta, 16 February 1993.

44 Michael Dols, "The Leper in Medieval Islamic Society," 902, citing al-Jahiz (d. ca. 868–69), *al-Bursan wa l-ᶜurjan* (Cairo-Beirut, 1972), 52.

45 Komogoba Sako, 7 November 1992. This plant was also used for protection against leprosy. Ousmane Konaté, "La place du Service Social dans une institution sanitare spécialisée, cas de L'Institut Marchoux" (*Mémoire*, Ecol ede Formation en Développement Communautaire, Bamako, 1985), 48.

46 Madu Marigo, 5 April 1993. Most phrases are excerpts from the Koran.

47 Buna Sawane, 26 October 1992.

The application and physical effects of all these treatments often intensified one's pain and discomfort. In the 1920s, Balafonci Diarra observed that the blistering induced by the caustic substance caused patients to "cry" (kasi).[48] Seni Koulibali once visited a healer, Kontembolo Tangara, every two weeks in the early 1950s. Kontembolo routinely made cuts on Seni's forehead, elbows, knees, and chest, and then daubed them with a dark medicine. After each treatment, Seni was forbidden from washing for a week.[49] Nènènkoro Balo, who received a similar treatment around that time, described the practice as very painful.[50] Consuming plant-based solutions often resulted in diarrhea and/or vomiting, an effect desired for medicines of many ailments, not just leprosy. Nana Keita vomited each time she drank a solution derived from the kunjè tree (Guiera senegalensis) while undergoing treatment as a child in the early 1940s.[51] Foni Doumbia more explicitly stated that patients often suffered from his healer's remedies (ca. 1910s or 1920s), derived from jakumakari (Psorospermum corym biferum) and tutudala (Parinari curatellifolia, tutu blanc) trees.[52]

For most patients, a total cure required an elimination of the signs of difference (the patches and sores) or, at the very least, prevention of further damage. Bambara and Malinké speakers, for example, interpreted the "reddening" (bilenya) of black skin as illness. The "blackening" (finya) of skin therefore demonstrated recovery, a return to normalcy. Nénénkoro Balo articulated his partial recovery from a marabout's medicines specifically in those terms.[53] After suffering diarrhea and vomiting, Adama Traoré similarly found that his medicines had removed the patches and "blackened" his skin (in the 1930s and 1940s).[54] Although his patches remained, Mamadou Dama felt that his own treatment with indigenous medicines in the 1930s at least spared him the shame of losing fingers or toes as happened to many other patients.[55] In some cases, simply the inducement of diarrhea or vomiting was interpreted as an improvement.[56]

Patients reacted with mixed enthusiasm towards these different treatments. Very few informants reported cases of complete and permanent cures. As one rare example, Madu Marigo's older brother believed that he was healed by African medicines.[57] Since certain forms of leprosy could go into remission on their own, it is impossible to determine whether such reported cures occurred naturally or from medical intervention. Some individuals experienced improvement from, for example, the blistering or incision remedies, but others found the same methods utterly useless.[58] Although several

48 Balafonci Diarra, 19 November 1992. Kasi means to cry with tears or to scream.
49 Seni Koulibali, 16 February 1993.
50 Nènènkoro Balo, 22 January 1993. Shea butter was and is used widely for many other ailments as well as in cooking.
51 Nana Keita, 29 November 1992.
52 Foni Doumbia, 19 January 1993.
53 Nènènkoro Balo, 22 January 1993.
54 Adama Traoré, 26 November 1992.
55 Mamadou Dama, 27 October 1992.
56 Sira Traoré, 21 April 1993.
57 Madu Marigo, 5 April 1992.
58 Malè Sissoko, 24 February 1993; Fanta Koita, 9 March 1993; Seni Koulibali, 16 February 1993; Nènènkoro Balo, 22 January 1993; Dramane Touré, 16 November 1992.

treatments could successfully remove patches, most people suffered relapses either a few months or years later. After several cycles of treatment, cure, and relapse, patients became skeptical of their healers' abilities to cure leprosy. The pain and frustration of their clinical experiences exacerbated the grief already induced by their social isolation.

Patients and Their Healers

Saran Keita's story illustrated how patients and healers developed relationships extending beyond their immediate clinical encounters. To continue her treatment, Saran followed her healer to the gold fields and was eventually drawn into his family life. Other patients mentioned in this chapter also traveled great distances for medical reasons. These "therapeutic journeys" transformed their lives, but only temporarily and in limited ways, especially when compared with their later dislocations connected with European practices (described in later chapters). Though occasionally meeting other patients along the way, they always returned home after consultation with indigenous healers.

Overall, patient-healer relationships outside one's family varied in conjunction with the amount of time spent together. Some healers merely supplied medicines or prescriptions without administering them. Saran Koulibali (b. ca. 1910) and Bakari Boré (b. ca. 1938), for example, always treated themselves at home with remedies obtained from others.[59] Many people, however, spent longer intervals with their healers and occasionally resided with them. In the process, such patients met others from neighboring villages or even distant regions. To receive his incision treatments, Seni Koulibali visited his healer every two weeks in the 1950s. The journey took an entire day; he and other patients from still more distant villages usually slept in the healer's compound for one night before returning home. Majan Fofana lived with his healer for three years (ca. 1958) during which he met several other leprosy, epilepsy, and mental patients.[60] In most cases, patients went alone, leaving spouses and other family members behind.[61] As discussed later, the limited duration of their stays generally prevented them from becoming full members of their healers' communities.

Over such long periods of time, patients underwent therapy in broken intervals. Regardless of whether they traveled or not, most received their medicines in the cold dry season when their labor was not needed in the fields and they could better handle the sometimes debilitating effects of their medicines. Madu Marigo, for example, took his remedies over the course of fifteen years (in the 1940s and 1950s) but only during the two or three months of the cold season (December through February).[62] Similarly, Gabriel Konaté spent only the three months of each cold season (in the 1940s) lodging with his healer in a distant village.[63] The temporary nature of clinical

---

59 Saran Koulibali, 27 March 1993; Bakari Boré, 22 March 1993.

60 Majan Fofana, 16 December 1992.

61 As one exception, Kanko Fofana and her child ate and slept in her healer's compound for four years. Kanko Fofana, 9 February 1993.

62 Madu Marigo, 5 April 1993.

63 Gabriel Konaté, 2 April 1993.

encounters, however prolonged, suggests that patients rarely displaced themselves permanently. Everyone eventually returned home.

Patients who lived with their healers usually contributed labor to their new households as would any prolonged guest. Treating leprosy and other illnesses near Koutiala in the late 1930s, Nyanyugu Dembélé hosted as many as ten patients at one time. These patients usually remained for several years; they ate together and worked Nyanyugu's fields.[64] Aminata Traoré similarly lived in her healer's compound for three years (also in the 1930s) and assisted with household work by pounding millet and chopping wood.[65] The meaning of this labor remained vague, appearing to some as a fair exchange for treatment or to others as an obligation expected of any household member. In a few rare cases, patients who did not reside with a healer still provided labor. Adama Traoré, for example, worked his healer's fields for one rainy season in the 1940s while two other women patients regularly fetched his firewood.[66]

In agrarian communities, the commercial meaning of healing, especially when practiced by family members, differed considerably from other enterprises. Rather than seek direct material gain, individuals or families derived status and enlarged their social networks through their medical reputations. Recall that Saran Keita believed that charging specific fees for her treatment of infants jeopardized the cure. For similar reasons, most healers believed that they should only accept "symbolic" remuneration (*wari songo*, literally, "the kola nut price").[67] They also avoided overt payments when treating relatives. Makan Dambélé, for example, never paid Mamadou Traoré for his services (in the 1940s), because the two men belonged to the "same family."[68] As a marabout-healer of considerable wealth, Kundasi Tolema lodged, fed, and sometimes clothed patients in the 1930s without expecting payment in return.[69]

While many healers practicing throughout the century considered charging fees dishonorable, factors such as taxation, forced labor, and the emergence of a cash economy no doubt transformed the meaning of such services from the very beginning of colonial rule. The "professionalization" of indigenous medicine occurred primarily in urban areas. Marabouts in particular developed reputations for charging exorbitant fees for their services. Patients did expect to offer something in return, usually if the treatment manifested positive results.[70] Malè Sissoko never paid his healer in the 1920s, because the blistering medicine failed to remove his patches.[71] Bala Samaké's father gave one healer the equivalent of two cows for lodging and treating his son for two years in the early 1930s. Although the treatment healed some of the sores, it did not arrest the disease.[72]

---

64 Mori Tangara, 20 January 1993.

65 Aminata Traoré, 6 April 1993.

66 Adama Traoré, 26 November 1992.

67 Saran Keita, 17 May 1993.

68 Makan Dambélé, 22 April 1993.

69 Alu Tolèma, 28 November 1992.

70 Kabiné Traoré, 16 December 1992.

71 Malè Sissoko, 24 February 1993.

72 Bala Samaké, 2 December 1992.

The total absence of cash in these transactions distinguished healing from more overtly commercial activities.[73] As shown by the last example, "payments" were made in the form of gifts, usually livestock. After satisfactory treatments in the 1940s, Kabiné Traoré and Mori Tangara paid their healers a sheep and a chicken respectively.[74] Aminata Traoré's father gave a cow after his daughter's three year stay in the 1930s.[75] Paying livestock usually lay within the means of most people, so healing rarely posed an economic burden. The size of the payment expected also depended on the patient's socioeconomic position. Sometime in the 1930s, Moussa Diakité visited one healer who, if the treatments worked, expected a sheep from patients of "slave" (jòn) status or a cow from those who were "free" (horòn).[76] In a very rare example of a burdensome use of cash, Nakan Doumbia's mother sold most of their livestock to pay for other remedies when her own failed in the 1940s.[77]

Though usually limited, contact with other communities accustomed patients to the idea that their disease might lead them in directions different from those followed by their friends and family at home. Like the bodily interventions, these other experiences contributed to a new sense of self among leprosy patients. Visiting healers facilitated encounters with people of different ethnic identities or from distant places. Some individuals even met other leprosy patients along the way. Kalifa Koulibali, for example, found his healer (in the late 1920s) treating more than a hundred others for a variety of illnesses including leprosy.[78] Fatogomo Kamara, a healer practicing in the region of Siby in the 1940s, received and lodged leprosy patients from as far away as Ségou and Mopti.[79] Contact with other patients with the same disease, who usually numbered about three or four at one time, sufficed in exposing some individuals to the commonality of their experiences and problems. Such contact could affect profoundly one's sense of self as a leper. In the end, however, it occurred too briefly and sporadically for patients to form themselves into recognizable groups as they eventually did through involvement with European institutions.

Conclusion

As noted in the introduction to this chapter, most people consulted for this study first became leprosy patients through contact with indigenous healers. Though temporary, the resulting physical displacement and bodily interventions reinforced their sense of difference from others in their rural communities. It also accustomed many

---

73 Even in many communities today, cash is considered an impersonal and inappropriate form of compensation for many types of services.

74 Kabiné Traoré, 16 December 1992; Mori Tangara, 20 January 1993.

75 Aminata Traoré, 6 April 1993.

76 Moussa Diakité, 14 November 1992. The exact meanings of "free" and "slave" do not correspond exactly to their meanings in antebellum America. For a detailed elucidation of slavery in turn-of-the-century Mali, see Roberts, *Warriors, Merchants, and Slaves*.

77 Nakan Doumbia, 17 November 1992.

78 Kalifa Koulibali, 11 December 1992.

79 Kabiné Traoré, 16 December 1992.

individuals to a life away from home. This dimension of a leper's social experience remained constant for most of the century. However, what did change was the manner and frequency in which patients abandoned these indigenous treatments for European ones. As the remaining chapters reveal, the transition to European institutions coincided with a profound transformation in their social identities as lepers.

5

Toubabs as Tabibs
Europeans as Doctors

One day late in August 1900, a leprous woman calling herself "Mousso Koura" (literally, "old woman") arrived soliciting alms at the Notre Dame de la Merci Mission run by the White Sisters in Ségou. The Sisters gave her some porridge and chatted with her briefly before retiring for the evening. The next morning they found her in the same place. Rather than return home as she had led them to believe, Mousso had slept in the open with the hyenas. Noticing that her condition had worsened, the Sisters began talking to her about "the good God, the great truths, the good remedy." The sick woman then implored them to grant her whatever was necessary to see this God; they happily obliged her. A short while later her family took her away on a mat. Describing the event, one of the Sisters entered in their mission diary, "This poor corpse which is nothing but a sore will be buried in the bush, but the soul—we hope for the day when it will go to God for eternity."[1]

The Sisters' interest in Mousso Koura reflected a widespread European preoccupation with the care, cure, and control of diseased and other disadvantaged peoples in the newly conquered colony. Indeed, the most common local word for European, *toubab*, derived from the Arabic term for doctor, *tabib*.[2] Throughout the nineteenth century, Europeans of all types had lived up to the reputation implied by this name by dispensing medicine to local populations in West Africa. In the first half of the twentieth century, missionaries and administrators continued in this role. "Healing" served as a pretext for extending their political or ideological control, while colonial authority extended their medical control.

The social isolation described in Chapter 3, in addition to the pattern of crossing cultural boundaries in the pursuit of cures, encouraged lepers like Mousso Koura and Saran Keita to leave their villages for European enclaves. By moving, such individuals exposed themselves to an entirely new configuration of beliefs and practices focused on their disease. They also entered a new economic and social environment

---

1 "Diaire," Ségou, 21 August 1900, Soeurs Blanches [hereafter SB] 271.9 D. Note the reference to burial of lepers in isolation. In most cases, mission diaries and annual reports do not refer to Sisters and Fathers individually. Since they document the experiences and observations of the missionaries as a group, this study also refers to them collectively.

2 Mungo Park, the first European traveler to reach the Niger River, reported its usage in the late eighteenth century. Mungo Park, *Travels in the Interior Districts of Africa* (1799; reprint, New York: Arno Press and the New York Times, 1971), 273.

which facilitated begging as a means of material survival. Throughout the colonial period, successive European responses to their presence constituted "ordering activities" which continually transformed their identities as lepers.[3] This chapter elaborates the principal political, technical, and social factors underlying those responses. Subsequent chapters will then examine their specific implications for patient identity.

Medicine for the "Natives"

Nineteenth- and early-twentieth-century reports written by colonial doctors and administrators reveal two primary motivations for establishing government medical services for Africans. On one hand, many officials considered such services necessary for demonstrating the advantages of colonial rule. Their presumed altruism served as a convenient rationalization for the larger colonial enterprise. As the director of the Health Service (Service de Santé) in St. Louis (Senegal) wrote in his 1824 report, medicine represented the most important science for "spreading civilization amongst ignorant peoples and making them enjoy the benefits of the sciences and arts."[4] On the other hand, the reports expressed repeated concern for the health of a growing European population. Protection from devastating scourges such as yellow fever required medical intervention in African communities. The haphazard and half-hearted nature of medical efforts, however, suggests that the concern for African health extended only to the point that it advanced either of these two objectives. Furthermore, the apathetic response of most Africans resulted from a failure to integrate these efforts with local medical culture.

In 1905, ten years after the formal creation of French West Africa, the colonial administration established the Assistance Médicale Indigéne (AMI) to provide health services—primarily smallpox vaccinations at first—to "native" (indigéne) populations.[5] The AMI vaguely resembled a number of earlier but smaller endeavors such as the colony's first Medical Assistance clinic (opened in Gorée, Senegal in 1837) and the Dakar hospital (1872).[6] Though primarily responsible for European personnel and African soldiers, doctors posted at military installations in the interior had also extended their services to local communities throughout the nineteenth century. The AMI itself was supposed to be a civilian agency, but nearly all its doctors belonged to the military. The few civilian doctors recruited into service needed a special certificate from institutes of colonial medicine in Bordeaux and Marseilles.[7]

Publicly, administrators portrayed the AMI as the métropole's natural duty to its colonies. In a 1906 address to a government council, Ernest Roume, French West Africa's governor general, insisted that the administration owed certain things to a population whose "direction" they had "assumed" and whose taxes they collected.

---

3 "Ordering activities" is a notion developed by Ainlay and Crosby in their discussion of stigma in "Stigma, Justice," 19–20.

4 "Rapport général sur le Service de Santé des établissements depuis le mois de mars 1819 jusqu'au 31 octobre 1823," 10 April 1824, Centre des Archives d'Outre-Mer [hereafter CAOM], SG Senegal XI dos 29.

5 French West Africa constituted a federation of France's colonies in the region. See Bado, Médecine coloniale, and Domergue-Cloarec, Politique coloniale, for a more detailed account of AMI's early years.

6 Dr. Blanchard, "L'Oeuvre sanitaire de la France en Afrique Occidentale," 31 December 1940, CAOM, Aff Pol 3240.

7 Domergue-Cloarec, Politique coloniale, 111.

The government's "end of the deal" included "not only security and works of public utility, but also medical assistance which every civilized nation owes to its subjects and which is the most immediately tangible benefit they can receive."[8] Beneath this public veil of civic altruism, however, officials viewed medicine as a means of demonstrating the utility of colonial rule for Africans. One doctor stationed in Bamako bluntly stated in an internal report that medical assistance constituted one of the best "tools" of colonization, because the "natives notice every day our good intentions." The "quasi-miraculous" effects of "modern medicine" does nothing but "heighten our prestige in their eyes."[9] Many others throughout the medical service shared this belief in their role as, in the words of one doctor, "collaborators of the administration."[10]

The presumed popularity of European medicine contrasts sharply with the actual situation already documented in doctors' own reports from the previous century. Although travel narratives from that era often portrayed Africans as pestering Europeans for medicines, most doctors stationed in the field for long durations complained of widespread disinterest.[11] Between the 1860s and 1880s, doctors working at military posts in Bakel, Kayes, and other places reported that patients usually arrived only as a last resort after consulting their own healers and marabouts.[12] One doctor posted in Ségou in 1895, three years after conquest, observed that the presence of French troops and their Senegalese contingents frightened most people away. To see "interesting" medical cases, he visited patients who gathered at the nearby Catholic mission.[13] Just before the AMI's creation, another doctor in Kayes noted that even the families of African chiefs consulted doctors only when the European *commandant* (the French equivalent of district officer) acted as an intermediary.[14]

As documented in successive AMI reports, the disinterest in European medicine continued in spite of the increase in services. The 1911 annual medical report for the Haut-Sénégal-Niger colony, for example, described African responses to the AMI as "refractory." One colonial administrator even tried to convince local chiefs of the "efficacy" of European medicine by reminding them that it was "free"—hardly an advantage for people whose own medical treatments posed little economic burden.[15]

---

8 "Rapport médicale annuel [hereafter RMA] de Kayes, 1906," Archives Nationales du Mali [hereafter ANM] 1H-62 FA.

9 "Rapport médical mensuel [hereafter RMM] de Bamako, octobre 1904," ANM 1H-49 FA.

10 Dr. Haueur to Gouverneur [hereafter Gouv.] de Haut-Sénégal-Niger [hereafter H-S-N], 12 January 1912, ANM 1H-8 FA.

11 Paul Soleillet visited Ségou in 1878 and 1879 and described many scenes of Africans seeking medicines in his published account, *Voyage à Ségou 1878 1879* (Paris: Challamel, ainé, 1887).

12 Alfred Borius, "Quelques considérations médicales sur le poste de Dagana (Sénégal), observations faites pendant l'année 1862" (*Thèse*, Faculté de Médecine de Montepellier, 1864), 60; Pierre Carbonnel, "La mortalité actuelle au Sénégal" (*Thèse*, Faculté de Médecine de Paris, 1873), 19; Andre A. Jollet, "Contribution à la géographie médicale du Soudan occidental, histoire médicale du poste de Koundon (1884-1886), étude d'hygiène et de pathologie exotiques" (*Thèse*, Faculté de Médecine de Bordeaux, 1887), 66; Anselme A. Lacarrière, "Contribution à l'étude de la géographie médicale, souvenirs médicaux du poste de Kayes (Haut-Sénégal, 1885-86)" (*Thèse*, Faculté de Médecine de Bordeaux, 1887), 37-38.

13 "Diaire," Ségou, 11 October 1895, Péres Blancs [hereafter PB].

14 "RMA de Kayes, 1902," ANM 1H-62 FA.

15 "RMM de H-S-N, février 1911," ANM 1H-44 FA.

Like nineteenth-century European travelers, a few AMI doctors described their popularity in terms of the large volume of consultations while overlooking their relatively insignificant influence in the rest of the district. For example, the 1905 medical report from Kayes cited the "flood" of "impatient" patients as evidence that the "native" understood the "so utilitarian and humane goal of the work for which he receives the precious benefits." The report included a photograph of people lined up at the dispensary.[16] Just a year later, however, Kaye's assistant-director of Health Services complained that patients with skin ailments fled upon the first application of a balm which the governor had asked him to test on Africans.[17]

The AMI was responsible for virtually all aspects of public health and medical service in a vast and culturally diverse region. Under these circumstances, the specific local reactions to AMI practices varied tremendously. For smallpox, doctors circulated in their regions administering vaccinations. During one such campaign in 1907, a doctor working in the Djenne district described the Muslim Fulani peoples as "refractory" but noted that the Bambara "fetishists" were "very trusting."[18] The doctor in Dédougou (located in what is today Burkina Faso) meanwhile observed that people resorted to European medicine only for ailments which could be easily arrested, namely surgical affections such as guinea worm and complications resulting from syphilis. They rarely consulted him for diseases requiring longer treatment.[19] In contrast, patients visiting the dispensary in Gaoua (about 150 kilometers southeast of Bobo-Dioulasso) tended to suffer from diseases such as leprosy and sleeping sickness which the doctor found "impossible to treat effectively."[20]

Poor infrastructure and a small staff also stymied the AMI's intended effect on local populations. The administration erected dispensaries only in district capitals and staffed them with one doctor and perhaps one or two African nurses. In other words, only a handful of doctors were responsible for the Soudan colony (Mali), a region roughly the size of California and Texas combined.[21] The annual medical report for 1905 noted that the distances and travel expenses discouraged people from visiting dispensaries and pushed them to look for cures in the "superstitious and dangerous practices of their sorcerers."[22] In most cases, doctors found patients by traveling through villages rather than by waiting for them vainly at their clinics. The previous chapter noted how patients were often accustomed to lodging with healers who lived great distances from their own villages. Doctors like those in Ouagadougou and Tahoua complained that they could not offer that same level of care.[23]

The AMI's limited influence partly resulted from the agency's complete detachment from local medical culture. During these early years, French doctors established

16 "RMA de Kayes, 1905," ANM 1H-42 FA.

17 Dr. Gourien to Lt. Gouv., no. 472, 7 March 1906, ANM 1H-2 FA. The reliability of such reports is questionable, since doctors frequently altered or fabricated consultation statistics. Bado, *Médicine coloniale*, 186-90.

18 "RMM de H-S-N, juillet 1907," ANM 1H-43 FA.

19 "RMA de H-S-N, 1914," ANM 1H-44 FA.

20 "RMM de Gaoua, octobre 1904," ANM 1H-66 FA.

21 See Bado, *Médecine coloniale*, for a more detailed discussion of AMI's limited resources.

22 "RMA de H-S-N, 1905," ANM 1H-42FA

23 "RMA de H-S-N, 1906," ANM 1H-42 FA.

a practice of competing rather than cooperating with African healers—a practice which continues today in Mali. This competitiveness is reflected in their reports. Typical of most colonial health workers, the doctor assigned to Djenne in 1908 boasted that his "superior" medicines and treatment drew patients away from the "blacksmiths" whom he viewed as the local equivalent of doctors.[24] Another doctor in Timbuktu meanwhile complained jealously that people remained under the "influence" of marabouts who used their moral authority to exploit patients.[25]

Like earlier attempts to deliver medicine in the nineteenth century, the AMI amounted to little more than a public relations effort during its first years of operation. As noted by other historians, its limited services also dwindled drastically during the First World War.[26] In 1920, AMI staff for all the West African colonies consisted of seventy military and thirty-six civilian doctors. [27]A medical school for local peoples had opened in Madagascar in 1896 and French Indochina in 1902, but no such equivalent existed in West Africa until 1918. Only in 1921 did this school, the Ecole de Médecine de Dakar, graduate its first African doctors (eight) and midwives (sixteen).[28] On the whole, medicine for the "natives" remained, in practice, a low priority during the first two decades of the twentieth century.

The Missionary's Mission

The difficulties encountered by government workers contrasted sharply with the perceived success of mission health facilities. In the late nineteenth century, Catholic missionaries belonging to the orders of the White Fathers and White Sisters had established their posts in important administrative centers such as Ségou, Kati, and Kita. The charters for both orders required that missionaries receive medical training to prepare them for running dispensaries and visiting the sick at their homes.[29] Compared to colonial documents, their diaries and reports communicate a more sincere commitment to caring for the ill. Their gushy prose style reflects a deep desire to emulate Christ's benevolence. However, these same diaries and reports show that caring for the sick served as a pretext for proselytizing or merely spreading the mission's influence. Dispensing medicine enabled missionaries to approach local peoples and initiate religious discussion in a less obtrusive manner.[30] Much like the efforts of medical missionaries in British Nyasaland, the "healing of the body took second place to winning of the soul."[31] In that sense, their vision of medicine as a public relations instrument resembled that of the colonial administration.

24 "RMM de Djenne, juillet 1908," ANM 1H-43 FA.

25 Ibid. Competition with marabouts concerned doctors in Kati as well. "RMA de H-S-N, 1906," ANM 1H-42 FA.

26 Bado, *Médecine coloniale*, 14 and 192.

27 Domergue-Cloarec, *Politique coloniale*, 111–13

28 Ibid., 61.

29 François Renault, "Principes missionnaires et action sanitaire des Péres Blancs et Soeurs Blanches du Cardinal Lavigerie (1868–1960)," in Jean Pirotte and Henri Derroitte, eds., *Churches and Health Care in the Third World* (New York: E. J. Brill, 1991), 28.

30 Ibid., 28.

31 Vaughan, *Curing Their Ills*, 65.

Over time, most White Fathers in the colony reduced their involvement in the day-to-day care of diseased and dispossessed peoples. Their diaries from the turn of the century reflect a waning interest in their affairs. At the Kita mission, for example, the Fathers still provided medicines at their dispensary, but their preoccupation with other responsibilities—expanding the parish, for example—prevented them from devoting much attention to itinerant lepers. The Sisters, therefore, gradually assumed full responsibility for opening and running their own dispensaries and hospices throughout the colony.

As was the case at missions throughout Africa, caring for the sick overlapped with a broader interest in marginal individuals who were more inclined to convert than "normal" members of society.[32] The creation of Catholic missions in the Niger River region coincided with an ongoing social upheaval induced by French conquest and occupation (completed in 1892). In the years prior to this occupation, Ségou's economy had become increasingly dependent on captive slave labor provided largely by Samory's wars. Soninké and Bambara "nobles" used these slaves for agricultural production in places such as Banamba. The French did not actively liberate these slaves, but their presence enabled many to escape without fear of retribution. To assist and control refugees, the army often created *"villages de liberté"* (freedom villages) next to their posts throughout the region. Many refugee slaves found these villages a mixed blessing, since the authorities often used them as sources of cheap or forced labor for colonial projects and trade. Former masters were also allowed to reclaim their captives for up to four months after escape.[33] By 1905, however, a series of slave desertions, acts of resistance , and revolts culminated in a massive exodus of several thousand.[34]

In 1895 the White Sisters established a dispensary near one such village in Ségou, and, within six months, they received an average of 137 patients a day.[35] The adjoining mission gradually became a refuge for slaves as well as outcasts and indigent peoples of all types.[36] In general, the dispensary's popularity resulted more from the personal care and attention provided to patients rather than any specific medical treatment. Referring to the many beggars, leprosy patients, and blind individuals who routinely appeared after Mass in Ségou, one 1902 report observed, "To help them live, we give them some cauri shells [the local currency] as alms; to help them die properly, we give them a small ration of catechism every two days." [37] During the first years of the century, the dispensary received roughly one thousand patients (of all types) every trimester.[38] Although some visitors suffering from ailments such as guinea worm sought only a physical cure, many others like Mousso Koura desired

32 Vaughan describes a similar phenomenon for missionaries working in British Nyasaland. Ibid., 61.

33 Roberts and Klein, "The Banamba Slave Exodus " Suret-Canale, *French Colonialism*, 63.

34 Roberts and Klein, "Slave Exodus," 386–94.

35 "Diaire," Ségou, 25 April 1895, 1 May 1895, and 15 November 1895, PB.

36 "Diaire," Ségou, 27 September 1895, 31 October 1897, and 20 March 1899, PB; "Diaire," Singobougou, 24 May 1900, SB D 271.9.

37 "Diaire," Banankourou, 1 July 1902, PB.'

38 "Diaire," Ségou, 31 January 1901, 29 July 1902, and 26 January 1903, SB 271.9 D.

other forms of care such as food and personal contact.[39] Some simply chose the mission as a place to die.[40]

In 1903 the French National Assembly passed the *Loi de Laicization* (Secularization Law) which formally barred the church's involvement in government services in France and its colonies. In accordance with this law, the colonial administration dismissed the Sisters from the military hospitals in Kati and Kayes where they had worked as nurses for several years.[41] Though at first a disappointment, this change of policy reinforced the differences between the two types of *toubabs* in the eyes of the local population. At government dispensaries, patients found doctors wearing the same uniforms as the district officers and *toubab* soldiers. In most cases they received no lodging and little or no attention outside the clinic.

The missionaries, on the other hand, provided a more appealing form of health care. In 1906 the Sisters closed their Ségou hospital and moved its patients to a new one in Banankourou, a nearby *village de liberté* where the Fathers had been running a mission since 1899. While colonial doctors throughout the colony reported general ambivalence towards their medical efforts, the Sisters received more patients than they could handle: for example, 1,541 in the second trimester of 1908 alone.[42] Praising this success in their annual report for 1908–09, the White Fathers wrote, "The government itself, which can not officially favor it [the hospital], expressed all its admiration to the Sisters . . . and, on two occasions, gave them some small donations."[43] The Banankourou center included a group of huts serving as a hospice which, by 1910, housed an average of eighteen "pensioners" including several with leprosy.[44] Of all the *toubab* institutions in the colony at the turn of the century, only the Sisters' attracted significant numbers of "sick" visitors.

As described in the following section, colonial officials viewed leprosy patients as a scourge requiring containment. The Sisters, by contrast, saw them as humans in need of spiritual as well as medical care. For example, in 1901 the French commandant in Ségou assigned one leprous woman to a hut outside of town because of the "infection" emanating from her body. Nearby residents later found her corpse devoured by hyenas, a fate apparently met by other abandoned lepers.[45] Meanwhile, just a year before, the Sisters had lodged a potentially "contagious" woman, Fatimata, in a private hut on the mission's own grounds.[46] Noting the "free" circulation of patients and the absence of a local leprosarium, one diary entry for 1902 stated, "It is only a question that we be entrusted again with this task [of caring for

39 "Diaire," Ségou, 18 July 1897, PB.
40 "Diaire," Ségou, 8 September 1900, SB 271.9 D.
41 "Notes historiques des postes d'Afrique Occidentale Française AOF 1897–1939," SB B 480/6, 9; Inspection du Service de Santé to Lt. Gouv., 26 July 1904, ANM 3E-8 FA.
42 "Diaire," Banankourou, 28 August 1908, SB 271.9 D. As Vaughan notes for other parts of Africa, these diaries and reports, relying on powerful Biblical imagery, inflated the mission's importance to attract funding. They also "contributed to the image of Africa as a sick continent." Vaughan, *Curing Their Ills* 61, 74, and 79.
43 "Rapport annuel [hereafter RA], 1908-09," PB.
44 "RA de Banankourou, 1909–10," PB.
45 "Diaire," Ségou, 9 September 1901, SB 271.9 D.
46 "Diaire," Ségou, 8 September 1900, SB 271.9 D.

lepers], for which we are delighted, because we will have the opportunity to do much good."[47]

As was the case among missionaries throughout Africa, melodramatic encounters with needy Africans, especially lepers, provided perfect copy for published reports and mission magazines directed at potential donors in Europe.[48] The Sisters' diaries and reports contain many brief but spirited anecdotes in which they overcome their fears of contagion to admit leprosy patients—along with others such as elderly individuals abandoned during famines—into the mission and hospice.[49] In 1902, missing both legs from leprosy, the daughter of a former Ségou "king" crawled more than a kilometer to the mission rather than the government clinic.[50] A year later the Mother Superior met a leprous man on her way to catechism and invited him to undergo treatment at their hospice. The local government doctor, who visited the mission frequently in search of "interesting cases," punctured an abscess on the man's skin causing him to bleed severely. As he lay dying, one of the Sisters proposed baptism, which he accepted, apparently saying, "Yes, I want it, and, in any case, I wouldn't know what it is exactly—I'll take your word for it, because you are so kind." The diary for that day reads,

> The poor man collected what remained of his strength to say "yes," and received baptism under the name of Hippolyte. . . . His body was buried in our cemetery to the great stupefaction of his family and the people of his village. Here the lepers are thrown into the bush where the wildlife devours their pitiful remains.[51]

The numerous descriptions of such incidents in the Sisters' diaries no doubt exaggerated the enthusiasm and significance of conversion on the patient's part. The Sisters invariably prided themselves on their religious achievements in spite of the convert's desperation and often imminent death. Though most patients like "Hippolyte" hardly understood the full meaning of the sacraments and other Catholic rituals, the experience of instruction and conversion provided them with a form of attention not available in their villages. In addition to providing food, lodging, and medical treatment, the Sisters talked to patients and invited them to become members of their community. The prospect of normal burial also reinforced this sense of acceptance which, from the patient's point of view, was more important than the largely ineffective medicines. Indeed, some patients temporarily left the hospice to continue receiving medical treatment from local healers.[52]

Like many colonial officials, the White Fathers and Sisters clearly regarded the provision of medicine as a means of expanding their influence. However, the Sisters quickly realized that clinical treatment alone hardly sufficed. Many diseased and marginal peoples desired care more than cures. Such desires complemented

47 "Diaire," Ségou, 24 October 1902, SB 271.9 D.
48 See Vaughan, *Curing Their Ills.*
49 "Notes historiques des postes d'Afrique Occidentale , 1897–1939," SB B 480/6.
50 "Souvenirs de Sr. Ursule," [undated], SB A5040/5. This is an excellent example of how leprosy was not confined exclusively to "lower classes."
51 "Diaire," Ségou, 17 July 1903, SB 271.9 D. Note again the practice of separate burial for lepers.
52 "Diaire," Banankourou, 16 August 1913, SB 271.9 D.

the Sisters' own aspirations for drawing people into their religion. Prolonged contact outside the clinic enabled missionaries to initiate discussions of more spiritual and philosophical issues. The Sisters also hoped that the level of assistance provided by the hospice would demonstrate for local populations the strength and sincerity of their commitment to helping people. As their reports and diaries reveal, lepers, more than any other patients, enabled the Sisters to fulfill their multiple duties as missionaries. Vaughan describes a similar situation in British Basutoland where leprosy gave missionaries an opportunity to engineer new African communities.[53]

The Leprosaria Revival

The Introduction described how the preoccupation with leprosy in Europe had long since faded by the beginning of the nineteenth century. Europeans traveling to West Africa, for example, were initially preoccupied by seemingly more devastating and common ailments such as malaria, yellow fever, smallpox, and cholera. Although René Caillié, a French explorer, had observed leprosy during his travels through the region in the late 1820s, most reports hardly acknowledged the disease.[54] Only after the discovery of the bacillus in 1873 and full-fledged colonial occupation did medieval fears begin to reappear and provoke the construction of leprosariums worldwide.

In French West Africa, perceptions of leprosy's incidence varied wildly and contributed to the colonial government's haphazard responses.[55] For example, in 1907 staff from the medical laboratory in Bamako conducted research in the zone between the Niger River and what is today western Burkina Faso. They estimated leprosy's prevalence at around two to three percent of the population.[56] The health services director in the Niger colony meanwhile reported an incidence of a half percent in 1913 (4,725 out of a population of 812,500).[57] Between 1904 and 1909, doctors in the towns of Dori, Bamako, and Timbuktu described the disease as "infrequent," while those in Bougouni and Sofara noted the opposite.[58]

These almost contradictory perceptions resulted in part from imperfect and inconsistent diagnosis. One doctor in Kayes admitted in a 1906 report that leprosy

53 Vaughan, *Curing Their Ills*, 79.

54 For examples, see medical reports in CAOM XI dos 29 and Archives Nationales du Sénégal [hereafter ANS] 1H-6, 1H-7, 1H-8, 1H-11, and 1H-13. René Caillié, *Journal d'un voyage à Tembouctou et à Djenne, dans l'Afrique Centrale . . . pendant les années 1824, 1825, 1826, 1827, 1828* (Paris: Editions Anthropos, 1965).

55 Bado describes the inconsistent manner in which doctors and administrators reported disease. Bado, *Médecine coloniale*, 132.

56 "Rapport sur une mission d'études scientifiques dans les territoires de la boucle de Niger, mai–septembre 1907," ANM 1H-43 FA.

57 "RMA de Niger, 1913," and for 1917, ANS 2G-13/23 and 14/17.

58 See "RMM" for Dori, October 1904, ANM 1H-56 FA; Bamako, November 1904, ANM 1H-49 FA; Tombouctou, March 1907 and February 1905, ANM 1H-43 and 1H-79 FA; Bougouni, December 1904, ANM 1H-53 FA; and Bandiagara, September and October 1909, ANM 1H-51 FA. In Zinder, a Hausa town situated in the westernmost part of French-controlled territory, a French doctor found large numbers of blind and leprous beggars. He also observed some villages populated almost entirely by lepers. "RMA de H-S-N 1905-06," ANM 1H-42 FA.

patches resembled many other "non-pathological" lesions (presumably the *kaba* described by so many informants) and that the seemingly anesthetized quality of these patches were a very uncertain sign of the disease.[59] Another observer in Côte d'Ivoire recognized that leprosy's slow evolution made its contagiousness less "evident" than other diseases such as smallpox.[60] As other historians have noted, European doctors during these years frequently confused leprosy with yaws, tertiary syphilis, and scabies.[61]

Colonial officials often disagreed among themselves over the proper method of diagnosis. One 1914 circular informed administrators in Côte d'Ivoire that leprosy manifested itself through three symptoms: "patches, cutaneous nodules, and ulcers." Noting the frequency of misdiagnosis, the circular suggested that administrators also test for the patch's anesthetized quality with a needle. That same year, however, the annual health report recommended that administrators collect tissue samples with a razor instead. Recognizing the inability to perform proper diagnosis in the field, the colonial governor wrote with unusual candor in the report's margin,

> How can one diagnose leprosy without a microscope? It suffices to realize the difficulties of surgical diagnosis. . . . Some label leprosy what others call syphilis, and what the third party treats under the heading of general illnesses taking them for parasites or fungus. The numbers don't have any value . . . and it is impossible to base . . . an anti-leprosy campaign [on them], and to specify where the segregation villages should be placed.[62]

The governor's skepticism also suggests that many people described as lepers in early reports probably suffered from other ailments.

With a few exceptions, most Europeans believed that leprosy was highly contagious and therefore attributable to the African way of life.[63] Their thinking reflected a general tendency throughout the continent to blame illness on a perceived lack of civilization.[64] The directors of Health Services in Côte d'Ivoire and Dahomey both linked the disease's transmission to itinerant traders and caravan routes.[65] More commonly, colonial doctors pointed to what they perceived as a widespread African ignorance of contagion. Following their 1907 study, Bamako's laboratory staff reported that "the natives take no isolation measures against these sick . . . the mutilated continue to live in contact with all."[66] A doctor posted in Gao similarly wrote in 1906, "The natives display no repulsion towards them [lepers] and, living the same existence, they [the lepers] draw by hand cous-cous from the communal calabash."[67] Notions of African fatalism also bolstered these perceptions. In Côte d'Ivoire, one

---

59 "RMA de Kayes, 1906," ANM 1H-62 FA.

60 "RMA de Côte d'Ivoire, 1907," ANS 2G-7/18.

61 Michael Tuck found examples of this confusion occurring in early twentieth-century Uganda. Personal communication. See also Vaughan, *Curing Their Ills*, 138.

62 "RMA de Côte d'Ivoire, 1914" and attached documents, ANS 2G-14/16.

63 In Kayes, one doctor noted that, even though they took no precautions to avoid the disease, "the blacks" easily recognized it and knew it to be contagious. "RMA de Kayes, 1906," ANM 1H-62 FA.

64 Packard, *White Plague*, 51; Vaughan, *Curing Their Ills*, 161 and 201.

65 "RMA de Côte d'Ivoire, 1908," ANS 2G-8/23; "RMA de Dahomey, 1907," ANS 2G-7/19.

66 "Rapport sur une mission . . . 1907," ANM 1H-43 FA.

67 "Rapport médical annuel de H-S-N, 1906," ANM 1H-42 FA.

doctor found that people in his area could diagnose the two forms of leprosy but that they took no prophylactic measures against it. "The Dioulas," he wrote, "disregard the contagious nature of leprosy and consider it a curse sent by Allah to punish their sins."[68]

For many officials, the leprosy problem appeared most acute around towns and administrative posts which had been attracting marginal individuals of all kinds—lepers, madmen (*fatow*), widows, freed slaves—since the beginning of colonial occupation. In these new locations, such individuals could earn money either through small jobs like porterage or, more commonly, through begging. Many of the African traders and bureaucrats who settled in burgeoning urban centers such as Bamako had money and prayed at mosque on Fridays. For the first time, one could easily venture into a town and solicit alms from a total stranger already predisposed to giving. Town markets also grew and contributed to the increasingly disproportionate concentration of wealth which made fulfillment of religious obligations just a bit easier for prosperous and pious inhabitants. In Ségou, for example, the White Sisters often found invalid persons in the markets either begging or working as porters.[69] A famine at the beginning of the century brought "bands of beggars" to their mission doors.[70] Blind and leprous beggars also circulated in the market and streets of Kayes although, by 1914, the police kept their numbers down by chasing them away as "vagabonds."[71]

Along with the perceived African ignorance of contagion, the migration of rural leprosy patients into towns became the principal pretext for segregation. Throughout the nineteenth century, French officials had used segregation as a public health measure in their small but growing West African territories. Health inspectors routinely quarantined ships suspected of carrying yellow fever or of originating from cholera zones. As noted in the introduction, European officials throughout the continent invoked health concerns to justify racial segregation. Reflecting a very prevalent attitude, one French doctor at the Service d'Hygiéne in Dakar urged in 1905 the creation of separate quarters for Europeans and Africans in order to protect the former from the "imminent danger" posed by the latter's lack of hygiene.[72] Even missionaries and other Europeans found themselves subject to quarantine at times if they happened to travel from an area "infected" with a presumably contagious disease.[73] The visible ravages of sleeping sickness throughout Africa at the turn of the century also inspired segregation policies in French, Belgian, and British colonies.[74]

---

68 "Rapport médical annuel de Côte d'Ivoire, 1907," ANS 2G-7/18. This reporting of "Allah's curse" seems very spurious. None of my informants ever suggested an association of leprosy or any other diseases with "sin" as was often the case in Europe.

69 "Diaire," Ségou, 2 May 1904, SB 271.9 D.

70 "Diaire," Singobougou, 25 June 1900, SB 271.9 D.

71 "RMA de Kayes, 1906," ANM 1H-62 FA; "RMA de H-S-N, 1914" ANM 1H-44 FA.

72 Dr. Ribot to Maire de Dakar, 14 June 1905, CAOM Aff Pol 3236. The connections between racial and medical segregation are well documented for other parts of Africa. See, for example, Swanson, "The Sanitation Syndrome" and "'The Asiatic Menace.'"

73 "Diaire," Ségou, 9 October 1901, SB 271.9 D.

74 See Bado, *Médecine coloniale*; Headrick, *Colonialism, Health, and Illness*; Lyons, *The Colonial Disease*; and Vaughan, *Curing Their Ills*;

Aside from a few sporadic decrees, French West Africa never developed a coherent leprosy policy until the 1930s, leaving doctors in the field to deal with the disease according to their own beliefs and means. In general, those posted at AMI clinics found it difficult to attract voluntary leprosy patients. One doctor working in Kayes in 1906 blamed chaulmoogra oil, the most common leprosy medicine at the time, for taking too long to show results. "The native," he wrote, "wants to see immediate effects."[75] Two years later a doctor in Bafoulabé more bluntly admitted that their medicines were "useless."[76]

Lacking a real cure for leprosy, many doctors advocated the physical isolation of patients. The first two International Leprosy Congresses had already recommended this approach which was supposed to eradicate the disease through containment. The director of Health Services in Koulikoro, for example, proposed in 1904 the creation of institutions modeled on the *villages de liberté* created for refugee slaves. "It would only take a little surveillance," argued one doctor in Koulikoro, "to prevent the lepers from leaving the limits which we would impose on them."[77] Doctors posted in the town of Kayes and in a village near Ouagadougou similarly suggested using force to place patients in leprosariums.[78]

In 1909 the minister of Colonies (Trouillot) followed the advice of the Société de la Pathologie Exotique, an influential medical association devoted to tropical medicine, by formally promoting isolation as a means of leprosy control for all of France's colonies. Noting the success of such measures in Norway and Ireland, he wrote, "I have every reason to believe that their [the isolation measures] adoption in the colonies would not be any less efficacious. . . ."[79]

Most early attempts at isolating patients, however, failed and embarrassed local authorities. For example, in 1904 Ségou's medical officer complained that "lepers" were delivering foodstuffs to the market as their only source of income. To resolve this problem, he proposed their incarceration in a special compound near the government dispensary where they would receive rations and medical treatment. The colonial governor responded that, though leprosy posed a danger, the budget did not permit this level of care. Instead, the governor recommended that the doctor simply isolate them far outside town. Following this suggestion, the local commandant ordered prison laborers to construct ten huts on the other side of the Niger River. Within a year, however, every patient placed in these huts disappeared and never returned to Ségou.[80]

---

75 "RMA de Kayes, 1906," ANM 1H-62 FA.

76 "RMM de Bafoulabé, juillet 1908," ANM 1H-48 FA.

77 "RMA, Koulikoro, 1904," ANM 1H-49 FA.

78 "RMM, Keo, octobre 1904," ANM 1H-71 FA; "RMA de Kayes, 1905," ANM 1H-42 FA.

79 Ministre des Colonies to Gouverneurs, no. 79, 23 August 1909, ANM 1H-4 FA. The French West African governor later dispatched a circular with the minister's recommendation and a copy of the Société's brochure to all the colonies. Gouv. Gén. to Lt. Gouverneurs, no. 190 C., 1 October 1909, ANM 1H-4 FA. On the role of the Société de la Pathologie Exotique, see Bado, *Médecine coloniale*, 166.

80 Administrateur [hereafter Admin.] du Cercle de Ségou to Lt. Gouv., no. 164, 8 August 1904, ANM 1H-35 FA; Lt. Gouv. to Admin. du Cercle de Ségou, no. 1363, 18 August 1904, ANM 1H-35 FA; Commandant [hereafter Comm.] de Cercle de Ségou to Lt. Gouv., no. 284, 20 December 1904, ANM 1H-35 FA; "RMA, 1905-06," ANM 1H-42 FA. Three years later the annual medical report for all of Haut-Sénégal-Niger bluntly stated that "the native population will not respond with enthusiasm towards this prophylactic measure [isolation]." "RMM de H-S-N, 1909," ANM 1H-44 FA.

The failure of this particular attempt revealed two general problems with segregation. First, as in other parts of Africa, colonial officials lacked the resources necessary for carrying out their intended goal.[81] Leprosariums required land, buildings, fences, and staff to guard and treat their residents. Second, the widespread hostility to physical isolation or treatment of any kind often required the use of force which further alienated patients. Between 1907 and 1915 virtually all French West Africa's isolation centers from Senegal to Côte d'Ivoire lost most or all of their patients within a few years of opening. In 1912 doctors traveling in the "bush" (*en brousse*) still found it impossible to collect the needed leprosy statistics. "As soon as they [the villagers] understand the purpose of the inquiry, the sick and their entourage become distrustful and run off and hide in the bush; even worse, some of the sick are friends or relatives of those responsible for informing the investigator." [82]

To remedy these problems, doctors proposed all sorts of rules which reflected an administrative preoccupation with social control and often obstructed more focused medical concerns. In theory, a 1911 decree legally obligated village chiefs to report leprosy along with eighteen other diseases including yellow fever, smallpox, and diphtheria.[83] One doctor in Côte d'Ivoire advocated punishment and fines—"suitably high in order to be effective"—for patients who violated segregation laws and advanced too close to isolation villages. The doctor also suggested making local chiefs responsible for catching escapees and fining healthy people for "penetrating" the confines of the camp.[84] On several occasions in the 1920s (including once on Christmas Eve) administrators in Bamako used the police to survey and round up patients, especially those caught begging.[85] "Make the sick understand," one commandant instructed his police commissioner, "that this is not a compulsory measure against them [the patients] but that, on the contrary, the local administration wants to come help them." [86]

In Bamako, the police usually deposited patients—sometimes as many as forty at a time-in the often dilapidated isolation village at Bako-Djikoroni located on the other side of the river. By 1928 this village included fields and provided rations much like other "leper colonies" elsewhere in the colonies. Its residents frequently escaped and resumed begging at the market only to be rounded up again. "On several occasions," one administrator noted in 1929, "I was made to notice that the lepers subsisting at the Djikoroni isolation village had come to Bamako. I had them driven back to their camp." [87] By 1930 the colonial governor had begun issuing decrees sentencing

81 Vaughan, *Curing Their Ills*, 78.

82 "RMA de H-S-N, 1912," ANS 2G-12/24.

83 *Journal Officiel* [hereafter *JO*], 15 June 1911, 238.

84 "RMA de Côte d'Ivoire, 1914," ANS 2G-14/16.

85 "Note de Service" to Commissaire, no. 551, 24 March 1925; Comm. de Cercle de Bamako to Gouv., no. 760, 15 April 1925, ANM 1H-56 FR; Dr. Nemorin, 6 February 1925, ANM 1H-56 FR; "RMA de Soudan, 1926" ANM 1H-75 FR; "Note du service" to Chef de la Subdivision de Bamako, no. 786, 26 June 1928; Chef de la Subdivision de Bamako to Lt. Gouv., no. 710, 22 September 1928, ANM 1H-56 FR.

86 Comm. de Cercle de Bamako to Commissaire de Police, no. 1089, 24 December 1927, ANM 1H-56 FR.

87 Chef de la Subdivision de Bamako to Comm. de Cercle de Bamako, no. 215, 20 September 1929, ANM 1H-56 FR.

people to "obligatory residence" at Bako-Djikoroni for periods as long as ten years as if it were indeed a prison.[88]

These police actions resulted in part from growing complaints among the local European population. "Not a day passes," wrote Dr. Laigret, director of the Laboratoire Central de Biologie which oversaw the leprosarium, "without me receiving the reproach of someone who saw a leper strolling through town."[89] One European businessman with the Société d'Entreprise Africaines complained to the mayor in 1928 that lepers and others with contagious diseases circulated too closely to European homes. He noted how one man, who "was nothing but a frightful sore," installed himself against his walls. The mayor in turn asked the police commissioner to hold the leper until the administration decided on his fate.[90] The fact that four of the seven hundred "whites" (one Syrian and three French merchants) living in Bamako had contracted the disease no doubt intensified people's fears.[91]

Despite increasing hostility among Europeans, indigent leprosy patients continued to find Bamako very conducive for begging. Prosperous Muslim residents in particular were remarkably tolerant. Bouboucar Diallo, whose father worked as a cook for a French officer, recalled how, in the late 1920s and early 1930s, lepers came to beg in Bamako during the dry season. Most African residences in town included a spare hut or room for visitors or strangers in need of shelter. Families like Bouboucar's allowed itinerant lepers and other beggars to sleep in their compounds, usually in the vestibule leading to the street. On any given night these temporary lodgers numbered as many as two or three in one vestibule. Other beggars preferred sleeping in the doorways of shops near the market. Bouboucar stressed that nearly all lepers in town originated from other places; he himself knew some from Kaarta and Kita.[92]

Given such relatively favorable conditions, many patients strongly resisted the government's increasingly coercive attempts to bar them from town. In one incident, Amadou Kanté, a village resident and former Bamako tailor, wanted to see his family in town and threatened to leave Bako-Djikoroni even without permission. Other patients threatened a hunger strike if they were not allowed to leave as well. Afterwards, Bamako's commandant recommended that the chief of the neighboring village

88 Terrason, "Arrêté," 21 February 1930; Terrason, "Arrêté," 21 June 1930, ANM 1H-56 FR. On one occasion, authorities at the Carabane prison school in Senegal sent Malamine Traoré, a fifteen-year-old "detainee," to the Bamako leprosarium because he had "become a danger to the other detainees." The doctor responsible for Djikoroni found that Malamine did not have leprosy after all. The next day Malamine disappeared, much to the chagrin of the police and administrators who did not find him until two months later. They sent him back to Carabane to finish his sentence. This incident also demonstrates how officials continued to misdiagnose leprosy. Gouv. de Soudan to Comm. de Cercle de Bamako, no. 4628, 24 June 1930; Commissaire de Police to Comm. de Cercle, no. 471D, 18 August 1930; Gourvil to Maire de Bamako, no. 126, 26 August 1930; Chargé d'Affaires to Comm. de Cercle de Bamako, no. 229, 30 August 1930; Comm. de Cercle de Bamako to Subdivison de Mourdiah, no. 2055, 29 September 1930; Comm. de Cercle de Koulikoro et Kolokani, no. 2578, 7 October 1930, ANM 1H-56 FR.

89 Dr. Laigret, "Laboratoire de Central de Biologie, Extrait du Rapport Annuel, 1929," Archives de l'Institut Marchoux [hereafter AIM], Bamako.

90 R. Bierray to Administrateur-Maire de Bamako, 7 June 1928, ANM 1H-56 FR.

91 Laigret, "Rapport sur le fonctionnement du Laboratoire, 1929," ANS 2G-29/26. One one of the "whites" had even fled into the bush after diagnosis by a French doctor.

92 Bouboucar Diallo, 3 February 1993.

be ordered to supervise the lepers' camp.[93] In the margin of his report, the commandant smugly wrote, "In regards to the threats of a hunger strike. . . .These poor people
would certainly prefer to die of indigestion than inanition."[94]

Success and Failures

In the course of the 1920s, a few colonial doctors discovered that treating patients
more or less as criminals frightened them away from medical treatment. Stiff patient
resistance once again provoked a rethinking of the government's approach. As early
as 1925 the doctor stationed at Bamako's clinic actually found that several patients
had settled voluntarily with their "calabashes, spoons, blankets, and mats" on the
clinic's grounds. This development led him to propose the construction of a special
adjoining house for sheltering "disinherited cases."[95] Dr. Laigret observed a sharp
contrast in behavior between patients isolated in Bako-Djikoroni and those who
reported "freely" to his clinic. "I wouldn't be surprised," he wrote, "if the fear of the
leprosarium was one of the principal factors behind the fidelity of my free patients."
In 1928 he "liberated" about half the leprosarium's residents because its distance
from town impeded regular treatment.[96] Dr. Laigret's successor, Dr. Gourvil, reported
that its inhabitants "do not enjoy any comfort, and seem to be abandoned by the
world and have very low moral." He recommended closing the site altogether.

> We wanted to do something to "fight" against leprosy. In creating [Bako-]
> Djikoroni we drove many lepers to flee from doctors. In the course of my
> diagnostic visits I saw many who hid for a year and more, never coming out
> except at night, out of fear of being taken to [Bako-] Djikoroni.[97]

The problems with the Bamako leprosarium mirrored those occurring at other isolation centers throughout the colonies. The 1925 medical report for all French West
Africa affirmed that the "grave problem of segregating and treating lepers" had not
yet been resolved except in Côte d'Ivoire where the leprosarium on Ile Désiré housed
one hundred patients.[98]

Years of stiff patient resistance precipitated the 1932 creation of a more accommodating institution on the outskirts of Bamako. Designed to serve as a central office
for coordinating French West Africa's leprosy policy and conducting scientific
research, the Institut Central de la Lépre also conveniently addressed the problem of
"itinerant lepers." It provided its residents with generous rations, comfortable
accommodations, and large fields for cultivation. Within a few years of its opening,
patients flooded "spontaneously" into Bamako rather than bother with the inferior

93 Chef de la Subdivision de Bamako to Comm. de Cercle de Bamako, no. 215, 20 September 1929, ANM 1H-56 FR.
94 Ibid.
95 Dr. Nemorin, 6 February 1925, ANM 1H-56 FR.
96 "RMA de Soudan, 1928," ANS 2G-28/25. See also Bado for similar references to the debate over segregation among colonial officials. Bado, *Médecine coloniale*, 141 and 166.
97 "RA sur le fonctionnement du Laboratoire Vaccinogène et de Biologie" [contained in "RMA de Soudan,
1930"], ANS 2G-30/22.
98 "RMA d'AOF, 1925," ANS 2G-25/27.

medical posts in their own districts. They had heard of the Institute and its privileges by word of mouth.[99] It was unquestionably more hospitable and better staffed than the old center in Bako-Djikoroni. Its location on the main road to Guinea and the absence of fences or gates minimized the sense of incarceration which ordinarily drove people away.

In the end, the Institute's perceived success obscured the endless failures and provided new inspiration for advocates of segregation. Noting in 1937 that at least 10,593 lepers lived within the colony, Soudan's lieutenant governor questioned the utility of concentrating all their attention on the *"blanchissement"* (literally, "whitening"—a euphemism for curing) of only five hundred patients. He urged the Health Service to organize its efforts better with a "multiplication of segregation villages" across the entire territory.[100] The annual report for that year announced the formation of "agricultural [leper] colonies" in other large towns such as San and Sikasso where patients would "benefit from regular treatment" while being assured of their "liberty."[101] A doctor with the Office de Niger, a vast state-run agricultural project in the Niger valley, also advocated segregation villages for the lepers living among its resident laborers.[102]

Without equivalent funding, most other attempts throughout French West Africa faced the same problems as before. As early as 1935, the new centers in the Soudan colony could not adequately supply food to their residents.[103] Two years later the annual medical report for French West Africa stated that "absolute isolation" could not work without causing patients to flee all their dispensaries and medical centers.[104] In 1942 only three of the Soudan's centers remained, housing only the most "mutilated or miserable" patients. Doctors in all other districts treated individuals at dispensaries and kept them isolated *"à domicile"* (in their homes).[105] One Health Service director described the effectiveness of their leprosy program as "illusory." The invalid residents in the "leper colonies" were not receptive to treatment, and in other locations patients reported to AMI facilities very irregularly.[106] Doctors in Niger and Guinea reported similar conditions.[107]

Many officials believed that their problems were merely a matter of "propaganda," that one day "the natives" would understand the utility of segregation.[108] One report cited the great distance between dispensaries and patients' homes.[109]In smaller localities, individuals with leprosy refused hospitalization at dispensaries

99 "Rapport semestriel [hereafter RS] du Service de Prophylaxie de la Lèpre [hereafter SPL], premier semestre, 1938," AIM. Interviews with former patients confirm this success in attracting voluntary patients by the late 1930s. See also Bado on the Institute's creation. Bado, *Médecine coloniale*, 279-83.

100 Lt. Gouv., "Observations et instructions," 5 June 1937, attached to "RMA de Soudan, 1936," ANS 2G-36/35.

101 "RMA de Soudan, 1937," ANS 2G-37/26.

102 "Rapport sur le fonctionnement du Service Sanitaire de l'Office de Niger. 1936." ANS 2G-36/36.

103 "RMA de Soudan, 1935," ANS 2G-35/22.

104 "RMA de l'AOF, 1937," ANS 2G-43/37.

105 "RMA de Soudan, 1941," ANS 2G-41/16; "RMA de Soudan, 1942," ANS 2G-42/19.

106 "RMA de Soudan, 1943," ANS 2G-43/13.

107 "RMA de Niger, 1939," ANS 2G-39/13; "RMA de Guinée, 1936," ANS 2G-36/37.

108 "RMA de l'AOF, 1938," ANS 2G-38/11.

109 "RMA de Soudan, 1942," CAOM Agence FOM 384.

altogether because, according to French observers, it conflicted with their previous living habits.[110]

Segregation also continued to overburden an already limited health budget. Acknowledging that one could not hold patients without feeding them, many doctors advocated "agricultural colonies" in which patients grew their own food. When the "asylum" in Sine-Saloum (an administrative *cercle* situated on Gambia's northern border and southeast of Dakar) fell under the control of the AMI, doctors sought to alleviate its budgetary demands by transforming it into a "village of cultivation producing for itself."[111] Even such supposedly "self-sufficient" institutions, however, required large budgets for staff and infrastructure. The Health Service director in Guinea complained that the Institute in Bamako could not accommodate enough patients from his colony and that he himself lacked money to create Guinea's own "agricultural" leprosariums.[112]

A few doctors vaguely acknowledged that the biological ineffectiveness of their leprosy treatments also contributed to the unpopularity of their dispensaries and leprosariums. Throughout the colonies doctors found that only "material advantages," not medical treatments, attracted patients.[113] One medical report noted that the "slowness" of government remedies caused the "natives" in Dakar to avoid the dispensaries in preference to their own healers.[114] Doctors in Guinea similarly admitted that Africans "had absolutely no confidence in a treatment which took so long."[115] One former patient confirmed this observation, noting that patients in Siguiri (Guinea) often escaped from the dispensary at night. "They were scared of the shots" and, rather than risk capture again by returning to their own villages, went to other locations and received treatment from indigenous healers.[116] From Dahomey to Senegal large numbers of patients continued to flee the segregation centers.[117]

In the volumes of reports and correspondence from this period, only one doctor explicitly admitted the ineffectiveness of their drugs. Dr. Botreau-Roussel, Health Service director for Côte d'Ivoire, wrote in his 1934 report, "[I]t is next to impossible to impose these treatments on the natives . . . the treatment is poorly welcomed by them because it is uncertain and . . . absolutely ineffective in the immense majority of cases." He complained that the Leprosy Service imposed treatments randomly upon each region, some receiving chaulmoogra oil while others receiving distilled ethers. "Native" patients often accepted an initial series of injections, sometimes for as long as two or three months, but in the end they experienced no improvements. In fact, the injections often caused additional problems such as intramuscular infections.[118]

---

110 "RMA de Soudan, 1938," ANS 2G-38/0.

111 "RMA de Soudan, 1936," ANS 2G-36/43.

112 "RMA de Guinée, 1935," ANS 2G-35/23.

113 "RMA de Sénégal, 1938," ANS 2G-38/0.

114 "RMA de Dakar et Circonscription, 1935," ANS 2G-35/21.

115 "RMA de Guinée, 1929," and for 1934, ANS 2G-29/31 and 34/21.

116 Drissa Makasuba, 5 November 1992.

117 "RMA de l'AOF, 1936," ANS 2G-36/43.

118 "RMA de Guinée, 1936," ANS 2G-36/27.

Botreau-Roussel argued that imposing these treatments on "natives" made for "bad politics" and would end up discrediting colonial medical methods to the advantage of indigenous ones, noting that "in many regions there exists native medication which gives incontestable results for the macular form of leprosy." He himself observed patients clinically and permanently cured from these remedies. For these reasons, he believed that the medical service could attract leprosy patients only when it possessed the "proper" remedy as it already did for yaws and sleeping sickness. In the meantime, he suggested, the Service should concentrate on improving living conditions; after all, leprosy had disappeared from Europe without the use of medical treatments.[119]

Botreau-Roussel's recommendations contrasted sharply with those of most other doctors who, though aware of their medicines' limitations, felt compelled to force them on Africans. Some officials envisioned leprosariums not so much to isolate lepers from the healthy population but to confine them in one location to facilitate regular and prolonged treatment.[120] Others believed it necessary to impose treatment by force and complained that they lacked the authority to do so. For a solution, they proposed new coercive laws to facilitate better "results."[121]

In addition to recognizing the ineffectiveness or, at least, unpopularity of their treatments, officials gradually acknowledged the narrow urban focus of their leprosy programs. In the 1930s and 1940s no other facility matched the relative success of the Bamako Institute in terms of the material advantages and comprehensive care provided for its residents. As one of its directors noted, the Institute's ability to attract voluntary patients could not be replicated elsewhere.[122] Most leprosariums serviced larger towns, but the majority of patients remained in rural areas. The administration therefore repeatedly called upon rural doctors posted at AMI clinics to assume some responsibility for the disease. These half-hearted appeals, however, hardly counted as a rural leprosy policy. Aside from a few scattered and feeble efforts, district doctors had, in the words of one 1939 report, "lost sight" of the leprosy problem altogether.[123]

Mobile Medicine

As early as 1930, the colonial government had begun, albeit slowly, to develop a different response to leprosy. With the creation of the Service de la Lépre as a sub-unit of Bamako's Laboratoire Central de Biologie, one agency assumed exclusive responsibility for

119 "RMA de Côte d'Ivoire, 1934," ANS 2G-34/23. See Bado, *Médecine coloniale*, for more insight into Botreau-Roussel's political relations within the medical service.

120 "RMM de Macina, septembre 1934," ANM 1H-12 FR. Bado also notes the beginning of a new philosophy in colonial public health at this time. Bado, *Médecine coloniale*, 227.

121 Gouv. Gén. de l'AOF to Gouv. de Soudan, no. 843, 19 October 1938; Gouv. de Soudan to Gouv. Gén. de l'AOF, no. 2720, 29 October 1938; Inspecteur Général de Service Sanitaire et Médicaux de l'AOF to Directeur des Affaires Politiques, no. 2440/1, 16 December 1938; Procureur Général to Directeur des Affaires Politiques, no. 146, 11 January 1939; Gouv. Gén. de l'AOF to Gouv. de Soudan, no. 42, 18 January 1939, ANM 1H-27 FR. "RMA de Sénégal, 1939," ANS 2G-39/14.

122 "RS du SPL, premier semestre, 1938," AIM.

123 "RMA de Soudan, 1935," ANS 2G-35/22; "RMA de Togo, 1938," and for 1939, ANS 2G-38/21 and 39/16; "RMA de Niger, 1939," ANS 2G-39/13.

the disease. By the end of its first year, the Service had about sixty-one leprosy patients who reported to the clinic for treatment. The number rose to 191 in 1931 and 224 in 1932.[124] Commenting on the increasing success, Dr. Gourvil wrote, "Our patients are free, live with their families, and lead a more or less normal existence." He also felt that segregation in a government institute was unnecessary since Bamako families already isolated patients in separate huts within their compounds.[125]

In recommending leprosy treatment at the clinic rather than the isolation center, Laigret and Gourvil reflected a change in philosophy already underway within the international medical community. The Third International Leprosy Congress held in Strasbourg in 1923 acknowledged the relative failure of segregation. After working in India, two well-known American doctors in the 1920s recommended outpatient care as a more effective approach to treatment.[126] In the end, however, the small minority of doctors like Laigret and Gourvil failed to convince the colonial administration. This new philosophy would not emerge as official policy in French West Africa until the late 1940s, and a few staunch proponents of isolation would even remain vocal up until independence.

Like its predecessor, the Second World War had strained the leprosy service's already limited resources.[127] Medical staff such as the Institute's director withdrew to join the war effort. Though not documented in health-related correspondence or reports, a rift between pro- and anti-Vichy colonial staff no doubt added to the disruption. Those who recognized problems in the leprosy program could do nothing until after the war.[128] When the war did end, they found that France's colonial authority had weakened considerably. Its defeat by Germany and the subsequent split between de Gaulle's government-in-exile and the German-controlled Vichy government reawakened colonial subjects to the possibility of challenging their overlords.

In return for providing a temporary foothold for the Free French and supplying troops for the liberation of the *métropole*, many Africans expected immediate and tangible concessions from the new post-war government. The 1944 Brazzaville Conference formally initiated a series of significant reforms of French West Africa's political and economic organization. As one important consequence of these developments, the government transformed the old colonies into federal territories and granted them limited representation in the French parliament. Beyond administrative restructuring, the Second World War also facilitated the emergence of new African political elites who would eventually lead the transition to independence in 1960.[129]

Dr. Rigou, the director general of French West Africa's Health Service, attended the Brazzaville Conference and presented a paper on the reorganization of all the

124 Dr. Gourvil, "RA, Laboratoire Vaccinogéne et de Biologie de Bamako, 1932," inside "RMA de Soudan, 1932," ANS 2G-32/34; "RMA de Soudan, 1931," ANS 2G-31/29.

125 "RMA de Soudan, 1932," ANS 2G-32/34.

126 Gussow, *Leprosy, Racism, and Public Health*, 151.

127 The next chapter will describe how the war specifically affected Bamako's Institut Central de la Lépre.

128 "RMA de Soudan, 1942," ANS 2G-42/19. See also Bado, *Médecine coloniale*, 290–98.

129 For more details on these political changes see William J. Foltz, *From French West Africa to the Mali Federation* (New Haven: Yale University Press, 1965), and Ruth Schachter Morgenthau, *Political Parties in French-Speaking West Africa* (Oxford: Clarendon Press, 1964).

agencies under his control. On the subject of leprosy, his paper praised the research and experimentation conducted in Djikoroni but acknowledged that the Institute was "not equipped or tooled for assuring, with its own means, diagnosis and systematic treatment for the [entire] Federal territory." Referring to the Service de la Lépre, Rigou described government attempts at controlling leprosy as "theoretical." In his view, their programs needed a much wider scope.[130]

Several officials working in the 1930s had already proposed alternatives to leprosariums so that they could extend medical treatment to patients in rural areas. In a 1935 report, for example, the Bamako Institute's interim director, Dr. Bernard, noted the urgency of creating *"quartiers de traitement"* (treatment quarters) in all the Soudan's districts for accommodating patients and providing them with fields for cultivation. At the same time, however, he suggested a "more practical" solution of training teams of "mobile nurses" who could then treat patients in their own villages.[131] Another Institute director, Dr. Beaudiment, believed that only ten percent of the Soudan's inhabitants ever saw a French doctor. To address this problem, he similarly proposed the use of mobile nurses. More specifically he suggested that nurses engaged in the sleeping sickness campaign should also conduct inspections for leprosy while on their tours.[132]

Mobile treatment campaigns for other diseases were already common practice throughout the continent. As noted earlier in this chapter, French doctors at the beginning of the century circulated in West Africa administering smallpox vaccinations. The most celebrated mobile campaigns focused on sleeping sickness in the Belgian Congo and French Equatorial Africa (Afrique Equitoriale Française, or AEF).[133] In 1932, after conducting the widely praised campaign in AEF, Dr. Eugéne Jamot moved to France's West African colonies to head a new service established especially for this disease. Jamot overcame vehemently jealous opposition from regional doctors to transform this service into a fully autonomous federal agency free to operate independently of the other health services, especially the AMI. Renamed the Service Général Autonome de la Maladie du Sommeil (SGAMS) in 1939, this agency constructed its own treatment clinics in locations which did not necessarily coincide with dispensaries in administrative centers. Its doctors and nurses traveled widely, unlike the more sedentary AMI staff. In essence, the SGAMS existed because the AMI could not cope with a disease regarded by the administration as an urgent danger. Centralizing control in one federal agency, its architects also sought to bypass entirely the authority of each individual colony.[134]

Jamot's apparently dramatic successes impressed doctors throughout Africa. To this day, many health professionals regard him as a hero of colonial and tropical medicine. In the wake of the Brazzaville Conference, reform-minded administrators therefore looked to mobile medicine as a solution to the seemingly incorrigible problem of leprosy. The

130 Rigou, Dir. Gén. de la Santé Publique de l'AOF, "Conference de Brazzaville, De la Reorganisation des Services Sanitaires et Médicaux en Afrique Occidentale Française," January 1944, AIM.

131 "RA de l'Institut Central de la Lépre [hereafter ICL], 1935," ANS 2G-35/118.

132 "RS du SPL, premier semestre, 1938," and for second semester, AIM.

133 See Bado, *Médecine coloniale*; Headrick, *Colonialism, Health, and Illness*; and Lyons, *Curing Their Ills.*

134 For more details on the sleeping sickness campaign, see Danielle Domergue, "La Lutte contre la trypanosomiase en Côte d'Ivoire, 1900-1945," *Journal of African History* 22, 1 (1981): 63-72.

Service de la Lépre merged with SGAMS in 1945 to become the Service Général d'Hygiène Mobile de Prophylaxie (SGHMP). Based in Bobo-Dioulasso, SGHMP also assumed control of the treatment of malaria, syphilis, smallpox, yaws, and yellow fever. It would also continue to operate in complete administrative and financial independence of AMI. This restructuring made AMI's defectiveness all the more apparent. Health administrators viewed the agency as too sedentary and overly concentrated on individual curative medicine as opposed to publicly-oriented mass prophylactic campaigns.[135]

The Bamako Institute fell under SGHMP's control and, for several years, its director remained in charge of the overall leprosy program. As a federal agency, SGHMP subdivided the colonies into "sectors" which did not always conform with the administrative boundaries of districts (*cercles*) and even the colonies themselves. Whether intended or not, this arrangement ensured that control of SGHMP activities remained firmly anchored in the hands of its own directors.[136] Within two years, the new leprosy program was fully underway. The old clinics used for the sleeping sickness campaign re-opened for leprosy treatment and the SGHMP assumed control of all the leprosariums formerly run by the AMI.[137] In 1948, Institute doctors began experimenting with newly developed sulfone-based antibiotics such as diaminodiphenyl sulfone (DDS) which the SGHMP nurses then employed in the first therapy trials in the Ouagadougou sector.[138] These drugs enabled doctors to arrest the disease in patients for the first time. Although many of the leprosariums and agricultural colonies survived for a number of years, the SGHMP considered them *"formations hopitaliéres"* (hospital units) reserved for experimentation and the prolonged treatment of "a few privileged patients"; in theory, they were no longer supposed to segregate patients from the rest of the population.[139]

Much correspondence circulating within the colonies, however, documented substantial limits to SGHMP's initial effectiveness. In 1950 the agency reported a total of 80,083 patients in all of its sectors. (That number did not include the many areas in which SGHMP still did not operate.)[140] A total of fifty leprosariums treated only 3,080 individuals. The other 297 outpatient clinics documented 31,562 visitors, and only 6,983 of those actually received the minimum dosage of chaulmoogra considered necessary for improvement. The distance—sometimes several days walk—between patients and dispensaries also perpetuated the "irregularity" of treatment.[141] Constructed in accordance

135 "RA du SGHMP, 1951," 2G-51/61.

136 This federal approach drew considerable opposition from administrators. Bado, *Médecine coloniale*, 299–303.

137 "RA du SGHMP, 1946," and for 1948, ANS 2G-46/65 and 48/74.

138 Laviron, "Fonctionnement du Secteur Lépre du SGHMP au cours de l'année 1950," 13 July 1951, AIM.

139 "RA du SGHMP, 1949," 2G-49/57. "Développement d'une campagne antihansenienne globale en AEF," [undated, ca. 1955–56], ANS 1H-73. Forced isolation also fell out of fashion in France as well. In 1932 an "exotic diseases" ward had opened at the Saint-Louis Hospital in Paris for the purpose of isolating people with leprosy and other "contagious" diseases. In 1952, however, the principles of this pavilion ran contrary to "contemporary notions of liberty." Doctors then transformed it into an "intra-hospital home" for "able-bodied" lepers who knew how to "profit" from the alarm caused by their disease outside the hospital. By 1956, hospitalization of lepers was reserved only for a very limited number of special cases. See extract from "Bulletin du Syndicat National des Médecins, Chirurgiens, et Spécialistes des Hopitaux Publics," no. 48 in published pamphlet, "Orientation actuelle de la lutte antihansenienne et rehabilitation sociale du lépreux en France Metropolitaine et d'Outre-Mer," 1956, ANS 1H-73.

140 Laviron, "Fonctionnement," 13 July 1951, AIM.

141 "RA du SGHMP, 1950," ANS 2G-50/61.

with the incidence of sleeping sickness, most of SGHMP's installations did not coincide with the distribution of leprosy which varied greatly from region to region.[142]

Most of SGHMP's problems originated from the very nature of France's colonial authority in West Africa. Long wary of tax collectors and military recruiters, many patients in the late 1940s still avoided contact with government agents. Doctors and administrators at that time perceived the post-Brazzaville African population as less pliant than it had been in the 1920s and 1930s. In 1947, for example, French West Africa's governor general attributed patient resistance to politics rather than ignorance, which had once been a more popular explanation.

> These difficulties originate to a large degree from certain elements of the population who, by interpreting in a regrettable fashion the liberties which have been conceded to them, consider themselves relieved of the obligation to respond to the convocations to which they are subject and refuse to report to the vaccination sessions or the medical visits [intended for] control and diagnosis.[143]

Even patients undergoing the more effective DDS treatment minimized contact with health officials. One 1949 report noted that such patients disappeared as soon as they felt themselves the least bit improved. When lesions reappeared a few months later, the same patients returned for more injections.[144]

While SGHMP's new leprosy program suggested a kinder spirit, some government officials persisted in advocating authoritarian health measures as a response to patient resistance. In 1946 the Institute's director, Dr. Laviron, called for legislation mandating the isolation of "contagious" cases and obliging "natives" to report for medical inspection and treatment.[145] A year later the governor general suggested granting mayors and district officers powers to restrict the liberty of "circulation" for people with "endemic" diseases.[146] Some even proposed a decree obliging all workers ("houseboys, cooks, merchants, transporters of food, butchers, etc.") to carry a medical certificate proving that they did not carry the Hansen's bacillus.[147] Concerned with the growing number of patients who "endangered" both passengers and staff on trains, one doctor in 1950 requested that station police identify suspected cases and report them to local dispensaries. These dispensaries would in turn interdict the "contagious" and "repulsive" individuals from traveling on the trains.[148] As late as the mid-1950s, some doctors requested administrative or judicial pressure to force patients to continue their regular treatment.[149]

142 "RA du SGHMP, 1951," ANS 2G-51/61.

143 Gouv. Gén. de l'AOF to Ministre [hereafter Min.] de la France d'Outre-Mer [hereafter FOM], Direction des Affaires Politiques, no. 5496, 1 August 1947, ANS 1H-48.

144 "RA du SGHMP, 1949," ANS 2G-49/57.

145 "Communication du Laviron à la séance de la Commission Consultative de la Lèpre du 1 octobre 1946 au Min. de la FOM," 10 october 1946, AIM.

146 Gouv. Gén. de l'AOF to Min. de la FOM, Direction des Affaires Politiques, no. 5496, 1 August 1947, ANS 1H-48.

147 "Projet Arrèté," September 1950, ANS 1H-48.

148 Controleur des Trains, "Rapport de tournée," no. 9, 11 July 1950; Médecin-Chef du Dakar/Niger to Directeurs Locals de Santé Publique de Sénégal et Soudan, no. 352, 16 August 1950; Dir. de la Santé Publique de Sénégal, no. 2969, 26 August 1950; Dir. Gén. de la Santé Publique to Laviron, no. 3302, 30 August 1950, ANS 1H-73.

149 "Développement d'une campagne antihansenienne," ANS 1H-73.

This preoccupation with controlling patients reflected a debilitating conservatism among many administrators and doctors who felt their colonial powers slipping away. Conservatism reached its extreme as some doctors persisted in using their old remedies which most leprosy specialists outside French West Africa regarded as ineffective. Despite DDS's recognized efficacy and the relative uselessness of chaulmoogra, SGHMP adopted the new drug slowly and reluctantly. By the end of 1950, only 294 patients scattered around the colonies had undergone sulfone treatments while 6,983 received chaulmoogra. Laviron, the Institute's director, claimed that DDS's format as an oral medication limited its use to hospitals where staff could strictly control their patients. He noted that Africans outside hospitals were "incapable of taking their pills according to the desired dose and date." Even the *"évolué"* (educated) patients failed in this respect.[150] Oral sulfone was therefore "impossible in the bush." [151] Laviron's attitude also reflected a widespread assumption in medical discourse that African patients were "decidely 'difficult.'" [152]

In response to this problem, the director of Public Health for all the colonies ordered that patients swallow their medicines in the presence of a doctor or nurse: "In no case, will we give the patient a provision of pills [to take on his own]." [153] Laviron felt that sulfone could only be used on a large scale if it became injectable. Towards that end, the Institute experimented with suspensions of DDS in chaulmoogra ether.[154] The director and his colleagues insisted that chaulmoogra might still play a "therapeutic role" in these injections despite mounting evidence to the contrary.[155] As late as 1953, the Institute's pharmacist openly criticized the abandonment of chaulmoogra at the International Leprosy Congress in Madrid.[156]

This type of conservatism prevented French West Africa from keeping pace with international developments in leprosy control. In 1951, while Laviron still advocated chaulmoogra, the World Health Organization called for an end to leprosariums and recommended mass treatment campaigns with DDS.[157] Two years later, even the SGHMP's equivalent in French Equatorial Africa (AEF) initiated its own "global" anti-leprosy program. Rather than work out of leprosariums and dispensaries, traveling teams of doctors and nurses visited villages in accordance with a well-organized schedule that enabled patients to receive their weekly pills and twice-monthly injections. Equipped with fairly curative sulfone drugs, these medical personnel were able for the first time to arrest the disease in a large number of patients. Many doctors in Africa and elsewhere considered the AEF program a model of success. According to one 1956 report, this "simple, efficacious" approach minimized the disturbances in

---

150 Laviron, "Fonctionnement," 13 July 1951, AIM.

151 Ibid.

152 Vaughan, *Curing Their Ills,* 165.

153 Circular, Dir. Gén. de la Santé Publique to Directeurs of Santé Publique Locale, no. 654, 16 February 1950, ANS 1H-73.

154 Laviron, "Fonctionnement," 13 July 1951, AIM.

155 "RA du SGHMP, 1950," ANS 2G-50/61.

156 Jardin, "Rapport de mission au Congrés International de Lèprologie de Madrid," no. 1162, 18 February 1954, ANS 1H-73.

157 Min. de la FOM to Haut Commissaire de la République en AOF, 14 May 1957, AIM.

the patient's life and permitted the complete avoidance of "segregation" and "detribalisation." [158]

Meanwhile, in French West Africa only 80,000 of an estimated 350,000 leprosy patients (based on a 1.36 percent incidence) were receiving regular and correct treatment as late as 1955.[159] To address this problem, the colonial government finally adopted WHO's recommendations. It initiated its own mobile campaign in which nurses circulated by any means available—car, bicycle, boat, horse—to deliver sulfone drugs to infected villagers in the remoter rural areas. Dr. Richet, the director of AEF's mobile campaign, then became SGHMP's new director.[160] In 1957 the minister of France d'Outre-Mer instructed the federal governor to abandon chaulmoogra altogether and rely only on DDS.[161] A few SGHMP doctors, however, still defended the utility of this ancient drug which they used, to WHO's consternation, through most of that year.[162]

Without question, the mobile campaign and DDS eventually cured thousands of leprosy patients throughout French West Africa. In some cases, prompt treatment prevented the permanent nerve and tissue damage which ordinarily transformed individuals into social lepers. Many doctors aspired to eradicate the disease completely. Others hoped that at least the promise of a cure would minimize its stigma. In the 1950s, Raoul Follerau, a French poet and journalist, devoted himself entirely to changing social attitudes towards leprosy throughout the world. As a self-designated spokesman for all lepers, he traveled widely espousing the virtues of Catholic charity.[163] His public embraces of disfigured leprosy patients and melodramatic speeches attracted considerable attention from journalists, doctors, and government officials on all continents. Follerau's theatrics embodied the optimism inspired by the new cure.

In the end, DDS empowered doctors to kill a bacillus in nature but failed to resolve a myriad of other problems impinging on its delivery to patients in society, especially one under French colonial rule. French doctors unaccustomed to rapid change continued to lament the erosion of their authority. The high costs and complexity of the mobile campaign gradually made France dependent on the World Health Organization and UNICEF for financial and technical support. This dependence reflected a new era in which international organizations directly participated in the administration of African health programs as they often do today. For example, in 1956 doctors meeting at the International Leprosy Congress in Rome questioned the merits of France's preference for administering sulfone with injections of

---

158 "Développement d'une campagne antihansenienne," ANS 1H-73.

159 Richet, "Bilan des moyens supplémentaires nécessaires pour mise sur pied d'une campagne globale anitihansenienne en AOF," no. 5404, 22 December 1955, ANS 1H-73.

160 Ibid.

161 Min. de la FOM to M. le Haut Commissaire de la République en AOF, no. 003309, 14 May 1957, AIM.

162 On continued use of chaulmoogra oil, see Richet's report and an extended exchange of correspondence. Richet, "Considerations sur le développement d'une campagne antihansenienne globale instituée en AEF depuis fin 1953. [undated, probably early 1955], AIM; 24 April 1956 to 30 July 1956. Note especially Kerbastard to Directeur de SGHMP, no. 540, 2 May 1956, ANS 1H-73; and Gay Prieto, "Mission en AEF, dans l'état du Cameroun et en AOF, septembre-octobre 1957," 8 October 1957, AIM.

163 For more details on his life, see Raoul Follerau, *"Vous aurez 20 ans en l'an 2000"* (France: Flammarion, 1986); and Etienne Thevenin, *Raoul Follerau: Hier et aujourd'hui* (Paris: Librairie Arthéme Fayard, 1992). See also Vaughan, *Curing Their Ills*, 93–94.

chaulmoogra oil suspensions. Already dependent on technical assistance from UNICEF, colonial administrators grudgingly admitted that they would have no say in the choice of specific medicines used.[164]

The French government and UNICEF also disagreed over the specific implementation of the mass campaign. Some UNICEF officials in New York wanted to begin with a trial program in only one West African colony. Fearing political repercussions from the other excluded colonies, French officials wanted to conduct the campaign in all of French West Africa at once.[165] In another instance, UNICEF requested a duty exemption for imported equipment and supplies designated for official use. The director of finance and customs refused, even though UNICEF ordinarily received such exemptions for its operations in France.[166] In a confidential note to the governor of French West Africa, the minister of France d'Outre-Mer (formerly the minister of colonies) complained that "international assistance" imposed additional financial obligations on the territories. The government also lacked personnel for properly conducting the recommended programs. The minister added that "the international organizations . . . have not only a control over the material and supplied products, but also a technical control over the operations."[167]

Though annoying for some doctors, the loss of power to patients and international agencies hardly compared with the gradual loss of power to politically active African staff. In the late 1950s, pressure to "Africanize" government agencies imposed new constraints on the SGHMP's recruitment and management of its personnel.[168] While implementing the global anti-leprosy campaign, Laviron sought to hire fifty more Europeans. The recent recruitment of two hundred African nursing assistants, in his view, gave Africans little reason to quibble. In the end, however, he hired only ten European *chefs d'equipe* (team leaders) to avoid "political incidents" which would have arisen from the perceived delay or indifference towards Africanization.[169] The SGHMP's African nurses also struck twice in 1957; their demands involved wages, work load, and treatment of specific employees. The high commissioner (formerly the governor general) for French West Africa complained that these strikes jeopardized the welfare of the patients as well as the continuation of funding from UNICEF.[170] (Chapter 7 will examine these strikes more closely.)

The prospect of independence for each individual colony threatened the long-term viability of federally organized agencies like the SGHMP. Following a 1956 inspection of the mobile leprosy program, a field representative from the World Health Organization observed that French West Africa was not far from some type of "self-government" either as a federation attached to France or as independent states. The SGHMP, he speculated, would remain French for several years since

164 Min. de la FOM to M. le Haut Commissaire de la République en AOF, no. 003309, 14 May 1957, AIM.
165 R. Marti, Représentant en Chef de l'UNICEF Bureau de l'Afrique to Richet, 11 June 1956, AIM.
166 Dir. Fédéral des Douanes to Directeur des Douanes de la Guinée Française, 22 January 1957; Haut-Commissaire de la République en AOF to Dir. Gén. de la Santé Publique, no. 3.960/FD-I, 2 April 1957, AIM.
167 Min. de la FOM to Gouv. de l'AOF, 15 June 1956, no. 0546, ANS 1H-73.
168 See Foltz, *From French West Africa*, 143–4 and 152–3.
169 Laviron to Dir. Gén. de la Santé Publique de l'AOF, [undated, probably September 1957], AIM.
170 Haut Commissaire de la République en AOF to Chefs de Territoire, [undated, probably October 1957], AIM.

African doctors preferred living in big cities and lacked interest in "fighting epidemic diseases and working in the bush."[171] Two years later, in the wake of still more political changes, SGHMP director Dr. Richet reflected nostalgically on the history of French doctors in West Africa:

> [France] always held to assisting as quickly as possible its Overseas Territories with the social benefits—health and cultural—brought by its administrators, scholars, educators, and missionaries. The very structure and philosophy of SGHMP conflicted with the prevailing political winds. Its sectors spread across borders dividing colonies and it was organized as a federal service, not colony by colony.[172]

Richet argued that "territorialization," brought on by the *loi-cadre* (the law which privileged local territorial governments at the expense of federation), would greatly hamper their leprosy control program.

Beyond these political issues, the very structure of the leprosy program limited access to patients in the long run. In relying on a vertically organized and separate colonial bureaucracy focused exclusively on leprosy, the mobile campaign enabled health care workers with the AMI to disengage themselves entirely from the disease. This trend had become apparent as early as 1951 when Laviron faulted the AMI for practicing "sedentary" medicine and thereby treating leprosy only on occasion. In his view, the SGHMP covered about six million people, but the AMI remained responsible for the rest of the population.[173] In a 1954 letter to the director of the SGHMP, Laviron quoted reports from AMI doctors who, in spite of their "good intentions," could not properly treat leprosy.[174]

An entirely separate structure for leprosy reinforced the disease's stigma among other health care workers—a stigma which persists to this day in Mali. In 1957 an official from the World Health Organization found that AMA (Assistance Médicale Africaine, formerly the AMI) staff refused to treat leprosy patients despite efforts to convince them that this was a disease "like the others."[175] During an inspection tour in one "sector," an SGHMP administrator learned that only two hundred of two thousand patients received regular treatment. The local AMA doctor absolved himself from all responsibility, insisting that leprosy was not his business: "I have absolutely no relationship with these nurses [of the SGHMP] who are strangers to my Service, who don't report to me, who don't even inform me of their work, their program, their difficulties. . . . "[176] In 1958 Richet stressed the importance of the AMA's participation in the leprosy campaign. "Every AMA nurse who does not understand this necessity [of diagnosing and treating lepers] would make a grave mistake."[177]

---

171 O. M. Lehner, Field Representative, AAO, "Rapport de visite, 20 fevrier 1956 à 11 mars 1956," 6 June 1956, AIM.

172 Richet, "Quelques notions sur le service commun de lutte contre les grandes endémies," 4 July 1958, ANS-1H 63.

173 "RA de l'Institut Marchoux [hereafter IM]," 8 March 1951, ANS 1H-73.

174 Laviron to Dir. du SGHMP, no. 1493, 9 December 1954, ANS 1H-73.

175 Gay Prieto, "Mission en AEF," 8 October 1957, AIM.

176 "Quelques réflexions à batons rompus," [undated and unsigned, probably late 1950s and perhaps Richet], AIM.

177 Richet to Médecins Chefs au Soudan, no. 3.077, 9 June 1958, AIM.

The difficulties created by the reliance on one specialized and vertically organized agency contrasted sharply with the relative success of approaches used in other parts of Africa. In 1959 Richet inquired about the leprosy campaign in British Nyasaland (Malawi). Dr. Currie, a specialist at the Kochira Leprosarium, commended the French mobile program but described the advantages of Nyasaland's own approach:

> We in Nyasaland have adopted the slower method of working through the staff of the Health Services without setting up a separate Leprosy Service. The benefit of this method is that medical staff in this country are now all familiar with leprosy and do not regard it as a disease to be read and treated only by volunteers or specialists.

Currie added that "few patients live more than fifteen miles from a medical centre" and doubted the utility of a mobile program for Nyasaland; "there has been no need to recruit a large specialized leprosy staff."[178]

More than anything else, SGHMP's difficulties in providing treatment for such a large and dispersed population demonstrated that, without corresponding improvements in education and infrastructure, drugs alone would not eradicate the disease. Unlike smallpox, for which one injection sufficed for all time, leprosy required at least one or two years of biweekly drug treatment. Health agents could either entrust patients with large supplies of medicines to take on their own or visit them every week or two. A nun working in Cameroon once attempted the former approach by giving patients entire packets of DDS sufficient for a month. The local government doctor, however, observed that these packets ultimately wound up for sale in the market.[179] Poorly educated—if at all—in Western biological concepts, most patients did not understand the necessity of consuming these medicines in a regimented manner even when they no longer felt ill.[180] The unorthodox use and circulation of Western pharmaceuticals remains a problem throughout Africa to this day.[181]

Though more certain, the second approach, regular visitation, required a substantial investment in personnel and transportation. To maintain control over drug use, an official with the World Health Organization recommended that all patients swallow their DDS pills in front of a nurse.[182] Distrusting of patients and unable or unwilling to rely on the AMA's network of dispensaries, the SGHMP sent its own

---

178 G. Curie to Richet, 10 March 1959, AIM.

179 Gay Prieto, "Mission en AEF," 8 October 1957, AIM. As documented in Chapter 9, this phenomenon eventually occurred in Mali as well.

180 For similar reasons, many tuberculosis patients in contemporary United States fail to follow their prescribed therapies which usually last at least a year. As discussed in Chapter 10, improper use of antibiotics contributed to the spread of resistant forms of leprosy and tuberculosis.

181 See, for example, Caroline Bledsoe and Monica Goubaud, "The Reinterpretation and Distribution of Western Pharmaceuticals: An Example from the Mende of Sierra Leone," in Sjaak van der Geest and Susan Reynolds White, eds., *The Context of Medicines in Developing Countries: Studies in Pharmaceutical Anthropology* (Dordrecht: Kluwer Academic Publishers, 1988), 253–76. Since tuberculosis medicines required sustained use often lasting a year or more, health agents in South Africa also encountered difficulties in monitoring patients. Much like individuals with leprosy in Mali, half-cured tuberculosis patients often disappeared from doctors' control only to suffer relapses later. Packard, *White Plague,* 277 and 285.

182 Gay Prieto, "Mission en AEF," 8 October 1957, AIM.

staff on exhausting tours through rural areas.[183] Commando-like teams of doctors and nurses swept through villages in Land Rovers or on bicycles, creating an illusion of military efficiency. In towns, health agents were similarly expected to monitor every patient.

The Soudan's poorly-developed transportation infrastructure severely limited the mobility of these teams. Furthermore, many patients still remained suspicious of government agents who disregarded local conceptions of disease and who administered treatments without fully explaining their meaning. In 1959 one inspector observed numerous problems with the colony's mobile campaign. The nurse in Macina had not conducted the last fifteen rounds of treatment while the SGHMP staff in Bandiagara saw only ten percent of its patients on a continued basis. The San sector "presented the maximum fantasy" with only twenty-five patients at its hospital. Throughout the colony, leprosy patients still failed to report for regular diagnosis and treatment. "The administration," complained the inspector, "is not favorable towards measures of constraint of any sort and estimates that 'persuasion' is the only way [to draw patients in.] Since a long time alas! we have been fixed on this point."[184] Richet similarly faulted the "mentality" of numerous "tribes" who either did not take the disease seriously or who treated it with such "degradation" that "their lepers" hid and avoided contact with health agents.[185]

When the colonies became independent in 1960, neither the mobile campaign nor the increased use of DDS had succeeded in extending leprosy treatment to the entire population. The SGHMP restructured itself twice in the final years to accommodate French West Africa's fragmentation and thereby preserve its own disease-control programs. In the first restructuring, the SGHMP changed its name to the Service Territorial d'Hygiéne Mobile et Prophylaxie (STHMP) and appointed directors representing each of the eight former colonies (now called territories). Disputes, however, immediately arose over the control of hiring and the responsibility for paying employees. The governor of Soudan, for example, challenged STHMP's request that each territory pay for its own director. Meanwhile, labor unions demanded a reduction in the number of leprosy treatment tours conducted by African staff. Individuals from all sides challenged STHMP's administrative and fiscal authority.[186] By the end of 1960, the last vestiges of federation collapsed leaving STHMP with no governmental parent and inducing a second restructuring. The new Organisation de Coordination et de Coopération pour la Lutte Contre les Grandes Endémies (OCCGE, known informally as the "Grandes Endémies") now acted as an "inter-state" agency whose members consisted of the former colonies and France.

The OCCGE retained nominal control over programs for leprosy and the other diseases. Although lacking the administrative and fiscal powers of its predecessors, the agency continued to play an important role in the formation and implementation of health policies for most of the independent states. As of 1996, the OCCGE had

183 "Conversations à Leopoldville," 1 October 1954, ANS 1H-73.

184 Labusquiére, Chef de la Section Lèpre, "Compte rendu de tournée partielle effectuée dans certains secteurs et C. M. de la République du Soudan en janvier et mars 1959," 1 May 1959, AIM.

185 Richet, "Quelques notions," 4 July 1958, ANS 1H-63.

186 See for example, "Procès-verbal de la Conference des Ministres de la Santé Publique," 12–14 fevrier 1958; Ministre de Santé Publique en Haute-Volta to Ministre de la Santé Publique de l'AOF, no. 0902, 18 March 1958, ANS 1H-63.

remained influential in Francophone West Africa and directly involved in Bamako's leprosy institute.

Conclusion

Without a conclusive understanding of leprosy's transmission, we cannot properly assess the impact of colonial rule on its incidence in Africa as other historians have for sleeping sickness and tuberculosis.[187] Factors such as diet, living conditions, migration, industrialization, and deforestation play no proven role in transmission. As noted in the Introduction, medical historians still do not understand how leprosy virtually disappeared from Europe centuries before the use of antibiotics. Nor can they explain its continued prevalence in other societies. Colonialism, therefore, did not necessarily spread the disease.

This chapter, however, does reveal that French colonial policies severely limited the treatment of patients, even after the introduction of antibiotics. The principal causes of this overall problem were: an authoritarian approach to healing; a failure to address indigenous attitudes and responses to leprosy; a complete separation of its treatment from regular health services; and the colonial state's limited investment in infrastructure and education.[188] Indeed, six of today's ten most endemic countries in Africa—Mali, Chad, Côte d'Ivoire, Guinea, Madagascar, and Niger—are all former French colonies.[189] In the remaining chapters, we will examine the consequences of these and other factors for the patients themselves.

187　Bado argues that African population displacements during the First World War contributed to the spread of sleeping sickness and leprosy. (Bado, *Médecine coloniale*, 197) While this may have been true for the former, there is no convincing epidemiological evidence for the latter.

188　Ibid., 277 and 290. Bado argues that the leprosy campaign partly failed because colonial policy focused more on economic success rather than improvements in health. He also faults "bureacracy."

189　"Leprosy Will Soon be Eradicated in Africa," L'Agence Panafricaine d'Information (21 April 1996), from http://www.nando.net/pana/.

6

Becoming a Community

Makan Traoré, the very first patient I interviewed, originally left his home in Bafou-labé in the early 1930s. Weary from years of social mistreatment, he traveled to Bamako where "lepers" like himself reportedly received special care. One day, however, "*chasseurs*" (hunters) working for the *toubabs* seized him on the street and brought him to the leprosarium in Bako-Djikoroni on the other side of the Niger River. Subjected to unusually strict surveillance, Makan felt more like a prisoner than a patient. Several months later, in 1934, colonial officials moved him again along with all the other residents back across the river to an entirely new site in the sister village Djikoroni. The *toubabs* called this new site the Institut Central de la Lépre. It was more spacious than the old leprosarium and included several large stone buildings. No longer surrounded by a wall, Makan found his new shelter more accommodating. Djikoroni thereby became his permanent home.[1]

Eleven years later—on August 24, 1945—a large group of the Institute's residents "revolted." The incident began early in the morning when the "able-bodied" patients refused to work and gathered in front of the director's office. When they began protesting the insufficiency of their daily rations and the severity of their labor obligations, Director Laviron ordered them to disperse. Their refusal angered the European doctor who responded by selecting ten protesters for expulsion from the Institute. This act enraged the remaining protesters who then called out the other patients. Within minutes, most (though not all) of the Institute's residents and their children had assembled in the courtyard with their mats, cooking utensils, hoes, and other possessions. They stridently yelled out their threats to leave en masse. Laviron then called in a contingent of gendarmes who drove everyone back to their quarters and took the ten expelled patients to Bamako.[2]

---

1 Makan Traoré, 9 August 1991.

2 I have documented this event with evidence supplied by several informants and a wide variety of written sources. Aldiouma Kassibo, 9–11 January 1993; Bala Diarra, 19 November 1992; Cèmoko Diarra, 20 November 1992; Foni Doumbia, 19 January 1993; Bréma Koulibali, 19 January 1993; Malé Sissoko, 24 February 1993; Chaka Tangara, 18 November 1992; Mori Tangara, 20 January 1993; Makan Traoré, 9 August 1991; Michel Traoré, 17 November 1992; "Diaire," Djikoroni, 24 August 1945, SB; Max Accart, "Rapport sur les incidents survenus à l'ICL les 23 et 24 août 1945," 1 September 1945, ANM 1H-67 FR; and letters submitted by Mamadou Fomba in the name of the patients, 24 and 25 August 1945, ANM 1H-67 FR.

In the eleven years between the arrival of the first patients like Makan and the outbreak of this "revolt," the social meaning of leprosy changed dramatically in Bamako. "Lepers" had been flowing into the colonial capital for several decades, but the Institute accelerated that flow and drew once marginal and dispersed peoples together into a dynamic community capable of collective action. Numbering over four hundred residents by the 1940s, this was the largest and most visible community of its kind in all of French West Africa. Its size and strength contrasted sharply with the smaller enclaves in Catholic missions and other isolation centers scattered around the colonies.

In one sense, the Institut Central de la Lépre exemplified the authoritarian nature of colonial medicine which other historians have similarly demonstrated elsewhere in Africa.[3] European doctors, Catholic nuns, and African staff subjected their patients to controls affecting both body and soul. Conducted in the name of healing, these controls nonetheless advanced the cause of colonialism. They also constituted a new array of "ordering activities" (as discussed in the Introduction) which reinforced leprosy's stigma, albeit in a manner different from the indigenous responses described in Chapters 3 and 4.

In another sense, however, the Institute exemplified the ability of otherwise marginal individuals to coalesce and exert some degree of control over their own lives. Borrowing the words of sociologist Barry Adam, the Introduction referred to this process as the "translation of commonality into community."[4] This colonial enterprise assembled patients in one space where they could discover the "commonality" of their past experiences. As subjects of medical treatment and experimentation, targets for "moral" reform and religious conversion, and objects of colonial domination, patients in Djikoroni underwent an entirely new array of experiences as a group. They thereby forged new bonds which transcended ethnic and regional differences. They intermarried, established families, and learned to use their stigma for "secondary gains."[5] All this occurred because they shared one common attribute: leprosy.

This chapter examines the Institute's historical significance as a locus of colonial authority and patient community. In the context of the preceding chapter, it also provides a sense of how broader developments transpired on a very local level. While specific memories of the Institute's first twenty years of operation, especially the "revolt," fade with the passing of individuals like Makan, their long-term effects on patient identity remain visible today. The remaining three chapters will elaborate that legacy within the larger context of historical changes occurring on the eve of independence and long after.

The Power of Persuasion

When the Institut Central de la Lépre was planned in 1931, French West Africa's director of Health Services, Dr. Sorel, intended it as a hospice, clinic, research center,

3 See Lyons, *The Colonial Disease;* Sadowsky, "Imperial Bedlam"; and Shapiro, "Medicine in the Service of Colonialism." Vaughan notes how leprosy centers in Africa reflected "larger colonial society and systems of control." Vaughan, *Curing Their Ills,* 88.

4 Adam, *The Survival of Domination,* 12.

5 Goffman, *Stigma,* 10.

and administrative headquarters for the colonial leprosy service.[6] Bamako, the capital of the Soudan, lay at the center of all the colonies and was connected to Dakar by railroad. It seemed an appropriate location for a leprosarium of this scale. For the actual site, the Institute's planners selected Djikoroni, a neighboring village directly south of Bamako on the road to Guinea.

The Institute's first patients came from an older makeshift leprosarium on the other side of the river. Many of them had first moved to Bamako on their own to beg or avoid the shame of living with leprosy in their villages. Medical inspectors and the local police then forced them into isolation. More patients were gradually brought in from Côte d'Ivoire, Guinea, Senegal, Niger, and more distant regions of the Soudan.[7] Within the first few years, the population grew from about two hundred to four hundred residents.

The patients themselves came from all walks of life. Many had originated from agrarian communities where medical inspectors first found them. The French army also periodically identified infected individuals among its African recruits or even within already established regiments. One of the Institute's African nurses, Aldiouma Kassibo, was charged with inspecting government functionaries, students, orphanage residents, and employees of European enterprises. Only the most serious or persistent cases ended up in the Institute, while the others received treatment as outpatients at a clinic in Bamako. Even when not severe, leprosy usually destroyed one's chances of ever working in the colonial service or for a European business. Reflecting a common attitude of the time, the Soudan's director of Health Services once bluntly stated, "It is useless to continue giving them [Africans with leprosy] an education which will not assure them any chance of success in local services."[8]

In its early years the Institute attracted only a handful of voluntary patients from Bamako and neighboring areas. The lingering reputation of the old makeshift leprosarium as a miserable place frightened many into hiding whenever the "leper hunters" appeared. Nurse Kassibo often participated in searches and worked through village chiefs to recruit patients.[9] In more distant regions, administrators and doctors also used their political authority to coax villages into sending their lepers to the Institute. Individuals such as Mariame Kouyaté were "caught" (*minè*) by the Europeans (*toubabs*) and driven to Bamako. As the first patients to leave their homes, they often remained frightened until it became clear that the Institute would provide them with food and clothes.[10]

As reported by many patients, fear of capture by *toubab* doctors existed throughout the colony. Residents in Sanankoroba, for example, believed that the *toubabs* threw lepers in the river.[11] Before leaving for the Institute himself, Yusufu Diarra had

6 Dr. Robineau, extract from *Les Grandes Endémies Tropicales*, 19 September 1936, SB C5167/4.

7 "RMA de l'AOF, 1934," CAOM, Aff Pol 383.

8 Chef du Service de Santé to Dir. de l'IM, no. 1.499, 9 December 1938, AIM, Bamako.

9 Aldiouma Kassibo, 9–11 January 1993.

10 Mariame Kouyaté, 18 November 1992. Vaughan argues that "the fight against leprosy' in colonial Africa is not . . . primarily a story of incarceration and segregation" (Vaughan, *Curing Their Ills*, 77). Testimony from former patients in Mali, however, suggests that subtle forms of coercion were used. Colonial records also document varying degrees of forced segregation in other parts of French West Africa. As indicated later, doctors concealed the coercive practices in their public reports.

11 Foni Doumbia, 19 January 1993.

known several people whom doctors had long before taken away by force.[12] Yoro
Boli similarly observed *toubabs* catching patients in his hometown of Nara.[13] In Faladyé, lepers slept in the bush for a night or two whenever health officials passed
through to record their names.[14]

This rounding up of patients in towns and rural areas coincided with other exer-
cises of colonial power, most notably compulsory labor and military recruitment. The
toubabs passed once a year through Séguésono (near Ouéléssébougou) to recruit people for the army as well as to "catch" people with leprosy and sleeping sickness.
Whenever this occurred, Bala Samaké was instructed by his father to hide in the bush
along with four others with the same disease.[15] Cèmoko Diarra was similarly ordered
by elders in Domila (near Kati) to hide in another village if the *toubabs* ever
appeared.[16]

While many patients regarded their recruitment as involuntary, administrators
and doctors believed (or at least pretended) that force was not employed. A 1936
medical journal article by the first director, Dr. Robineau, proudly noted, "The first
innovation of the Service stems from the fact that no coercion is exercised against the
patients admitted to the establishment." [17] The realities of power relationships within
the colonial environment, however, blurred the distinction between force and "persuasion," an ambiguous word chosen by many doctors and administrators to
describe their actions. For example, in January 1940, Bamako's commandant accompanied a team of White Sisters, then working as nurses at the Institute, in their search
for patients who no longer came for their treatments. Already notified by the mayor's
office, the African chiefs for each of Bamako's quarters received the *toubabs* and
assisted them in re-registering their patients.[18]

In theory, the Institute did not hold its patients by force. No wall or fence locked
them in. The expansive grounds consisted of open patient villages, fields, hospital
buildings, laboratories, residences for Europeans, and a special pavilion for "mulat-
tos." On special holidays, patients were allowed to return to their families for a day.[19]
A chaplain visiting from another colony was actually surprised that the Institute permitted its patients to circulate in town.[20] Kassibo noted that, on one occasion, a large
number of residents easily escaped when they learned that seven people had died in
the hospital the previous night. Others left fearing that the *toubabs* burned patients in
the garbage incinerators.[21] Madu Sako, a patient at the time, recalled similar
"escapes" occurring in the early years when the *toubabs* still recruited lepers by

12 Yusufu Diarra, 21 March 1993.
13 Yoro Boli, 28 January 1993.
14 Bernadetti Traoré, 11 March 1993.
15 Bala Samaké, 2 December 1992.
16 Cèmoko Diarra, 20 November 1992.
17 Robineau, extract, SB C5167/4.
18 "Diaire," Djikoroni, 23 January 1940, SB.
19 "Diaire," Djikoroni, 4 March 1936, SB.
20 "Diaire," Djikoroni, 2 June 1941, SB.
21 Kassibo, 9–11 January 1993, 27. The Sisters' diaries for these years document numerous cases of people
    dying for unspecified reasons at the hospital.

force.[22] For a brief period in the late 1930s, patients began leaving when they were unable to receive treatment as a result of an interruption of medical supplies.[23]

In practice, the Institute's directors fostered a martial atmosphere which maintained patient obedience without the use of walls or guards. Nearly all doctors in the colonial service belonged to the military and wore their uniforms on the job; patients addressed them as "colonel" and "commandant." When a number of Institute residents began "escaping" without permission to beg in town, Kassibo and other staff members were obliged to conduct roll call in the mornings and evenings.[24] One old woman in particular found herself rounded up by Institute employees whenever she slipped out to the market to beg.[25] According to several former patients, the doctors also routinely denied leave or cut rations for the "undisciplined" patients or those who failed to report for treatment.

The European staff assumed that, as stigmatized and often poor members of society, lepers had no reason to go elsewhere. It was thought that generous rations and lodgings sufficed to keep patients under control. Reports from this time demonstrate little sympathy for other needs such as family obligations. For example, after learning of his brother's death, one patient named Victor sought permission to return to his village. When the director refused on account of his "contagious" condition, Victor fled on his own.[26] On another occasion, Director Beaudiment complained that many patients gave "a thousand" excuses for leaving while others departed without warning. He attributed their flight to an overconfidence in the "improvements" resulting from their medical treatment. "They are pushed by their restlessness and arrogance to return to parade in their villages with their hoard and new clothes."[27]

The Institute's manner of obtaining and retaining its patients reflects the subtle and not-so subtle ways in which people with leprosy experienced colonial power. In her chapter on leprosariums, Vaughan suggests that "faith in the possibility of a cure . . . brought large numbers of leprosy sufferers into voluntary isolation in 'leper colonies' and 'leper villages' all over Africa."[28] This gradually became the case in the 1940s and 1950s but hardly corresponds to the situation in the 1930s. Official discourse indeed created an illusion of segregation without coercion, but actual practice, as reported by patients themselves, makes it clear that the Institute would never have filled its wards without an initial exercise of colonial authority.

---

22 Madu Sako, 11 November 1992.

23 "RS du SPL, deuxième semestre, 1938," AIM.

24 Kassibo, 9-11 January 1993.

25 "Diaire," Djikoroni, 26 May 1941, SB. Kassibo mentions a strikingly similar case which may actually be the same. Kassibo, 9–11 January 1993.

26 "Diaire," Djikoroni, 14 April 1936, SB.

27 "RS du SPL, deuxième semestre, 1938," AIM.

28 Vaughan, *Curing Their Ills*, 78.

The Medical Mission

As suggested above, the Institute's land and buildings created a physical space in which doctors exercised considerable power. The extent of this power manifested itself most poignantly in the preliminary medical exams performed on newly arrived patients. After registering, both men and women met privately with a *toubab* doctor in a stark white consultation room. According to Nurse Kassibo, patients disrobed and allowed the doctor to inspect their bodies closely, genitals included. They also endured the acute pain caused by the removal of skin tissue samples without anesthesia.[29]

More significantly, the Institute empowered doctors to conduct medical research under the guise of "treatment." Until the 1950s, there was no effective cure for leprosy. The remedies most commonly employed throughout the colonies were chaulmoogra and other hydnocarpus oils imported from French possessions in India and Indochina.[30] Doctors also experimented with a number of other substances in different formats including ethers of gorli (a nut found in Guinea and Côte d'Ivoire), olive, shea, and peanut oils.[31]

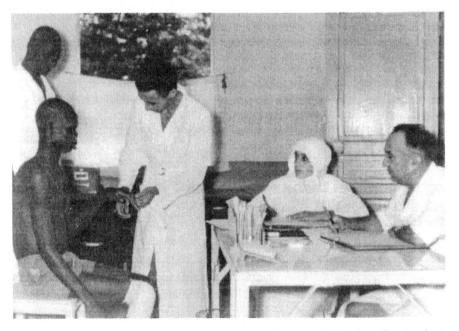

Photo 2: Medical consultation at the Institut Marchoux (ca. 1957). Kassibo stands at left and Laviron sits at desk. Several former patients have identified the seated White Sister as Soeur Agnes. Patient and standing doctor are unidentified. [Photographer unknown, courtesy of the Institut Marchoux]

---

29 Kassibo, 9–11 January 1993.
30 "RMA de Soudan, 1935," ANS 2G-35/22.
31 "RA de la mission à Djikoroni, 1934-35," SB B5167/3.

Most often these substances were injected either intravenously, intradermally, intramuscularly, or in some combination of the three. In one therapy trial, thirty-eight people received weekly injections of tellurite soda (a compound made from an element usually used in metals and ceramics). The patients quickly complained of a nasty odor in addition to nausea, vomiting, and anorexia. Since only two of the thirty-eight reported any kind of improvement, doctors discontinued the experiment.[32] In another trial, injections of xylol (usually used as an antiseptic) gave patients only temporary relief before they suffered relapses. Doctors later tried blue methylene, also an antiseptic which, after much praise, was eventually abandoned because "it [too] hadn't given any improvement."[33]

In general, patients' clinical experiences varied considerably in accordance with the wide range of experimental injections administered during these years. For example, in one study, each member of a group of forty-one people received between twenty and over forty injections of chaulmoogra oil in the course of a month. The report on this experiment indicated that the patients claimed to feel better—"good morale, good appetite, activities are less painful"—but that their lesions were hardly affected. Only 6.6 percent of those receiving less than forty injections and 54.6 percent of those receiving more than forty experienced "improvement." Even those who received sixty injections totaling 700 cc of the solution continued to test positive in their nasal mucous samples (considered the path of contagion). In addition to its costliness and delicate preparation, this form of treatment necessitated daily or, at least, three times a week intravenous injections which proved especially difficult for women and children with less accessible veins. Nearly all patients suffered painful reactions and inflammation.[34] Kassibo observed that, at best, chaulmoogra injections succeeded in removing a few lesions while also generating unpleasant side-effects such as large abscesses.[35] Much praised as a locally available remedy, gorli produced similar "violent local reactions" in which lesions became encrusted with pus and numerous vesicles containing a "thick and yellowish" serum appeared on the skin.[36]

Doctors were well aware of the suffering caused by their experimental treatments, but, assured of a large supply of patients at the Institute, displayed only mild concern. For example, Beaudiment recommended that the chaulmoogra experiment described above continue even though he acknowledged "the repulsion felt by the patients towards the oil."[37] In 1945, after several years of intensive experimentation, the Institute still reported that intradermic gorli injections produced "violent reactions" and little improvement, especially in individuals with numerous large lesions. After repeated resistance by patients, doctors concentrated their efforts on individuals with "few patches."[38] In other words, they treated people most likely to show

32 "RS du SPL, deuxième semestre, 1938," AIM.
33 "RA de la mission à Djikoroni, 1936–37," SB B5167/3.
34 "RS du SPL, deuxième semestre, 1938," AIM.
35 Kassibo, 9–11 January 1993.
36 "RS du SPL, deuxième semestre, 1938," AIM; Kassibo also observed the violence of this reaction. Kassibo, 9–11 January 1993. Bado also mentions these gorli experiments. Bado, *Médecine coloniale*, 339.
37 "RS du SPL, deuxième semestre, 1938," AIM.
38 "RA du SPL, 1945," AIM.

signs of improvement or enjoy the spontaneous remission known to occur in some leprosy cases. The Institute's staff also found patients resistant to other forms of medical intervention. In 1943 a man who was supposed to have part of his foot amputated disappeared during the night.[39] That year the Institute was obliged to temporarily cease surgical operations (amputations in most cases) because the "results were hardly satisfactory and the effects on native morale disastrous."[40]

In secluding a population of nearly four hundred patients, the Institute provided doctors with a degree of sustained clinical power not possible in most other places in the colonies. Patients arrived there having already suffered intense stigma and social isolation in their villages or on Bamako's streets. Many saw nothing malicious in the doctors' treatments which they understood as genuine attempts at healing, however painful or harmful. Through prior experiences with indigenous medical practices such as scarification and purging, many were already accustomed to the discomfort and complications involved with healing. Saran Keita observed that, in the early years, some people died simply because the *toubabs* did not yet know how to use gorli properly. Nonetheless, she was willing to risk her life rather than return to her intolerant village.[41] Doctors were aware that their medicines did not effect permanent cures, but, as Director Laviron noted in 1945, patients considered themselves healed with the slightest disappearance of leprosy patches.[42]

In essence, the Institute represented a harnessing of colonial power to extend medical control and facilitate research. The sleeping sickness campaigns in the Belgian Congo revealed a similar process in which soldiers rounded up patients, and doctors performed lumbar punctures on Africans stretched out on the ground by force.[43] Though controversial by today's ethical standards, the Institute's clinical practices aroused little, if any, concern in the international medical community. Its staff regularly reported their findings in prominent medical journals and contributed to the dialogue on leprosy in recognized forums such as the Fourth International Leprosy Congress (1938) in Cairo. Archival and oral sources do not suggest that the Institute's practices ever approached the level of brutality associated with Nazi doctors then working in concentration camps and mental asylums in Europe. However, the two seemingly unrelated situations reveal a similar pattern of medical power deriving from the state's ability to confine stigmatized patients within a highly controlled physical space.

The Colonial Mission

In the same manner that colonial power facilitated medical intervention, the pretext of healing empowered European staff to colonize their patients in ways not possible elsewhere. As noted in the preceding chapter, French policy derived from perceptions of leprosy as a social as well as medical problem. The administration and local

---

39 "Diaire," Djikoroni, 12 March 1943, SB.
40 "RA de la mission à Djikoroni, 1943–44," SB B5167-3.
41 Saran Keita, 17 May 1993.
42 "RA du SPL, 1945," AIM.
43 Lyons, *The Colonial Disease*, 80 and 84–85.

European populations regarded the free circulation of lepers as unbecoming for their growing towns. In this vein, the Institute's planners and operators sought not just to cure people but to keep them off the streets and transform thoroughly their manner of living. The Institute organized patients into a permanent community over which it exercised considerable social, in addition to clinical, control.

This control lay in the hands of the Institute's European staff, which initially consisted of a director, his assistant, two "auxiliary" doctors, an "auxiliary" pharmacist, and three White Sisters who worked as nurses.[44] The first four directors were military doctors drawn from the African colonial service.[45] Most had some background in leprosy before they arrived, but all developed reputations as specialists from their highly visible positions and through their subsequent publications. They usually maintained close ties to medical schools and research institutes in France and assumed higher posts in the health service upon leaving the Institute. Not knowing any local languages, the directors and other European doctors used their multilingual African employees like Kassibo for communicating with patients and carrying out their orders.

Lacking a real cure for leprosy, the Institute's doctors rationalized social control as a means of healing. The preceding chapter has already noted how colonial officials often attributed the disease's incidence to the African way of life. In the words of one report, prevention of the disease therefore resided "to a large degree in the transformation of the native's living conditions."[46] Director Laviron similarly attributed improvement among his patients to their "regulated life, good food, reduced work."[47] As a corollary to this reasoning, doctors viewed African living habits and thinking as obstacles to recovery. Noting the greater difficulty of treating ulcers on Africans as opposed to Europeans, Director Beaudiment faulted "native negligence" and the custom, despite repeated warnings, of walking without shoes.[48] On another occasion, the Institute staff tried to separate babies from their leprous mothers, a practice then common at leprosariums worldwide.[49] When the Institute first opened, Muslim patients were even forbidden, for "health reasons," from fasting.[50]

All members of the Institute community, including the French doctors and their families, lived on the premises. Much like earlier efforts in Côte d'Ivoire, the Institute contained four residential "villages" designed so that patients could continue "native" life. French planners had even gone out of their way to construct some homes in either Bambara or Senufo style.[51] In an attempt to replicate family life, they arranged huts in clusters of four with a fifth designated for cooking. Residents in each of these villages elected a chief who oversaw the distribution of rations and

44 "RMA de Soudan, 1933," ANS 2G-33/21.
45 The first four directors were Dr. Robineau (1934-36), Dr. Tisseuil (1936-38), Dr. Beaudiment (1938-42), and Dr. Laviron (1942-57).
46 "RS du SPL, premier semestre, 1938," AIM.
47 "RA du SPL, 1945," AIM.
48 "RS du SPL, deuxième semestre, 1940," AIM.
49 "Rapport annuel de la mission à Djikoroni, 1940–41," SB B5167/3.
50 Kassibo, 9–11 January 1993.
51 "La lutte contre la lèpre en AOF," typed on Union Coloniale Française letterhead and found in file of press releases and newspaper clippings, No. 145, November 1934, CAOM, Agences FOM 383.

other supplies and served as an intermediary between patients and staff. The Institute also provided a primary school for younger residents expelled from orphanages and for patients' children.

Except for individuals temporarily placed in the Institute's hospital wards, medical exams and treatment occupied only a fraction of a patient's time. A wide variety of other activities absorbed the remainder. The Institute provided land for people wishing to cultivate crops and also demanded that "able-bodied" patients perform tasks as a form of recompense for the many benefits they received.[52] As was the case at leprosariums throughout Africa, the European staff discouraged idleness among the patients.[53] One inspector congratulated Beaudiment for "utilizing the lepers" through the creation of small industries "adapted to their strength."[54] Every morning women spun cotton thread until 11 a.m. when they began preparing meals. Some individuals such as Saran Keita were engaged in processing medicines. Men assumed tasks like cleaning the Institute grounds, weaving, and, during the war, sewing their own clothes. One of the most demanding jobs involved retrieving building stones from the nearby hills. Some patients, such as Bala Diarra, were engaged as masons and used these stones in the construction of Institute buildings.[55] Those who worked usually received a salary that amounted to only a fraction of wages paid to "healthy" laborers in town.[56] A handful of patients with European educations assumed more advanced responsibilities. Mamadou Fomba, a former schoolteacher, instructed students at the primary school, while Suzanne, a young "mulatto" woman, also worked as a nurse.[57]

The directors' preoccupation with social control manifested itself most clearly in their almost self-contradictory use of expulsion as a means of discipline. As early as 1938, Beaudiment felt that the Institute was losing control over its patient community. In that year the leprosarium reached capacity and began turning new patients away. "One of the troublesome consequences of this absence [of other leprosaria]," Beaudiment wrote,

> is the monopolization of a certain number of places by the extremely irritable, helpless, incurable [patients] who are of no interest for experimentation and whom the Institute cannot remove except little by little in order to avoid troublesome repercussions. . . .

He also complained that the government had no "legal powers" for removing the many lepers then flooding into Bamako. These patients, in his view, came mainly for the Institute's privileges such as free food, clothing, lodging, cinema, and other "distractions." They insisted on receiving treatment as outpatients yet disregarded all recommendations concerning isolation.[58] In 1941, the Institute expelled several "bad characters" in order to improve the overall "mentality" of the others.[59] Once patients

52 "Diaire," Djikoroni, 4 October 1935, SB.

53 Vaughan, *Curing Thier Ills*, 89.

54 "Diaire," Djikoroni, 24 January 1942, SB.

55 Bala Diarra, 19 November 1992.

56 "Diaire," Djikoroni, 10 August 1943, SB.

57 "Diaire," Djikoroni, 23 July 1942, SB.

58 "RS du SPL, premier et deuxiéme semestre, 1938," AIM.

59 "RA de la mission à Djikoroni, 1940–41," SB B5167/3.

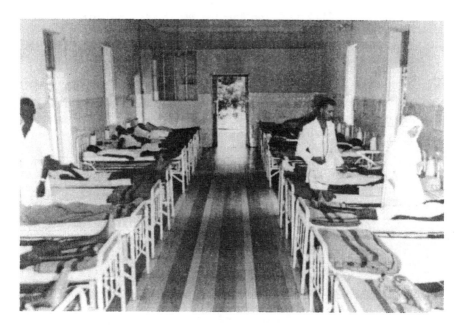

Photo 3: Unidentified nurse, doctor and White Sister, visiting Institute patients (ca. 1957). [Photographer unknown, courtesy of the Institut Marchoux]

began arriving on their own volition and entrenching themselves in the community, the European staff regarded the Institute as a privilege. As demonstrations of their power, the directors restrained patients who wished to leave and expelled those who wanted to stay. This seemed to contradict the policy of isolating lepers, but such was the contrary and, from a patient's point of view, confusing nature of domination.

Of all the European staff, the White Sisters maintained the closest and most regular contact with patients. With limited knowledge of Bambara and Malinké, they also oversaw the patient villages and acted as go-betweens for the other Europeans. Given this privileged role, they sought to expand their Christian community. In the hospital wards the Sisters discreetly raised religious issues with bedridden patients usually on the brink of death. Their perceived success was mixed. In 1934 one badly infected but "very Muslim" woman repeatedly interrupted the conversation whenever it shifted to Catholicism. The attending Sister persisted unsuccessfully until the woman's physical condition suddenly worsened and she became more "accepting." Seemingly more concerned with her success as a missionary than her failure as a nurse, the Sister praised the woman's new "intelligent disposition." "The disease," she wrote, "does its work as well as its grace. This morning she listened to me."[60] Other patients such as Amidou Bair, meanwhile, never accepted even on their

---

60 "Diaire," 5–6 October 1934, SB B 5167/4. For a similar example, see "Diaire," Djikoroni, 15 December 1935, SB.

deathbeds. They died "in error" with only the Sisters' hope that God would have pity on them.[61]

Outside the hospital wards the Sisters engaged in activities including teaching catechism, showing religious films, and paying social visits to residents at their huts.[62] Once in 1941 they purchased cloth and sandals for the patients who were not allowed in European stores.[63] The Sisters also conducted weekly sewing classes for young girls. Like the work details ordered by the directors, the sewing classes were designed to ward off idleness and teach patients or their families useful skills. Beyond those ostensibly practical aims, however, the Sisters used the classes to conduct informal discussions on "morality." On one occasion Beaudiment openly thanked them for "raising the intellectual and moral level of the native woman."[64]

The preceding chapter noted how French administrators and Catholic missionaries often pointed to their medical services as a humanitarian justification for their presence. At the Institute, doctors similarly used their patient community as a showpiece for the colonial and medical enterprises. The Leprosy Service's 1935 annual report, for example, proudly stated, "A number of French and foreign visitors, on official missions, or tourists passing through Bamako, are received at the Leprosy Institute and contribute to our publicity." A documentary film about the Institute then circulating in France also advanced this objective.[65] Visitors ranged from curious journalists and writers to countless missionaries received by the Sisters.[66]

As a colonial showpiece, the Institute brought patients face to face with some of the highest officials at the time. Over the years, it became a standard stop for government delegations passing through Bamako. In April 1937 the patients and staff assembled on the Institute grounds to receive the minister of colonies, governor, and director of Health Services. The French tricolor decorated all the buildings and grand festivities ensued. Mamadou Fomba, the school instructor, delivered a speech in which he "translated the gratitude of all the patients."[67] In 1943 all the patients lined up on the "avenue" to welcome still again the governor general from Dakar. Director Laviron selected a very "mutilated" newlywed couple to greet the guest personally and perform a dance to demonstrate their unweakened spirit.[68]

The greatest publicity for the Institute came in the form of a feature film called *L'Homme du Niger* which opened at the Olympia Theater in Paris in the autumn of 1939.[69] The film recounted the fictional story of a colonial engineer working on the Markala Dam. After contracting leprosy, the engineer disguises himself as a Tuareg,

61 "Diaire," Djikoroni, 20 April 1936, SB.

62 "Diaire," Djikoroni, 13 October 1935, SB; "RA de la mission à Djikoroni, 1934–35," SB B5167/3.

63 "RA de la mission à Djikoroni, 1939–40," and for 1941–42 and 1942–43, SB B5167/3.

64 "Diaire," Djikoroni, 15 June 1935 and 3 November 1941, SB.

65 "RA de l'ICL, 1935," ANS 2G-35/118.

66 "Diaire," Djikoroni, 4 January 1938, SB.

67 "Diaire," Djikoroni, 18 April 1937, 21 July 1937, 28 March 1938, SB.

68 "Diaire," Djikoroni, 19 August 1943, SB.

69 Riovalen to Beaudiment, 7 November 1939, AIM. Video recording of film in author's possession.

goes into hiding, and receives secret treatment from the Institute's charitable doctor. Parts of the film were shot on the actual Institute grounds and, more importantly, several scenes feature real patients. In short, the portrayal of the Institute in *L'Homme du Niger* reinforced for *métropole* audiences the importance of France's colonial power in the fight against Africa's exotic diseases.

By taking people off the street or out of their villages and placing them in the Institute, the European staff asserted control which extended far beyond the clinical sphere. Providing food, housing, and fields in addition to care empowered the staff to enlist patients for work details and subject them to their "moral" influences. On the streets, lepers constituted an embarrassment to the achievements of colonialism. On the grounds of a well-organized Institute, they became a showpiece of its success. In this way, the Institute exemplified the power of colonialism to advance medical control and the power of medicine to return the favor.

A Community in Revolt

The revolt described at the beginning of this chapter exposed the inseparability of medical and colonial power but also revealed the capacity of patients to resist it. Though originally coerced to leave their villages, most patients did not want to return once they had settled at the Institute. Whatever hardships they endured there could not compare to the stigma and social isolation suffered at home. Their protest expressed a desire for greater control rather than, as had always been possible, escape. For this reason, it focused specifically on rations and work, two loci of the Institute's power over patients.

For most of its history, the Institute's success in retaining patients depended on its provision of rations. The European staff considered free food a privilege, but the patients saw it as a right which came with living under the direct tutelage of *toubabs*. Once, during the first years of operation, Director Robineau reduced rations at a moment when millet in the market was especially expensive. In response, "all the lepers nearly made a small revolution." "In their home [villages]," one White Sister observed, "they are far from having as much [food as they do here], but they believe that this is owed to them."[70] The Institute's European staff, particularly Laviron, also used their control over rations to discipline patients who failed to report for medical treatments or who were found begging in Bamako.[71]

In mid-1945, as a result of the war, Laviron reduced patient rations by substituting unthreshed for threshed rice.[72] Around the same time, patients engaged in retrieving stones had begun to complain of fatigue, especially when they had to walk out to the hills rather than ride by car. On August 16, eight days before the open protest, Mamadou Fomba, the school instructor, expressed the patients' grievances in a letter to a colonial administrator in Dakar. The letter stated that Laviron imposed the strenuous work details as a "pretext for organization and for camouflaging his hate

70 Random notes by Sister Marie de Pontamain, undated but probably late 1930s, SB D5167/5.
71 Kassibo, 9–11 January 1993.
72 "RA du SPL, 1943," AIM.

for his patients and his inability to manage such a big institution."[73] On the eve of the revolt, several other patients asked Kassibo to request a work exemption and inform Laviron of their inability to feed themselves with the new rations. When informed of the request, Laviron immediately berated Kassibo for challenging the director's judgment and authority.[74]

Immediately after the demonstration, both Fomba and Mamadou Diakité (a patient-nurse) submitted three more letters of complaint on behalf of the patients to the governor. In addition to the insufficient rations, they decried Laviron's severity and unfairness. A letter dated the 24th read, "We work too hard (nine hours a day) and we are badly paid 25 [francs] a month! Even more, they distribute [sic] to us kicks and punches like donkeys! This is a prison! We demand to leave!"[75] Another letter blamed Laviron for firing Fomba from the school in 1943 and, more recently, for cutting Diakité's salary.

Kassibo attributed the revolt directly to the excessively hard work for which patients received meager compensation. Their expulsion merely provoked the rest of the community to support them.[76] A government investigator sent by Bamako's commandant similarly observed that patient-workers initiated the protest, but, unlike Kassibo, he described their complaints as exaggerated. Citing their "demanding spirit," he reported that most of the patients had been there for over five years and "considered the living compounds their own property and all the other advantages their right." "Many remember the good old days when the Institute opened and [they] inform the new arrivals of those times. Everyone considers himself wronged." Out of sixty-seven designated laborers, only about thirty ever reported to their jobs. The crew of thirty-four gardeners tended to sit around in small groups and the weavers produced very little. The investigator believed that such laziness did not justify larger rations. Following Laviron's "medical opinion," he declared the food allotment sufficient and attributed the patients' unanimous complaints to the simple fact that their rations had once been greater.[77]

To underplay the larger political significance of the revolt, the investigator accused Fomba and Diakité of manipulating patient discontent in order to satisfy their own personal spite against Laviron.[78] The transcripts of their interrogations suggest that the questioning was intended as much for reinforcing and brandishing colonial power as it was for collecting information. In his testimony, Fomba revealed a clear personal dislike of Laviron and claimed to represent the views of the other patients. He accused the director of being "against him" and orchestrating his dismissal from the school by informing the education administration of his "contagiousness." Responding to several more aggressive questions, Fomba explained how, since

73 Fomba to Haut Commissaire de l'AOF Française à Dakar, 16 August 1945, ANM 1H-67 FR.

74 Kassibo, 9–11 January 1993.

75 "Une Révolte des Malades," [signature illegible, but Fomba later admitted that Diakité wrote the letter for him], 25 August 1945, ANM 1H-67 FR.

76 Kassibo, 9-11 January 1993.

77 Accart, "Rapport ," ANM 1H-67 FR.

78 Ibid. Also Procès-Verbal, with Mamadou Fomba, 29 August 1945; and Procès-Verbal, with Mamadou Diakité, 30 August 1945, ANM 1H-67 FR.

1940, he had to pay for his rations and construct his lodging without material or labor assistance from the Institute.

In the course of his questioning, Diakité admitted writing two of the letters for Fomba. Digressing with, perhaps, the intent of intimidation, the investigator then informed him of the regulation requiring all "public writers" to include their names on whatever they write. Diakité claimed to know nothing about the regulation. The questioning then shifted to Diakité's role in the events. "Do you consider yourself to be associated with Mamadou Fomba in the complaints and denunciations against your director?"

"I only served as writer."

"You are here as an auxiliary agent normally paid and are under the orders of the Médecin Commandant [Laviron]. Didn't you think that it was your duty to inform your chief of the request made of you by Mamadou Fomba?"

"I should have done it. If I didn't do it, it is because the Médecin Commandant suspended [sic] the salary which I had been receiving before."[79]

The investigator's manner of questioning and his subsequent report emphasized the "personal" nature of the conflict while ignoring evidence of Laviron's abuse of medical and colonial power over patients. By all accounts—those of former patients, Kassibo, and the Sisters—Laviron was a severe man fixated on discipline and order. This fixation exacerbated a number of tensions already developed under two previous directors. As Kassibo observed, in this era of "total colonialism," both Robineau and Beaudiment had maintained the "fixed line" separating Africans and Europeans.[80] Most patients noted Laviron's preoccupation with control: the slightest disorder, such as an unclean path or an absence from treatment, made him frightfully angry. Expressing a sentiment held by many other patients from that time, both Bala Diarra and Jean-Marie Kamara described Laviron's rules and orders as "mean spirited" (*ka farin*).[81]

The investigator's report also conspicuously underplayed the status of Institute residents as physically ill persons in need of medical treatment and as stigmatized individuals in need of social rehabilitation. In many ways, Fomba's life embodied the tragedy of being both a leper and an African colonial subject at the Institute. The investigator, however, mentioned none of the following details which might have better explained his discontent to other administrators.

Originally from Banamba, Fomba worked as a schoolteacher at posts in Sikasso and Bougouni.[82] His first leprosy patches appeared around the time he began considering marriage. Initially, a doctor granted him six months leave for treatment, but after showing no signs of recovery, Fomba moved to the newly opened Institute in Djikoroni. There he quickly became the school's director as well as the *chef de canton* for all four patient villages.

According to a French journalist who met him in 1935, the thirty-five-year-old Fomba suffered "from his insertion between the whites whom he understands, but with whom he cannot have relations, and the blacks, his brothers in misery, too far from him [in terms of] their brains." Teaching cheered him considerably but he suffered

79 Procès-Verbal, with Mamadou Diakité, ANM 1H-67 FR.

80 Kassibo, 9–11 January 1993.

81 Bala Diarra, 19 November 1992; Jean-Marie Kamara, 9 July 1993.

82 "Décision," found in Bamako correspondence folder, 1927, ANM 1H-75 FR.

"more than the other patients and [spends] hours in profound despair, because he knows that he will never find again the face of his youthful years and will exercise his profession [only] with difficulty elsewhere." Fomba was "forced to renounce forever the normal life which he had so well earned [for himself]. He continues, nevertheless, to courageously serve his country, our country."[83]

The Sisters described Fomba in less flattering words. In her report of a visit to the Institute in 1938, Sister Andrée-Marie singled him out as an example of the "fanatic Muslim" patients who happened to be educated. She noted his despondent though intelligent personality and said that the Sisters first found him "unapproachable and even hostile." After a few years, he supposedly grew to admire "the goodness, and serenity" of the missionaries whom he found different from other "whites." The Sisters hoped that he, the African nurses, and other évolués would eventually convert to Christianity.[84] However, when a visiting school inspector called for Fomba's early retirement from his post as director and teacher, the Sisters "rejoiced." He was replaced by Raymond, a prominent Catholic patient closely involved with the mission.[85]

By 1945 Fomba had greatly suffered physically and emotionally. Five years earlier he had been partially blinded from keratitis for which he underwent a series of injections of mercury cyanide and another series of "hydrocotyle," a substance whose effects were questioned even by the doctors who administered it.[86] His dictation of letters to Diakité suggests that he had also lost the use of his hands. Kassibo observed that Fomba was very jealous of his healthy wife, especially when she fraternized with young African staff members. She eventually left him at an unspecified time before the revolt.[87]

The absence of these biographical details in the investigator's report reveal the level of indifference towards the physical and social hardships experienced by leprosy patients in those times. In addition to the report, the final actions taken against Fomba and the other "ringleaders" demonstrated a disregard for the medical needs for which the Institute was originally intended to satisfy. After the revolt, Fomba spent his last days in custody at the Institute while he awaited completion of an unrelated legal matter. Laviron asked the governor of Soudan to expedite his case so that he could send Fomba back to his village. The stern director exercised his authority over the rebellious patient to the very end: "the grave state of his illness does not permit me to allow him to roam about in town."[88]

Meanwhile, the director general of public health sent a letter to Laviron commending him for handling the events with "calm." Seemingly aware of the doctor's penchant for excess, however, the director general also requested that Laviron, in accordance with his "medical and human" spirit, not pursue judicial retribution for the two patients (presumably Fomba and Diakité) whom he was

83 Dr. Claude Tery-Tranin, "Un Bel effort français," hand-typed but found in a folder with press releases and other news clippings, [undated but probably 1935 or 1936], CAOM Agences FOM 383.

84 Djikoroni Visit Report, 1938, SB B5167/1.

85 "Diaire," Djikoroni, 5 September 1943, SB.

86 "RS du SPL, deuxième semestre, 1940," AIM.

87 Kassibo, 9–11 January 1993.

88 Laviron to Gouverneur du Soudan, no. 672, 28 September 1945, ANM 1H-67 FR.

incriminating. "The reprehensible deeds for which they are reproached can be attributed, for a large part, to the special mental state resulting indirectly from their disease."[89] According to Kassibo and other patients, Fomba eventually returned to the Ségou region and was never seen in Djikoroni again. The nine other "ring-leaders" were also expelled as Laviron originally planned. An Institute vehicle discharged them on the different roads leading towards their respective villages.[90]

The little-known revolt at the Institute occurred at a moment when direct and active challenges to French authority were becoming more visible throughout the colonies. After the Second World War, the contradictions between France's fight for liberty in Europe (in which Africans directly participated) and its oppressive colonial policies in Africa inspired more overt demands for change. The 1944 Brazzaville Conference therefore dismantled some of the most hated excesses of colonial rule such as the *indigénat* legal code which permitted an unjust judicial system, tax collection, forced labor, and military conscription. At the end of that same year, about 1,280 African former prisoners of war mutinied at their Thiaroye barracks near Dakar.[91] The war had significantly weakened France's authority and motivated Africans to confront it directly. Although the Sisters viewed the patient revolt as a "reappearance of the communist spirit," none of the evidence suggests that it received inspiration, direction, or support from any centrally organized "resistance" movement outside the Institute.[92] In that sense, it was a purely internal affair. However, the colonial and racial relationships which gave rise to the conflict were hardly different from those at work in the Thiaroye mutiny.

The investigator's report painted the event as a circumstantial friction between "personalities." In reducing political agency to individual acts of self-advancement, revenge, and even dementia, it ignored the existence of larger and no less real problems and issues. According to the transcript of their testimonies, Fomba and Diakité themselves admitted that personal grudges against Laviron partly motivated their actions. Kassibo's account further corroborates this. However, personality conflict does not explain how most of the other patients also readily mobilized themselves against Laviron. The director's position as a military officer and an agent of the state combined with his role as a doctor gave him an unusual amount of power, even within the colonial context, to control other people's lives. The patients' position as both colonial subjects and victims of leprosy made them especially vulnerable, though not totally helpless, before this power.

Though sparked by a rivalry between particular individuals, the revolt nonetheless belonged to a larger global pattern of leprosy patients collectively resisting the institutions which dominated their lives. Similar protests and disturbances occurred at isolation centers in British East and Southern Africa between the 1920s and 1950s.[93] In 1936, between 100 and 150 lepers escaped from the Tichilesti Hospital in Bucharest.

---

89 Dir. Gén. de la Santé Publique to Laviron, no. 261, 22 September 1945, ANM 1H-67 FR.

90 Bala Diarra, 19 November 1992.

91 Myron Echenberg, "Tragedy at Thiaroye: The Senegalese Soldiers' Uprising of 1944," in R. Cohen, J. Copans, and P. Gutkind, eds., *African Labor History* (Beverly Hills: Sage Publications, 1978).

92 "Diaire," Djikoroni, 24 August 1945, SB.

93 Vaughan, *Curing Their Ills*, 86–87.

According to one report from the time, "townspeople, horrified at the gruesome sight, rapidly quitted the streets and barricaded themselves in shops and houses." The lepers marched to Town Hall and demanded more food before being "herded" back to the hospital by police.[94] In 1937, several hundred patients at the San Lazaro Hospital in Manila "overpowered" the hospital guard, "paraded" through the streets for several hours, and finally marched to the palace where the presidential secretary met with them. Their protests included complaints that people with tuberculosis, a far more contagious disease than leprosy in their view, were allowed to "run loose" while they as lepers were held as prisoners. The police arrested eleven protesters and "herded" the rest back to the hospital.[95] That same year, about eleven hundred patients at an island leprosarium in Japan beat the police superintendent assigned to guard them and launched a hunger strike to demand "better pay, self-government, and the dismissal of the superintendent."[96] In the context of these strikingly similar patient protests, the revolt in Djikoroni represented as much a challenge to excessive medical control as it was a response to abusive colonial authority.

Conclusion

When asked to explain why they remained in Djikoroni, many former Institute patients consulted for this study replied, *"Yan, an bé kelen."* (Here we are one.) This expression articulated a sense of community which contrasted with the shame and alienation experienced in their villages. The precise meaning of this community varied among them and changed over time. Some individuals such as Saran Keita did not participate in the revolt, but nonetheless shared deep ties with other patients (in Saran's case, most notably her husband). Through this community, patients also became directly involved in the broader historical developments of their day. The following chapters examine the continuation of this phenomenon through the last years of colonial rule and long after independence.

---

94 "Lepers Escape and Hold Town at Bay," *Leprosy Review* 7, 3 (1936): 127.

95 "Lepers Get Free March in Manila," *Leprosy Review* 8, 1 (1937): 48.

96 "Lepers on Strike in Japan," *Leprosy Review* 8, 1 (1937): 48.

7

Healing and Politics

The previous chapter illustrated tight connections between the identities of leprosy patients and the institution responsible for their care. In the late colonial and post-colonial periods, this and other leprosy control institutions changed in ways with profound implications for those identities. The changes resulted in part from the specific changes in policy and technology described in Chapter 5. They also resulted from concurrent political struggles affecting all of society.

In August 1958, Dr. Jean Languillon, the new director of the Institut Marchoux (formerly the Institut Central de la Lèpre), met with two labor unions to discuss his proposed dismissal of several nurses.[1] When the unions demanded that he also dismiss the White Sisters, Languillon stormed out, threatening to resign if this ever happened. Aldiouma Kassibo represented the union for Assistance Médicale Africaine (formerly AMI). He and his counterpart for SGHMP responded to Languillon's outburst with a written complaint accusing the missionaries of proselytizing on the job and privileging Christian patients over others. Their complaint also described Languillon's comportment as "brutal and racist," because he often insulted African personnel in front of patients. Languillon "reigns like a despot over the Africans while . . . the Europeans abusively use the vehicles and gas belonging to the service [the Institute]."[2]

Two days later Languillon intercepted a copy of the complaint which Kassibo had submitted for publication in the African newspaper *Barakela* ("The Worker"). Some of the Sisters believed that their African colleague was more interested in provoking his boss than actually driving them out of the Institute. Nonetheless, they notified the head of Bamako's Catholic mission who then beseeched a *Barakela* editor to prevent its publication "at any cost."[3] When Mali became independent in 1960, one Sister still resented Kassibo for "shooting them in the back" while pretending to be friends. She described him as a "fanatical Muslim" who tried to force patients into his own religion as soon as they entered the Institute.[4] Kassibo had meanwhile become

---

1 Emile Marchoux had been a well-known colonial doctor who worked extensively on leprosy between 1908 and his death in 1943. Bado, *Médecine coloniale*, 221.

2 Aldiouma Kassibo and Mohamed Balla Niambélé, Comité d'Entente des Syndicats du SGHMP et de l'AMA du Soudan, "Motion," 11 August 1958 [attached to "Rapport de visite de Djikoroni, 6 août 1960"], SB C 5167/1.

3 "Diaire," Djikoroni, 13 August 1958, SB.

4 Sr. M. Nathanael, "Rapport de visite de Djikoroni, 6 août 1960," SB C 5167/1.

head of Djikoroni's branch of the ruling Union Soudanaise-Rassemblement Democratique Africain (US-RDA) party and apparently no longer resisted their presence. The Catholic order ended up surviving the transition to independence and remained a part of the Institute for another thirty years.

These seemingly local tensions between the Institute's African and European staff reflected the effects of larger political developments on the delivery of health care in the twilight of colonial rule. As revealed in earlier chapters, medical institutions served a variety of political and ideological purposes for both colonial administrators and Catholic missionaries. Hospitals and dispensaries demonstrated European civilization and altruism while simultaneously facilitating social control. The act of caring and treating placed the White Sisters in direct contact with people whom they could then target for conversion.

African staff also gradually learned how to use their positions in medical institutions for non-therapeutic ends. As with other government employees, their education and daily contact with Europeans heightened their awareness of colonial injustices such as racial discrimination. The dependence of colonial agencies on their labor empowered them to challenge the government directly through strikes. These agencies also provided African employees with an expansive network for coordinating political activity across French West Africa. After independence, their positions gradually became a means for preserving their fragile socioeconomic status in Malian society. The limited infrastructure inherited from colonial rule and the steady deterioration of Mali's economy severely undermined what remained of their therapeutic utility.

The enduring non-therapeutic dimension of health care described in this chapter has profoundly shaped patient experiences to this day. Much like soldiers in a battlefield, Djikoroni's leprosy patients became pawns in the political struggles between their healers. Their marginal social positions facilitated manipulation and exploitation which changed over time but rested on the same foundation of medical authority. In the 1950s the Sisters and politically active Muslims entangled patients in a religious rivalry which represented a larger contest between colonizers and colonized, whites and blacks. Independence ultimately served the interests of government workers who suffered most directly from colonial and racial subjugation. From the 1960s onward, these workers constituted a privileged but always threatened class which occasionally profited from resources explicitly intended for patients. This development partly reflected a more widespread trend in which health systems in Africa ultimately served the interests of "dominant groups."[5] The final two chapters of this book reveal how this mix of neglect and exploitation, like so many other "ordering activities," deepened the sense of social isolation among Mali's lepers.

Religious Struggles

As exemplified by the nineteenth-century Muslim states led by Umar Tall and Shehu Amadu, political and economic affairs in precolonial Mali often played out within a religious framework. French military officers and administrators partly established their

---

5 Judith Lasker, "The Role of Health Services in Colonial Rule: The Case of the Ivory Coast," *Culture, Medicine, and Psychiatry* 1 (1977): 277–97.

authority by manipulating this framework.[6] When it appeared necessary, they selectively supported Islamic institutions and activities. This policy often impeded the efforts of Catholic missionaries whom the government appreciated as cultural emissaries but also disliked as a threat to its delicate entente with Muslim leaders. The contradictory relationship between administrators and missionaries manifested itself quite clearly in the domain of health.[7] In spite of the Secularization Law (*Loi de Laicization*), officials frequently donated government money to mission dispensaries and, more notably, employed Sisters at the Institute. Since many Malians interpreted this as tacit support of mission activities, their challenges to colonial authority within the Institute often involved religion.

From the moment of their arrival at the Institute in 1934, the Sisters were conscious of their potentially controversial dual role as nurses and missionaries. One "inspector" from the parent mission in Bamako advised them to be "prudent" in regards to "religious relations" with the patients and African staff who were overwhelmingly Muslim.[8] In spite of this and other warnings, however, the Sisters remained relatively uninhibited in actively promoting their religion. Their diary for those early years contains many entries documenting aggressive attempts at conversion, some of which the previous chapter describes.

Though exaggerated, the Sisters' diaries and reports reveal that patients and staff often resented bedside proselytizing. Muslim patients were said to divert new converts from the "path" while relations with the African staff were described as "not always supple nor polite."[9] One "hostile" Muslim nurse in particular interfered with the religious instruction of patients until his dismissal in 1942.[10] The school director who succeeded Mamadou Fomba similarly opposed the Sisters' offer to show their films and documentaries to students.[11] Even patients who initially agreed to "listen" often withdrew, especially when they became preoccupied with their own survival.[12] The desperate emotional and physical condition of most converts suggests that healthier patients remained ambivalent towards the Sisters' religious efforts. The mission's 1943–44 Annual Report, for example, documented its success by noting proudly that twenty-three out of twenty-five adults allowed the Sisters to "regenerate" them before dying.[13]

In 1948 the Sisters estimated that a tenth of the four to five hundred patients were either Christian or catechumen.[14] Seven years later the number remained about the same.[15] Only those confronted with imminent death tended to adhere and, at times,

---

6 Stephen Harmon, "The Expansion of Islam Among the Bambara Under French Rule: 1890 to 1940" (Ph.D. dissertation, University of California, Los Angeles, 1988).

7 For a full account of relations between missionaries and the colonial administration, see Joseph-Roger de Benoist, *Eglise et pouvoir colonial au Soudan Français: Les relations entre les administrateurs et les missionaires catholiques dans la Boucle du Niger, de 1885 à 1945* (Paris: Editions Karthala, 1987).

8 "Rapport de visite de Djikoroni, 1934," SB B 5167/1.

9 "Rapport annuel de la Mission à Djikoroni [hereafter RAMD], 1943–44," SB B 5167/3; "Rapport de visite de Djikoroni, 1938," SB B 5167/1.

10 "RAMD, 1941–42," SB B 5167/3.

11 "RAMD, 1955–56," SB B 5167/3.

12 "Diaire," Djikoroni, 5–6 October 1934, SB B 5167/4. For a similar example, see "Diaire," Djikoroni, 15 December 1935, SB 5167/4

13 "RAMD, 1943–44," SB B 5167/3.

14 "RAMD 1947–48," SB B 5167/3.

15 "RAMD, 1954–55," SB B 5167/3.

even they were hard to approach. The Sisters blamed the "Islamic environment" for hindering their converts' perseverance and suspected that some of the more "fanatical" Muslims warned patients against Catholicism before entering the Institute.[16] In 1953 the Muslim community erected two mosques with Koranic schools on the other side of the road to accommodate the growing number of former patients and other non-leprous migrants. A marabout had also begun visiting the hospital to spend time at the sides of the very sick.[17]

The Sisters interpreted such activities as direct challenges to their own efforts. Alleging that marabouts bribed or even menaced non-Muslims into converting, they visited new patients immediately to capitalize on any potential interest in the Christian "path."[18] Once, after losing five patient converts, they accused Djikoroni's marabouts of employing a "discourse of lies and promises of an easy life" in order to extinguish the "flame of their faith."[19] Becoming a Muslim, in their view, took "little effort": "shave the head, take a Muslim name, and say a prayer."[20] When two more of their "best" converts apparently went mad, the Sisters denounced the Muslims for using the tragedy as a demonstration of what would happen to others if they too converted.[21] They also accused the nurse who registered new patients of threatening them with expulsion if they dared become Christian.[22]

Confronted with such opposition, the Sisters repeatedly devised new ways of communicating their messages or elevating their status within the community. Ever since the Institute opened, they had organized sewing lessons as a pretext for "moral discussions" with girls and young women whom they hoped to prepare for marriage.[23] To "access" the families of African employees, they often received non-leprous children and wives as patients for medical consultations conducted on the side.[24] In 1956 the missionaries opened a small library for the nurses and hoped that it would help "propagate Christian morality."[25] Recognizing that most Muslims mistrusted them, the Sisters also invited their rivals to "study circles" in which they were free to discuss whatever topics they chose: "Indochina, leprosy, evolution of French civilization, the riches and beauty of France."[26] When a Dominican Father passed through and recommended using local folklore to excite more interest in their teachings, they enlisted the help of Amadou Hampate Ba, an eminent African historian. "Although a Muslim himself," Hampate Ba proved to be "sincerely interested in raising the spiritual level of Africans." He agreed to provide the Sisters with some appropriate material.[27]

---

16 "RAMD, 1947–48," SB B 5167/3.

17 "RAMD, 1953–54," SB B 5167/3.

18 "RAMD, 1954–55," SB B 5167/3.

19 "RAMD, 1956–57," SB B 5167/3.

20 "RAMD, 1955–56," SB B 5167/3.

21 "RAMD, 1955–56," SB B 5167/3.

22 "RAMD, 1956–57," SB B 5167/3.

23 Sr. M. Annonciata, "Lettre de visite aux soeurs," 28 June 1952, SB B 5167/1.

24 "RAMD, 1941–42," SB B 5167/3.

25 "RAMD, 1956–57," SB B 5167/3.

26 "RAMD, 1954–55," SB B 5167/3.

27 "RAMD, 1956–57," SB B 5167/3.

The Sisters also wanted their small community to assume some responsibility for attracting more converts on its own. In 1954 a group of Christians organized "processional demonstrations" to display their religiosity publicly.[28] Within a year they formed a "legion" for the purpose of "demonstrating their faith outside." The legion saved enough money for a Christmas party in which members provided musical entertainment and distributed kola nuts and cigarettes to all the patients at the Institute.[29] Noting the importance of the "legionnaires," one mission report stated, "When a patient enters the Institute, it is necessary to attract him before the Muslims are able to take him in their nets."[30]

In the twenty-six years between the Institute's opening and Malian independence, the Sisters read their successes in rather modest and often contradictory signs. For example, the same 1938 report which described relations with African nurses as "not always supple nor polite" also noted, in another section, that the staff was "perfectly respectful and correct."[31] A 1950 report attributed a slight improvement in relations with Muslims to parties thrown for Easter and Christmas.[32] The Sisters similarly rejoiced when Muslims attended midnight mass for the first time in 1953. "Fortunately," one Sister commented, "there are no mosques so far in the village of the Institute, although for the first time patients gather several times a day for prayer."[33]

On the eve of independence, however, it became clear that the mission would never attract enough converts to rival the strength and influence of the Muslim community. In 1958 only eight members—all male—remained in the legion.[34] That same year the director of the *Presse Divine*, a Muslim newspaper, began a collection for constructing a mosque on the Institute grounds; it opened in 1959 much to the Sisters' dismay.[35] The Sisters also now found it impossible to "lead" new or dying patients to God. Whenever they attempted to give "summary instruction" sufficient for baptism, patients turned their heads and explained that they were Muslim. One member of the mission believed that Muslims had pressured them to say this regardless of its veracity. Another Sister accused Djikoroni's "Grand Marabout" of sending his acolytes into the hospital to threaten people with improper burial if they did not participate in Muslim prayer.[36]

As suggested by Kassibo's letter mentioned at the beginning of this chapter, African patients and staff particularly resented the Sisters for receiving tacit support from the European doctors. For example, their 1940–41 Annual Report noted how Director Beaudiment "likes the natives in general, but looks to favor the Christians." When a Christian mulatto patient died, Beaudiment ordered that every Christian grave in the cemetery be marked with a tombstone to distinguish

---

28   "RAMD, 1954–55," SB B 5167/3.
29   "RAMD, 1955–56," SB B 5167/3.
30   "RAMD, 1957–58," SB B 5167/3.
31   "Rapport de visite de Djikoroni, 1938," SB B 5167/1.
32   "RAMD, 1950–51," SB B 5167/3.
33   "RAMD, 1953–54," SB B 5167/3.
34   "Rapport de visite de Djikoroni, 5 décembre 1958," SB B 5167/3.
35   "RAMD, 1958–59," SB B 5167/3.
36   Sr. M. Nathanael, "Rapport de visite de Djikoroni, 6 août 1960," SB C 5167/1.

it from Muslim graves.[37] In a similar demonstration of favoritism, Director Laviron allowed the Sisters to conduct catechism during work hours and expelled one patient accused of "terrorizing" a woman considering conversion.[38] When the Sisters suspected the above-mentioned nurse of threatening converted patients with expulsion, they appealed to one of the French doctors for his dismissal.[39] The marabout who had been visiting patients in the hospital was similarly expelled.[40]

The most apparent display of the Institute's sympathies for the mission occurred in 1956 when Muslim landlords in Djikoroni reportedly requested that their Christian tenants either convert to Islam or leave. This continued for two years until, after repeated protests, several Christians obtained from the Institute a small piece of land adjacent to the church. Ironically, the Christian patient who had farmed this plot for years initially refused to relinquish it until Laviron intervened on behalf of the other Christians. All those "threatened with expulsion [from their residences] because of their religion" were then allowed to build their own homes in this area.[41] In the eyes of most patients and staff, such initiatives exemplified the Institute's collaboration with the Catholic mission.

In their preoccupation with conversion and creating a Christian community, the Sisters clearly overstepped the bounds of narrowly defined clinical therapy for which the Institute had hired them. Muslim patients, staff, and other community members sought to contain these ideologically-minded activities by promoting their own religion. In this way, the Institute became as much a forum for larger political struggles as it was a place of healing. The medical institution swept leprosy patients from the margins of society and transformed them into pawns at the center of those struggles.

Political Struggles

The Institute and other leprosy programs began as instruments of colonial authority. They enabled urban administrators and colonial doctors to isolate leprosy patients and gave missionaries easy access to potential converts. Over time African employees learned how to use these same institutions for the advancement of their own interests. As in other government agencies, direct contact with Europeans placed health care workers in a unique situation which subjected them to colonial domination on a daily basis but also positioned them well to resist it. They emerged at independence as a new class of government functionaries who, like the Sisters, used their special positions for non-therapeutic ends.

As described by Nurse Kassibo and others who worked in the colonial administration, subjugation characterized their relationships with most of their European colleagues and superiors. From the moment of conquest to the end of the Second

---

37 "RAMD, 1940–41," SB B 5167/3.
38 "RAMD, 1942–43," and for 1943–44, SB B 5167/3.
39 "RAMD, 1956–57," SB B 5167/3.
40 "RAMD, 1954–55," SB B 5167/3.
41 "RAMD, 1956–57," SB B 5167/3; "Rapport de visite de Djikoroni, 1958," SB B 5167/1; Jean Marie Kamara, 9 July 1993.

Photo 4:   Aldiouma Kassibo (1993) [Photograph by Eric Silla]

World War, the French government provided Africans with few opportunities to educate themselves sufficiently for high-level positions within its agencies.[42] In the Health Service, Africans were restricted to "auxiliary" positions. The Ecole de Médecine de Dakar opened just after the First World War and, as of 1936, had trained hardly more than one hundred *médecins auxiliaires* (doctor's assistants) for all of French West Africa.[43] A 1932 report suggests that many officials in the administration deliberately kept Africans in inferior positions. Since the end of the First World War, a staff shortage had limited the effectiveness of the Health Service. Rather than train and hire Africans, the administration turned to French and foreign "contract" personnel in spite of their "notoriously insufficient technique" and lack of "conviction and enthusiasm." The report even admitted that the European *chefs de service* did not always possess the necessary aptitude for their positions. Although some exercised their jobs "honorably," African staff were considered to lack "professional and moral qualities" necessary for entrusting them with more elevated responsibilities. Auxiliary African doctors and pharmacists were to remain

---

42 Morgenthau, *Political Parties*, 13.

43 Domergue-Cloarec, *Politique coloniale*, 340.

under the "permanent direction and control of European doctors." "It is necessary,"
the report concluded, "to wish for a sufficient augmentation of European staff so
that the totality of our native auxiliaries can be returned to their normal situation of
technical and administrative subordination."[44]

As noted in Chapter 6, the Institute's European staff often regarded African personnel with suspicion. In a 1950 report, for example, Director Laviron described
Mamery Sidibé, a nursing intern at the Institute, as "very susceptible but conscien-
tious." The report praised Sidibé for resisting his colleagues' efforts to make him a
"*revendicateur*" (activist, a term used to describe politically motivated individuals
who openly pressed their demands). Laviron thought that Sidibé could become a
"good nurse" because he was not as political as the others.[45] This association of political quiescence with professional competence reflected a widespread contempt for
outspoken employees.

In general, Europeans dealt with their African staff by erecting what Kassibo
referred to as "barriers." This practice continued even after the Second World War
when the government finally began promoting Africans to higher positions. Dr.
Safouné Traoré, for example, finished his studies at the Ecole de Médecine in 1949
and assumed a post as *médecin chef* (head physician) for a garrison at the Camp de
Thiaroye, site of the famous 1944 mutiny of African soldiers. Until he arrived, this
post had been reserved for Europeans who were usually issued a jeep as one of
their added benefits. Traoré, however, never received a vehicle and found himself
obliged to "make a commotion" so his protests would be heard. When he later
assumed a post in Niger, the local French commandant routinely humiliated him
by scolding him in front of his patients and refusing to shake his hand. Traoré
responded first by silence and, when the commandant became more aggressive, by
shouting back and ignoring his orders.[46]

Traoré's resistance to mistreatment reflected a more general transformation of
African employees after the Second World War. Staff at the Institute were now more
likely to challenge or disagree with the Sisters and other Europeans with whom they
worked closely. In 1946 Sister Paul Miki observed that the Institute's nurses manifested "a spirit of independence and arrogance which makes all subordination painful for them." Revealing again the degree to which the mission and Institute
bolstered each other's authority, Miki warned that the Sisters could encounter
"obstacles" if the administration [presumably Laviron] no longer backed them.[47] A
confidential attachment to their 1947–48 Annual Report similarly noted how both
patients and African staff were affected by the political atmosphere. Citing a recent
spree of thefts at the Institute, the report added, "only the presence of the Sisters
helps with the maintenance of order and discipline." In their view, Laviron needed
them more than ever.[48]

44 Inspecteur Mobile d'Hygiène to Inspecteur Gén. des Services Sanitaires et Médicaux de l'AOF, "Rapport
    d'ensemble sur une tournée d'inspection effectuée dans les colonies . . .," 25 August 1932, ANS 1H-26.

45 Laviron, "Bulletin individuel de notes," 27 March 1950, AIM. Bado notes similar friction between Euro-
    pean and African medical personnel. Bado, *Médecine coloniale*, 217.

46 Safoune Traoré, 22 March 1993.

47 "RAMD, 1945–46," SB B 5167/3.

48 Sr. Marguerite du S. C., "Avenant au rapport," attached to "RAMD, 1947–48," SB B 5167/3.

Unable to understand the staff's seemingly contradictory behavior, the Sisters often interpreted political awareness and activity as conspiracy. For example, their 1950 Annual Report praised the dedication of an African doctor who always responded to their calls for assistance. The same report, however, lamented his failure to monitor the nurses and patients, and his tendency to "excuse" their indiscipline. He and the other nurses worked together politically and often conducted "long *palabras* [interminable and meaningless discussions] which usually terminate in 'it's the government's fault.'" The Sisters preferred the "simple *broussards*" (people of the bush) over the "*évolués*" (educated Africans), most of whom were Muslim.[49] In reference to his departure a year later, one Sister observed, "He was devoted to the patients but had a bad influence in terms of religion and politics; we will not miss him."[50]

In 1954 the Sisters similarly applauded the African nurses for their polite and respectful behavior but then condemned them, especially the younger ones, for becoming increasingly "sensitive." "They easily consider themselves scorned as 'black' for the smallest of remarks which we make to them in regards to the service."[51] A report submitted one year later noted that the "nefarious" influence of two "communist" nurses disrupted their work and obliged them to enlist one of the European doctors for support. Out of necessity, the Sisters grew even more "conciliatory, [and] understanding" and searched for ways of "creating a spirit of collaboration and entente."[52]

As the drift towards independence became more apparent in the second half of the 1950s, the Sisters gradually recognized the importance of political neutrality for their own future. The *loi cadre* passed by the French parliament in 1956 granted each colony greater political autonomy and representation. Beginning in late 1955, the African staff at the Institute and other SGHMP installations organized several strikes which often interrupted treatment campaigns. On one occasion in early 1956, employees in the Soudan and Guinea struck for several months leaving nurses with Assistance Médical Indigène to assume some of their responsibilities in rural areas. Although the Institute's nurses continued working night shifts for the sake of patients at risk of dying, the Sisters complained that many leprosy patients elsewhere in the Soudan were not receiving their medicines. They also feared that the situation would worsen in the approaching rainy season when delivery of medical supplies became more difficult. In spite of their discontent, the Sisters decided to avoid politics altogether so that Africans would consider them apart from the rest of the European community—a task which the Sisters admitted was not easy since they maintained close and constant relations with European functionaries and received European-level salaries.[53]

By 1957, the Sisters recognized fully the African nurses' aspirations "for the day when they alone will govern their country and when they will no longer need the aid

49 "RAMD, 1949–50," SB B 5167/3.

50 "RAMD, 1950–51," SB B 5167/3.

51 "Rapport de visite de Djikoroni, janvier 1954," SB B 5167/1.

52 "RAMD, 1955–56," SB B 5167/3.

53 "RAMD, 1956–57," SB B 5167/3; Ministère de la Fonction Publique, Territoire du Sénégal, "Protocole de fin de gréve," 3 June 1957, ANS 1H-63.

of Europeans."[54] A third SGHMP strike ended in December of that year and pro-voked the Institute's new director, Dr. Languillon, to call for the dismissal of nurses on whom he "couldn't count"; he wanted to replace them with "more reliable" Euro-pean or African specialists.[55] In January 1958, just a few days before the festivities for International Leprosy Day, the SGHMP nurses struck again and Languillon repeated his demands.[56] The controversy concerning the Sisters' dismissal arose directly from these developments.

At one time the Sisters considered Kassibo a "just" man with "integrity," "even though" he was a Muslim. Now they regarded his union leadership and participa-tion in a May Day march as a negative influence on the other Institute employees. Their reports described similar union activists as "fanatical Muslims" or, if they were non-religious, as "Marxists."[57] Given their precarious situation, however, the Sisters still considered it prudent to keep their opinions quiet. They even distanced themselves from Languillon, whom they found too "reserved and authoritarian" towards African nurses.[58]

On the eve of independence, members of the African staff demonstrated their burgeoning power by defending their interests at the Institute and successfully checking the Sisters' political influence. The latter clearly disliked the rapid changes but nonetheless wanted to position themselves favorably for whatever conditions arose under African rule. As members of a small elite of Western-educated Africans, health professionals throughout French West Africa participated actively in national and labor politics as Kassibo did.[59] Their multiple social roles were not unlike those of indigenous healers who, in earlier years, occupied positions of power in initiation societies and other institutions not directly related to health and medicine. Like the Sisters, African employees used the Institute to further their own political ambitions which, up to that point, centered on independence.

Economic Struggles

From the perspective of many people at the margins of society, independence in 1960 merely represented a changing of the guard, not a social revolution. Whereas African political parties tempered the abuse of governmental authority in the pre-ceding decade, no comparable entities existed to balance the power of Mali's first two regimes. The newly formed Republic of Mali continued using French as an official language and retained most of the old colonial administrative structure, replacing European commandants with Africans. Its French educational system hardly changed and the Health Service maintained a centrally-planned European

---

54 "RAMD, 1956–57," SB B 5167/3.

55 "RAMD, 1957–58," SB B 5167/3.

56 Sr. M. Agnes to Mére Supérieure, 29 January 1958, SB B 5167/2.

57 "Rapport de visite de Djikoroni, 6 août 1960," SB C 5167/1.

58 "RAMD, 1956–57," SB B 5167/3; Sr. M. Annonciata, open letter, 5 December 1958, SB B 5167/1.

59 Patton similarly notes the political role of health professionals in both Anglophone and Francophone West Africa. Adell Patton, *Physicians, Colonial Racism, and Diaspora in West Africa* (Gainesville: University Press of Florida, 1996), 18–19.

system of clinical therapy and public health programs. Modibo Keita and his party, the US-RDA, assumed control of Mali in 1960. With inspiration and influence from China and the Soviet Union, Keita and his party pursued a "socialist" path to development. By the close of 1962 Mali had abandoned the franc zone (which maintained a common currency for the former French colonies) and began printing its own money. The economy declined steadily as the government established state-owned industries and commercial monopolies.

Under these conditions, the same medical institutions once used for the collective goal of liberation became instruments for individual survival. Health professionals along with other government workers constituted a new class of privileged but increasingly disaffected functionaries. Their status differed dramatically from that of their patients who enjoyed few of the celebrated benefits of African rule (as will be noted in the following chapter). For that reason, the relationship between healers and patients remained colonial in nature. Like their colonial forebears, nurses and doctors rarely belonged to the communities in which they worked and often ignored local attitudes and practices. They still failed to address the underlying causes of patient dislocation and the broader economic and political problems impinging on mobile treatment. To this day, many rural patients do not receive prompt and adequate care, especially since health professionals outside the mobile campaign continue to avoid treating patients with leprosy altogether.

The division between this functionary class and the rest of society grew out of sharp differences in their perceptions of the colonial experience. In Kassibo's view, government workers like himself had suffered racism and the "burden" of colonialism more than other Africans living in the rural areas. The French went out of their way to make employees feel inferior, reminding them each day of their "subordination." Kassibo believed that people in the "bush" felt differently about independence, because they had not experienced this sense of inferiority daily. Government functionaries were therefore more passionate about establishing African rule at any expense. "Since we became colonized, to become independent, that was the essential in life—the rest didn't matter."[60]

Indeed, the African staff at the Institute enjoyed a new sense of control most clearly manifested in their relationship with the Sisters whose presence was no longer a *fait accompli*. At independence, an African priest contacted the new nation's vice-president to ensure that the government would not completely "Africanize" the Institute.[61] Three years later the Sisters sought permission from the Organisation de Coordination et de Coopération pour la lutte contre les Grandes Endémies (OCCGE, formerly the SGHMP) in order to continue residing in a pavilion on the Institute grounds.[62] The African staff's new powers became most apparent when, at Kassibo's urging, it prevented the replacement of a retiring Sister by another who had worked at the mission several years earlier. This time the other mission members admitted that, in the colonial years, the unwelcome Sister had often allowed Christians into medical consultation ahead of other patients. The tense personality conflict between

---

60 Kassibo, 9–11 January 1993.
61 Abbé Traoré to Mère Domin, 29 June 1960, SB C 5167/2.
62 SB, "Rapport de visite de Djikoroni, 11–19 mars 1963," SB C 5167/1.

her and Kassibo was so well known that even a European pharmacist at the Institute recommended that she not return.[63] The Sisters' weakened political position at the Institute severely inhibited their religious activities. Heeding new laws which the Muslim nurses actively enforced, a visiting Sister from Bamako warned the mission not to proselytize openly with patients.[64] The Sisters also observed that many people, especially women, were reluctant to join a religion which would leave them even more isolated when they returned to their home villages. According to one report, the strength of the Muslim influence, combined with the timidity of the Catholic legion, prevented any growth at all in the Christian community. The Sisters therefore became less concerned with direct conversion and more interested in maintaining good social relations with everyone including Muslims. They routinely visited the marabouts and their wives as well as évolué (educated) women. Once they even invited a nurse to relate the story of his pilgrimage after he returned from Mecca.[65] Given their precarious position, the Sisters also cultivated close contacts with Bamako's elites and "monde métis" (mulatto society).[66] By 1966 one mission member reported "excellent" relations between the Sisters and the African staff—Kassibo included: "what a difference [compared] with the ambiance of the years between 1960–62."[67]

The mission's subsequent diary entries and annual reports reveal the extent to which the African staff redirected the Sisters' thinking and activities. Over time the mission became less interested in conversion and more preoccupied with the latest developments in medicine. This change corresponded with a broader secularization of missionary medicine throughout Africa.[68] Overwhelmed with the care of patients, the Sisters no longer had enough time for developing their local language skills or visiting people in the community.[69] Now they rarely discussed issues with "the Muslims" and seemed resigned to the fact that young people were more interested in music and dance than religion.[70] One report acknowledged their limited religious appeal and observed that there was only one Christian out of 190 patients at the Institute.[71] In 1975 Djikoroni's Christian community numbered only 150.[72] Given such a limited audience, the Sisters' religious attentions shifted away from Djikoroni and focused primarily on the observance of holidays with the greater Christian community in Bamako and elsewhere in Mali. When their contract came up for renewal at

---

63　SB, "Rapport de visite de Djikoroni, 11–19 mars 1963," SB C 5167/1; Sr. M. Nathanael to Mère Supérieure, 27 November 1962; Sr. Laurentius to Mère Supérieure, 23 and 27 November 1962; SB C 5167/2.

64　Sr. M. Nathanael, "Lettre de visite aux soeurs," 24 March 1963, SB C 5167/1; SB, "Rapport de visite de Djikoroni, 30 avril à 11 mai 1966," C 5167/1.

65　"RAMD, 1963–64," SB C 5167/3.

66　"RAMD, 1964–65," SB C 5167/3.

67　"Rapport de visite de Djikoroni, 30 avril à 11 mai 1966," SB C 5167/1.

68　Vaughan, Curing Their Ills, 71.

69　"RAMD, 1970–71," SB C 5167/3.

70　"RAMD, 1973–74," SB C 5167, and "RAMD, 1975–76," SB D 5167/3.

71　"RAMD, 1973–74," SB D 5167/3.

72　"RAMD, 1974–75," SB D 5167/3.

the end of 1973, the Sisters limited the new one to only two years; the rapid changes at the Institute made them unsure of their long-term commitment.[73]

Independence no doubt relieved individuals like Kassibo from the burdens of racial subordination and enabled them to prevent the Sisters from expanding their religious influence. Unlike earlier events, an ongoing dispute between Languillon and his African staff climaxed in July 1971 and obliged the European director to leave with nobody except the Sisters to accompany him to the airport.[74] Such triumphs, however, were tempered by a new set of problems which jeopardized the delivery of health care to patients. As noted in the previous chapter, the new Malian government cut its health budget by one-third, making it difficult to finance properly the mobile leprosy program. According to Ahmed Dédaou, a nurse then stationed in Bandiagara, employees no longer wanted to conduct their treatment tours without sufficient per diem payments and funding for fuel and vehicles. Mali's abandonment of the franc zone and creation of its own currency severely weakened the real purchasing power of government functionaries who neglected their official jobs in order to supplement their incomes with outside work or businesses.[75] This development belonged to a more general trend of declining job satisfaction and government medical services throughout West Africa.[76]

As the quality of health services in Bamako declined and demand increased, the Institute's staff began informally treating outsiders without leprosy to earn extra cash or other non-monetary benefits. In 1959 the Sisters observed that Bamako's central dispensary and Point G hospital lost the population's confidence because their staffs lacked "conscientiousness."[77] Dissatisfaction with Bamako's "dirty" maternity wards, "rude" midwives, and prohibitive hospitalization costs drove many women to the Institute as well.[78] By 1962, the Institute's African nurses had forced Director Languillon to allow the treatment of "non-lepers" in their own hospital and dispensary. These new patients were often related to the nurses themselves, the nurses' friends, or important officials such as the police chief and soldiers from neighboring Camp Para. The Sisters similarly treated other Catholic missionaries—priests and abbots included—because the latter no longer trusted the Government hospital at Point G.[79] The Institute's electrocardiograph, the only working one in Mali, also attracted the diplomatic corps.[80] In 1963 investigators caught the Institute's laundry manager distributing items from the storehouse to his friends and family. Many expensive medicines were also disappearing from the Institute's pharmacy.[81] Though troubled by these and other developments, Director Languillon found that he no longer had the

---

73 "RAMD, 1972–73," SB D 5167/3.

74 "RAMD, 1971–72," SB D 5167/3.

75 Ahmed Dédaou, 28 December 1992.

76 Patton, *Physicians*, 37–39.

77 "RAMD, 1959–60," SB C 5167/3.

78 "Rapport de visite de Djikoroni, 30 avril à 11 mai 1966," SB C 5167/1.

79 Ibid.

80 "RAMD, 1964–65," SB C 5167/3.

81 "Rapport de visite de Djikoroni, 11–19 mars 1963," SB C 5167/1.

authority to change the situation.[82] One Sister lamented, "The Institute, while remaining an experimentation center for leprosy, won't it become a Hospital-Dispensary for an entire quarter of Bamako? The nurses' union seems to greatly wish for that."[83]

The problems associated with President Modibo Keita's rule culminated in the "cultural revolution" of 1967–68 when many government functionaries found themselves directly threatened. Drawing on the Chinese example, the ruling party embarked on its own "cultural revolution" in 1967. The Popular Militia, originally created at independence, assumed increasing control of the streets and wielded power rivaling that of the army and police.[84] In one infamous incident known as "Operation Taxi," the young stalwarts of the Militia seized all the taxis owned by government functionaries as part of their fight against capitalist speculation.[85] Since his return to Mali in 1965, Dr. Safouné Traoré had worked as *médecin chef* in Macina. Confronted with too many difficulties imposed by the Militia, he requested a transfer to San where he had once served several years earlier. In a seeming reversal of the principles of independence, a team of Chinese doctors then took over his post in Macina.[86] Although head of the ruling US-RDA party in Djikoroni, Kassibo also suffered from the disruptions caused by the Militia.[87]

Moussa Traoré's 1968 coup halted the abuses of the cultural revolution but failed to reverse the economic deterioration hampering activities at the Institute and elsewhere in Mali. As both Ahmed Dédaou and Dr. Traoré observed, health care workers could no longer support their families with such low salaries.[88] The crumbling of an already poor infrastructure and the insufficient provision of vehicles and fuel worsened the delivery of medicines to remote areas. These two factors, largely outside the control of ordinary functionaries, left patients vulnerable to neglect and occasional exploitation throughout the ensuing years.

As early as 1969, Director Languillon attempted to forbid the treatment of non-lepers at the Institute, but Malian employees angrily protested and continued accepting friends and family as they had been for some time.[89] The Sisters found that nurses devoted themselves even more to the pursuit of money on the side, "much to the detriment of the most poor [patients]." "We cannot speak for a long time with a nurse or worker without him raising the question of insufficient salary."[90] Due to a scarcity of medicines elsewhere in Bamako, non-leprous patients, especially associates of the staff, continued receiving medicines at the Institute. In one case a nurse charged a leprosy patient for antibiotics and then, moments later, administered three

82 Ibid.; also"RAMD, 1961–62," SB C 5167/3.

83 "RAMD, 1961–62," SB C 5167/3.

84 Pascal Imperato, *A Wind in Africa: A Story of Modern Medicine in Mali* (St. Louis: Warren H. Green, 1975), 26–30.

85 Bintou Sanankou, *La Chute de Modibo Keita* (Paris: Editions Chaka, 1990), 73; Moussa Konaté, *Mali, Ils ont assassiné l'espoir: réflexion sur le drame d'un peuple* (Paris: Edition l'Harmattan, 1990), 27; also interview with Aliou Bagayogo, 7 June 1993. As their purchasing power declined, functionaries had supplemented their salaries with other income-generating activities such as leasing taxis or transport trucks.

86 Safouné Traoré, 22 March 1993.

87 Kassibo, 9–11 January 1993.

88 Ahmed Dédaou, 28 December 1992; Safouné Traoré, 22 March 1993.

89 "RAMD, 1969–70," SB D 5167/3.

90 "RAMD, 1970–71," SB D 5167/3.

free injections to the friend of his colleague.[91] On another occasion, an administrator in the accountant's office was transferred to a position of lesser responsibility after a series of conspicuous thefts from the Institute.[92] Frequent interruptions of electricity ruined vaccines in the refrigerators and interrupted surgery, sometimes when patients were already under anesthesia. Deprived of adequate care, patients became increasingly difficult and demanding.[93] In the early 1980s, non-leprous visitors from Djikoroni continued "invading" the Institute's facilities which they considered the community's dispensary; the older nurses never dared turn them away.[94]

The mobile leprosy campaign run by the Grandes Endémies elsewhere in the country similarly suffered from a demoralized staff. For example, in 1975 doctors at the Institute received a number of patients suffering from advanced lepromatous leprosy. None of these patients had ever been diagnosed or treated before, and they all happened to originate from the Kayes region where a mobile nurse should have identified them first. A subsequent inquiry found that the Grandes Endémies nurse responsible for the Kayes sector could not monitor the treatment teams in outlying areas because he had no vehicle. His register of patients dated back to 1962, and, of the 2,864 individuals listed, only 508 were receiving regular treatment. The register indicated neither deaths nor disappearances and contained no new entries. In another sector, a dispensary employee notified the Grandes Endémies of fifteen new cases, but the mobile nurse responsible for that area could not confirm the diagnosis because, again, he too had no means of transportation. The Institute doctors concluded from the inquiry that the leprosy campaign had been "dormant" for years and recommended that the old register be completely abandoned.[95]

A similar inquiry conducted in the Bougouni region a year later found that nearly half of the 214 patients surveyed were actually cured. The Grandes Endémies nurses responsible for their care had been reluctant to declare them cured and, as a result, many continued to be treated with drugs "in an abusive manner" for years. About twenty percent of the patients also suffered from disabling neurological damage, a consequence of starting treatment at a late stage of the disease. The inquiry concluded that bad roads had prevented their early diagnosis and treatment.[96]

On the basis of these and other inquiries, Institute doctors speculated that the prevalence of leprosy in Mali was probably less than one percent as opposed to the official figure of two percent. Virtually none of the patients diagnosed between 1957 and 1960 had been removed from the lists. While doctors lauded the competence of Grandes Endémies nurses in diagnosing and treating their patients, they also complained that those same nurses neglected their administrative responsibilities, namely keeping accurate statistics. The doctors confirmed their findings by surveying ninety random patients who frequented the Institute's dispensary. These patients, ranging in ages from fourteen to sixty-four, had been undergoing treatment for an

---

91 "RAMD, 1969–70," SB D 5167/3.

92 "RAMD, 1973–74," SB D 5167/3.

93 "RAMD, 1972–73," SB D 5167/3.

94 Dr. Chevalard to Président de l'Association Raoul Follereau Française, 24 November 1982, AIM.

95 Dr. Louvet and Dr. Bernard, "Organisation de la campagne lépre dans la Region de Kayes," January 1975, AIM.

96 Dr. Louvet, "Compte rendu de mission dans la Region de Bougouni," February 1976, AIM.

average of eighteen years. An average of four years had passed between the appearance of the disease's first signs and the moment when patients finally began European treatment.[97]

When, in 1979, the Institute identified some of the first sulfone-resistant cases in West Africa, the Malian government and OCCGE began restructuring the country's leprosy program for the first time since its development in the 1950s.[98] Until that point, the program had been organized vertically, operating autonomously from the regular Health Service whose staff never bothered with leprosy patients. Sulfone-resistant leprosy, however, now necessitated the introduction of more complicated therapies which further burdened an already demoralized and insufficiently financed medical staff. The old approach depended on specially trained nurses repeatedly traveling long distances to often inaccessible places. The new program shifted responsibility for leprosy back to the regular Health Service for the first time since 1944. Under this "horizontal" system, all health professionals would treat the disease. This dramatic change in policy also coincided with the development of a new primary health care system known as the Soins de Santé Primaire (SSP).

Designed to widen the delivery of basic health services in rural areas, SSP provided nurses' aids (aide-soignants) of minimal training to communities which funded and constructed their own dispensaries (usually a simple one- or two-room structure). These nurses in turn worked with village "health councils" organized and trained to oversee their own care and address public health problems. Each council included a local midwife and other individuals assigned to specific responsibilities such as maintaining a small case of medical supplies (including mercurochrome, bandages, and antimalarial medicines) or monitoring village hygiene. Doctors or more advanced nurses based in the nearest administrative centers periodically visited the SSP nurses at their posts and addressed more major medical needs. By minimizing the distance between healers and patients, SSP, in theory, obviated the need for "mobile" teams to track individuals with leprosy.

Though the new leprosy program effectively bypassed the Grandes Endémies, it remained vulnerable to the old problems. In an experimental leprosy program in the Kolokani district, SSP nurses were supposed to oversee treatment of patients in their communities. A 1985 inspection conducted by Institute epidemiologists, however, found that the program barely functioned (if at all) as planned; the theoretically thorough structure of SSP did not exist. Unpaid for many months, the aide-soignants had completely abandoned their "medical role." Members of the health councils had disappeared, often with the medical supplies, while drought and famine preoccupied most other villagers. As a consequence of this disorganization, leprosy patients did not receive the drugs as prescribed. On some of his periodic visits, a doctor from the administrative center distributed medicines himself, but only in bulk, so that he could not control their specific use. The inspectors found that in practice the program had remained vertically organized and dependent entirely on the doctor's visits. The nurse specialist responsible for overseeing the leprosy program in the cercle blamed the failures on the absence of a moped. A car

---

97 Drs. Louvet, Saint-André, and Bernard, "Epidémiologie de la lépre en Afrique de l'Ouest," [n.d., probably 1976], AIM.

98 Institut Marchoux, "Rapport général," 11 November 1986, AIM.

given specifically for the project was never used for conducting "leprosy tours." During their visit, inspectors learned that the then absent *médecin chef* had driven it more than five hundred kilometers to Koutiala where, for at least a month, he was conducting unrelated business.

In another district, Nossombougou, the inspectors found medical records falsified to create an illusion that the nurses had been fulfilling their responsibilities. Six patients documented as having taken all their medicines had in fact received none. Others had received their medicines from a third party and took them without proper supervision. They included two pregnant women and an eight-year-old child who consumed an adult's dose. When questioned, one nurse admitted that he could not conduct his tours since his moped broke down often and he could rarely find gas.[99]

The extent and consequences of these problems remained evident even in 1993. That year Saran Keita, cured of her disease at least two or three decades before, purchased leprosy medicines (DDS) from an Institute employee. Like other "cured" patients, she feared a relapse of the disease whenever she felt ill. Even non-leprous individuals such as local farmers purchased these medicines for alleviating general illnesses.[100] Around the same time, Institute inspectors found other leprosy antibiotics for sale in the Bamako market. International organizations had supplied these medicines to the Grand Endémies specifically so that patients could receive free treatment.[101] Outside Bamako, a nurse in San frequently charged his patients for their pills.[102] In Macina, a lack of fuel money prevented the dispensary nurse from regularly visiting one leprous man in a village about forty kilometers away.[103] As these examples illustrate, the leprosy program suffered from seemingly endemic dysfunctions stemming from the continued tendency of some health care workers to use "healing" for non-medical ends and, in other situations, from the absence of funds and infrastructure necessary for a sustained delivery of medicines in rural areas.

Colonial medical institutions including those which dealt with leprosy facilitated the formation of a new class of "healers" whose social roles extended well beyond medicine. Through Western education and involved contact with Europeans, many of these health professionals assumed active political roles in the 1950s for the collective goal of independence. After independence, however, they encountered the new challenges of severe economic decline and increasingly oppressive government policies. In response, they used their occupations to protect their fragile but privileged economic and social positions, even at the expense of their far more destitute and ostracized patients. Many people involved with leprosy treatment in the postcolonial era agreed that the quality of medical care had deteriorated as a result of insufficient salaries and poor infrastructure. As early as 1963 one Sister observed how, due to neglect by employees and the lack of funds, the Institute's buildings had fallen into disrepair: "The Institute which once was so dainty . . . with its flower-beds, has

---

99 Dr. Daumerie and Dr. Husser, "Rapport de tournée dans le Cercle de Kolokani, Cadre de la polychimiothérapie operationnelle," 7 January 1985, AIM.

100 Saran Keita, 11 June 1993; Fousseyni Sow, 7 July 1993.

101 Pierre Bobin, 4 May 1993; Leopold Blanc, 10 December 1992.

102 De Rasilly, 23 March 1993.

103 Mamadou Koulibali, 17 February 1993.

lost its 'chic'."[104] Even Kassibo acknowledged, "Before [independence] there was discipline, and after there were different ways of doing things." In his view, however, the weakening of "order" hardly mattered when compared with their liberty: "There were no regrets for that."[105]

Conclusion

As other scholars have argued, healing should be studied within its wider political context.[106] This chapter has therefore elucidated the role of far-ranging historical developments—such as the transition to independence and subsequent economic stagnation—within the seemingly marginal world of Mali's leprosy patients. The next two chapters extend the analysis by examining how patients themselves responded to these and other developments. Such an approach will reveal patients as significant and complex historical actors who gradually asserted themselves more actively in defining their social identities.

104 "Rapport de visite de Djikoroni, 11–19 mars 1963," SB C 5167/1.

105 Kassibo, 9–11 January 1993.

106 Steven Feierman, "Struggles for Control: The Social Roots of Health and Healing in Modern Africa," *African Studies Review* 28, 2/3 (June/September 1985): 73–147.

8

Dislocations

Major changes in policy and politics only partly explain changes in identity. At some point, our attention must return to the trajectory of people's lives, so that we can refine our sense of how they changed as individuals and members of a social group. Their lives, when examined collectively, reveal both common patterns and distinct variations. In turn, these patterns and variations help us to feel the inherently rough texture of historical change.

As albinos (*yefugew*) in the village of Dialakoro (Koulaye Arondissement), Joseph Koulibali and his two brothers endured a level of social isolation comparable to what individuals with advanced leprosy often experienced. Joseph's father never treated them as proper sons, and fellow students often chased them from school. Hearing that "fetishers" (*bolitigiw*) sacrificed albinos in their rituals, they never walked alone in the bush. "An albino's blood is better than your own," people often said. On one occasion a hostile villager attempted to kill Joseph with a boulder from a nearby road then under construction. The boulder missed his head but injured his hand. One of Joseph's brothers eventually married a blind woman while the other was only able to find a wife with a "bad head" (mental problems).

At the age of 19, shortly after the Second World War, Joseph's parents identified a patch on his chest as leprosy. Believing that local healers could not cure the disease, he immediately consulted an African SGHMP nurse (originally from Côte d'Ivoire) who regularly passed through the village to administer injections. A few people saw Joseph with the nurse and, before long, everybody knew that he had "the big disease."

One night Joseph walked out into the fields alone. He sat beneath a moonless sky and talked to himself and to God. He felt that nobody, not even God, wanted him. After falling asleep, he entered a dream which instructed him to go to a place with "lots of people." A few days later he left for Bamako without telling anyone except his mother. "Are you coming back?" she asked. "Never," he replied. He kept his word.

Joseph settled in Djikoroni in 1953. Since the Institut Marchoux was full, he received treatment from the Grandes Endémies clinic in town. He worked as a wage laborer for nine years and then began selling used schoolbooks in Bamako's Dibida market. Joseph prospered and built a collection of 3,600 volumes. At the height of the Cultural Revolution in 1968, however, the Popular Militia seized his entire stock.

That same year he converted to Catholicism, because the Bible, which a friend had read to him in Bambara, "put his mind to rest" (*hakili bè sigi*). It took Joseph another twelve years to rebuild his book collection. With his savings, he married a "healthy" woman in 1980 and subsequently had four children. The onset of blindness in 1991 forced him to abandon his bookselling business. During my year of research, I often saw him begging with an old tomato-paste can in Djikoroni or Bamako's center.[1]

From diagnosis to destitution, Joseph underwent several core experiences through which his identity as a leper changed. Most of these experiences were associated in some way with social and physical dislocation. As illustrated by his multiple statuses as an albino, Catholic, and, more recently, beggar, this disease-based identity often intersected with identities rooted in other attributes. Indeed, his identity as an urban migrant placed him in a social category which embraced millions of individuals throughout Africa. In the end, however, Joseph's residence in Djikoroni and eventual membership in an association of patients (described in the next chapter), suggest that his leper identity predominated over these others.

Photo 5: Joseph Keita (1993). Patient residences at the Institut Marchoux are are in the background. [Phtograph by Eric Silla]

---

1 Joseph Koulibali, 8 December 1992.

This chapter examines two of the most significant core experiences for leprosy patients in twentieth-century Mali: migration and begging. Drawing on life histories such as Saran Keita's and Joseph's, it reveals how patients responded to the changes in government treatment programs and national politics analyzed in previous chapters. Variations in their experiences translated into variations in the meaning of their identities as lepers. For many individuals, migration and begging reinforced their sense of separation from "normal" society. At the same time, however, these experiences facilitated new forms of collective action which the following chapter will elucidate in more detail.

Cause to Leave

Though they failed to cure the desired number of patients, the nurses from the mobile campaigns of the SGHMP and OCCGE succeeded in introducing otherwise isolated rural populations to the power of European leprosy medicines. A month or two of DDS treatment usually produced immediate results. As news of these medicines circulated from the 1950s onward, leprosy patients consulted local healers less and less frequently. The mobile campaign's designers had assumed that this tangible efficacy alone would convince patients to stay in their villages. Instead, it merely awakened more people to the idea that even better treatment might be found in towns. Chapters 5 and 7 noted how politics, limited infrastructure, and low morale often impeded the proper care of rural patients. By resettling near permanent clinics, patients bypassed this problem altogether and assured themselves of more reliable therapy. Like earlier migrants, they also escaped the shame of social isolation in their villages. Antibiotics, after all, could eliminate the bacillus from their bodies but never reverse the permanent nerve and tissue damage which made them social lepers for life.

Before the SGHMP's mobile campaign, responses to leprosy in most rural communities remained relatively uninfluenced by European health policies. Unless visited by colonial "leper hunters" recruiting patients for the Institute and other leprosariums, individuals with the disease rarely encountered practitioners of European medicine for long periods of time. Moving into colonial society through activities such as military service, education, trade, or urban begging facilitated contact with leprosy inspectors, but this usually occurred outside one's own village.[2] For example, several members of Issaka Traoré's family first went to Bamako to fulfill their forced labor obligations in the 1930s. Afterwards they settled in Bamako permanently and became traders of millet and cloth. Issaka later joined them and, after developing leprosy, underwent treatment at the Institute as an outpatient rather than return home.[3]

Beginning in the 1950s, the mobile campaign gradually reduced the role of local medical knowledge in the diagnosis and treatment of leprosy. Increasing numbers of patients such as Fuseni Diakité and Moussa Sokoba received their first diagnosis from SGHMP nurses passing through on routine visits.[4] Even when fellow family

2 "RMM de Macina, fevrier 1935," ANM 1H-12; "Rapport médico-chirugical de H-S-N, août 1909" and for June/July 1915, ANM 1H-44; Folder 6 in Box 1937–38 contains correspondence documenting numerous school inspections, AIM.

3 Issaka Traoré, 5 November 1992.

4 Fuseni Diakité, 4 November 1992; Moussa Sokoba, 18 February 1993.

members or villagers recognized the disease first, patients often preferred sulfa drugs over indigenous medicines. Alfa Inamoud, a Tuareg nomad who settled near Timbuktu, disregarded family pressure to use local healers and relied entirely on European medicine.[5] After observing positive results in individuals returning from Bamako, once-dubious healers in Buna Sawane's village began advising their own leprosy patients to go there as well.[6]

Also beginning in the 1950s, African nurses became the predominant dispensers of *toubab* leprosy medicine in rural areas. Most of them did not originate from the communities in which they worked, so patients still regarded them as government agents and outsiders. Ahmed Dédaou, for example, grew up in Timbuktu but worked in distant places such as Djenne, Bandiagara, and Konna.[7] Through repeated contact which often lasted several years, however, patients and nurses gradually developed close relationships. When interviewed, many former patients remembered one or two specific government health workers like Ahmed who oversaw their entire treatment and, as a result, minimized the role of family members and other villagers in the diagnostic and healing processes.

Government medical intervention also changed the manner in which leprosy generated stigma. Sulfone drugs enabled many patients to continue working without suffering permanent handicaps and offensive open sores which had been common causes of shame and social isolation in the past. In theory, one could avoid becoming a leper—in the social sense of the word—altogether. In practice, new forms of stigma developed on top of the old ones. The coercive isolation programs of the preceding decades signaled to people that the *toubabs* also regarded leprosy as a disease apart. The continued separation of leprosy treatment from regular health services in the 1950s further justified social exclusion of lepers.

Through government policies and biologically based definitions of leprosy, individuals became identified publicly as lepers more easily and sooner than in earlier times. As noted in previous chapters, the simple appearance of patches did not necessarily indicate leprosy. One became a leper in the eyes of the community usually with the development of open sores or other blemishes. In the eyes of the government, however, anyone carrying the bacillus was a leper. Official identity cards often included a note indicating that their bearers had the disease.[8] Schools routinely examined students and expelled those who tested positive. (They could return only if they tested negative six months after completing treatment.) Government functionaries similarly lost their jobs, and the army considered leprosy "absolutely incompatible with military service."[9]

Since the SGHMP nurses traveling from village to village treated only one disease, rural patients seen with those nurses automatically revealed themselves as lepers. Likewise, patients in towns reported to a specific building designated for leprosy.

5 Alfa Inamoud, 24 December 1992.

6 These healers initially refused to believe that *toubabs* could cure leprosy. Buna Sawane, 26 October 1992.

7 Ahmed Dédaou, 22–28 December 1992.

8 In 1993 Brèma Touré still possessed his identity card from 1957. "Lépreux" had been entered next to the heading "*Signes particulier.*" Brèma Touré, 2 April 1993. "Medical passports" were also used in the Belgian Congo. Lyons, *The Colonial Disease,*128.

9 Dir. Gén. de la Santé Publique, "Au sujet de l'éviction des malades lépreux du milieu scolaire, administratif et militaire," no. 3290, 30 June 1956, AIM.

Photo 6:   Colonial identification card indicating Brèma Touré's status as a leper. [Photograph by Eric Silla]

By separating treatment from other health services, the government transformed all carriers of the bacillus into social lepers regardless of whether they exhibited any of the outward signs. In other words, medical treatment itself engendered social stigma. This new situation provoked some individuals of otherwise high status to seek their medicines in secret, as they often do even today. Dr. Philippe Dembélé, for example, encountered (near Gao in the early 1980s) one prominent Songhay marabout who refused to admit that he had leprosy in spite of repeated diagnoses. The marabout took only milk and honey until his condition worsened. He then approached Phillipe secretly and requested European medicines. The marabout insisted on concealing his condition for fear that public knowledge would ruin his life and career.[10]

Without question, the widening distribution of leprosy medicines after the 1950s enabled many individuals to remain in their villages. Those who lived close to SGHMP clinics found little reason to leave their homes. Mousa Koulibali never went to Bamako because of the easy availability of treatment in Kangaba.[11] After unsuccessful attempts with local healers, Bala Samaké considered going to Djikoroni until he learned that a closer clinic in Ouéléssébougou could cure him as well.[12]

---

10   Philippe Dembélé, 11 December 1992. Ahmed Dédaou, who worked as a mobile nurse in Nioro, Diré, and Gao in the 1960s and 1970s, observed that nomadic peoples tried to conceal their disease. He too treated a prominent marabout in secret. Ahmed Dédaou, 22–28 December 1992. A White Father in San similarly noted cases of individuals from notable families who received medicines in secret and concealed their disease from the public; Bernard de Rasilly, 21 March 1993.

11   Mousa Koulibali, 6 February 1993.

12   Bala Samaké, 2 December 1992.

The large numbers of patients drifting into towns and administrative centers, however, suggest significant limitations to the mobile campaign's ability to sustain treatment over the long term and alleviate social problems related to the disease. Patients such as Fuseni Diakité eventually left their homes because poor infrastructure and unreliable nurses prevented the SGHMP from delivering the steady and prolonged drug therapy necessary for obtaining a permanent cure.[13] For many, the desire to leave even outweighed strong opposition from family members. Lasine Berté's father, for example, feared that his son would never return and consented to his departure in 1954 only after his wife divorced him.[14] Malè Sissoko learned of the Institute from a Dyula trader passing through his village near Nioro. After his family refused to let him go, Malè escaped one night (ca. 1953) without telling anyone and then embarked on a nineteen-day journey to Djikoroni by foot.[15]

The dislocation resulting from the region's increasingly uneven economic development also hampered the SGHMP's efforts to keep patients stationary and under treatment. In some cases, people developed leprosy in the course of an extended odyssey through several colonies or, after independence, countries. In the late 1950s Nègè Barri left his village (Pita) in northern Guinea and, looking for work as a driver, wound up near Timbuktu. He married a local woman and several years later showed the first signs of leprosy. At the time he knew no other "lepers" in town. He underwent European treatment administered by a French doctor and continued working.[16] Magara Sidibé of Wuru (near Keleya, southern Mali) similarly left for Abidjan to make money in the late 1940s. His first patch appeared in 1956 when he was about twenty-five years old and, in his words, "very attractive." A *toubab* doctor diagnosed it as leprosy and sent him to "Petit Paris," a local treatment center much like the Institute in Djikoroni. He spent six years there before moving to Bobo-Dioulasso to continue his trading. There he also received *toubab* medicine and found another leper community. After a year in Bobo, however, he moved still again to Korhogo (Côte d'Ivoire) where he underwent both *toubab* and "Bambara" medical treatment. His healer, Siriki Koulibali, lodged Magara along with other patients suffering from leprosy and other diseases. For six years Magara sold kola nuts and worked in a local silver mine. He found that Siriki's medicines succeeded in removing his patches. After returning to Wuru, he suffered another relapse and, in 1968, finally settled in Djikoroni.[17]

In short, most patients who settled permanently in administrative centers and towns sought easy access to medical treatment. As a result of the mobile campaign, rural populations learned of the effectiveness of new *toubab* leprosy medicines. For some, that campaign obviated the need to leave. For others, however, it merely increased expectations that better care lay elsewhere. Already mobile individuals who developed leprosy knew more than anyone that living near a clinic assured one of proper treatment and minimized shameful experiences common in villages.

---

13 Fuseni Diakité, 4 November 1992.

14 Lasine Berté, 16 November 1992.

15 Malè Sissoko, 24 February 1993.

16 Nègè Barri, 25 December 1992.

17 Magara Sidibé, 2 February 1993. Magara's story reveals how interrupted treatment prevented permanent cure.

Djikoroni: In the Company of Others

As suggested by the examples above, the growing capital of Bamako became the primary destination for leprosy patients throughout the colony. The Institut Marchoux had maintained its reputation for providing food and shelter but could no longer accommodate everyone seeking entrance. From the 1940s onward, most newcomers had to accept treatment as outpatients and live by their own means in Djikoroni. To absorb the heavy patient load, the SGHMP established another clinic a few kilometers away in the center of town. Despite the distance, its patients preferred to live in Djikoroni with the others. The community originally formed by the Institute now grew on its own as both its former patients (such as Saran Keita) and these newcomers settled permanently on the other side of the road. The community's rapid growth reflected strong desires to remain near each other as well as fears of returning to unfriendly villages and of losing access to the best leprosy care in the region.

As noted earlier, sulfa drugs could rid patients of the leprosy bacillus but could not reverse the stigmatizing nerve and tissue damage. For the rest of their lives, they would manifest leprosy's characteristic infections and amputations. Socially they would always remain lepers even though biologically they no longer carried the disease. For this reason, many patients continued to choose Djikoroni as their permanent refuge throughout the late- and post-colonial periods. Individuals such as Mamadou Dama never returned to their villages, fearing that people would only shun them as before.[18] Nènènkoro Balo found that, in Djikoroni, the company of others with the same disease "put his mind at rest" (*hakili bè sigi*). If he had returned to his village, he would have been the only leper there.[19] Issa Traoré believed that poverty and an inability to work made most lepers, even when cured, unwanted in their villages.[20]

In receiving treatment in Djikoroni and Bamako, even as outpatients, people became accustomed to a level of care which they knew was unavailable in their villages. Buna Sawane, for example, went to Djikoroni in 1955 and stayed there, because doctors trained in *toubab* medicine never came to his village.[21] In a few cases, the prolonged nature of therapy itself encouraged patients to settle permanently. Banci Doumbia arrived in 1954, three years after another patient from his village had settled there. He rented a house and received outpatient treatment at the Institute for the next fifteen years.[22]

In most cases, the decision to settle permanently in Djikoroni was based on several factors. For example, Mamadou Diallo, who first arrived at the Institute during the early part of Laviron's tenure in the 1940s, returned occasionally to his village near Kayes but always wanted to be near medicine in Djikoroni. He also preferred the company of other lepers rather than that of "healthy people." His own villagers never directly insulted lepers, but they did often mention the disease (*bana fo*) in the course of an argument. In Mamadou's eyes, leprosy caused peoples' "hearts to hurt"

---

18 Mamadou Dama, 27 October 1992.

19 Nènènkoro Balo, 22 January 1993.

20 Issa Traoré, 7 April 1993.

21 Buna Sawane, 26 October 1992.

22 Banci Doumbia, 12 November 1992.

(*dusu bè dimi*).[23] A need for medicines and community combined with a dread of ostracism in his village kept him in Djikoroni.

The transition to a permanent life in Djikoroni also occurred gradually. Nèkoro Traoré first spent five years in the 1950s at the Institute before returning to her village. At the time she had not yet suffered any permanent physical damage. Fifteen years later, however, the disease manifested itself again, making it painful to pound millet or cook over fire. As blisters and sores multiplied, she and her husband began arguing frequently. Complaining that she could no longer work, he left her to marry another woman. With nowhere else to go, Nèkoro returned to Djikoroni and resumed outpatient treatment at the SGHMP clinic.[24]

Lepers manifested their attachment to Djikoroni most vividly by building homes and establishing families there. Technically the land outside the Institute belonged to the original inhabitants of the area. To build a compound and obtain fields, settlers usually paid Djikoroni's chief (who was not a leper) a symbolic fee of ten kola nuts. Many former patients also continued farming land on Institute grounds. While some individuals such as Balafonci Diarra and Soumana Traoré brought their spouses and children from their villages, most people arrived alone.[25] Over time they married other community residents, usually though not always lepers. Saran Keita, her sister, Kanko Fofana, Malè Sissoko, and Michel Traoré, for example, all found leprous spouses, but Bakari Kanoté married a "healthy" woman.[26] Other individuals such as Dramane Touré and Sirima Diabaté returned to their villages temporarily in search of a leper to marry and bring back to Djikoroni.[27] In short, connections to family and property anchored one permanently to this community, and, for many individuals, conveniently served as an additional reason for not returning home.[28]

Djikoroni's patient community clearly originated within the Institute, but, by the late 1940s, this government center, with a capacity for only about four hundred residents, could no longer handle the growing flood of patients. The high concentration of people suffering from the same disease and undergoing the same treatment furthered the development of the collective identity described in Chapter 6. In Djikoroni, leprosy constituted a new basis for family and social ties. For many, the community offered an attractive escape from the alienation and irregular medical treatment endured in villages.

Alternate Destinations

The significant presence of former leprosy patients in other administrative centers and towns throughout Mali in the 1990s reveals the extent to which the disease continued

---

23 Mamadou Diallo, 9 April 1993.

24 Nèkoro Traoré, 19 May 1993.

25 Balafonci Diarra, 19 November 1992; Soumana Traoré, 25 November 1992.

26 Bakari Kanoté, 5 November 1992. The Sisters' diaries document many other similar unions between leprosy patients.

27 Dramane Touré, 16 November 1992; Fanta Koita, 9 March 1993.

28 Mamadou Dama, 27 October 1992; Abdoulaye Diarra, 27 November 1992. Both Mamadou and Abdoulaye gave those reasons for not returning.

to provoke migration despite government efforts. From Kita to Timbuktu, these individuals underwent a common experience of moving away from their villages. When settled in new locations, however, they did not always coalesce into recognizable communities as in Djikoroni. As the following examples illustrate, the development of a strong group identity often required an institutional catalyst and a critical mass of individuals with similar attributes.

Of all the locations researched for this study, Timbuktu manifested the sharpest contrast with Djikoroni. Patients in the region never settled in any one place and remained dispersed across great distances. Originally from a Songhay village near Bomba (situated on the Niger River between Gao and Timbuktu), Hadiatou Mohammadun settled in Timbuktu in the early 1960s when she became sick and wanted to live close to European medicines. She never married and lodged with an old woman healer who specialized in gynecological problems.[29] Most people who moved away from their home "communities" were originally Tamachek-speaking nomads who could not keep up with their families because of their illnesses. For example, in the early 1960s Alfa Inamoud settled with his wife and children on the outskirts of Timbuktu. Unable to function as a pastoralist, Alfa similarly wanted to live near a government dispensary.[30] El Mehdi Ag Rhally, also from a nomadic Tuareg group, first developed leprosy while working near Mopti just before independence in 1960. He initially consulted a government nurse in Mopti, but preferred to live closer to his region of origin in the north. El Mehdi then moved to Kabara, a small village adjacent to Timbuktu. When his condition improved, he began traveling again. However, he eventually suffered a relapse while in Niamey and resumed European treatment. Two years later he returned to Kabara where he settled permanently.[31]

An unusually aggressive and methodical mobile treatment campaign led by a French doctor between the 1950s and 1970s also minimized the need to settle near the dispensary in Timbuktu. Virtually every patient in the region at the time knew Dr. Depinay who traveled by whatever means possible—canoe, bicycle, foot—to ensure regular distribution of medicines.[32] Ousmane Sabaguna, for example, operated a canoe in Hondibomo, a river village about twenty kilometers east of Timbuktu.[33] He initially consulted healers on an island about thirty kilometers upstream until European treatments became available through a traveling team organized by Depinay.[34] The reliable distribution of medicines also provided nomads with several options for

29 Hadiatou Mohammadun, 23 December 1992.

30 Alfa Inamoud, 24 December 1992. Tuareg peoples in this area are often stratified socially between "noble" and "slave" status. Alfa identified himself as Tuareg but did not mention his social rank. Generally people of slave status are called Bella. The other "Tuaregs" mentioned here also only identified themselves as Tuareg.

31 El Mehdi Agh Rhally, 25 December 1992.

32 Depinay's efforts are documented in a thirty-minute film, *En Pirogue sur le Niger* [seen by author at the Association Raoul Follerau, Paris]. Depinay married a local Songhay woman and, when he died in the 1970s, was buried in Goundam. He is still remembered by lepers and non-lepers throughout the Timbuktu–Goundam region.

33 Spelled officially as Houndou-Bomon, but Hondibomo corresponds more closely to its contemporary pronunciation.

34 Ousmane Sabaguna, 26 December 1992.

settling. Muhammad al-Her, for example, chose to live in Hondibomo rather than Timbuktu.[35]

Other factors such as the relatively thin population density no doubt contributed to the absence of leper communities. A sufficient critical mass of patients never existed. In places where they did settle, leprosy proved to be a weaker social tie than family and ethnicity. El Mehdi chose to settle in more familiar Kabara as opposed to Mopti, Muhammad in Hondibomo rather than Timbuktu. Individuals who did desire a community or better treatment traveled over seven hundred kilometers to Bamako. Djikoroni's sizable population of Tuareg, Songhay, and Fulani lepers from the Timbuktu area and other northern regions suggests that at least some people did not consider their own urban communities sufficient havens for people with their disease. It also demonstrates their willingness to live in a Bambara- and Malinké-dominated milieu for the sake of perceived medical advantages or the company of other lepers.

Unlike Timbuktu, the Niger town of Macina attracted notable numbers of patients over the years. Created by the colonial government in 1921, Macina served

Photo 7:   Muhammad al-Her (1993) [Photograph by Eric Silla]

---

35 Muhammad al-Her, 26 December 1992.

as the administrative center for a newly formed district which eventually encompassed large parts of the Office de Niger river irrigation project. In the 1950s the SGHMP based one of its mobile teams in the town. Over the years, patients settled there to ensure easy and regular access to the latest and most effective medicines. For example, after one year of unsuccessful indigenous treatment, Haraba Dembélé followed the advice of other villagers in Bendugu and moved to Macina with her husband. There a *toubab* doctor amputated one of her fingers and provided her with pills and injections which eventually cured her blisters and sores. In her interview, Haraba stressed that she left Bendugu on her own volition, that people in Bambara and Bozo communities never chased undesirable individuals away. After finishing treatment she preferred to stay in Macina where she and her husband were able to farm. Other non-leprous residents in town also took good care of her, providing her with additional millet, sugar, and soap.[36] In ensuing years Macina became a refuge for many other patients from throughout the area.

Leprosy clearly served as a reason for individuals to settle permanently in Macina but hardly constituted a basis for visible group identity. The town lacked an institution which would have brought patients closer together and thereby helped them to become more conscious of their commonalities. Although Ouéléssébougou similarly lacked this kind of institution, its proximity to Bamako (about eighty kilometers to the south) facilitated an awareness that patients in some places did live as a community. As a small but conveniently located roadside town, Ouéléssébougou became involved in colonial society much earlier than other more remote rural areas. In 1936 the White Fathers opened a mission dispensary where, for the next two decades, many leprosy patients received their first treatments. By 1958, however, the SGHMP had installed its own clinic and the mission dispensary subsequently closed.[37]

Throughout these and later years, many people who settled in Djikoroni originated from the Ouéléssébougou area. While most patients went on their own, a few like Jean-Marie Kamara were brought by the White Fathers in the early 1950s.[38] Occasionally, patients arrived in Djikoroni only to find the Institute full and the cost of living too high. Jeriba Doumbia first developed leprosy shortly after the Second World War. At the time he already knew of one leprous man from his village, Manabougou, who left for Djikoroni and never returned. Jeriba himself went, but doctors at the Institute turned him away and informed him that he could receive the same medicines in Ouéléssébougou. After only fifteen days in Djikoroni he followed their recommendation.[39] Even patients who never set foot in the well-known leper community usually knew of others who did.

No equivalent institution in Ouéléssébougou provided food or lodging, but, as one former patient observed, all the leprosy patients knew each other.[40] After all, they reported to the same place for treatment often for several years. Like the Institute, the town's clinic brought people from otherwise disparate backgrounds together. Anna

36 Haraba Dembélé, 15 February 1993.
37 Wim Schakenraad, 2 December 1992.
38 Jean-Marie Kamara, 9 July 1993.
39 Jeriba Doumbia, 30 November 1992.
40 Anna Bagayogo, 30 November 1992.

Bagayogo grew up in a distant village about fifty kilometers away. In 1949, after five
years of unsuccessful indigenous treatment, she and her first husband moved to
Djikoroni as had another leprous woman from their village. Within a few months,
however, they returned home when her husband failed to find work. He died just a
few years later, at which point she followed the advice of a *toubab* doctor and settled
again in Ouéléssébougou. There she met and married Jeriba Doumbia.[41] Overall,
former patients in Ouéléssébougou demonstrated a strong sense of group identity
even though they did not physically live in a distinct community.

The importance of institutions in shaping collective identity is most evident in
San where, despite its great distance from Bamako (about five hundred kilometers by
road), patients developed a strong sense of community. In the 1930s the Health Service operated a small but fairly active leprosarium in this rapidly growing commercial town situated at the intersection of major roads connecting Mopti, Ségou, and
Bobo-Dioulasso. However unsuccessful in the actual fight against leprosy, this institution served as an alternate refuge for people unable or unwilling to trek to Bamako.
Before moving to Djikoroni in the 1940s, Kalifa Koulibali first went to San where he
found a number of other patients being housed and fed at the leprosarium. Patients
there were free to walk around in town and had their own chief.[42]

In the 1950s the leprosarium closed, but its residents moved onto the premises of
the SGHMP clinic also known as the "trypano" (a holdover name from the days when
the SGHMP treated only trypanosomiases, sleeping sickness). Yusufu Diarra lived
there for a number of years with about twenty-five other residents. Yusufu had actually traveled to Bamako, but the Institute's staff instructed him to return to San where
the medicines would be "the same."[43] According to Ferdinand Jessana, another
patient at the time, the "trypano" provided patients with generous rations of food in
addition to fields for farming.[44] Shortly before independence the patients' houses collapsed from heavy rains, so Yusufu, Ferdinand, and the others began sleeping on the
premises of the town's dispensary.[45] After independence, newly arrived patients continued to settle and marry each other in this small community. The leprosarium,
though closed, had established San's reputation as a haven for lepers.

From the 1950s onward, moving away became one of the most common experiences for people with leprosy in Mali. The spectrum of their destinations reflects the
diversity of their objectives and resulting identities. Attracted to European dispensaries, many individuals settled in small towns where they either lived separately or in
the company of others like themselves. The contrasts between Timbuktu, Macina,
Ouéléssébougou, and San reveal the long-term effects of colonial institutions on collective identity. However, whether they lived separately from each other or as a community, virtually all patients remained socially identified by their disease as they had
been in their villages.

41 Ibid.
42 Kalifa Koulibali, 11 December 1992.
43 Yusufu Diarra, 21 March 1993.
44 Ferdinand Jessana, 21 March 1993.
45 Yusufu Diarra, 21 March 1993.

Becoming a Beggar

The third chapter examined the numerous factors which contributed to a leper's sense of shame and motivated flight to urban areas. Handicapped and unable to work at normal capacity, many individuals considered themselves burdens on their families, especially in subsistence farming communities subjected to periodic droughts and famines. In most cases, they could not compensate their decreased productivity by publicly begging (*delilikè, garibuyakè*) in the village because, as many informants explained, others would fault the family for neglect. Families generally regarded begging as a source of both shame and insult.[46] People said that it "ruined one's name" (*tògò tiyèn*).[47] Likewise, those who no longer had families to support them could not beg outright in or around their villages lest they embarrass the entire community. In such situations people received more discreet forms of assistance. For example, earlier in the century, families in Saran Keita's village often allowed destitute individuals to collect the remains of threshed rice.[48]

Public begging as practiced in administrative and commercial centers did exist in slightly different forms before the imposition of colonial rule. As the French traveler René Caillié observed in 1827, the religious obligation of giving alms made large Muslim communities in towns such as Timbuktu and Djenne especially tolerant.[49] Both Koranic students and mystics begged as part of their lessons in or demonstrations of humility. Two major religious revival movements led by Shehu Ahmadu and Umar Tall spread these practices to many other communities in the northern and western regions of present-day Mali.[50] Kasoume Tangara, one of the healers mentioned in Chapters 3 and 4, insisted that Bambara societies forbade begging until Umar Tall conquered the Bambara states and encouraged the practice. Kasoume explained that begging began in villages with the arrival of a "marabout" (religious teacher) who was allowed to instruct children without the villagers realizing exactly how this would "ruin" their customs.[51] In most places, such as Aminata Tall's village near Tojon (in present-day Burkina Faso), overt begging was tolerated only for Koranic students, not lepers or invalids.[52] However, even in large Muslim communities which encouraged alms-giving, Koranic students usually ventured to marabouts in other locations to avoid the stigma of begging around one's own home.

Other types of solicitation also existed in rural societies, but they hardly resembled the specific form of begging as later practiced in towns. For example, Silvestré Kamaté identified griots (*jeliw*) as people who once begged (*délilikè*) in his village.[53] Although known historically as bards and custodians of oral tradition for "nobles," many griots were merely born with the title—much like blacksmiths and leather

---

46 See, for example, Bezo Kamaté, 23 March 1993.

47 For example, Malè Sissoko, 24 February 1993.

48 Mentioned in the course of Saran Koulibali's interview, 27 March 1993.

49 He also observed the relative absence of public begging outside of these two locations.

50 See Robinson, *Holy War*; Ba and Daget, *L'Empire peul*; and Roberts, *Warriors*.

51 Kasoume Tangara, 18 February 1993.

52 Aminata Tall, 6 April 1993.

53 Silvestré Kamaté, 23 March 1993.

workers—and never learned the skills necessary for practicing the "caste's" craft.[54] They remained griots in name only but continued to profit from their special status by collecting gifts from their patrons who had likewise inherited their positions from birth. As another example, some Bambara oral traditions portray other types of indigent individuals venturing to local rulers in search of alms.[55] Both these cases, however, did not constitute public begging, because only specific individuals—as opposed to the general public—were targeted for solicitation. Furthermore, most of such solicitations probably occurred in private spaces. In short, nearly all informants reported that begging did not occur in their small rural villages, Muslim and non-Muslim alike. Before the development of colonial towns, lepers had little choice but to remain in their home communities and accept the support, however limited, of their families or neighbors.[56]

Chapter 5 explained how religious piety and the concentration of wealth in urban centers attracted mendicants with leprosy. Colonial leprosariums, particularly the Institut Marchoux, were partly designed to cope with this phenomenon. The Institute provided resident patients with generous rations and other supplies, so that they would not beg. Over time, however, former patients and newcomers who settled on the other side of the road had to find other ways to support themselves. Either because of stigma or handicaps, these individuals were often unable to assume "normal" Bamako wage jobs such as driving lorries or taxies. Occasionally the Institute hired former patients such as Issaka Traoré to work as janitors or gardeners. Most other patients, however, resorted to informal or temporary occupations such as collecting firewood from the nearby bush for sale in town.[57] Lasine Berté collected wood for fifteen years, starting in the late 1950s. He earned little, however, because physical weakness prevented him from carrying the larger, more profitable pieces. After much hardship he learned to make straw and cotton mattresses which yielded more money.[58] Several of his friends also took up mattress-making and other trades such as small-scale farming and petty commerce.[59]

Most lepers lived in perpetual economic insecurity, shifting from one vocation to another. For about four years in the 1960s Soumana Traoré earned small change as a table vendor until his money ran out and he was forced to cut straw for mattresses.[60] Fuseni Diakité worked around the same time as a cook for the Institute's European staff. He eventually lost his job when he fell out of favor with an employer's wife.[61] Kanko Fofana first performed odd jobs such as pounding millet and washing clothes

---

54 See McNaughton, *The Mande Blacksmiths*.

55 Harold Courlander with Ousmane Sako, *The Heart of the Ngoni, Heroes of the African Kingdom of Segu* (New York: Crown Publishers, 1982).

56 The origins and meaning of begging in West Africa has been the subject of interesting historical debate. See Iliffe, *The African Poor* and J. D. Y. Peel, "Poverty and Sacrifice in Nineteenth-Century Yorubaland: A Critique of Iliffe's Thesis," *Journal of African History* 31 (1990): 465–84. Iliffe responds to Peel's critique in, "Poverty and Transvaluations in Nineteenth-Century Yorubaland," *Journal of African History* 32, 4 (1991): 495–500.

57 Issaka Traoré, 5 November 1992.

58 Lasine Berté, 16 November 1992.

59 Buna Sawane, 26 October 1992; Dramane Touré, 16 November 1992; Bakari Kanoté, 5 November 1992.

60 Soumana Traoré, 25 November 1992.

61 Fuseni Diakité, 4 November 1992.

until she and her leprous husband, Malè Sissoko, began farming just before indepen-dence.[62] As Djikoroni's population swelled and land grew scarce in the 1960s and 1970s, farming itself became problematic. Balafonci Doumbia for example, lost his fields to the government as it resettled Malian refugees following the collapse of the Mali Federation in 1960.[63]

More than any other occupation, begging exemplified the extent of this eco-nomic insecurity. Some individuals such as Fanta Suko and Nci Doumbia began soliciting alms as soon as they arrived in Djikoroni in the 1950s; without any friends or family to house them, they had to pay rent.[64] Komogoba Sako begged because her older brother could not provide for all the dependents living in his household.[65] In San, just after independence, the SGHMP clinic stopped supplying food, and the mayor's office barred about thirty patients from farming land which did not belong to them. (According to Dr. Safouné Traoré, San's chief doctor at the time, the new Malian government had reduced the Ministry of Health's budget to a third of its original size before independence.[66]) Patients such as Sabari Sokoba suddenly found themselves obligated to solicit alms in the market.[67] A few people returned to their villages, but Ferdinand Jessana remained in San since he had chil-dren and was still undergoing treatment. About twenty years later, when the Malian government forbade people from living on clinic premises, still more lep-rosy patients began begging.[68]

Most people entered the occupation with a sense of anguish since it had been a highly stigmatized activity in their villages. As Sabari Sokoba noted, begging shamed the entire community.[69] Bakari Boré found that his fellow villagers willingly fed elderly and blind people but somehow resented the burden of supporting lepers unable to work. Bakari therefore moved (in the 1970s) to San where he knew that he could beg freely.[70] Of all informants, only one, Fatoma Kamaté, begged openly in his village and only at the expense of great humiliation. People said he smelled; they yelled the insult *"kunato"* and spit while chasing him away. He lived alone this way for six years before moving (just before independence) to San which was more con-ducive to begging.[71]

In the same manner that the company of other lepers enabled people to live comfortably with their disease, the substantial presence of other beggars (of all types, not just lepers) made the practice more acceptable and fostered a sense of group identity. As Aminata Tall discovered in the late 1960s, seeing others in the same position alleviated one's fears.[72] Like the disease itself, begging brought

62 Kanko Fofana, 9 February 1993.
63 Balafonci Doumbia, 19 November 1992.
64 Fanta Suko, 7 December 1992.
65 Komogoba Sako, 7 November 1992.
66 Safouné Traoré, 22 March 1993.
67 Sabari Sokoba, 21 March 1993.
68 Ferdinand Jessana, 21 March 1993.
69 Sabari Sokoba, 21 March 1993.
70 Bakari Boré, 22 March 1993.
71 Fatoma Kamaté, 21 March 1993.
72 Aminata Tall, 6 April 1993.

together people from a wide variety of backgrounds and enabled them to help each other on and off the streets. Jean-Baptiste Dambélé, for example, learned Bambara from another leper so that he could beg more effectively in San.[73] Nana Keita overcame her initial shame only after joining a group of women who begged together at the mosque on Fridays.[74] Throughout the 1960s and 1970s, beggars such as Nèkoro Traoré also often slept together in central locations such as the mayor's office or Bamako's main pharmacy.[75]

As noted in earlier chapters, villagers in general did not tolerate begging in their own communities, but town-dwellers, especially Muslims, wittingly or unwittingly encouraged it through their generosity and even partial hospitality. The marabout Sékou Fanta Madi, for example, attracted many blind and leprous people to Kankan (Guinea) by providing them with free food until his death in 1958.[76] In Bamako, wealthy or high-status individuals often assumed the role of patron for one or several beggars. The *chef de canton* (local African ruler appointed by the French) of Kita often supplied food to Musomari Nomogo's husband for distribution to others in the 1950s. Musomari's husband had been one of the town's oldest mendicants and acted as "chief" of their "association." After independence the African commandant of Kita allowed him and his wife to lodge in an adjoining compound.[77] A tolerant homeowner in Bamako similarly allowed Karunga Doumbia to sleep in his empty garage. Wojima Sako, a retired policeman, later became Karunga's patron and occasionally presented him with gifts of clothes and millet. By the close of the 1950s, Karunga had pooled enough money to marry a woman and rent a house in the Hamdallaye quarter of Bamako.[78]

In general, begging resulted from a complex and changing interplay of physical disability, social stigma, and poverty. A few individuals moved into towns for the sole purpose of soliciting alms, but most people simply sought better medical treatment or sanctuary from unpleasant social conditions. Only when confronted with the demands of paying rent or procuring food did such people subject themselves to the shame and fear associated with begging. The company of others engaged in the same activity often alleviated the emotional trauma and strengthened the collective identity associated with their disease. In cosmopolitan towns such as Bamako, widespread toleration and support of beggars made their occupation profitable and somewhat acceptable when compared with its contemptible status in villages. Not all lepers became beggars and not all beggars were lepers. The two identities often fused together, since the "normal" populations of these towns usually encountered lepers only as mendicants in the market or in front of the mosque. In the end, however, begging intensified the stigma of leprosy and, as revealed in the following sections, made lepers vulnerable to persecution.

---

73 Jean-Baptiste Dambélé, 21 March 1993.

74 Nana Keita, 29 November 1992.

75 Nèkoro Traoré, 19 May 1993.

76 Majan Fofana, 16 December 1992.

77 Musomari Nomogo, 21 April 1993.

78 Karunga Doumbia, 15 December 1993.

Beggars and the Colonial State

Since the beginning of the century, leprosy constituted both a medical and a social problem for colonial government officials. Their policies sprang as much from a desire to cure the disease as from a desire to control the scourge of lepers moving into towns and cities. Though never fully implemented, their repeated plans to fight begging through segregation reflected an unwillingness or inability to resolve the deeper causes of migration. The following examples of Bamako and Dakar illustrate how colonial authorities in the post-Brazzaville era lacked autocratic powers or sufficiently "medical" pretexts for removing these undesirable mendicants from towns. Nonetheless, their attitudes and scattered attempts established a precedent for harsher actions pursued by Mali's postcolonial regimes.

Throughout the early 1950s, begging lepers constituted an unsolvable nuisance for Dakar administrators who, according to one official, knew not whether to treat lepers as "patients" or as "vagabonds."[79] In 1952, for example, the police arrested twenty-four begging lepers for "vagabondage and mendicancy" and sentenced them to eight days in prison and a one-year *"interdiction de séjour"* (prohibition against entering the town). Authorities from the Hygiene Service then transported them to the leprosarium in Peycouk (Thiés). Not long after, they escaped and returned to Dakar in spite of the interdiction. The following year the police "transferred" about fifty to sixty more lepers to Peycouk in a similar manner. Some of them had already been "rounded up and transferred several times."[80]

In 1954, one French official was disturbed by the sight of Danish sailors photographing a group of five lepers beside a war memorial in Dakar. The official acknowledged that imprisonment was no longer a solution, since "healthy" inmates refused to live alongside those with the "repulsive disease." (They even refused to ride on the same vehicles despite vigorous washing and disinfection.)[81] Instead he suggested that the SGHMP construct detention units adjacent to the M'Bour and Peycouk leprosariums in which patients—who, in some cases, had already spent two months in jail—could serve out their "theoretical" prison sentences.[82] Two years later the governor of Senegal recommended that the Office of Social Affairs and the Health and Hygiene Services systematically contact each leper individually and offer two options: treatment at M'Bour or prison for "vagabondage."[83]

The American consul in Dakar also described the "noticeable" gatherings of lepers outside the town's Cathedral, the Government General, and the American Consulate. "[T]hey [the lepers] are not conducive," he wrote, "to the Government's present strenuous attempts to make Dakar an attraction for tourists." The problem resulted

79 Délégué du Gouv. to Gouv. du Sénégal, no. 959, 3 September 1954, ANS 1H-73.

80 Dir. de la Santé Publique du Sénégal–Mauritanie to Dir. Gén. de la Santé Publique, no. 595, 4 February 1954, ANS 1H-73

81 Délégué du Gouv. to Gouv. du Sénégal, no. 959, 3 September 1954, ANS 1H-73.

82 Ibid.; Délégué du Gouv. Sénégal to Gouv. du Sénégal, no. 16.392, 24 September 1954; Délégué du Gouv. du Sénégal to Admin. de la Subdivision de M'Bour, no. 17.759, 16 October 1954; Délégué du Gouv. du Sénégal to Gouv. de Sénégal, no. 22.029, 27 December 1954, ANS 1H-73.

83 Délégué du Gouv. du Sénégal to Gouv. Gén., no. 2074, [undated but probably February or March 1956]; Gouv. Gén. to Délégué du Gouv. du Sénégal, no. 2561, 17 February 1956; no. 1718, Gouv. du Sénégal to Délégué du Gouv. du Sénégal, 16 March 1956; Gouv. du Sénégal to Gouv. Gén., no. 533, 16 March 1956, ANS 1H-73; Gouv. de Sénégal to Gouv. Gén., no. 1062, 22 May 1956, ANS 1H-73.

from the administration's inability to isolate "patients with repulsive but non-contagious sores."

All leprosaria in French West Africa have two functions: treatment and isolation for those actively contagious, and asylum for the incapacitated. While most of these institutions are obliged to turn away patients for lack of space, in certain cities, particularly Dakar, many sufferers, while receiving "outpatient" treatment at the dispensaries, refuse hospitalization in these special institutions because it interferes with their lucrative profession of begging.[84]

Though not contagious, lepers aroused considerable concern among the non-African residents who pressured the government to clear them off the streets.

Meanwhile, in Bamako, the Institute's director, Paul Laviron, similarly abhorred the increased circulation of lepers in Bamako. He complained that "sanctions and exclusions" imposed on the Institute's "recalcitrant" patients bore no results. "The leper is an itinerant, a merchant, a beggar." His patients sold their rations and supplies for cash and even lodged and fed "non-leprous" laborers working at the airport. Laviron lacked a "permanent text" empowering him to "force" lepers back to their places of origin. After discovering three leprous "houseboys" (servants) working for Europeans, he asked the administration to reconsider his decree first proposed several years earlier. This decree would have obligated laborers to carry health cards indicating if they had any contagious diseases.[85]

By attracting so many patients from rural areas, the Institute had suddenly appeared as a health hazard of its own. The Sisters cited the example of Bamako's sixty leprous "whites" as evidence that its proximity to town constituted a "big danger of contagion." Along with government officials, they identified a site twenty-nine kilometers south of Djikoroni for lodging two thousand more lepers.[86] Most of the international medical community at this time no longer considered leprosariums necessary or useful means for controlling the disease, but, as late as 1958, French administrators and doctors still found a large isolation center appealing.[87]

As noted in Chapter 5, the circulation of begging lepers in towns and cities posed a recurring problem for the colonial government since the beginning of the century. In the 1950s, however, the political climate had changed considerably; administrators no longer wielded the same level of autocratic power as had their predecessors who once ruled by decree. Forced removal of non-contagious patients, no matter how "repulsive," had also become unacceptable in medical circles. In this new context, the outdated plans for an even larger leprosarium outside Bamako never materialized. Efforts to stem the problem with police roundups and special detention units in Dakar also failed. While the government possessed a cure for leprosy, it lacked an effective remedy for begging, one of the disease's most notorious social consequences.

84 C. Vaughan Ferguson, "Leprosy in French West Africa," Foreign Service Despatch, 18 May 1954, U.S. National Archives, Washington, D.C.
85 Laviron to Dir. de la Santé Publique, no. 108, 5 July 1950, ANS 1H-48. See also Gouv. de Soudan to Gouv. Gén., no. 2076, 27 July 1951, ANS 1H-73.
86 Untitled and unsigned notes, SB D 5167-5.
87 "RAMD, 1954–55" and "RAMD, 1957–58," SB B 5167-3.

Beggars and the Postcolonial State

As noted in the previous chapter, people on the margins of society gradually viewed independence in 1960 more as a changing of the guard than a social revolution. Colonial methods of administration, justice, health, education, and law enforcement endured. For Mali's leprous mendicants, this meant that penal codes prohibiting their occupation would remain on the books and allow police to remove them at will.[88] Their experiences with postcolonial state authority therefore deepened their sense of alienation, which the next chapter examines in more detail. Above all, repeated attempts to remove beggars from Bamako reflected the combined influence of European notions of urban order and indigenous prejudices against lepers and other stigmatized people.

Much like the colonial administration in Dakar, the first independent Malian government periodically sought to clear beggars, the *"sans travailles"* (literally, without work), from Bamako's streets.[89] Amadou Diakité, who served as US-RDA party chief in the Bamako district of Quinzambougou, saw no malicious intent behind these roundups. He regarded them as acts of "generosity," attempts to provide beggars with a better life. The government, in his view, considered mendicants inappropriate for an "organized country" (*pays organisé*).[90] Aliou Bagayogo served as Minister of Interior under Modibo Keita in 1968 and similarly regarded the roundups as a routine police action for "cleansing" the streets, not a concerted policy of persecution. However, he acknowledged that the Popular Militia—which bypassed the usual chain of government authority and, between 1967 and 1968, took the law into its own hands—may have organized its own roundups.[91]

Individuals subjected to these roundups, of course, felt deliberately persecuted. Once, in the early 1960s, the police beat Nci Doumbia as they arrested him.[92] Jeneba Traoré found the last three years of Keita's rule especially unpleasant. In 1967 the police constructed a special "house" for incarcerating beggars at their station in the N'Tomikorobougou quarter of Bamako.[93] After holding individuals such as Jeneba for the day, the police would dump them all in Djikoroni, regardless of whether they lived there or not.[94] Adama Traoré was also held once at the station until he paid a fine of 1,500 francs. He and the other imprisoned beggars received only a gourd of porridge in the morning and one of rice in the afternoon and evening. Some beggars spent as many as two or three days in captivity. Upon release, the police usually forbade them from begging near their most lucrative spots: the pharmacy, the post office, the central market, the mosque, and the *toubab* quarters.[95]

88 Gaoussou Traoré, "Le Phénomène de la mendicité à Bamako et dans les centres urbains," *Aurore* (1 April 1993), 3.

89 Moussa Konaté briefly refers to these roundups (*rafles*) directed against the *"sans travail"* (*Mali*, 27).

90 Amadou Diakité, 2 March 1993.

91 Aliou Bagayogo, 7 June 1993.

92 Banci Doumbia, 12 November 1992.

93 Danzeni B. Koné, "Les aspects socio-économiques et religieux de la mendicité dans le District de Bamako" (*Mémoire*, Philosophy, ENSUP, Bamako, 1989).

94 Jeneba Traoré, 7 November 1992.

95 Adama Traoré, 13 November 1992. Most of the *toubab*s at this time were expatriates.

Often the police tried to remove leprous and other handicapped beggars physically from town. Mamadou Koulibali witnessed one incident in which the police abandoned a number of lepers far down the road to Siby.[96] On another occasion, the police drove thirty kilometers towards Ségou and unloaded Adama Traoré along with about thirty-five other lepers far in the bush. A few individuals managed to walk back to Bamako on their own, but about sixteen handicapped men and women had to crawl to the road where they waved to cars for help.[97]

By 1968 Modibo Keita's government and the Popular Militia became perceptibly more repressive. The National Assembly disbanded at the beginning of the year, and in June the suppression of a small revolt in Ouéléssébougou resulted in two deaths. On November 19 a group of military officers led a successful coup, and shortly thereafter Lieutenant Moussa Traoré became Mali's second president.[98] Within a few years, the initial promises of a restoration of democracy were forgotten; Mali became a party-less military dictatorship run by the Comité Militaire de Libération Nationale (CMLN).

As before, political change brought only a temporary reprieve for beggars; by September 1969 the police resumed their roundups.[99] Arouna Dembélé, director of the Office of Social Affairs from 1970 to 1979, described these efforts as even more severe than they had been under Modibo Keita's rule. The socialist state had cared for most people's needs, but in the wake of the coup, begging escalated dramatically. Between 1970 and 1971, Malian beggars in Abidjan and Ghana had been collected and flown back to Bamako. Even more distant countries such as Saudi Arabia, Zaïre, and Congo were repatriating Malians, many of whom had become beggars while abroad.[100] As the number of beggars increased with the great drought of 1972–73, President Traoré ordered the removal of "human garbage" (les ordures humaines) from Bamako. The director general of security then collected all the blind and leprous beggars and left them behind in Sanankoroba, a small town thirty kilometers to the south.[101]

Traoré's regime became visibly more repressive throughout the 1970s as military officials gradually dominated the entire administration. Historian Moussa Konaté described the first ten years under the CMLN as "one of the most somber points" in Malian history.[102] Modibo Keita died in captivity in 1976 and the suppression of a number of "attempted coups" resulted in more arrests. The government banned political activity and manipulated labor unions to its advantage.

The lepers who begged during these years endured some of the harshest treatment they were ever to experience. Nanténé Keita, mentioned earlier, usually begged in the mornings with her children. Each day she collected enough money to buy *sana* (leftover cooked rice) and some basic ingredients for sauce. The police rounded her up several times during Traoré's rule. Once they stuffed her into a crowded car with other

---

96 Mamadou Koulibali, 12 March 1993.

97 Adama Traoré, 13 November 1992.

98 Sanankou, *La Chute de Modibo Keita*, 175.

99 Moussa Konaté, *Mali*, 27.

100 Arouna Dembélé, 10 August 1993; see also Gaoussou Traoré, "Le Phénomène de la mendicité," 3.

101 Arouna Dembélé, 10 August 1993; see also Gaoussou Traoré, "Le Phénomène de la mendicité," 3.

102 Moussa Konaté, *Mali*, 41.

beggars whom they abandoned again near Sanankoroba.[103] Moussa Diakité and several others were frequently beaten, and some people believed that a few individuals died.[104] Nakan Doumbia, for example, never again saw three of her friends after the police dumped them all (Nakan included) far from town on the road to Siby.[105]

Nearly everyone subjected to these roundups in the 1970s believed that Tiékoro Bagayogo, director of police services and internal security, had orchestrated all the roundups. Intimidated by his widely perceived power and ruthlessness, victims often offered little resistance or simply avoided the city's center. After spending three nights at the police station, Yoro Boli gave up public begging altogether, as had so many others.[106] Only on a few rare occasions, usually after particularly vicious roundups, did lepers fight back. Their direct resistance amounted to little more than yelling insults and throwing stones at police from concealed places.[107] As an indirect response, however, a number of beggars formed small associations to organize better their activities on the streets and to provide each other with mutual support.[108] The following chapter will examine these associations in more detail.

As the brutality became intolerable in 1978, Nurse Kassibo and other staff from the Institut Marchoux voiced a complaint directly to the president.[109] To the relief of many Malians, Bagayogo and several other officials were arrested later that year for plotting a coup. Though no doubt responsible for corruption and many atrocities, Bagayogo served as a scapegoat for assuaging popular discontent with Moussa Traoré's regime.[110] He died in 1983 while serving a prison sentence in Taoudeni, the notorious desert village where Modibo Keita also expired.

Bagayogo's arrest reduced the harshness of police activities, but the government's preoccupation with controlling beggars continued. In late 1979, not long after these developments, the Republic of Mali's Ministry of Defense, under instruction from President Traoré, handed down a confidential letter ordering the police and the Ministry of Health and Social Affairs to "liberate public places from the beggars who had become too invasive in Bamako." [111] Nantènè Keita was among the many blind, leprous, and handicapped people rounded up in the resulting sweep. The police took her to their station and held her overnight before agents from the Ministry of Health and Social Affairs arrived to record names and take photographs. The police released her after she agreed to pay 500 francs (about $2, supposedly the cost of the photograph). Others, however, were held longer because they had no money.[112]

103 Nantènè Keita, 29 November 1992.

104 Mamadou Koulibali, 12 March 1993; Moussa Diakité, 14 November 1992. None of my informants, however, could ever identify specific individuals who died.

105 Nakan Doumbia, 17 November 1992. She did not know if they had died or simply given up living in Bamako.

106 Yoro Boli, 28 January 1993.

107 Nantènè Keita, 29 November 1992.

108 For example, in the late 1970s Komogoba Sako established an association of women lepers which remains active today. Komogoba Sako, 7 November 1992.

109 Moussa Diakité, 18 November 1992.

110 Pascal Imperato, *Historical Dictionary of Mali* (Metuchen, NJ: Scarecrow Press, 1986), 92–93.

111 Direction National des Affaires Sociales, "Enquête sur la mendicité à Bamako," 7 May 1980, Direction National des Affaires Sociales, Bamako.

112 Nantènè Keita, 29 November 1992.

As part of this effort, the Department of Social Affairs surveyed 260 mendicants and found that 55.6 percent of them were blind and 18.3 percent were leprous. Nearly half of all 260 said that they had settled in Bamako for medical treatment. The resulting report concluded,

> The mendicants see their salvation only in the practice of begging. They rebel against any effort at emancipation. The beggars see their future only in the care provided by the state and in [the generosity of] the believers [pious Muslims]—for them, asking alms is a duty. . . . The resettlement of mendicants in their villages of origin is the only solution to their problem, but this must be accompanied or complemented with preliminary training in a trade which would enable them to live once and for all at their homes.[113]

This recommendation reflected a relatively new belief that medical treatment for lepers required some form of complementary social rehabilitation. In the 1960s Dr. Languillon, Laviron's successor, transformed the Institute from a patient hospice into a more focused research center. As doctors preoccupied themselves almost exclusively with clinical matters, the Institute assumed a less active role in the day-to-day lives of its current and former patients. Languillon nonetheless recognized the broader needs of most lepers and recommended establishing a rehabilitation camp next to the village of Samanko on the road to Guinea.[114] The Order of Malta (an international charitable organization) and Bamako's Lions Club financed its construction and initial maintenance. In 1970 the Malian prime minister presided over its inauguration.[115]

Both the Sisters and Nurse Kassibo visited the settlement weekly while the Friends of Samanko association (composed of civic leaders) oversaw its general management. Originally designed to provide three years of vocational training so that patients could reintegrate themselves into their home villages, the Village de Post-Cure de Samanko was not supposed to be a permanent asylum. As the Social Affairs report suggests, however, Samanko could not possibly address the needs of hundreds of indigent lepers. By 1975 it had "rehabilitated" only fifty-five patients, many of whom preferred to settle next to the center rather than return to their villages.[116] Within a few more years, most of its residents ensconced themselves permanently in the housing units, leaving no room for new patients.[117] Samanko became more of a showpiece for the charity of a few individuals and organizations than an effective antidote to begging. In a 1975 promotional pamphlet extolling its success, two large photographs of President Moussa Traoré—the man who ordered the removal of "human garbage" from the streets—and his wife appear next to the caption, "The Friends of Samanko."[118]

---

113 Direction National des Affaires Sociales, "Enquête sur la mendicité à Bamako," 7 May 1980, Direction National des Affaires Sociales, Bamako.

114 This was most likely the site purchased for the planned but never realized leprosarium of the late 1950s.

115 "RAMD, 1964–65" and for 1965–66, SB C 5167-3; "Précis historiques du Poste de Marchoux," SB C 5167-4.

116 "RAMD, Djikoroni, 1969–70" and for 1970–71 and 1971–72, SB D 5167-3. Lions Club, "Village de Post-Cure de Samanko," booklet in author's possession, January 1975.

117 Dawda Koita, 23 August 1993.

118 Lions Club, "Village de Post-Cure de Samanko," 17.

In the early 1980s the perceived begging problem prompted two more attempts at social assistance. Samanko's limited effectiveness had become especially apparent in 1982 when the Department of Social Affairs conducted another investigation and identified 782 mendicants who slept in public places. Government officials also learned that beggars had formed associations to organize their activities on the streets and pool their earnings for more even distribution at the end of each day.[119] With the support of the Association Raoul Follerau (a French organization devoted to improving the welfare of leprosy patients), the Institute allocated part of its land for gardens and supplied a well and solar pump. Indigent lepers were given small plots on which they could cultivate produce as a source of income.

Around the same time, the White Sisters and other charitable organizations arranged the construction of a small cluster of cement homes adjacent to the Samanko center. Like so many similar institutions throughout the century, it was designed to keep begging lepers far from the streets. This new "village," known as Samanko-Invalides, provided food and housing for about fifty indigent and invalid persons without a family or other means of support. Without question it relieved a few people from the misery of begging for survival in the capital of one of the world's poorest countries.

In the end, however, Samanko-Invalides and the gardens alone could not possibly eliminate the problem. Concern for public begging continued throughout the decade. Nanténé Keita and Komogoba Sako, leaders of one of the most active mendicants' associations, believed that Bala Kalen, the imam of Bamako's Grand Mosque who maintained close ties to the government, discouraged Friday begging because it competed with his own efforts to collect alms at prayer. Whenever they became too numerous, he instructed them to sit in the shade and not bother others. Nanténé and Komogoba also believed that "black" Christians once called the police to remove begging lepers from the area around Bamako's Cathedral.[120] In December 1988, ten years after Bagayogo's arrest, the police conducted still another roundup.[121]

These repeated attempts to clear begging lepers from Bamako's streets echoed a period in Mali's early colonial past when health agents and administrators removed people to the leprosarium in Bako-Djikoroni. For the victims of police roundups, African rule made life even more difficult. Whatever hardships one experienced in a village hardly compared to the persecution suffered in the capital which was assumed to provide better medical care. After the brutalities of the 1970s, many lepers would forever distrust and resent their African *famaw* (rulers, those who wield power). Nothing accentuated their separation from society more than a drive out of town and abandonment in the bush.

Conclusion

Without question, migration is one of the principal components of historical change, especially in Africa. It also plays an important role in the definition of social identities.

---

119 Gaoussou Traoré, "Le Phénomène de la mendicité," 3.

120 Nantènè Keita, 29 November 1992.

121 Danzeni Koné, "Les aspects . . . de la mendicité," x.

In his analysis of national identities, Benedict Anderson notes how "administrative organizations create meaning." Drawing on Victor Turner's concept of the "journey" as a "meaning-creating experience," Anderson cites religious pilgrimages to places like Rome and Mecca as institutionalized mechanisms drawing together different people from "*otherwise unrelated* localities." [Anderson's emphasis.][122] Government leprosy programs in Mali functioned in a similar manner. Having introduced once-isolated communities to the power of new European medicines, the mobile campaign unintentionally created a new incentive to resettle near clinics, if not the Institute itself. Leprosy-based social identities already existed in rural areas, but these institutions spawned communities in which people became conscious of themselves as a group bonded together by a common attribute.

Along with social experiences at home, the specific manner of resettlement directly affected one's identity as a leper. In locations such as Djikoroni where institutions provided extensive care and material support, once-alienated patients often developed a strong sense of community. SGHMP clinics in administrative centers rarely offered comparable support, but nonetheless served as common destinations for people from disparate localities, religions, or ethnicities. Such people did not necessarily settle together, but they at least developed some degree of group awareness. Over time, leper identities assumed many forms reflecting different levels of alienation and varied patterns of resettlement. In all cases, however, moving away demonstrated the continued, though always changing, power of difference in shaping social organization.

Begging represented an even greater degree of social dislocation. In both the colonial and postcolonial periods, government officials regarded beggars as a blemish on their capitals. The constant circulation of disfigured and disabled peoples in need of support betrayed deep inadequacies in the provision of medical care and other forms of socioeconomic assistance to rural areas. Failing to redress these inadequacies, officials pursued the short-term solution of removing the blemish physically. Beggars with leprosy and other disabilities (such as blindness) gradually responded to these hostile actions by forming small associations. As the following chapter reveals, these and subsequent associations became the clearest expression of their group identity.

---

122 Anderson, *Imagined Communities*, 53–54.

9

Becoming an Association

Throughout the twentieth century, identities rooted in leprosy underwent continual change while always manifesting deep connections to the past. This study began by examining the formation of those identities in rural societies, especially where government programs had little influence. Stigma was shown to derive from the disease's incurable and chronic nature. The resulting physical disfigurement and handicaps often barred sufferers from work and marriage, two essential components of a "normal" identity in agrarian communities. Lepers left their villages and settled in places like Djikoroni largely to escape the social isolation which impinged on their day-to-day lives. In forming communities on the basis of their disease, however, they merely reinforced their difference from others. Their stigma assumed new but no less onerous forms as they became vulnerable to medical and colonial domination. Economic depravity drew many into begging, which compounded their stigma and, especially under African rule, subjected them to police persecution. The dysfunctions of a colonial medical system, which persisted in the postcolonial era, prevented many patients from enjoying the potential benefits of antibiotic treatment. Social and political conditions had changed considerably since independence, but these individuals remained vulnerable to permanent nerve and tissue damage, the principal cause of physical and social suffering. In the 1990s, Mali entered still another period of dramatic change. Leper identities once again underwent a transformation which nonetheless followed a recognizable historical trajectory.

A popular revolt and subsequent coup unseated President Moussa Traoré in 1991, nearly twenty-three years after he first took power. A year later, Malians enthusiastically participated in their first multiparty elections and chose Alpha Omar Konaré as their president. Bamako residents could now listen to at least eight fully independent FM radio stations. New newspapers and journals appeared every week. Rival bus lines competed with each other, and a construction boom created a new demand for labor. Students demonstrated freely in the streets without fear of violent retaliation. Of all these momentous changes, the blossoming of independent associations most clearly revealed the aspiration of many Malians to participate in a new civil society. These associations focused on a variety of issues and activities including the environment and the arts.

Founded in 1991 shortly after the March Revolution, the Association des Malades Lépreux du Mali (AMLM) exemplified a similar zeal for political activism among Dijkoroni's former and current leprosy patients. Their activism entered the public eye most notably during the presidential campaign. While debating his rivals on national television, candidate Demba Diallo employed a proverb about lepers to question the sincerity of his rival's appeal to voters. The well-known proverb says, "One befriends a leper, because one knows that, if he finds a ring, he will give it to you. However, if the leper dares to hang the ring from the cord around his neck, one breaks with him."[1] In other words, one chooses friends on the basis of what they can give in return.

Diallo's ill-timed proverb enraged the leper community in Djikoroni, because its imagery reinforced the stereotype of lepers without fingers. Their ensuing protests embarrassed him before the entire electorate and won them a visit from Alfa Omar Konaré, Diallo's most formidable opponent and eventual vanquisher.[2] Use of the proverb on television represented one of the many ways in which society continued to wrong those affected by the disease. In addition to manifesting discontent with their popular image, their vocal reaction uncovered a deeper, long-standing resentment of the misery associated directly with three decades of African rule.

This latest expression of group identity also coincided with other important developments occurring on an international level. In August 1993, two years after the AMLM's founding, the Fourteenth International Leprosy Congress convened in Florida to discuss, among other things, the World Health Organization's (WHO) proposed goal of eliminating leprosy by the year 2000. WHO's ambitious goal rested on the capability of antibiotics to render most patients non-infectious within forty-eight hours. It also relied on a narrow clinical definition of leprosy based solely on the presence of bacilli. From this perspective, most of the AMLM's members were not "Hansen's Disease patients" since they had long since completed their treatments and no longer carried the bacillus. While the international medical community discussed the eradication of a disease, its sufferers were becoming all the more visible as a self-conscious social group. The incongruity between WHO's optimistic vision of the future and the recent developments in Djikoroni underscored the degree to which practitioners of scientific medicine had detached themselves from the social milieu of patients. Even if, according to WHO's projections, leprosy as a biological affliction would disappear at the century's close, the AMLM demonstrated that leper as a social identity would endure for at least one more generation.

Lepers and their "Healers"

When viewed in historical context, the AMLM's creation fits into a long-term pattern of patient discontent which began with the first attempts at leprosy control earlier in the century. Discontent of all types resulted to a large degree from the dissonance between patients' social needs and their healers' therapeutic and non-therapeutic endeavors. The Institute's 1945 "revolt" illustrated how patients perceived the Institute as a refuge and home, while their European doctors thought of it

---

1 Kounato fè teria koun ye, n'a ye bolo la nèguè tomo, k'a di'i ma; nka ni min ko a b'a ta do a kan na dyourou la, i bè fara a la." I was unable to obtain an official transcript of the debate. This particular version of the proverb is from Mgr. Molin, *Recueil de proverbes*.

2 Famory Keita, 6 December 1992. The incident was well publicized. Many other people in Bamako related this incident during informal conversations.

as research center which they alone controlled. As the world's medical practitioners became more biologically focused from the 1950s onwards, the Institute intensified its research activities and gradually reduced its provisions of food, clothing, and shelter. By the early 1990s, Djikoroni's lepers articulated their discontent by contrasting the Institute's former largesse during "European times" (*toubab tuma*) with its subsequent parsimony under independent rule.

Over the years, the White Sisters had also noted this decline in the Institute's concern for the general welfare of its current and former patients. As early as 1954, one report observed that Director Laviron had become "very difficult" and was interested "in the disease but not the patients."[3] His successor, Dr. Jean Languillon, appeared similarly preoccupied with his status as a respected leprosy specialist. According to mission reports, he busied himself only with experiments and rarely visited the hospital rooms.[4] In the 1970s the Sisters complained that the European doctors worked "almost exclusively for their advancement" and were only interested in patients to the degree that they served their medical "reputations."[5]

The Institute's complicated status after independence also contributed to the perceived decline. As noted in Chapter 5, the OCCGE, a multinational organization whose members consisted of France and the former colonies, succeeded the SGHMP in 1960 and transformed the Institute into one of its official research centers. While most colonial and clerical institutions quickly fell under African leadership, the Institute—and its growing staff of African doctors, administrators, and nurses—remained under the direction of French doctors: Dr. Languillon (1958 to 1971); Dr. Saint-André (1971 to 1981); Dr. Nebout (1981 to 1989); and Dr. Bobin (1989 to 1995). The Association Raoul Follereau Française (ARFF) and other European charitable organizations committed to leprosy eradication gradually assumed responsibility for most of its operating budget. In 1978 the Institute also became a "collaborative center" for WHO's leprosy campaign.

By 1981, roughly 14 percent of the Institute's budget came from WHO, while most of the remainder came from the ARFF. The Institute's annual report for that year complained that the ARFF used financial assistance as a pretext for meddling in its affairs. More specifically, the report cited the association's refusal to fund some technical equipment and to supply thalidomide, an important drug used in treating a particular condition of leprosy.[6] A combination of budgetary problems, financial improprieties on the part of one of its African administrators, and personal rivalries between the director and the ARFF strained the Institute considerably for most of the 1980s.

In 1989, the OCCGE brought in Dr. Bobin to revitalize the languishing Institute. Bobin had been director of a similar ARFF-funded institute in New Caledonia, a French Overseas Department. He immediately initiated the renovation of its run-down buildings and reformed the management of its personnel and finances. He then reorganized its departments to sharpen the Institute's focus as Mali's only dermatological clinic and as a research and training center committed to leprosy control. A marble sign which read "Institut Central de la Lépre - A.O.F."

---

3 Mére Louise-Marie, "Rapport de visite de Djikoroni, 28 octobre au 1 novembre 1954," SB B 5167/1.

4 Mére Nathanael, "Rapport de visite de Djikoroni, 11 au 19 mars 1963," SB C 5167/1.

5 "RAMD, 1972–73," SB D 5167/3; "RAMD, 1973–74," SB D 5167/3.

6 [Title page missing, probably the Institut Marchoux's Rapport Annuel for 1981], AIM.

still hung above the entrance as if the colonial era had only recently passed. Upon Bobin's instructions, the Institute's caretakers removed it. As of 1993 when I completed my research, the Institut Marchoux remained under OCCGE's control. While the ARFF provided about 80 percent of its operating budget, the OCCGE and Malian government paid the salaries for its African staff. As *coopérants* (technical advisors similar to Americans employed by the U.S. Agency for International Development), Bobin and most of the other French doctors were technically employed by the French government.

Bobin believed that a near "revolt" of Djikoroni's lepers in 1991 was provoked specifically by his reforms of Institute policy. Former patients, many of whom had finished their treatments years before, had grown accustomed to receiving free medicines, quality care for ailments unrelated to leprosy, and other privileges at the Institute. Much like earlier directors, Bobin felt that former leprosy patients in Mali and other places including New Caledonia considered themselves entitled to these benefits. Past medical and social policies had conditioned them to expect special and separate care. In his view, however, it was the responsibility of other organizations like the ARFF to change social attitudes through education so that lepers and the world around them would view leprosy as they would any other disease. Since modern treatments could render people non-infectious within forty-eight hours and arrest the disease before the onset of permanent physical damage, people with leprosy no longer needed treatment outside of regular medical services.[7]

Though well intentioned, Bobin's views exemplified the limitations of an exclusively clinical understanding of leprosy. For nearly a century, medical policies had treated lepers separately from the general population. Even prior to colonial rule, local societies regarded the disease differently from other afflictions. The ability of doctors to eradicate a bacillus hardly empowered them to eradicate stigma. As Bobin reformed the Institute and hoped that new thinking would spread to the general population, lepers in Djikoroni and throughout Mali remained preoccupied with day-to-day struggles similar to those endured by previous generations. From their point of view, an "education" campaign alone would not undo a seemingly inevitable way of life rooted in the distant past.

While the government's leprosy service frequently malfunctioned from inadequate infrastructure and demoralized staff, the regular health service remained even less prepared to attend to the welfare of leprosy patients and survivors. As late as the 1980s, its staff regularly discriminated against individuals manifesting this disease. In 1983 Director Nebout complained to the minister of health that doctors and nurses had been turning away "lepers" suffering from ailments unrelated to leprosy. That year a radiologist at Bamako's hospital refused to see a man who had long since been cured.[8] On another occasion the hospital turned away a similar man with a strangulated hernia, a potentially fatal condition if not treated promptly.[9] Four years later, a surgeon at Bamako's hospital refused to operate on a cured leper with appendicitis. The patient was sent to the Institute where doctors were forced to operate despite the

---

7 Pierre Bobin, 20 October 1992.

8 Nebout to Président de l'Association Raoul Follereau Malienne, "Demande d'intervention au ministre de la santé pour éviter la ségrégation des malades atteints de lèpre," 19 May 1983, AIM.

9 Dr. Chevallard, 8 July 1987, AIM.

absence of proper equipment.[10] Throughout the 1980s the surgical unit at the Institute also received increasing numbers of severely mutilated patients—often from great distances away—who had been refused treatment for infections caused by injuries stemming from permanent neurological impairments.[11] Such delays merely exacerbated the infections and often necessitated amputation.

Outside Bamako, some health agents manifested even harsher contempt for leprosy survivors. In early 1993, for example, a local business in San gave seventy-five kilograms of powdered milk to a young nurse who was supposed to distribute it to his patients; he ended up selling the donation for his own profit. On earlier occasions he had pilfered the dispensary's medicines, including those for leprosy, and sold them at exorbitant prices. One patient had even paid for medicines for the wrong disease and died as a result. The stolen milk merely compounded leprosy patients' disaffection with the dispensary which, as part of a reform of the medical system, had begun charging user fees of 250 CFA (about $1) per visit. Many individuals could barely gather the 100-150 CFA necessary for a day's supply of food. Even with a free consultation, they could not afford the prescribed drugs or supplies. The dispensary also lacked basic items such as bandages and disinfectants.[12] Given these unfavorable conditions, San's lepers turned to the Père de Rasilly, an aging White Father first stationed at the local Catholic Mission in 1948. Starting in the late 1980s, de Rasilly provided basic care for their sores and infections as he once did before the advent of the mobile campaign. He also organized a gardening project for the lepers and occasionally slipped the most desperate individuals some money for survival.[13]

The daily gathering of ten or fifteen lepers at de Rasilly's doors—which I observed in 1991 and 1993—echoed scenes from an earlier age. Nearly a century before, the same disease under different circumstances had induced individuals to seek refuge at the Ségou mission. The stigma of leprosy, which clearly existed before colonialism, survived decades of dramatic political and social change. In dealing with the disease separately from all others, both European and African health officials added a new component to this stigma. Their fixation on leprosy's biological aspects also led them to overlook their patients' social predicaments.

New Struggles, Enduring Identities

The reaction to Demba Diallo's proverb demonstrated how, despite Bobin's aspirations, former and current leprosy patients continued to view themselves as a distinct social group meriting specific rights and respect. Their very existence betrayed the cumulative effects of past misdiagnosis and interrupted treatments. Their long-term struggles constituted the fabric of their identities. As the AMLM and its leaders' personal histories reveal, the nature of those struggles assumed new forms as the political and social contexts changed. Their identities, however, remained forever rooted in the disease.

---

10 Nebout to Madame le Ministre de la Santé Publique, 17 July 1987, AIM.

11 "Rapport annuel d'activité, Unité Chirurgie, Institut Marchoux," 1986, AIM.

12 Bernard de Rasilly, 2 and 21–23 March 1993.

13 Ibid.

As noted briefly in the previous chapter, unofficial patient associations existed long before the AMLM. Recall that Saran Keita belonged to one briefly before her limited resources obligated her to quit. Some of these associations formed specifically in response to the challenges of begging. Others simply reflected a widespread tendency among Bamako's inhabitants to join together in informal groups or *tonw* (plural for *ton*). The notion of a *ton* originates in Mali's deep past when agrarian societies organized themselves into associations based on gender, occupation, age, or initiatory status. *Tonw* created structures for mutual assistance, entertainment, and the sharing of knowledge. In the colonial and postcolonial urban milieu, new *tonw* based on new attributes—such as common profession, village of origin, or religion—often fulfilled the same purposes. In most cases, they were either exclusively male or female, although the latter's associations were more visible.[14]

One of the most active and vocal *ton* in Djikoroni originated in the 1970s and brought together a large group of women lepers, most of whom begged. As of 1993, this *ton* was still active, pooling resources for mutual assistance as well as social events such as dances, baptisms, and weddings. For special celebrations, they wore "uniforms" made from the same cloth. The *ton*'s leaders, Komogoba Sako and Jeneba Traoré, aggressively sought out charitable organizations and made sure their members received assistance on specific occasions such as International Leprosy Day. Their importance in the community became most evident when, in 1991, the AMLM's founders invited them to join their efforts.

Before the 1991 March Revolution, the largest and most visible leper associations consisted only of women. Men tended to organize themselves into smaller groups (*grenw*) of five to ten members and gathered daily for conversation beneath a tree or near a workshop. Banci Doumbia and his friends, for example, assembled next to a roadside overhang where their friends, also lepers, made straw mattresses. Having settled in or around the Institute as early as the 1930s or 1940s, several of Banci's group ranked among Djikoroni's oldest residents. Their *gren* was therefore widely known and, in 1991, encouraged to join the AMLM. In general, men's *grenw* were much less active and assertive than women's groups such as Komogoba's. Limited time and resources, however, prevented me from investigating the causes of these differences more concretely.

Whether male or female, these informal groupings of lepers provided little more than mutual support and a forum for socializing. They were largely powerless politically, because their members generally lacked basic literacy, formal education, an understanding of government institutions, and the requisite social ties. Mali's first two regimes had also restricted independent political activity. In contrast, the AMLM's two main leaders, Mamadou Koulibali and Fousseyni Sow, possessed the skills and background necessary for protecting or even advancing their interests through more formal channels. They also knew how to use Mali's newly won freedoms of expression and association to their collective advantage.

14 Claude Meillassoux, *Urbanization of an African Community: Voluntary Associations in Bamako* (Seattle: University of Washington Press, 1968); Kate Modic, "Negotiating Power: A Study of the Ben Ka Di Women's Association in Bamako, Mali," *Africa Today* 41, 2 (1994): 25-37; for a more general discussion of women's associations in Africa, see Audrey Wipper, "Women's Voluntary Associations," in Margaret Jean Hay and Sharon Stichter, eds., *African Women South of the Sahara*, 2d ed. (New York: Longman Publishing, 1995), 164-186.

Photo 8: Association (*tonw*) of women lepers in Djikoroni (1993). [Photograph by Eric Silla]

Mamadou was born at the Institute in 1948 while his mother was undergoing leprosy treatment.[15] His father had served in the French army and fought in France during the Second World War. After his retirement in 1948, the entire family settled in the father's Bambara village, Moromoro, situated about eighty kilometers northeast of Kita. Mamadou returned to Djikoroni in 1959 and lived with a cousin, also an Institute patient, so that he could continue his schooling. Six years later Mamadou received his first diagnosis of leprosy and underwent a year of sulfamide treatment administered by the Sisters. Considered cured at the time, Mamadou finished his studies and, after a year in Lemer, Holland, obtained a diploma in tourism. He spent 1973 working out of a hotel in Mopti leading tours through Sangha and Dogon country.

Dissatisfied with tourism, Mamadou studied journalism by correspondence and moved to Germany with the hope of obtaining a scholarship to enter a university in Holland. When this plan failed, Mamadou went to Paris where he found a job with the Institut National Géographique Français. In 1976 this job led him to Libya where he met several American agricultural specialists who, two years later, brought him to Washington state for a month's visit. The Americans had promised to employ him in the United States after his contract ended in December 1980. In September of that

---

15 Mamadou Koulibali, 12 March 1993.

year, however, he suffered a relapse. After unsuccessful treatment by an Egyptian doctor at a Libyan clinic, Mamadou's condition worsened and he returned once again to Djikoroni for more treatment. In 1986 he lost a toe as a secondary consequence of the disease. He remained in Djikoroni and never found regular employment again.

By virtue of his background and education, Fousseyni (b. 1954) was a similarly atypical "leper."[16] He belonged to a privileged class of government administrators assumed to be immune to "diseases of poverty."[17] His paternal grandfather was a Fulani merchant from Dara, Senegal, who settled in Kita in the late nineteenth century and married a granddaughter of Umar Tall, founder of the Tukolor Empire which once controlled most of the region. Born in 1906, Fousseyni's father, Abdoul Karim, worked as an administrator for the colonial government, became a *commandant de cercle* upon independence, and served as Kita's mayor from 1965 until his death in 1970. Fousseyni himself grew up in Kita before attending the Institut Pédagogique et Rurale (IPR) in Katibougou (near Bamako). From 1970 to 1981, he worked as an agricultural technician with Opération Arachides, a vast state-owned peanut cultivation project near his hometown. The project went bankrupt in 1981, so he moved in with his older sister Adam in Bamako.

Fousseyni's first symptoms had appeared in 1979, but a Grandes Endémies nurse assured him that they were not caused by leprosy. For five years he went untreated. In 1984, when the patches began multiplying, he finally consulted a French doctor at the Institut Marchoux. The doctor was unable to identify the particular form of his disease and sent a tissue sample to France for analysis; however, the results never returned. A few months later Fousseyni felt sufficiently cured and stopped his treatment on his own. More patches appeared around 1987. Doctors at the Institute then recognized his condition as the multibacillary form which required multidrug therapy consisting of strong doses of DDS and Rifampicin, the most widely used antibiotics. Fousseyni returned to his sister's house after a brief stay at the Institute's hospital, but this time he continued to report for treatment every month.

A deepening sense of social isolation in his sister Adam's compound prompted Fousseyni to move to Djikoroni in 1987. There he established a common bond with other leprosy patients despite their differences in education and socioeconomic status. One of the White Sisters, Dorothé, gave him a job at the pharmacy where he worked until the mission closed three years later. He then obtained a small plot in the gardens reserved for needy ex-patients. Even in Djikoroni, Fousseyni's sense of alienation endured. In 1990 he married Asa Keita, a young "healthy" woman who cooked for Institute patients. She knew of many patients with "healthy" spouses and therefore saw no reason to fear his disease. Her mother and friends, however, never accepted him, insisting that she too would become a leper. His subsequent conversion from Islam to Catholicism angered them even more.

In interpreting his alienation, Fousseyni found that his education threatened administrators who were more comfortable with compliant and unsuspecting lepers.

16 Fousseyni Sow, 28 October 1992; 14 May 1993; 5, 7, and 15 July 1993.

17 In informal conversations, a number of middle- and upper-class Bamako residents expressed a widespread assumption that the disease affected only the poor.

In 1992, for example, he spent only one month at the Samanko rehabilitation center before its directors turned him out. They claimed to lack operating funds, but Fousseyni believed that they did not want literate residents who might challenge their authority. During his brief stay, Fousseyni tried unsuccessfully to reform the center's management which had allowed a select group of quiescent patients to ensconce themselves permanently to the detriment of others who were waiting to enter. Although the Institute subsequently allowed Fousseyni to live in one of its own patient houses, some of its staff circulated rumors that he was dealing illegal drugs and causing other unspecified trouble.[18]

The experiences of Fousseyni and Mamadou echo those of an earlier patient activist, Mamadou Fomba, who led the 1945 "revolt" at the Institute. All three belonged to a minority of Western-educated Malians before disease precluded them from professional advancement and severed them from their peers. Their activism defied peoples' expectations of weak, indigent, and submissive lepers. They spoke French, could read and write, and, most importantly, knew how to deal with government institutions. The relatively unaffected exterior physical appearances of Fousseyni and Mamadou Koulibali

Photo 9: Fousseyni Sow (1992) [Photograph by Eric Silla]

---

18 Leopold Blanc, 10 December 1992.

Photo 10: Members of the Association Malienne des Handicapés de la Lèpre (1996). The three individuals in the center standing from right to left: Mariame Sanogo, Banci Doumbia, and Fousseyni Sow. [Photograph by Eric Silla]

did not automatically reveal their disease to others, as was the case for Mamadou Fomba. Their interiors, however, did change. In the end, they too became lepers as a result of the disease's repeated and prolonged occurrence.

The AMLM

Three factors contributed to the AMLM's creation: a history of informal association among Djikoroni's lepers; political liberalization following the 1991 coup; and the leadership of Mamadou Koulibali and Fousseyni Sow. Mamadou provided the first initiative in June 1990 when, as an outpatient, he wrote a letter to Bobin complaining that lepers no longer received the necessary medicines and adequate care. After the 1991 coup, he pronounced these grievances openly on national radio. Bobin feared a "revolt" and encouraged him to establish a formal association so that patients could express their complaints calmly. Mamadou then assembled most of Djikoroni's lepers for a meeting, and on August 14, 1991, the AMLM received formal authorization from the Malian government. As secretary general, Mamadou read a declaration on national television announcing the association's creation and goals. Fousseyni then began registering new members, issuing them photo-identification cards, and collecting dues. They eventually built a small cement block building at the edge of the Institute grounds which served as a forum for both formal and informal meetings.

Referring to themselves as *banabatow* (lepers) and others as *mogow kéné* (healthy people), AMLM's members embraced their new association as a means of collective empowerment. They sought to redress numerous injustices as they saw them. Shortly after the 1991 coup, the association complained to Bobin that lepers had seen little if any of the seventy-two million CFA (about $250,000) donated three years earlier to the Malian chapter of the Association Raoul Follereau (ARFM). The chapter was headed by Alu Cissé, a former health minister whom many lepers suspected of misusing funds originally intended for their benefit.[19] The ARFM's office was also located in another quarter of Bamako not easily accessed by people with disabilities or little money. As a result of its protests, the AMLM won greater control over the distribution of donations as well as the management of other ARFM programs.[20]

The AMLM demonstrated its capacity for collective action most forcefully in its response to one of the greatest challenges to Djikoroni's lepers ever. In mid-1993 the newly elected municipal government initiated a massive urban development project (*lotissement*) for Djikoroni. In imposing a grid of wide streets, the project threatened to displace a number of people from their homes and to destroy completely the lepers' gardens on the Institute grounds. A bulldozer had already razed, in the rainy season of 1992, the fields which former patients had cultivated for decades. At the time, government officials told them that "bandits" were hiding in the tall millet and corn stalks. When the bulldozers returned in 1993 and razed Banci Doumbia's meeting place, the real reasons became clear.

The project reinforced the lepers' sense of vulnerability. For nearly a century, social attitudes and government policies had subjected them to sundry forms of isolation and persecution. When the Institute opened in 1934, Djikoroni was a sparsely populated village. For years, Bamako's residents considered it *the* quarter for lepers, since former patients and those unable to enter the Institute settled in the vicinity. The growing capital, however, slowly encroached on the once secluded community. An extension of the neighboring airstrip cut straight through the center of the fields. In the 1950s individuals not affiliated with the Institute had begun taking over small plots and pressuring the director to relinquish patient land.[21] Nine years later the newly independent government assumed control of a large area for settling Malian refugees who fled Senegal with the break-up of the Mali Federation.

In subsequent years the eastern parts of Djikoroni between the road and the river—which had also once belonged to the Institute—were gradually developed to accommodate the growing population of urban (non-leprous) immigrants. "Development" involved plowing over existing homes and fields in order to construct a grid of streets

---

19 Mamadou Koulibali, 12 March 1993; Fousseyni Sow, 14 May 1993; Bernard de Rasilly also questioned ARFM's handling of funds, 2 and 21–23 March 1993.

20 Fousseyni Sow, 28 October 1992.

21 Djigui Diakité to Laviron, 22 September 1951, AIM; Administrateur to Laviron, no. 438, 4 July 1957; Laviron to Administrateur, 8 July 1957, AIM.

for new housing. According to the Catholic mission records, each of these development schemes displaced a number of former patients and allowed outsiders to settle in their place.[22] By 1981 Djikoroni's population had increased sixfold to about thirty thousand. Unable to purchase plots in the developed sections, many people built "illicit" homes on land which patients had been farming.[23] One Institute doctor even complained unsuccessfully to the minister of health about the "illicit occupation" and the unauthorized construction of a gas station on Institute property.[24]

With the 1993 project, the mayor's office intended to complete Djikoroni's development, considered by some to be long overdue.[25] It specifically targeted the oldest quarter which had remained a maze of dirt paths lined with adobe compounds as in a rural village. This was also the quarter where many of the Institute's former patients had settled over the years. People whose compounds lay in the path of a planned street were supposedly given the option of moving to a new plot on the other side of the road. However, in order to obtain the plot they had to pay several hundred dollars in administrative fees and begin building immediately. Those unable to afford these expenses could sell their rights to any number of eager merchants who would resell the plot for ten times its original value.

At first, the government excluded former patients from all discussions concerning the project, acting as if they had no rights to the land. When the bulldozers arrived and people found construction markers in their gardens, many of Djikoroni's lepers began meeting regularly at the AMLM to plan a response. On several occasions angry members marched directly to the mayor's office to voice their complaints. They also ripped out the construction markers and piled them in front of the Association building. After repeated demonstrations, the mayor's office finally invited Mamadou Koulibali to negotiate on behalf of the community. Officials then offered a new garden plot several kilometers away. AMLM members ridiculed this proposition since many of them were either disabled or too poor to pay for transportation. The proposition also ignored the minimum two years of hard work required to develop an equally prosperous and stable garden with banana plants and papaya trees. The level of the community's discontent and suspicion manifested itself most clearly when several members began suspecting even Mamadou of selling out and not advocating their interests forcefully enough. At that point AMLM meetings became acrimonious and divisive.[26]

As Djikoroni's lepers fought to protect their interests, another development conveniently stalled the project. In late August 1993 one of Bamako's newspapers documented a scandal in which commission members had assigned new plots to friends and family rather than Djikoroni residents. This discovery fueled the protests of non-leprous individuals who also felt threatened by the development project. As renters of homes targeted for removal, many people suddenly found themselves without a place to live and unable to afford a plot of their own. Even

22 "RAMD, 1966–67," SB C 5167/3.

23 [Title page missing, probably the Institut Marchoux's "Rapport annuel" for 1981], AIM.

24 Chef Baquillon to Ministre de Santé, "Occupations illicites de terrain sur le domaine de l'Institut Marchoux," 4 September 1981, AIM.

25 In informal conversations about Djikoroni, Bamako residents often complained of the quarter's dirty and disorganized condition.

26 Microfilm of minutes taken at AMLM meetings in author's possession.

home owners feared losing their property rights altogether since many could not pay the government fees or costs of new construction. A year later, the development project had hardly advanced and the AMLM members were still embroiled in their fight to retain control of their gardens.[27]

None of these new struggles—a politician's hurtful rhetoric, cutbacks in health and welfare services, unscrupulous bureaucrats, ruthless urban development—were unique to lepers in Djikoroni. People of all types in Africa and abroad have also dealt with them in one form or another. However, by participating in civic life collectively as lepers, these particular individuals revealed the capacity of disease to define identity as forcefully as more common attributes rooted in language, religion, or ethnicity.

Conclusion

The ensemble of narratives presented in this and previous chapters illustrates the tight connections between contemporary identities and the past. It reveals an uncanny tendency of identities to outlast the institutions and conditions which had engendered them in the first place. Several lepers have observed that, in some villages, their disease no longer prevents marriage or causes social isolation; villagers know that *toubab* medicines can arrest it before the onset of disfigurement and handicaps. Even the notion of contagion, once used to rationalize exclusion, has become less prevalent. However, people such as Fousseyni Sow, Mamadou Koulibali, Saran Keita, the beggars, the gardeners, and other survivors all feel as vulnerable to stigma as had their predecessors. The stigma of leprosy has endured vast sociopolitical changes and medical advances; it still permeates the society in which they live.

In late January 1993 the Institute prepared itself for International Leprosy Day which was scheduled for the 31st. Director Bobin led a French television crew on a tour of the laboratories, hospital wards, and other buildings so that they could broadcast footage to French audiences on the actual day. Radio France International also passed through to report on the Institute for global audiences.[28] Meanwhile, Mamadou Koulibali and other AMLM members busied themselves with the planning of their own festivities.

When the day arrived, Djikoroni's lepers lined the road to Guinea to welcome Alpha Omar Konaré, Mali's new president. Several small but active associations of women lepers had dressed in smart matching outfits. After much fanfare produced by groups of leper drummers and dancers, the president took his place beneath a canopy standing in front of the entrance to the Institute's main building. Behind him sat government officials, military officers, members of Bamako's diplomatic corps, and several prominent Malian businessmen. They all faced a podium behind which stood a group of well-dressed young children holding a large banner which read, "We are all children of patients, but we ourselves are not sick." ("Nous sommes tous des enfants des malades, mais nous ne sommes pas malades.") A crew of Malian television technicians darted about with their cameras and microphones. The entire area

---

27 Fousseyni Sow to author, 8 August 1994, private correspondence in author's possession.

28 Audio recording of this broadcast in author's possession.

was shaded by two rows of tall kapok trees planted when the Institute first opened in 1934.

After Dr. Bobin's opening address, Mamadou Koulibali welcomed the president and other visitors on behalf of all the lepers. He then delivered a brief speech in French which argued against the stigma of his disease. Bobin then led the president and other guests inside the Institute where representatives of Samanko's rehabilitation center displayed various crafts made by lepers. For the rest of the day, former patients gathered on Institute grounds for dancing, feasting, and celebration on a scale usually reserved for important religious holidays.

This one "tradition" had survived so many changes at the Institute. Throughout its nearly sixty-year history—even before the first International Leprosy Day in 1954—patients and staff had welcomed with similar fanfare dignitaries ranging from French presidents and colonial governors to Malian presidents and other African leaders. On each of those occasions, "educated" individuals like Mamadou Fomba and Mamadou Koulibali stood at the podium in the name of their fellow lepers. In assembling year after year before such important personages, Djikoroni's lepers ceremoniously reinforced their collective identity. Although Bobin viewed this identity as an anachronism, this one tradition, created by his forebears, obliged him to recognize it publicly. International Leprosy Day was originally intended to celebrate a new era in which scientific medicine would eradicate a disease and its stigma. The crowds of lepers who gathered to mark the event, however, betrayed the inability of medicine alone to achieve such ends.

Photo 11: Malian stamp commemorating International Leprosy Day, Emile Marchoux, and the institute which bears his name. [Printed with permission from Mali's Office Nationale de la Poste]

Postscript

I returned to Mali in the autumn of 1996, three years after completing the original research for this book. Bamako had become noticeably more congested and polluted as a result of rapid economic growth (about six percent annually). Acres and acres of new housing developments sprawled out into the surrounding countryside in every direction. In an effort to inspire national pride, the government had erected monuments and statues at virtually every major intersection.

Signs of dramatic change appeared in other parts of the country as well. Multinational mining companies such as South Africa's Anglo-American had moved in to work the old gold fields in the southwest. A network of relay stations made television reception possible in every corner of the country for the first time. Once-dilapidated roads were being restored and widened to facilitate a visible explosion in trade. Even in Timbuktu, a large construction crane (for a new water tower) rose high above the town's otherwise flat skyline. The Malian government was also in the process of decentralization, conferring administrative powers back to local communities for the first time since the beginning of colonization one hundred years earlier.

Change in Djikoroni was equally manifest. Dr. Bobin retired in 1995 and, as of December 1996, no new director had assumed his place. The OCCGE and Malian health ministry were once again in the process of redefining the Institute's role. A memorial plaque for Aldiouma Kassibo, who had passed away in late 1993, hung above the entrance to one of its buildings. Plaques honoring other Malian nurses and even a White Sister hung in other locations. Between 1990 and 1996, the number of registered leprosy cases in Mali dropped from 12,817 to 4,804, and the incidence of the disease fell from 13.48 to 4.74 per 10,000.[1] Dr. Tiendrebeogo, the Institute's epidemiologist, attributed this dramatic decline to the aggressive use of improved multidrug therapies from 1992 onwards.

Though "clinical lepers" were disappearing, social lepers were all the more visible and active. In 1995 the Association des Malades Lépreux du Mali (AMLM) altered its name to the Association Malienne des Handicapés de la Lèpre (AMHL). The alteration resulted from a new perception that the term "lépreux" (lepers) was somewhat derogatory. The association's signs and stationary now included as its symbol a hand with missing digits. The AMHL's leadership had remained essentially the same, with Fousseyni Sow and Mamadou Koulibali at the helm. Its membership had grown from approximately 400 in 1993 to 2,566 in December 1996. Such numbers made it one of the largest civic associations in Mali. In addition to a cooperative store in

---

1 World Health Organization, Weekly Epidemiological Record 71, 20 (1996): 149ñ56.

Djikoroni, the association now operated several small diesel mills for threshing grain in other Bamako quarters.

As with many other new organizations which had emerged under Mali's democracy, the AMHL's activities demonstrated a heightened consciousness of its status as a civic association with political rights. In informal conversations, Fousseyni explained how much he and others had learned in this regard. "Little by little," he said, "we are learning how to fight for our rights." Similar patient associations with links to the AMHL had sprouted in towns including Kita, Kayes, San, and Diré. The AMHL had also joined the Fédération Malienne des Associations pour la Promotion des Personnes Handicapées which belonged to a similar association for Francophone West Africa. Mamadou had also traveled to other countries in Africa and Europe to attend conferences for handicapped persons.

Quite clearly, increased global communication and Mali's emerging democratic culture were adding new layers to leper identities—identities rooted in the indigenous and European practices described in previous chapters. In 1994, former Hansen's Disease patients and health care professionals met in Brazil to form the International Association for Integration, Dignity and Economic Advancement (IDEA). This new association joined together patient associations scattered mainly throughout the Americas and Asia. Its main goals centered on involving former patients in eradication programs and in projects aimed at improving their socioeconomic status. At the time of my 1996 visit to Djikoroni, I informed the AMHL of this new organization. Mamadou, Fousseyni, and other members appeared eager to join.

In contrast to these encouraging initiatives, one setback reminded AMHL members of their continued vulnerability. For three years, the association had successfully prevented Bamako's urban development project from completely overtaking the patient gardens adjacent to the Institute. The mayor's office had even assured them that their plots would not be touched. In October 1996, however, bulldozers suddenly appeared without warning, cutting large swathes through the dense maze of banana plants and onion patches. One swath aimed directly at the AMHL's meeting house. In the vacant plain which once served as Bamako's airstrip, one could make out the first signs of a large traffic circle with wide boulevards radiating out in every direction much like the Place d'Etoile in Paris. I later learned that a luxury housing development would be built on these last vacant tracts. As he showed me around, Fousseyni shrugged his shoulders in defeat and acknowledged that the mayor's office had lied to them. Several times he repeated the following proverb with a cynical chuckle: "If the *fama* (ruler) wants to put a road on your head, then it's your neck which must be cut."

From my perspective, all of these latest developments followed the historical trajectory traced in this book. Mali's leprosy survivors were once again using their stigma for "secondary gains" only to confront the limits of their social power.[2] Sociologist Erving Goffman once observed that people who organize themselves on the basis of their stigma must "resign" themselves to a "half-world."[3] In other words, stigma can become the basis of collective action and empowerment but rarely becomes a means of accessing all the resources and institutions available to "normal"

---

2 Goffman, *Stigma*, 10. See the introduction to Chapter 6 for an earlier use of this concept.
3 Ibid., 21.

members of society. For Djikoroni's lepers, this factor severely limited their defenses against the stronger forces of rapid urban change.

These latest developments also reinforced this book's underlying premise—that the example of a seemingly marginal social group can enrich our understanding of broader historical change. From their first encounters with missionaries and colonial health agents to their vigorous participation in civic life, individuals with leprosy have been directly involved with the major social and political changes of their time. Identity has served as a useful paradigm for interpreting these changes from individual, national, and international perspectives. It has advanced our academic understanding of health and disease in Africa. Moreover, it has allowed us to focus on the issues most important to patients themselves.

SOURCES

Archives

[With the exception of CEDRAB, all archival sources were originally in French. All quotations used in this study were translated by the author.]

Archives de l'Institut Marchoux, Bamako (AIM) [Note: These archives are not formally catalogued and were in considerable disarray when I consulted them.]

Archives Nationales du Mali, Bamako (ANM)

Archives Nationales du Sénégal, Dakar (ANS)

Archives des Pères Blancs, Rome (PB)

Archives des Soeurs Blanches, Rome (SB)

Centre des Archives d'Outre-Mer, Aix-en-Provençe (CAOM)

Centre de Documentation et de Recherche Ahmad Baba (CEDRAB), Timbuktu

Selected Bibliography

Abdalla, Ismail Hussein. "Islamic Medicine and its Influence on Traditional Hausa Practitioners in Northern Nigeria." Ph.D. dissertation, University of Wisconsin, Madison, 1981.

Abdalla, Ismail Hussein, and Brian M. du Toit, eds. *African Healing Strategies*. New York: Trado-Medic Books, 1985.

Adam, Barry. *The Survival of Domination, Inferiorization and Everyday Life*. New York: Elsevier North-Holland, 1978.

Adjanohoun, E. J., et al. *Contribution aux études ethnobotaniques et floristiques au Mali*. Paris: Agence de Coopération Culturelle et Technique, 1985.

Afrique Occidental Française. *Coutumiers juridiques de l'A.O.F.* Vol. II., Soudan. 1939.

Ainlay, Stephen C., Gaylene Becker, and Lerita M. Coleman, eds. *The Dilemma of Difference: A Multidisciplinary View of Stigma*. New York: Plenum Press, 1986.

Altman, Lawrence. "Looking to the End of Another Plague." *New York Times*, 29 August 1993, 5(E).

Amselle, Jean-Loup. *Logiques métisses, anthropologie de l'identité en Afrique et ailleurs*. Paris: Editions Payot, 1990.

Anderson, Benedict. *Imagined Communities, Reflections on the Origin and Spread of Nationalism*. New York: Verso, 1991.

Anspach, Renee. "From Stigma to Identity Politics: Political Activism among the Physically Disabled and Former Mental Patients." *Social Science and Medicine* 13A (1979): 765–73.

Arnold, David, ed. *Imperial Medicine and Indigenous Societies*. Manchester: Manchester University Press, 1988.

Arnold, Harry. "Correspondence: Leprosy and Social Class in the Middle Ages." *International Journal of Leprosy* 54, 4 (December 1986): 647.

Ba, Amadou Hampaté, and J. Daget. *L'Empire peul du Macina*. Paris: Mouton and Co., 1962.

Bacou, P. "Traitement de la lèpre chez un Bambara de Koulikoro (Soudan)." *Notes africaines*, n.s., 22 (1944): 10.

Bado, Jean-Paul. *Médecine coloniale et grandes endémies en Afrique 1900–1960: lèpre, trypanosomiase humaine et onchocercose*. Paris: Editions Karthala, 1996.

Bailleul, Charles. *Petit dictionnaire: bambara-français, français-bambara*. England: Avebury Publishing Company, 1981.

Balslev, Knud. *A History of Leprosy in Tanzania*. Nairobi: African Medicine and Research Foundation, 1989.

Barber, Malcolm. "Lepers, Jews, and Moslems." *History* 66, 216 (February 1981): 1–17.

Bastien, Christine. *Folies, mythes, et magies d'Afrique noire: propos de guérisseurs du Mali*. Paris: Editions L'Harmattan, 1988.

Beck, Anne. *A History of British Medical Administration of East Africa, 1900–1950*. Cambridge: Harvard University Press, 1970.

"Belgian Congo: Attitude of Patients." *International Journal of Leprosy* 17, 4 (1949): 482–83.

Beriac, Françoise. *Histoire des lépreux au moyen âge: une société d'exclus*. Paris: Imago: Diffusion P.U.F., 1988.

Bird, Charles and Martha Kendall. "The Mande Hero," ed. Ivan Karp and Charles Bird, *Exploration in African Thought*. Bloomington: Indiana University Press, 1980: 13–24.

Bloch, Don. *The Modern Common Wind*. London: Heinemann, 1985.

Bocquene, Henri. *Moi, un mbororo, autobiographie de Oumarou Ndoudi, peul nomade du Cameroun*. Paris: Editions Karthala, 1986.

Borius, Alfred. "Quelques considérations médicales sur le poste de Dagana (Senegal), observations faites pendant l'année 1862." *Thèse*, Faculté de Médecine de Montepellier, 1864.

Bosman, William. *A New and Accurate Description of the Coast of Guinea*. 1705. New York: Barnes and Noble, 1967.

Bourdieu, Pierre. *Outline of a Theory of Practice*. Translated by Richard Nice. Cambridge: Cambridge University Press, 1977.

Bragg, Rick. "Lives Stolen by Treatment, Not by Disease: The Last Lepers." *New York Times*, 19 June 1995, 1(A) and 6(B).

Brandt, Allan. *No Magic Bullet: A Social History of Venereal Disease in the United States Since 1880*. Oxford: Oxford University Press, 1985.

Brasseur-Marion, Paule. *Bibliographie générale du Mali*. Vol. 1. Dakar: I.F.A.N., 1964.

———*Bibliographie générale du Mali*. Vol. 2. Dakar: I.F.A.N., 1976.

Braud, Paul. *Trois siècles de médecine coloniale française*. Paris: Vigot Frères, 1931.

Breitha, Olivia. *Olivia: My Life of Exile in Kalaupapa*. Arizona Memorial Museum Association, 1988.

Brenner, Louis, ed. *Muslim Identity and Social Change in Sub-Saharan Africa*. Bloomington: Indiana University Press, 1993.

Brewer, Douglas. *Fish and Fishing in Ancient Egypt*. Warminster, England: Aris and Phillips, 1989.

Brody, Saul. *Disease of the Soul: Leprosy in Medieval Literature*. Ithaca: Cornell University Press, 1974.

Brown, William. "The Caliphate of Hamdullahi 1818–1864: A Study in African History and Tradition." Ph.D. dissertation, University of Wisconsin, Madison, 1969.

Caillié, René. *Journal d'un voyage à Tembouctou et à Djenne, dans l'Afrique Centrale . . . pendant les années 1824, 1825, 1826, 1827, 1828*. Paris: Editions Anthropos, 1965.

Camara, Josephe. "Les problèmes psychosociologiques de la reinsertion des lépreux." *Mémoire*, Psycho-Pédagogique, Ecole Normale Supérieure, Bamako, 1987.

Camara, Philomene. "La reinsertion socio-économique des handicapés physiques, étude de cas: les hanseniens à Bamako." *Mémoire*, Psycho-Pédagogique, Ecole Normale Supérieure, Bamako, 1990.

Carbonnel, Pierre. "La mortalité actuelle au Sénégal." *Thèse*, Faculté de Médecine de Paris, 1873.

Cashion, Gerald. "Hunters of the Mande: A Behavioral Code and Worldview Derived from a Study of Their Folklore." Ph.D. dissertation, Indiana University, 1984.

Cauvin, Jean. *L'Image, la langue, et la pensée, vol. ii: receuil de proverbes de Karangasso*. St. Augustin, Germany: Anthropos-Institut—Haus Volker und Kulturen, 1980.

Chapman, Ronald. "Leonard Wood and the Culion Leper Colony, 1921–1927: A Study in American Character." Ph.D. dissertation, University of Hawaii, 1979.

Cohen, William B. "Malaria and French Imperialism." *Journal of African History* 24, 1 (1983): 23–36.

Comaroff, Jean. "Healing and Cultural Transformation." *Social Science and Medicine* 15B (1981): 367–78.

Comaroff, Jean, and John Comaroff. *Of Revelation and Revolution: Christianity, Colonialism, and Consciousness in South Africa*. Vol. 1. Chicago: University of Chicago Press, 1991.

Conrad, David. "A Town Called Dakalajan: The Sunjata Tradition and the Question of Ancient Mali's Capital." *Journal of African History* 35, 2 (1994): 355–77.

Conrad, David, and Barbara Frank, eds. *Status and Identity in West Africa: Nyamakalaw of Mande*. Bloomington: Indiana University Press, 1995.

Coombes, Annie. *Reinventing Africa: Museums, Material Culture, and Popular Imagination in Late Victorian and Edwardian England*. New Haven: Yale University Press, 1994.

Cooper, Frederick. "Conflict and Connection: Rethinking Colonial African History." *American Historical Review* 99, 5 (December 1994): 1516–45.

Copans, Jean. *Anthropologie et impérialisme*. Paris: Maspéro, 1975.

Coppo, Piero, and Arouna Keita. *Médecine traditionnelle: acteurs, itinéraires thérapeutiques.* Trieste: Arti Grafiche Noghere, 1990.

Courlander, Harold, and Ousmane Sako. *The Heart of the Ngoni: Heroes of the African Kingdom of Segu*. New York: Crown Publishers, 1982.

Curtin, Philip. *The Image of Africa: British Ideas and Action, 1780–1850*. Madison: University of Wisconsin Press, 1964.

Darby, William. *Food: The Gift of Osiris*. New York: Academic Press, 1977.

de Benoist, Joseph-Roger. *Eglise et pouvoir colonial au Soudan Français: les relations entre les administrateurs et les missionaires catholiques dans la Boucle du Niger, de 1885 à 1945*. Paris: Editions Karthala, 1987.

de Rasilly, Bernard. Unpublished collection of Bobo proverbs in author's possession. Mission Catholique, San, Mali.

Derrida, Jacques. *Writing and Difference*. Translated by Alan Bass. Chicago: University of Chicago Press, 1978.

de Wildeman, E. *A Propos de plantes contre la lèpre (Crinum sp. Amaryllidacées)*. Brussels: Institut Royal Colonial Belge, Section des Sciences Naturelles et Médicales, 1932.

Dharmendra. "Leprosy in Ancient Indian Medicine." *International Journal of Leprosy* 15, 4 (1947): 424–30.

Diakité, Djigui. "Essai sur les traditions sanitaires et médicinales bambara du Bélédougou." *Thèse*, Ecole de Médecine, Bamako, 1988.

Diakité, M. "Lèpre, le combat social." *L'Essor*, 2 February 1993, 6.

Diallo, Koura. "L'indigence et les méthodes d'interventions sociales institutionalisées." *Mémoire*, Psycho-Pédagogique, Ecole Normale Supérieure, Bamako, 1986.

Diarra, Ibrahima. "Contribution à l'étude de quelques aspects des dermatoses en médecine traditionelle au Mali." *Thèse*, Ecole de Pharmacie, Bamako, 1991.

Diarrah, Cheick Oumar. *Le Mali de Modibo Keita*. Paris: L'Harmattan, 1986.

Dieterlen, Germaine. *Essai sur la religion bambara*. Paris: Presses Universitaires de France, 1951.

Dols, Michael. "The Leper in Medieval Islamic Society." *Speculum* 58, 4 (1983): 891–916.
————."Leprosy in Medieval Arabic Medicine." *Journal of the History of Medicine* 34 (July, 1979): 314–33.
Domergue, Danielle. "La Lutte contre la trypanosomiase en Côte d'Ivoire, 1900–1945." *Journal of African History* 22, 1 (1981): 63–72.
Domergue-Cloarec, Danielle. *Politique coloniale française et réalités coloniales: la santé en Côte d'Ivoire, 1905–1958.* Toulouse: Association des Publications de l'Université de Toulouse-Le Mirail, 1986.
Dory, Electra. *Leper Country.* London: F. Muller, 1963.
Doumbia, Soumana. "Bako-Djicoroni, évolution d'un village suburbain vers un quartier urbain de Bamako." *Mémoire*, Geography, Ecole Normale Supérieure, 1973.
Dubois, A. *La lèpre dans la région de Wamba-Pawa (Uele-Nepoko).* Brussels: Institut Royal Colonial Belge, Section des Sciences Naturelles et Médicales, 1932.
Dubois, A., and L. van Hoof. *La lèpre au Congo Belge en 1938.*Brussels: Institut Royal Colonial Belge, Section des Sciences Naturelles et Médicales, 1940.
Duncan, M. Elizabeth. "Leprosy and Procreation—A Historical Review of Social and Clinical Aspects." *Leprosy Review* 56, 2 (1985): 153–62.
Echenberg, Myron. "Tragedy at Thiaroye: The Senegalese Soldiers' Uprising of 1944." In R. Cohen, J. Copans, and P. Gutkind, eds., *African Labor History.* Beverly Hills: Sage Publications, 1978.
Ell, Stephen. "Leprosy and Social Class in the Middle Ages." *International Journal of Leprosy* 54, 2 (June 1986): 300–305.
————. "Plague and Leprosy in the Middle Ages: A Paradoxical Cross-Immunity?" *International Journal of Leprosy* 55, 2 (June 1987): 345–50.
————. "Three Times, Three Places, Three Authors, and One Perspective on Leprosy in Medieval and Early Modern Europe." *International Journal of Leprosy* 57, 4 (December 1989).
Evans–Pritchard, Edward Evan. *Witchcraft, Oracles, and Magic among the Azande.* Oxford: Clarendon Press, 1937.
Fassin, Didier. "Influence of Social Perceptions of Leprosy and Leprosy Patients on Public Health Programs." *International Journal of Leprosy* 58, 1 (1990): 111–14.
————. *Pouvoir et maladie en Afrique: anthroplogie sociale dans la banlieue de Dakar.* Paris: Presses Universitaires de France, 1992.
Feierman, Steven. "History of Pluralistic Medical Systems: Changes in African Therapeutic Systems." *Social Science and Medicine* 13B (1979): 277–84.
————. *Peasant Intellectuals: Anthropology and History in Tanzania.* Madison: University of Wisconsin Press, 1990.
————. "Struggles for Control: The Social Roots of Health and Healing in Modern Africa." *African Studies Review* 28, 2/3 (June/September 1985): 73–147.
Feierman, Steven, and John Janzen, eds. *The Social Basis of Health and Healing in Africa.* Berkeley: University of California Press, 1992.
Field, Margaret. *Religion and Medicine of the Ga People.* New York: Oxford University Press, 1937.
Follerau, Raoul. *"Vous aurez 20 ans en l'an 2000": les appels à la jeunesse 1961–1977.* France: Flammarion, 1986.
Foltz, William J. *From French West Africa to the Mali Federation.* New Haven: Yale University Press, 1965.
Ford, John. *The Role of the Trypanosomiases in African Ecology: A Study of the Tsetse Fly Problem.* Oxford: Clarendon Press, 1971.
Foucault, Michel. *The Birth of the Clinic: An Archaeology of Medical Perception.* Translated by A. M. Sheridan Smith. New York: Vintage Books, 1975.

————. *Discipline and Punish: The Birth of the Prison.* Translated by Alan Sheridan. New York: Vintage Books, 1979.

————. *Madness and Civilization: A History of Insanity in the Age of Reason.* Translated by Richard Howard. New York: Vintage Books, 1988.

————. *Power/Knowledge, Selected Interviews and Other Writings, 1972–1977.* Edited by Colin Gordon. New York: Pantheon Books, 1980.

Frankel, Richard. *Hansen's Disease, A Synopsis for Health Care Professionals.* Honolulu: Hawaii Department of Health, 1991.

Gaide, Dr., and Dr. Bodet. *La Prévention et le traitement de la lèpre en Indochine.* Hanoi: Imprimerie d'Extrême-Orient, 1930.

George, K., K. R. John, J. P. Mulingil, and A. Joseph. "The Role of Intrahousehould Contact in the Transmission of Leprosy." *Leprosy Review* 61, 1 (1990): 60–63.

Gibbal, Jean-Marie. *Les Génies du fleuve, voyages sur le Niger.* Paris: Presses de la Renaissance, 1988.

Gilman, Sander. *Difference and Pathology: Stereotypes of Sexuality, Race, and Madness.* Ithaca: Cornell University Press, 1985.

————. *Disease and Representation: Images of Illness from Madness to AIDS.* Ithaca: Cornell University Press, 1988.

————. *Picturing Health and Illness: Images of Identity and Difference.* Baltimore: Johns Hopkins University Press, 1995.

Gleason, Philip. "Identifying Identity: A Semantic History." *Journal of American History* 69, 4 (March 1983): 910–31.

Goffman, Erving. *Stigma: Notes on the Management of Spoiled Identity.* New York: Simon and Schuster, 1963.

"Gold Coast: Public Warned of Leprosy Cure.'" *International Journal of Leprosy* 21, 4 (1953): 392.

Gottlieb, Alma. *Under the Kapok Tree: Identity and Difference in Beng Thought.* Bloomington: Indiana University Press, 1992.

Gourvil, E. "La lèpre au Soudan." *Bulletin de la Société de Pathologie Exotique.* Séance du 9 janvier, 1935: 7–11.

Gray, John. *Ashe, Traditional Religion and Healing in Sub-Saharan Africa.* New York: Greenwood Press, 1989.

Grayzel, John. "The Ecology of Ethnic–Class Identity Among African Pastoral People: The Doukoloma Fulbe." Ph.D. dissertation, University of Oregon, 1977.

Greene, Graham. *A Burnt-Out Case.* London: Heinemann, 1961.

Greene, Linda. *Exile in Paradise: The Isolation of Hawaii's Leprosy Victims and Development of Kalaupapa Settlement, 1865 to the Present.* Denver: U.S. Department of Interior, 1985.

Gregory, Dorothy. "Aids—The Leprosy of the 1980s: Is There a Case for Quarantine?" *Journal of Legal Medicine* 9, 4 (1988): 547–60.

Griffiths, P. Glyn. "Leprosy in the Luapula Valley, Zambia." *Leprosy Review* 36, 2 (1965): 69–67.

Grmek, Mirko. *Diseases in the Ancient Greek World.* Translated by Leonard and Mireille Mueller. Baltimore: Johns Hopkins University Press, 1989.

Grön, K. "Leprosy in Literature and Art." *International Journal of Leprosy* 41, 2 (1973): 249–83.

Grosz-Ngate, Maria. "Bambara Men and Women and the Reproduction of Social Life in Sana Province, Mali." Ph.D. dissertation, Michigan State University, 1986.

————. "Hidden Meanings: Explorations into a Bamana Construction of Gender." *Ethnology* 28, 2 (1989): 167–83.

Gruner, O. Cameron. *A Treatise on the Canon of Medicine of Avicenna, Incorporating a Translation of the First Book.* New York: Augustus M. Kelley, 1970 [1st edition, 1930].

Gugelyk, Ted, and Milton Bloombaum. *Ma'i Ho'oka'awale: The Separating Sickness.* Honolulu: University of Hawaii Foundation and the Ma'i Ho'oka'awale Foundation, 1979.

Gussow, Zachary. *Leprosy, Racism, and Public Health: Social Policy in Chronic Disease Control.* Boulder: Westview Press, 1989.

Gussow, Zachary, and G. S. Tracy. "The Phenomenon of Leprosy Stigma in the Continental United States." *Leprosy Review* 43, 2 (1972): 85–93.

———. "Stigma and the Leprosy Phenomenon: The Social History of a Disease in the Nineteenth and Twentieth Centuries." *Bulletin of the History of Medicine* 44 (1970): 425–49.

Haidara, Lalla Badji. "Prévention et contrôle des endémies majeures par les practiciens traditionnels." *Thèse,* Ecole de Pharmacie, Bamako, 1986.

Hall, Stuart. "Ethnicity: Identity and Difference." *Radical America* 23, 4 (1989): 9–20.

Hand, Wayland, Anna Casetta, and Sondra B. Thiederman, eds. *Popular Beliefs and Superstitions: A Compendium of American Folklore.* Boston: G. K. Hall and Company, 1981.

Harley, G. W. *Native African Medicine.* Cambridge: Harvard University Press, 1941.

Harmon, Stephen. "The Expansion of Islam among the Bambara under French Rule: 1890 to 1940." Ph.D. dissertation, University of California, Los Angeles, 1988.

Harms, Robert. *Games Against Nature: An Eco-Cultural History of the Nunu of Equatorial Africa.* Cambridge: Cambridge University Press, 1987.

———. *River of Wealth, River of Sorrow: The Central Zaire Basin in the Era of the Slave Trade, 1500–1891.* New Haven: Yale University Press, 1981.

Hartwig, Gerald, and K. David Patterson. *Schistosomiasis in the Twentieth Century: Historical Studies on West Africa and Sudan.* Los Angeles: Crossroads Press, 1984.

———, eds. *Disease in African History: An Introductory Survey and Case Studies.* Durham: Duke University Press, 1978.

Hastings, Robert. *Leprosy.* Edinburgh: Churchill Livingstone, 1994.

Headrick, Rita. *Colonialism, Health, and Illness in French Equatorial Africa 1885–1935.* Atlanta: African Studies Association Press, 1994.

Hedges, Chris. "Yemen's Lepers Still Outcasts as in Ancient Times." *New York Times,* 20 March 1993, (Y)2.

Heidegger, Martin. *Identity and Difference.* Translated by Joan Stambaugh. New York: Harper and Row, 1969.

Henry, Josephe. *The Soul of African People: The Bambara, Their Psychic, Ethical, Religious, and Social Life.* Translated by Anne Coleman. New Haven: Human Relations Area Files, 1960.

Hirsch, Emil G. "Fish and Fishing." In *The Jewish Encyclopedia,* Vol. 5. New York: Funk and Wagnalls Co., 1903.

Hunter, J. "Hypothesis of Leprosy, Tuberculosis, and Urbanization in Africa." In R. Akhtar, ed. *Health and Disease in Tropical Africa: Geographical and Medical Viewpoints.* New York: Harwood Academic Publishers, 1987.

Hunwick, John. "Notes on a Late Fifteenth-Century Document Concerning 'al-Takrur." In Christopher Allen and R. W. Johnson, eds., *African Perspectives: Papers in the History, Politics, and Economics of Africa Presented to Thomas Hodgkin.* Cambridge: Cambridge University Press, 1970.

———. "A Region of the Mind: The Arab Invention of Africa." Unpublished paper in author's possession, dated 17 February 1993.

Iliffe, John. *The African Poor: A History.* New York: Cambridge University Press, 1987.

———. "Poverty and Transvaluations in Nineteenth-Century Yorubaland." *Journal of African History* 32, 4 (1991): 495–500.

Imperato, Pascal. *African Folk Medicine: Practices and Beliefs of the Bambara and Other Peoples.* Baltimore: York Press, 1977.

———. "The African and Western Pharmacopeias." Paper presented to the African Studies Association Conference, 1978.

———. *Historical Dictionary of Mali.* Metuchen, New Jersey: Scarecrow Press, 1986.

———. "Interaction of Traditional and Modern Medicine in Mali." *Issue* 9, 3 (1979): 14–18

———. *A Wind in Africa, A Story of Modern Medicine in Mali.* St. Louis: Warren H. Green, 1975.

Irgens, L. M., F. Melo Caeiro, and M. F. Lechat. "Leprosy in Portugal 1946–80: Epidemiologic Patterns Observed During Declining Incidence Rates." *Leprosy Review* 61, 1 (1990): 32–49.

Jacobson-Widding, Anita, and David Westerlund. *Culture, Experience and Pluralism: Essays on African Ideas of Illness and Healing.* Uppsala: Almqvist and Wiksell International, 1989.

Jacoby, Ann. "Felt Versus Enacted Stigma: A Concept Revisited, Evidence from a Study of People with Epilepsy in Remission." *Social Science and Medicine* 38, 2 (1994): 269–74.

Janzen, John. "The Need for a Taxonomy of Health in the Study of African Therapeutics." *Social Science and Medicine* 15B, 3 (1981): 185–94.

———. *The Quest for Therapy: Medical Pluralism in Lower Zaïre.* Berkeley: University of California Press, 1978.

Jeanselme, E. *La lèpre.* Paris: Gaston Doin, 1934.

Jewsiewicki, Bogumil, and David Newbury, eds. *African Historiography: What History for Which Africa?* Beverly Hills: Sage, 1986.

Jollet, Andre A. "Contribution à la géographie médicale du Soudan occidental, histoire médicale du poste de Koundon (1884–1886), étude d'hygiène et de pathologie exotiques." *Thèse,* Faculté de Médecine de Bordeaux, 1887.

Jones, Eldred. *The Elizabethan Image of Africa.* Washington: Folger Books, 1971.

Kaba, Lansine. *The Wahhabiyya: Islamic Reform and Politics in French West Africa.* Evanston: Northwestern University Press, 1974.

Kalisch, Philip. "Lepers, Anachronisms, and the Progressives: A Study in Stigma." *Louisiana Studies* 12 (1973): 489–531.

———. "An Overview of Research on the History of Leprosy." *Leprosy Review* 43, 2 (1975): 129–44.

———. "Tracadie and Peninkese Leprosaria: Comparative Analysis of Societal Response to Leprosy in New Brunswick, 1844–1880, and Massachusetts, 1904–1921." *Bulletin of the History of Medicine* 17 (1973): 480–512.

Kasturiaratchi, Nimal. "Interaction of Medical Systems and the Cultural Construction of Leprosy in Sri Lanka." Ph.D. dissertation, Princeton University, 1989.

Kati, Mahmoud ibn al-Mukhtar. *Tarikh el-Fettach.* Translated by O. Houdas and M. Delafosse. Paris: Ernest Leroux, 1913.

Kaur, Paramjit, U. C. Sharma, S. S. Pandey, and Singh Gurmohan. "Leprosy Care Through Traditional Healers." *Leprosy Review* 55, 1 (1984): 57–61.

Kermorgant, A. "Quelques us et coutumes des indigènes de la Côte d'Ivoire." *Annales d'hygiène et de médecine coloniale* III (March 1901): 146–51.

Kieffer, M. "Sénégal et Soudan; hopitaux; morbidité et mortalité en 1899." *Annales d'hygiène et de médecine coloniale* IV (April 1901): 248–58.

Kivits, M. *La lutte contre la lèpre au Congo Belge en 1955.* Brussels: Académie Royale des Sciences Coloniales, 1956.

Kjekshus, Helge. *Ecology Control and Economic Development in East African History: The Case of Tanganyika, 1850–1950.* London: Heinemann, 1977.

Kleinman, Arthur. *The Illness Narratives, Suffering, Healing and the Human Condition.* New York: Basic Books, 1988.

Konaté, Moussa. *Mali, Ils ont assassiné l'espoir: réflexion sur le drame d'un peuple.* Paris: Edition l'Harmattan, 1990.

Konaté, Ousmane. "La place du Service Social dans une institution sanitaire spécialisée, cas de l'Institut Marchoux." *Mémoire*, Ecole de Formation en Développement Communautaire, Bamako, 1985.

Koné, Abdoul Karim, and Bakary Nouhoum Diarra. "Essai sur la 'science' des sorciers guérisseurs du Mande et de Tiakadougou." *Mémoire*, Philosophy, Ecole Normal Supérieure, Bamako, 1983.

Koné, Danzeni. "Les aspects socio-économiques et religieux de la mendicité dans le District de Bamako." *Mémoire*, Philosophy, Ecole Normale Supérieure, Bamako, 1989.

Konipo, M. "Traitement de la lèpre chez les Bozo." *Notes africaines*, n.s. 81 (1959): 8.

Kristof, Nicholas. "For Chinese, an Ancient Scourge Loses Its Terror." *New York Times*, 11 December 1991, (A)4.

Labusquière, René. *Santé rurale et médecine préventive en Afrique: stratégie à opposer aux principales*. Paris: Le François, 1975.

Lacarrière, Anselme A. "Contribution à l'étude de la géographie médicale, souvenirs médicaux du poste de Kayes (Haut-Sénégal, 1885–86)." *Thèse*, Faculté de Médecine de Bordeaux, 1887.

Lasker, Judith. "The Role of Health Services in Colonial Rule: The Case of the Ivory Coast." *Culture, Medicine, and Psychiatry* 1 (1977): 277–97.

Laveran, L. "Soudan." *Dictionnaire encyclopédique de science médicale*, Paris, 1880.

le Clech, Louis, and Jean Vuillet. "Plantes médicinales et toxiques du Soudan Français." *Annales d'hygiène et de médecine coloniale* (1902): 223–57.

League of Nations. Health Organization. *The Principles of the Prophylaxis of Leprosy, III. Health.* 1931.

"Lepers Escape and Hold Town at Bay." *Leprosy Review* 7, 3 (1936): 127.

"Lepers Get Free March in Manila." *Leprosy Review* 8, 1 (1937): 48.

"Lepers on Strike in Japan." *Leprosy Review* 8, 1 (1937): 48.

Le Roux de Lincy, M. *Le Livre des proverbes français*. Paris: Adolphe Delahays, 1859.

Levtzion, Nehemia. *Ancient Ghana and Mali*. London: Methuen, 1973.

———— and J. F. P. Hopkins, eds. *Corpus of Early Arabic Sources for West African History*. Cambridge: Cambridge University Press, 1981.

Lewis, Bernard. *Race and Slavery in the Middle East, An Historical Enquiry*. New York: Oxford University Press, 1990.

Lewis, Gilbert. "A Lesson from Leviticus: Leprosy." *Man* 22, 4 (1987): 593–612.

Lions Club, "Village de Post-Cure de Samanko." Bamako, 1975.

Long, Esmond. "The Social Stigma of Disease." *International Journal of Leprosy* 33, 1 (1965): 98–102.

Longe, Dr. "Note sur la prophylaxie anti-lépreuse dans le cercle du Sine-Saloum (Sénégal)." *International Journal of Leprosy* 6, 1 (1938): 51–56.

Lyons, Maryinez. *The Colonial Disease: A Social History of Sleeping Sickness in Northern Zaire, 1900–1940*. Cambridge: Cambridge University Press, 1992.

MacDonald, A. *Can Ghosts Arise?: The Answer of Itu*. London: British Empire Leprosy Relief Association, 1952.

Maier-Weaver, Donna. "Nineteenth Century Asante Medical Practices." *Comparative Studies in Society and History* 21, 1 (1979): 63–81.

Mali, Direction Nationale de la Santé. *Enquête socio-culturelle dan le cadre de la lutte contre les T.D.C.I. dans le cercle de Tominian*. 1989–90.

Mark, Peter. *Africans in European Eyes: The Portrayal of Black Africans in Fourteenth and Fifteenth Century Europe*. Syracuse: Syracuse University, Foreign and Comparative Studies Program, 1975.

Mauny, Raymond. "The Antiquity of Vaccination in Africa." *Présence Africaine* 36, 8 (1961).

McKelvie, A. "Proposed Leprosy Settlement for Ashanti." Appendix VI, 27 January 1948, *Minutes of the Thirteenth Session of the Ashanti Confederacy Council*, 18–21, 23, and 25–26 February 1948. [Courtesy of Ivor Wilks]

McNaughton, Patrick. *The Mande Blacksmiths: Knowledge, Power, and Art in West Africa.* Bloomington: Indiana University Press, 1988.

McNeill, William. *Plagues and Peoples.* New York: Doubleday, 1976.

Meillassoux, Claude. *Urbanization of an African Community: Voluntary Associations in Bamako.* Seattle: University of Washington Press, 1968.

Meyer, Gerard. *Proverbes malinkés.* Paris: Conseil Internationale de la Langue Française, 1985.

Molin, Mgr. *Recueil de proverbes, bambara et malinkés.* Moulineaux: Les Presses Missionnaires, 1960.

Monteil, Charles. *Les Bambaras du Ségou et du Kaarta.* Paris: Larose, 1924.

Moore, Henrietta, and Megan Vaughan. *Cutting Down Trees: Gender, Nutrition, and Agricultural Change in the Northern Province of Zambia, 1890–1990.* Portsmouth, N.H.: Heinemann, 1994.

Moore, R. I. *The Formation of a Persecuting Society: Power and Deviance in Western Europe, 950–1250.* New York: B. Blackwell, 1987.

Morgenthau, Ruth Shachter. *Political Parties in French-Speaking West Africa.* Oxford: Clarendon Press, 1964.

Nebout, Guy-Michel. "L'Institut Marchoux ou 50 ans de lutte contre la lèpre en Afrique noire." *Thèse,* Ecole de Médecine, Université de Paris VII, 1984.

Ngubane, Harriet. *Body and Mind in Zulu Medicine.* London: Academic Press, 1977.

Niane, Djibril T. *Sundiata: An Epic of Old Mali.* Translated by G. D. Peckett. London: Longmans, 1966.

Nordeen, S. K. "Editorial: Elimination of Leprosy as a Public Health Problem." *Leprosy Review* 63, 1 (1992): 1–4.

———."A Look at World Leprosy." *Leprosy Review* 62, 1 (1991): 72–86.

Nwude, N., and Omotayo O. Ebong. "Some Plants Used in the Treatment of Leprosy in Africa." *Leprosy Review* 51, 1 (1980): 11–18.

Ousmane, Mohamed. "La médecine traditionnelle tamachèque en milieu malien." *Thèse,* Ecole de Médecine, Bamako, 1981.

Packard, Randall. *White Plague, Black Labor: Tuberculosis and the Political Economy of Health and Disease in South Africa.* Berkeley: University of California Press, 1989.

Pankhurst, Richard. "The History of Leprosy in Ethiopia to 1935." *Medical History* 28 (1984): 57–72.

Park, Mungo. *Travels in the Interior Districts of Africa.* (1799) New York: Arno Press and The New York Times, 1971.

Parry, E. H. O. *Principles of Medicine in Africa.* 2d ed. Oxford: Oxford University Press, 1984.

Patterson, K. David. "Disease and Medicine in African History: A Bibliographic Essay." *History in Africa* (1974): 141–48.

Patton, Adell. *Physicians, Colonial Racism, and Diaspora in West Africa.* Gainesville: University Press of Florida, 1996.

Peel, J. D. Y. "Poverty and Sacrifice in Nineteenth-Century Yorubaland: A Critique of Iliffe's Thesis." *Journal of African History* 31 (1990): 465–84.

Person, Yves. *Samori: une révolution dyula.* Dakar: I.F.A.N., 1968.

Pirotte, Jean, and Henri Derroitte, eds. *Churches and Health Care in the Third World.* Leiden: E. J. Brill, 1991.

Ponnighaus, J., et al. "Is HIV Infection a Risk Factor for Leprosy?" *International Journal of Leprosy* 59, 2 (1991).

Pulvenis, Claude. "Une Epidémie de fièvre jaune à Saint-Louis du Sénégal (1881)." *Bulletin de l'IFAN* XXX, ser B, 4 (1968): 1353–73.

al-Qayrawani, Ibn Abi Zayd. *Al-risala.* Algiers: Editions populaire de l'armée, 1990.

Quinn, Frederick. "How Traditional Dahomian Society Interpreted Smallpox." *Abbia* XX (1968): 151–66.

Ramsey, Matthew. *Professional and Popular Medicine in France, 1770–1830.* Cambridge: Cambridge University Press, 1988.

Ranger, Terence. "The Invention of Tradition in Colonial Africa." In Eric Hobsbawm and Terence Ranger, eds.,*The Invention of Tradition.* Cambridge: Cambridge University Press, 1983.

Reitman, Valerie. "Banishment of Lepers in Japan May End, But Not the Anguish." *Wall Street Journal,* 19 March 1996, 1(A) and 10(A).

Renez-Stable, Elisso. "Cuba's Response to the HIV Epidemic." *American Journal of Public Health* 81, 5 (May 1991).

Richards, P. *The Medieval Leper and His Northern Heirs.* Totawa, New Jersey: Rowan and Littlefield, 1977.

Roberts, Richard. *Warriors, Merchants, and Slaves.* Stanford: Stanford University Press, 1987.

Roberts, Richard, and Martin Klein. "The Banamba Slave Exodus of 1905 and the Decline of Slavery in the Western Sudan." *Journal of African History* 21, 3 (1980): 375–94.

Robineau, M. "La Lèpre en Afrique Occidentale Française, étude bibliographique." *International Journal of Leprosy* 1, 4 (October 1933): 459–62.

Robinson, Charles. *Hausaland.* London: Sampson Low, Marston and Company, 1897.

Robinson, David. *The Holy War of Umar Tall: The Western Sudan in the Mid-Nineteenth Century.* Oxford: Clarendon Press, 1985.

Rosenberg, Charles. *The Cholera Years in 1832, 1849, and 1866.* Chicago: University of Chicago Press, 1962.

Rothman, Sheila. *Living in the Shadow of Death: Tuberculosis and the Social Experience of Illness in America.* New York: Basic Books, 1994.

Rutherford, Jonathan. *Community, Culture, and Difference.* London: Lawrence and Wishart, 1990.

Ryan, Frank. *The Forgotten Plague: How the Battle Against Tuberculosis Was Won—and Lost.* Boston: Little, Brown and Company, 1993.

Sabben-Clare, E. E., D. J. Bradley, and K. Kirkwood, eds. *Health in Tropical Africa During the Colonial Period.* Oxford: Clarendon Press, 1980.

Sadowsky, Jonathan. "Imperial Bedlam: Institutions of Madness and Colonialism in Southwest Nigeria." Ph.D. dissertation, Johns Hopkins University, 1993.

Sagara, Issiaka. "Le rôle de l'Institut Marchoux dans la vie sanitaire et socio-éducative des lépreux." *Mémoire,* Institut National des Arts, Bamako, 1988.

Salamanta, Ousmane "Etude épidemiologique de l'épilepsie dans l'arrondissement central de Bandiagara." *Thèse,* Ecole de Médecine, Bamako, Mali, 1989.

Samaké, Gaoussou. "La reinsertion socio-économiques des aveugles du Mali: cas du District de Bamako." *Mémoire,* Géographie, Ecole Normale Supérieure, Bamako, 1991.

Sanankou, Bintou. *La Chute de Modibo Keita.* Paris: Editions Chaka, 1990.

Sankale, M. *Médecins et action sanitaire en Afrique noire.* Paris: Présence Africaine, 1969.

Saunders, Suzanne. *'A Suitable Island Site': Leprosy in the Northern Territory and the Channel Island Leprosarium, 1880–1955.* Darwin, Australia: Historical Society of the Northern Territory, 1989.

Schneider, Harm. *Leprosy and Other Health Problems in Hararghe.* Haarlem: n.p., 1975.

Schneider, William. *An Empire for the Masses: The French Popular Image of Africa,1870–1900.* Westport: Greenwood Press, 1982.

Scott, James. *Weapons of the Weak: Everyday Forms of Peasant Resistance.* New Haven: Yale University Press, 1985.

Shapiro, M. "Medicine in the Service of Colonialism." Ph.D. dissertation, University of California, Los Angeles, 1983.

Shiloh, Ailon. "A Case Study of Disease and Culture in Action: Leprosy Among the Hausa." *Human Organization* 24, 2 (1965): 140–47.

Silla, Eric. "'After Fish, Milk do not wish': Recurring Ideas in a Global Culture," *Cahier d'Etudes Africaines* 144 (1996).
Sissoko, Sambou. "Le problème d'assainissement à Djikoroni-Para: cas de Djenekabougou." *Mémoire*, Geographie, Ecole Normale Supérieure, Bamako, 1984.
Skinsnes, Olaf. "Leprosy in Society: I. 'Leprosy Has Appeared on the Face,'" *Leprosy Review* 35, 1 (1964): 21–35.
———. "Leprosy in Society: II. The Pattern of Concept and Reaction to Leprosy in Oriental Antiquity." *Leprosy Review* 35, 3 (1964): 106–22.
———. "Leprosy in Society: III. The Relationship of the Social to the Medical Pathology of Leprosy." *Leprosy Review* 35, 4 (1964): 175–81.
———. "Leprosy in Society: IV. The Genesis of Lepra-Angst." *Leprosy Review* 39, 4 (1968): 223–28.
———. "Notes from the History of Leprosy." *International Journal of Leprosy* 41, 2 (1973): 220–233.
Skinses, Olaf, and Robert Elvove. "Leprosy in Society: V. 'Leprosy' in Occidental Literature." *International Journal of Leprosy* 38, 3 (1970): 294–303.
Skinses, Olaf, and Linda Peterson, "Photographic Gallery of Contributors of the Century." *International Journal of Leprosy* 41, 2 (1973): 156–76.
Snowden, Frank. *Blacks in Antiquity.* Cambridge: Harvard University Press, 1970.
Soleillet, Paul. *Voyage à Ségou 1878–1879.* Paris: Challamel, ainé, 1887.
Sontag, Susan. "AIDS and Its Metaphors." *New York Review of Books* (27 October 1988): 89–100.
———. *Illness as Metaphor.* New York: Farrar, Straus, Giroux, 1977.
Stevenson, Burton. *The Home Book of Proverbs, Maxims, and Familiar Phrases.* New York: Macmillan Company, 1948.
Suret-Canale, Jean. *French Colonialism in Tropical Africa, 1900–1945.* Translated by Till Gottheiner. London: C. Hurst and Company, 1971.
Susman, Joan. "Disability, Stigma, and Deviance." *Social Science and Medicine* 38, 1 (1994): 15–22.
Swanson, Maynard. "'The Asiatic Menace': Creating Segregation in Durban, 1870–1900." *International Journal of African Historical Studies* 16, 3 (1983): 401–21.
———. "The Sanitation Syndrome: Bubonic Plague and Urban Native Policy in the Cape Colony." *Journal of African History* 18, 3 (1977): 387–410.
Tauxier, L. *La Religion bambara.* Paris: Librairie Orientaliste Paul Geuthner, 1927.
Theroux, Paul. "The Lepers of Moyo," *Granta* 48 (1994): 127–91.
Thévenin, Etienne. *Raoul Follerau, hier et aujourd'hui.* Paris: Librairie Arthème Fayard, 1992.
Thomas, Howard. "A Study of Leprosy Colony Policies." M.A. thesis, Cornell University, 1943.
Tobimatsu, Jingo. *Hannah Riddel, Known in Japan as "The Mother of Lepers.* Translated from Japanese. [Publisher not listed], 1937.
Traoré, Dominique. *Médecin et magie africaine.* Paris: Présence Africaine, 1983.
Traoré, Gaoussou. "Le Phénomène de la mendicité à Bamako et dans les centre urbains." *Aurore*, 1 April 1993, 3.
Traoré, Marie. "Contribution au problème de l'integration socio-économique des aveugles: le cas de l'Institut National des Aveugles du Mali." *Mémoire*, Psycho-Pédagogique, Ecole Normale Supérieure, Bamako, 1984.
Trimingham, J. Spencer. *A History of Islam in West Africa.* London: Oxford University Press, 1962.
Turk, J. L., and R. J. W. Rees. "Aids and Leprosy." *Leprosy Review* 1, 59 (1988): 193-94.
Turshen, Meredith. *The Political Ecology of Disease in Tanzania.* New Brunswick, New Jersey: Rutgers University Press, 1984.
Unterman, Alan. *Dictionary of Jewish Lore and Legend.* London: Thames and Hudson, 1991.
Vance, Randolph. *Ozark Magic and Folklore.* New York: Dover Publications, 1947.

Vansina, Jan. *Living with Africa: Reminiscences and Historiography.* Madison: University of Wisconsin Press, 1994.

Vaughan, Megan. *Curing Their Ills: Colonial Power and African Illness.* Stanford: Stanford University Press, 1991.

Verbov, J. L. "Biblical Leprosy—A Comedy of Errors." *Journal of the Royal Society of Medicine* 83 (1990): 127–28.

Volinn, Ilse. "Issues of Definitions and Their Implications: Aids and Leprosy." *Social Science and Medicine* 29, 10 (1989): 1157–62.

Waddington, Ivan. "General Practitioners and Consultants in Early Nineteenth-Century England: The Sociology of an Intra-Professional Conflict." In John Woodward and David Richards, eds., *Health Care and Popular Medicine in Nineteenth Century England.* New York: Holmes and Meier Publishers, 1977.

Waite, G. M. "The Indigenous Medical System in East-Central African History." Ph.D. dissertation, University of California, Los Angeles, 1981.

Waxler, Nancy. "Learning to Be a Leper: A Case Study in the Social Construction of Illness." In G. Mishler, ed., *Social Contexts of Health, Illness, and Patient Care.* Cambridge: Cambridge University Press, 1981.

Weeks, Jeffrey. "Questions of Identity." In Pat Caplan, ed., *The Cultural Construction of Sexuality.* London: Tavistock Publications, 1987.

Wetherall, William. "A Bridge Not Too Far for Those with Leprosy: Sanitariums on Nagashima Island, Japan." *Far Eastern Economic Review* 141, 29 (21 July 1988): 41–43.

Wilks, Ivor. *Wa and the Wala, Islam and Polity in Northwestern Ghana.* Cambridge: Cambridge University Press, 1989.

Winifred, Norge Jerome. "Food Habits and Acculturation: Dietary Practices and Nutrition of Families Headed by Southern-Born Negroes Residing in a Northern Metropolis." Ph.D. dissertation, University of Wisconsin, 1967.

Winterbottom, Thomas. *An Account of the Native Africans in the Neighborhood of Sierra Leone, To Which is Added an Account of the Present State of Medicine among Them.* 1803; reprint, London: Frank Cass and Co., 1969.

Wondji, Christophe. "La Fièvre jaune à Grand Bassam (1899–1903)." *Revue française d'histoire d'outre-mer* 59 (1972): 205–39.

Woodward, John, and David Richards, eds. *Health Care and Popular Medicine in Nineteenth Century England.* New York: Holmes and Meier Publishers, 1977.

World Health Organization. "Leprosy Situation in the World and Multidrug Therapy Coverage." *Weekly Epidemiological Record* 67, 21 (22 May 1992): 153–60.

———. "Progress towards the Elimination of Leprosy as a Public Health Problem." *Weekly Epidemiological Record* 71, 20 (17 May 1996): 149–56.

Zahan, Dominique. *The Bambara.* Leiden: E. J. Brill, 1974.

———. "Principes de médecine bambara." *Zaïre* 2, 9–10 (November–December 1957).

Zouber, Mahmoud. *Ahmad Baba de Tombouctou (1556–1627): sa vie et son oeuvre.* Paris: G.-P. Maisonneuve et Larose, 1977.

Unpublished Arabic Manuscripts

al-ʿAlawi, Abu ʿabd Allah al-Mustafa b. Ahmad b. ʿAthman b. Mawlud. *Nawazil* [undated], CEDRAB, no. 277, Timbuktu.

al-ʿAlawi, Muhammad ibn Bakr b. al-Hashim (d. 1098 A.H./1687 A.D.). *Nawazil* [ca. 1600s, copied 1356 A.H./1937 A.D.], CEDRAB, no. 521, Timbuktu.

b. al-ʿAmshi, Muhammad b. al-Mukhtari. *Nawazil* (1199 A.H./1848 A.D.), CEDRAB, no. 4064, Timbuktu.

Anbuya ibn al-Talib ʿabd al-Rahman. *Majmuʿ li-Nawazil al-Takrur* (1236 A.H./1821 A.D.), CEDRAB, no. 627, Timbuktu.

al-Burtali, Ahmad al-Jayyid Ibn al-Talib Muhammad b. Abu Bakr al-Sadiq (d. 1230 A.H./
    1815 A.D.). *Sharh al-Ajurmiyya* (ca. 1800), CEDRAB, no. 5629, Timbuktu.
Ahmad b. abd. al-ᶜAraf. *Al-Nawazil al-Mufida* CEDRAB, no. 711, Timbuktu.
b. al-Qasri, Ibn Muhammad b. al-Mukhtar. *Nawazil* [ca. 1800s], CEDRAB, no. 603,
    Timbuktu.
al-Tinbukti, Ahmad Baba. "Fasl al-khiyar." *Manh al-Jalil ᶜala Mukhtasar Khalil* [ca. 1600,
    copied 1106 A.H./1694 A.D.], CEDRAB, no. 5661, Timbuktu.
al-Tinbukti, Saᶜid al-Habib Baba b. Muhammad al-Hadi al-Wadani. *Ajwiba* [early 1800s,
    copied 1266 A.H./1850 A.D.], CEDRAB, no. 1038, Timbuktu.
[Untitled]. Manuscript no. 836, Falke Collection, Northwestern University Library,
    Evanston, Illinois.
al-Warzazi. *Nawazil* [undated], CEDRAB, no. 2749, Timbuktu.

List of Informants

Explanation of Column Headings and Abbreviations

Name: In Mali most names are spelled in several different ways (e.g., Magan or
Makan, Koulibaly or Koulibali, Bagayoko or Bagayogo) and do not follow the official
phonetic orthography specified by the government's Direction Nationale de l'Alphabetisation Functionnelle et la Linguistique Appliquée (DNAFALA). For consistency
and ease of pronunciation, I arbitrarily selected only one spelling for each name
unless the person clearly pronounced it differently from others (e.g., Dambélé
instead of Dembélé).
Age: These ages reflect estimates made by informants themselves at the time of their
interview. Most people did not know the precise year of birth.
Ethnicities: Informants specified their own ethnicities (*siyaw*) in response to the interviewer's request. A few individuals stated that they were *numuw* (blacksmiths)
which usually denotes hereditary professional status. When appropriate, the individual's first language is also indicated. As stated in the Introduction, the precise meaning of these different ethnic labels varies tremendously over space and time. They are
used here only for rudimentary classification.
Current Home and Place of Birth: To facilitate locating the place of birth on a map, I usually asked informants to identify their home village's administrative *arondissement*,
cercle, or the nearest large town. These are indicated in parentheses. If the village is
located outside Mali's present-day borders, then the country is indicated in parentheses as well. Place names are spelled in accordance with the Official Standard Names
approved by the U.S. Board on Geographic Names (1965 edition) or with those
appearing on the Michelin map for West Africa. A few names such as Timbuktu follow English spellings.
Profession/Position: Virtually none of the former leprosy patients interviewed ever
held a government job or position which can be indicated conveniently with one
word. Most started their lives as farmers in rural villages and subsequently engaged
in a variety of activities. The heading is reserved for health care workers and other
"non-leper" informants.
>   (B): Indicates that the individual speaks Bambara as a first language despite Fulani
>   ethnicity.
>   (r): Indicates retired at time of interview.
>   —: Dashes indicate that data was not obtained for corresponding category.

Former Leprosy Patients (listed by current place of residence]

Name [Age/Sex; Ethnicity; Place of Birth] Date of Interview/Conversation.

Bamako (Djikoroni)

Agh Tabago, Sita [42/M; Bella (Tuareg); Timbuktu] 10 December 1992, 26 July 1993.

Bagayogo, Sédou [58/M; Bambara; Toumou (Sanko)] 11 November 1992.

Balo, Nènènkoro [50/M; Bambara (*numu*); Wolanyanbougou (Ségou)] 22 January 1993.

Berté, Lasine [60/M; Bambara; Konina (Koulikoro)] 16 November 1992.

Boli, Yoro [62/M; Fulani; Nara] 28 January 1993, 21 July 1993.

Cissé, Amadou [40/M; Fulani; Kondo (Ténenkou)] 20 November 1992.

Dama, Mamadou [67/M; Minianka; Wassoulou (Yanfolila)] 27 October 1992.

Diakité, Fulako [60/F; Fulani; Kita] 26 July 1993.

Diakité, Fuseni [54/M; Fulani (B); Blendio (Sikasso)] 4 November 1992.

Diakité, Moussa [60/M; Fulani (B); Wasala/Fransikoura (Bafoulabé)] 14 November 1992.

Diallo, Kamara [40/F; Fulani (B); Kouroulamini (Wassalou)] 11 December 1992.

Diarra, Abdoulaye [61/M; Bambara; Domila (Kati)] 27 November 1992.

Diarra, Bala [72/M; Bambara; Sanamba (Kati)] 19 November 1992.

Diarra, Balafonci [85/M; Bambara; Yéguénébougou (Kati)] 19 November 1992.

Diarra, Bè [73/M; Bambara; Tatrema (Dioro)] 12 November 1992.

Diarra, Cèmoko [70/M; Bambara; Domila (Kati)] 20 November 1992.

Diarra, Mamadou [64/M; Bambara; Fékoun (Koulikoro)] 21 July 1993.

Diarra, Nanyuma [45/F; Malinké; Karamakola (Siby)] 26 July 1993.

Diko, Bani [61/M; Moor; Dogodabaye (Nioro)] 10 November 1992.

Doumbia, Banci [58/M; Bambara; Cèkèna (Baguinéda)] 12 November 1992, 21 July 1993.

Doumbia, Demba [72/M; Bambara; Nianguena (Kangaba)] 27 November 1992.

Doumbia, Foni [80/M; Malinké; Kola (Sanankoroba)] 19 January 1993.

Doumbia, Kama [57/M; Malinké; Baga (Sanankoroba)] 25 November 1992.

Doumbia, Nakan 50/F; Malinké; Kondjiguila (Yanfolila)] 17 November 1992.

Fall, Samba [47/M; Fulani; Polenjowbé (Senegal)] 5 August 1993.

Fofana, Kanko [62/F; Malinké; Bafoulabé] 9 February 1993.

Fofana, Soulaymane [55/M; Dyula; Mounzou (Baguinéda)] 2 February 1993.

Garba, Hamadun [40/M; Songhay; Doyciré (Timbuktu)] 26 July 1993.

Gouro, Abdoulaye [75/M; Dogon; Douranguru (Bandiagara)] 13 November 1992.

Kamara, Jean-Marie [76/M; Malinké; Ouéléssébougou] 9 July 1993.

Kamara, Magan [70/F; Khassonké-Malinké; Nari (Oualia)] 18 May 1993.

Kamara, Nakunté [43/M; Kakolo (Soninké); Koungo (Nioro)] 21 July 1993.

Kanoté, Bakari [71/M; Malinké; Dalafin (Senegal)] 5 November 1992.

Keita, Falela [72/M; Malinké; Faraba (Kita)] 28 November 1992.

Keita, Modibo [43/M; Malinké; Sandianbougou (Djidian)] 13 November 1992.

Keita, Nana [60/F; Malinké; Kourousalé (Siby)] 29 November 1992.

Keita, Nantènè [60/F; Malinké; Kéniéroba (Siby)] 29 November 1992.

Keita, Nasira [54/F; Malinké; Naréna (Kangaba)] 26 July 1993.

Keita, Saran [80/F; Malinké; Gwansolo (Siby)] 9 November 1992, 21 January 1993, 22 January 1993, 14 April 1993, 4 May 1993, 11 May 1993, 17 May 1993, 7 June 1993, 9 June 1993, 11 June 1993, 29 June 1993, 2 July 1993, 5 July 1993, 6 July 1993, 8 July 1993, 12 July 1993.

Keita, Tenen [60/F; Malinké; Karakoudo (Guinea)] 9 December 1992.

Koita, Dawda [66/M; Bobo; Koosédugu (Tominian)] 23 August 1993.

Koita, Fanta [65/F; Malinké; Diéliba (Kangaba)] 9 March 1993.

Konta, Diké [35/F; Bozo; Sa (Yourou)] 5 August 1993.

Kontaga, Nyo [60/M; Malinké; Balandougou (Bafoulabé)] 29 July 1993.

Koulibali, Brèma [79/M; Bambara; Tajena (Sanankoroba)] 19 January 1993.

Koulibali, Joseph [52/M; Bambara; Dialakoro (Koulaye)] 8 December 1992.
Koulibali, Kalifa [73/M; Soninké; San] 11 December 1992.
Koulibali, Laye [67/M; Bambara; Golebekolo (Zinzana)] 5 November 1992.
Koulibali, Madu [40/M; Malinké; Kangaba] 29 July 1993.
Koulibali, Mamadou [44/M; Kakolo/Bambara; Djikoroni] 12 March 1993.
Koulibali, Nouhoum [60/M; Fulani; Macina] 5 November 1992.
Koulibali, Saran [85/F; Malinké; Siby] 27 March 1993.
Koulibali, Sékou [38/M; Khassonké; Fangala (Oualia)] 7 November 1992.
Koulibali, Seri [66/M; Bambara; Dounba (Koulikoro)] 5 August 1993.
Kouyaté, Mariame [80/F; —; Bougouni] 14 November 1992.
Maiga, Abdoulaye M. [53/M; Songhay; Bourem Sidé (Diré)] 5 August 1993.
Maiga, Bouré [42/M; Songhay; Goundam] 17 December 1992.
Makasouba, Drissa [49/M; —; Siguiri (Guinea)] 5 November 1992.
Sako, Komogoba [64/F; —; Dentoukoro (Ouéléssébougou)] 7 November 1992.
Sako, Madu [75/M; Malinké; Kunja (Siguiri, Guinea)] 11 November 1992.
Sangaré, Jeneba [70/F; Fulani; Diankaréla (Dioila)] 26 July 1993.
Sanogo, Bakari [75/F; Dyula; Bozola (Bamako)] 28 October 1992.
Sanogo, Mariame [36/F; Bozo; Mankarala (Zinzana)] 10 November 1992.
Sanogo, Tijane [63/M; Samogo; Sikasso] 5 August 1993.
Sawane, Buna [58/M; Soninké; Gabou (Kayes)] 26 October 1992.
Siby, Shaikna [38/M; Moor; Kankossa (Mauritania)] 5 August 1993.
Sidibé, Magara [60/M; Fulani; Ourou (Kéléya)] 2 February 1993.
Sidibé, Mané [60/M; Fulani; Kita] 26 July 1993.
Sidibé, Marè [60/M; Bambara; Gorobougou (Sirakoro)] 9 November 1992.
Sidibé, Soulaymane [67/M; Fulani; Makono (Sirakoro)] 4 December 1992.
Sinado, Bala [65/M; Soninké; Sirajè (Koulikoro)] 3 December 1992.
Sissoko, Malè [75/M; Soninké; Lambidou (Nioro)] 24 February 1993.
Sissoko, Moussa [50/M; Soninké; Kinkarè (Diéma, Kayes)] 3 December 1992.
Sissoko, Tunko [48/M; Malinké; Oualia] 10 November 1992.
Sow, Fousseyni [38/M; Fulani (B); Kita] 28 October 1992, 14 May 1993, 5 July 1993, 7 July
    1993, 15 July 1993.
Suko, Fanto [50/F; Malinké; Guéninférou (Kita)] 7 December 1992.
Sylla, Mariame [55/F; Soninké; Touba (Banamba)] 21 July 1993.
Tangara, Mori [74/M; Bambara; Tona (Bla)] 20 January 1993.
Tangara, Shaka [76/M; Bambara; Mimana (Farako)] 18 November 1992.
Tolèma, Alu [65/M; Dogon; Lafiéra (Tominian)] 28 November 1992.
Touré, Dramane [65/M; Djenneka[1]; Niamina (Koulikoro)] 16 November 1992.
Traoré, Abdoulaye [60/M; Bambara; Boditomo (Sananjo)] 9 November 1992.
Traoré, Adama [70/M; Bambara; Diéna (Baguinéda)] 26 November 1992.
Traoré, Adama [63/M; Bambara; Jegenwere (Sanando)] 13 November 1992.
Traoré, Bernadetti [63/F; Bambara; Faladyé] 11 March 1993.
Traoré, Duba [38/F; Bambara (numu); Mbéla (Kolokani)] 9 December 1992.
Traoré, Issaka [75/M; Dyula; Belenga (Boulougonna, Burkina Faso)] 5 November 1992.
Traoré, Jeneba [55/F; Bambara; Tiélé (Baguinéda)] 7 November 1992.
Traoré, Makan [—/M; Malinké; Bafoulabé] 9 August 1991.
Traoré, Michel [71/M; —; Konyobla (Sanankoroba)] 17 November 1992.
Traoré, Ousamane [63/M; Dafing; Toun (Bankass)] 25 November 1992.
Tunkara, Abdramane [40/M; Soninké; Mindiè (Mopti)] 4 December 1992.
Yirango, Musa [82/M; Dafing; Sornéré (Bandiagara)] 20 December 1992.

---

1 Father from Djenne and mother was Malinké.

Sources

Bamako (Lafiabougou)
Cissé, Jakini [60/M; Soninké; Siribougou (Ségou)] 28 January 1993.
Doumbia, Karunga [65/M; Malinké; Kondjiguila (Yanfolila)] 15 December 1992.

Conakry (Guinea)
Touré, Bouboucar [43/M; Malinké; Faranah] 6 February 1993.

Falan (Ouéléssébougou)
Doumbia, Bala [80/M; Bambara; Falan] 22 November 1992.
Doumbia, Mariame [52/F; Malinké; Yansana] 23 November 1992.

Houndou-Bomon (Timbuktu)
al-Her, Muhammad [—/M; Tuareg; Kel Horma (a nomadic group)] 26 December 1992.
Sabaguma, Ousamane [—/M; Songhay; Houndou-Bomon] 26 December 1992.

Kabara (Timbuktu)
Agh Rhally, El Mehdi [—/M; Tuareg; nomad from Gourma region] 25 December 1992.
Barri, Nègè [72/M; Fulani; Mamou (Guinea)] 25 December 1992.
Mohammadun, Hadiatou [67/F; Songhay; Abakoira (Bourem)] 23 December 1992.

Kangaba
Keita, Nantènè [68/F; Malinké; Déguéla (Kangaba)] 6 February 1993.
Koulibali, Mousa [60/M; Malinké; Kangaba] 6 February 1993.

Kita
Dambélé, Makan [60/M; Malinké; Tougounbaré (Toukoto)] 22 April 1993.
Juko, Mba [70/F; Malinké; Siguiri (Guinea)] 22 April 1993.
Kamara, Bakari [65/M; Malinké; Kouragué (Sagabari)] 22 April 1993.
Nomogo, Musomari [80/F; Malinké; Katabantankoto (Kokofata)] 21 April 1993.
Sidibé, Mbajala [50/F; Malinké; Founia (Sirakoro)] 22 April 1993.
Traoré, Adama [80/M; Malinké; Kita] 22 April 1993.
Traoré, Jasig [80/M; Malinké; Siraninkoro (Kokofata)] 22 April 1993.
Traoré, Mbajala [80/F; Malinké; Dionfa Kourou (Kokofata)] 22 April 1993.
Traoré, Sira [60/F; Malinké; Gahan (Mafina)] 21 April 1993.

Macina
Dembélé, Haraba [80/F; Bambara; Bendougou] 15 February 1993.
Dramè, Adama [55/M; Bambara; Tabara (Si)] 17 February 1993.
Kanta, Koko [53/M; Bozo; Tongué (Sarro)] 16 February 1993.
Katilé, Umu [60/F; Bambara; Yolo (Dioro)] 15 February 1993.
Koulibali, Seni [60/M; Bambara; Kokri (Kolongo)] 16 February 1993.
Sokoba, Moussa [53/M; Bambara; Sagabougou (Ségou)] 18 February 1993.
Tangara, Asata [70/F; Bambara; Ouana (Siyanro)] 17 February 1993.

Ouéléssébougou
Bagayogo, Anna [75/F; Bambara; Sienbougou (Kéléya)] 30 November 1992.
Doumbia, Farima [75/F; Bambara; Manabougou] 1 December 1992.
Doumbia, Jeriba [80/M; Bambara; Manabougou] 30 November 1992.

Samanko (Invalides)
Bokum, Aminata [50/F; Fulani; Dari (Niafounké)] 19 May 1993.
Diakité, Lassana [60/M; Fulani; Nafadji (Sébékoro)] 5 April 1993.
Diarra, Madu [90/M; Samogo; Ouagadougou (Burkina Faso)] 2 April 1993.

Fofana, Majan [66/M; Malinké; Kankan (Guinea)] 16 December 1992.
Guindo, Aljuma [39/M; Dogon; Kouna (Bankass)] 5 April 1993.
Konaté, Gabriel [64/M; Bambara; Mamaribougou (Faladyé)] 2 April 1993.
Marigo, Madu [100/M; Soninké; Fana] 5 April 1993.
Sangaré, Uma [83/F; Fulani; Niongono (Bankass)] 7 April 1993.
Tall, Aminata [70/F; Fulani; Wajiya (Tojon, Burkina Faso)] 6 April 1993.
Touré, Brèma [77/M; Samogo; Nimi Tougan (Burkina Faso)] 2 April 1993.
Traoré, Aminata [65/F; Malinké; Traoléla Guimbala (Kita)] 6 April 1993.
Traoré, Issa [54/M; Bambara; Taga (Bougouni)] 7 April 1993.
Traoré, Kabiné [64/M; Malinké; Niaganbougou (Siby)] 16 December 1992.
Traoré, Nèkoro [75/F; Bambara; Safo (Bamako)] 19 May 1993.

Samanko (Nouhoumbougou)
Dambélé, Dramane [70/M; Bambara; Joso (Macina)] 9 April 1993.
Diallo, Mamadou [60/M; Soninké; Bada (Kayes)] 9 April 1993.

San
Boré, Bakari [55/M; Minianka; Jebèlè (Kimparana)] 22 March 1993.
Dambélé, Jean-Baptiste [54/M; Bobo; Kona (Mandiakui)] 21 March 1993.
Dembélé, Sita [35/F; Minianka; Siraba (Kimparana)] 22 March 1993.
Diarra, Anu [40/F; Bobo; Konokan (Tominian)] 22 March 1993.
Diarra, Herasen [60/F; Bobo; Kunakan (Tominian)] 23 March 1993.
Diarra, Yusufu [60/M; Bambara; Da (Sorontona)] 21 March 1993.
Jessana, Ferdinand [67/M; Bobo; Konino (Mandiakui)] 21 March 1993.
Kamaté, Bezo [74/M; Bobo; Kuma (Tominian)] 23 March 1993.
Kamaté, Fatoma [60/M; Bobo; Koba (Tominian)] 21 March 1993.
Kamaté, Silvestré [77/M; Bobo; Torola (Tominian)] 23 March 1993.
Konaté, Yolonba [40/F; *numu*; Morobugu] 21 March 1993.
Koné, Dogoderma [30s/F; *numu* (Minianka); Morobila (Nientieso)] 22 March 1993.
Koulibali, Bintou [40/F; Bambara; Debena (Djenne)] 22 March 1993.
Sokoba, Sabari [50/M; Bobo; Kanyanso (Tenen)] 21 March 1993.
Théra, Arabaha [35/F; Bobo; Torola (Yasso)] 22 March 1993.
Théra, Chaka [43/M; Bobo; Dabudugu (Tominian)] 21 March 1993.
Théra, Félicité [50/F; Bobo; Siyandugu (Tominian)] 22–23 March 1993.
Théra, Nsi [40/F; Bobo; Bakarikui (Tominian)] 22 March 1993.

Séguésono (Ouéléssébougou)
Samaké, Bala [78/M; Bambara; Séguésono] 2 December 1992.

Timbuktu
Cissé, Tabakari [50/M; Songhay; Doua (Niafounké)] 26 July 1993.
Inamoud, Alfa [62/M; Tuareg; Kel Inachéria (nomadic group)] 24 December 1992.

Tinèma (Macina)
Koulibali, Mamadou [60/M; Bambara; Tinèma] 17 February 1993.

Health Workers (organized by place of interview)
Name [Age/Sex; Ethnicity; Place of Birth; Profession/Position] Date of Interview/Conversation

Bamako
Blanc, Leopold [—/M; French; —; Epidemiologist at Institut Marchoux] 12 October 1992;
17 October 1992; 10 December 1992.

Bobin, Pierre [—/M; French; —; Director of Institut Marchoux] 20 October 1992; 4 May 1993.

Cissé, Ali [—/M; —; —; Minister of Social Affairs (r)/President of Association Raoul Follerau Malienne] 22 October 1992.

Dembélé, Philippe [—/M; —; —; Directeur, Section Lèpre, Grandes Endémies] 11 December 1992.

Ounougo, Mamourou [49/M; —; Koutiala; Infirmier d'Etat, Grandes Endémies] 3 November 1992.

Sogodogo, Daba [54/M; Senoufo; Furu (Sikasso); Surgeon, Hôpital Gabriel Touré] 24 October 1992.

Timité, Bourèma [42/M; —; San; Infirmier d'Etat, Grandes Endémies] 3 November 1992.

Konna

Kassibo, Aldiouma [79/M; Bozo; Konna; Infirmier Majeur (r)] 9–11 January 1992.

Ouéléssébougou

Bane, Demba [—/M; Fulani; Konakari (Kayes); Infirmier d'Etat] 2 December 1992.

San

Dembélé, Ousmane [65/M; Bambara; Dieli; Infirmier (r)] 24 June 1991

Traoré, Safouné [70/M; Bambara; San; Médecin-Chef (r)/President of San branch of Association Raoul Follerau Malienne] 22 March 1993.

Timbuktu

Ahmed Mohamed Dédaou [—/M; Songhay; Timbuktu; Infirmier d'Etat (r)] 22–28 December 1992.

Saloume, Baba [75/M; —; Timbuktu; Dispensary employee (r)] 27 December 1992.

Indigenous Healers (organized by current location)

Name [Age/Sex; Ethnicity; Place of Birth] Date of Interview/Conversation

Bamako

Cissé, Ali Baba [48/M; Mandé/Hausa; Wa (Ghana)] 18 April 1993.

Maiga, Alassana [37/M; Songhay; Hinagoi (Haibomo)] 25 April 1993.

Macina

Tangara, Kasoume [83/M; Bambara; Konomani (Monipè); —/father was a healer] 18 February 1993.

San

Koné, Moussa [—/M; Bobo; Cèkelenso (San)] 25 June 1991.

Koulibali, Moussa [—/M; Bambara; Nankasso (San)] 24 June 1991.

Koulibali, Sidiki [—/M; Bambara; Ségou] 25 June 1991.

Sokoba, Issa [—/M; Soninké; Sorontouna (San)] 26 June 1991.

Traoré, Souleymane [—/M; Bambara; Sorontouna (San)] 25 June 1991.

Traoré, Seku [—/M; Soninké; —] 24 June 1991

Timbuktu

Cissé, Alpha Baba [—/M; —; Timbuktu] 14 July 1991; 5 January 1993.

Yattara, Bagna [—/M; —; —] 14 July 1991.

Other

Name [Age/Sex; Ethnicity; Place of Birth; Profession/Position] Date of Interview

Bamako

Abocar, Asoumane [—/M; Songhay; Goundam; Language Teacher] 6 November 1992.
Bagayogo, Aliou [—/M; Fulani; —; Ministre de l'Intérieur (1968, r)] 7 July 1993.
Dembélé, Arouna [—/M; Minianka; Directeur Affaires Sociales (r)] 10 August 1993.
Diakité, Amadou [75/M; Sarrokolé; Bamako; Tailor (r)/RDA Chief for Quinzambougou
    (r)] 2 March 1993.
Diakité, Samu [72/M; Fulani (B); Djikoroni; Chief of Djikoroni] 29 October 1992.
Diallo, Bouboucar [35/M; Fulani; Safouroulaye; Librarian] 19 October 1992.
Diallo, Bouboucar [74/M; Fulani; Nioro; Carpenter (r)] 3 February 1993.
Koné, Cémoko [81/M; Dyula; Djikoroni; Djikoroni resident] 30 October 1992.
Sow, Hamadou [36/M; Fulani; Sègè; cattle herder] 19 October 1992.

Houndou-Bomon

Suda, Baba [—/M; —; Houndou-Bomon; resident] 26 December 1992.

Kangaba

Doumbia, Mariame. [80/F; Malinké; Sanankoro; —] 6 February 1993.

Macina

Kamara, Kinjé [58/M; Bambara; Sumuni (Sirobilen); Gendarme (r)/Father was a healer] 18
    February 1993.

Ouéléssébougou

Schakenraad, Wim [—/M; Dutch; White Father missionary] 12 December 1992.

San

de Rasilly, Bernard [—/M; French; France; White Father missionary] 2 March 1993; 21–23
    March 1993.

Timbuktu

Baber, Moulaye Ahmed [79/M; —; Timbuktu; Muslim Scholar] 26–29 December 1992.
Boularaf, Mouhamad A. [84/M; —; Timbuktu; Muslim Scholar] 29 December 1992.

INDEX

Société de la Pathologie Exotique,
98
Soeurs Blanches. *See* White Sisters
Sofara, leprosy incidence in, 95
Soins de Santé Primaire (SSP), 150
Sokoto Caliphate, 45
Songhay, 16, 157, 161
  Empire, 44
  healers, 58, 80
  languge, 11 n34
  migration to Bamako, 162
  term for leprosy, 51
Soninké, 15, 61
  use of slaves, 92
Sontag, Susan, 19
Sorcery, 35, 40, 61–62, 69
  and Health Service, 90
Sorel, Dr., 118
Soudan Français. *See* French
  Soudan
South Africa, 6, 7, 16
Soviet Union, 145
Sow, Fousseyni, 11, 182, 184–185,
  186, 187, 189, 191, 192
Sri Lanaka, 24
Stamps, postage, 190
Status, 62, 69
  and healing, 84, 157
Stigma, 1, 6, 17–19, 22, 43, 52–53,
  60, 63, 177, 180, 181, 189, 190
  and activism, 192–193
  in Arabic manuscripts, 48, 49
  and begging, 155, 165, 166,
    167, 168, 171, 177
  and cures, 110, 156
  and institutionalization, 118,
    121, 124, 129, 131
  and leprosy policy, 112, 157
  and medical treatment, 80,
    156, 180
  persistence of, 181, 189
  in rural areas, 55, 71–73
  speeches against, 190
St. Louis, Health Service in, 88
Strikes, 111, 135–136, 143–144
Suicide, 71
Sulfone. *See* DDS,
Sundiata, 1, 15, 72–73
al-Suyuti, 46, 78, 79
Syphilis, 23, 47, 48, 50–51, 90, 96,
  107

Taboos, 58–60
  food, 35, 36, 48–49, 58–60
Tahoua, Health Service in, 90
Talmud, 49, 58
Tamachek. *See* Tuareg
Tamari, Tal, 50
Tanzania, 80
Taoudeni, 173
Tarikh el-Fettach, 3
Taxes, 31, 32, 84, 88, 108, 133
Ténenkou, 79
Thalidomide, 179

Theroux, Paul, 25
Thiaroye, Campe de, 142
  revolt at, 133
Tiendrebeogo, Dr., 191
Timbuktu, 2,3, 11 n33, 44, 46, 48,
  49, 77, 78, 79
  begging in, 165
  development of, 191
  Health Service in, 91
  leprosy incidence in, 95
  migration to, 156, 158, 161–
    162
al-Tinbukti, Ahmad Baba, 3, 46–48
Tinea. *See* Kaba
Tirailleurs Sénégalais
Tombouctou. *See* Timbuktu
Tominian, 56, 61, 67
Toubab, origins of, 87
Toulouse, 23
Touré, Samory, 30–31, 37, 45, 68
  and slavery, 92
Traders,
  and scholarly networks, 79
  and transmission of leprosy,
    96
Traditional healers. *See* African
  medicine; Healers
Traditional medicine. *See* African
  medicine; Healers
Traoré, Dr. Safouné, 142, 148, 167
Traoré, Moussa, 173, 174
  coup d'état, 39, 148, 172
  overthrow of, 177
Trypanosomiasis. *See* Sleeping
  sickness.
Tuareg, 16, 77, 156, 161–162
  European disguised as, 128
  medical beliefs, 58
Tuberculosis, 6, 19, 48
Turner, Victor, 176

Umar Tall, 16, 44–45, 136, 184
  and begging, 165
UNICEF, 110, 111
Union Soudanaise-Rassemble-
  ment Democratique Africain.
  See US-RDA
Unions, labor, 114, 135–136, 148,
  172
Upper Volta,
Urban growth, 167, 187–188, 191–
  193
  and begging, 166
US-RDA, 136, 145, 148, 171

Vaughan, Megan 6, 9, 12, 27, 95,
  121
Vichy government, 105
Villages de liberté, 92, 93, 98
Vitiligo, 22, 47, 58

Wa, 79
Walata. *See* Oualata,
White Fathers 91–92, 163, 181

comments on White Sisters, 93
  practicing African medicine,
    10
White Sisters,
  archives, 2
  assitance for beggars,
    174–175
  dismissal from government
    hospitals, 93
  and Fousseyni Sow, 184
  and independence, 136, 139
  at the Institut Marchoux, 118,
    120, 125, 127–128, 137–
    140, 142–144, 145–147, 183
  in Kati, 91
  in Kita, 91
  and labor dispute, 135–136
  on Mamadou Fomba,
    132
  medical role, 89, 91–95
  memorial plaques for, 191
  in photographs, 122, 127
  popularity of health services,
    93
  propaganda, 94
  proselytism and medical care,
    87, 91–92, 94–95, 117, 127–
    128, 135, 137–138, 146
  recruitment of Institut Mar-
    choux patients, 120
  relations with African staff,
    135, 137–140, 142–144,
    145–146, 148
  relations with colonial medi-
    cal service,89, 93, 94, 137,
    139–140, 142
  relations with European doc-
    tors, 131, 179
  relations with Muslims, 137–
    140, 145–146
  relations with OCCGE, 145
  in Ségou, 87, 91, 92–93
  on urban development,
    188
WHO. *See* World Health Organization
Wife beating, 33, 40, 68
Witchcraft. *See* Sorcery,
Women's associations, 38, 182
Work,
  in exchange for medicine, 84
  and healing, 83
  and jealousy, 70
  and shame, 70
  significance of, 27, 30, 31, 61–
    62, 63, 66, 67, 68, 72, 73,
    160, 177
World Health Organization, 109,
  110, 111, 113, 178, 179

Yaws, 95, 96, 97, 104, 107
Yellow fever, 6, 88, 99, 107

Zaire, begging in, 172